The Videomaker Guide to Video Production
Fifth Edition

The Videomaker Guide to Video Production
Fifth Edition

From the Editors of Videomaker Magazine
Introduction by Matt York, Publisher/Editor
Preface by Mike Wilhelm, Executive Editor

Editorial Staff
Jennifer O'Rourke – Managing Editor
Jackson Wong – Associate Editor
Greg Olson – Associate Editor

Production Staff
Production Director – Melissa Hageman
Art Director/Photographer – Susan Schmierer

Focal Press
Taylor & Francis Group

NEW YORK AND LONDON

First published 2013
by Focal Press
70 Blanchard Road, Suite 402, Burlington, MA 01803

Simultaneously published in the UK
by Focal Press
2 Park Square, Milton Park, Abingdon, Oxon OX14 4RN

Focal Press is an imprint of the Taylor & Francis Group, an informa business

Library of Congress Cataloging-in-Publication Data
The videomaker guide to video production / from the editors of Videomaker magazine ; introduction by Matt York, publisher/editor ; preface by Mike Wilhelm, executive editor.—5th ed.
   p. cm.
ISBN 978-0-240-82434-5 (pbk.)—ISBN 978-0-240-82467-3 (eBk.)
1. Video recordings--Production and direction. I. York, Matt. II. Wilhelm, Mike.
III. Videomaker, Inc. IV. Videomaker.

PN1992.94.V56 2012
777—dc23

                                                            2012033635

ISBN: 978-0-240-82434-5 (pbk)
ISBN: 978-0-240-82467-3 (ebk)

Typeset in Melior LT Std
by MPS Limited, Chennai, India
www.adi-mps.com

Printed and bound in the United States of America by Sheridan Books, Inc. (a Sheridan Group Company).

This book is dedicated to Thomas Jefferson for his commitment to pluralism, diversity and community. He would be happy to see readers of this book exercising freedom of the electronic press.

Civil liberty functions today in a changing technological context. For five hundred years a struggle was fought, and in a few countries won, for the right of people to speak and print freely, unlicensed, uncensored and uncontrolled. But new technologies of electronic communication may now relegate old and freed media such as pamphlets, platforms and periodicals to a corner of the public forum. Electronic modes of communication that enjoy lesser rights are moving to center stage.

Ithiel de Sola Pool
Technologies of Freedom
(Harvard University Press, 1983)

Contents

PREFACE   **xi**

IF YOU ARE NEW TO MAKING VIDEO: WELCOME!   **xiii**

PART I   **VIDEO GEAR**   **1**
    1 Cameras Need Lovin' Too: Camera Maintenance and Cleaning   3
    2 CMOS vs CCD   7
    3 Adjust Shutter Speed for the Best Video Images   12
    4 Weighing In on the Tapeless World   15
    5 Lens Accessories for Your Camcorder   20
    6 Stabilization: Tools and Techniques   24
    7 DSLR Workflow Tips: a Pro's Eye View   31
    8 Shooting with Interchangeable Lenses   36
    9 Guide to Buying Camcorder Tripods   40
   10 The Right Mic for the Job   45
   11 Cut the Cord   50
   12 Portable Lighting Equipment   54
   13 Monitors   59
   14 Choosing a Video Switcher   64
   15 Battery Basics   67
   16 Recommendations for the Best Video Editing Computer   71

PART II   **PRODUCTION PLANNING**   **75**
    17 Director's Chair: Secrets of Storytelling   77
    18 Pre-Production Planning: Approaches to Creating a Video
        Treatment that Works for You   82
    19 Video Production Scheduling   87
    20 It's All in the Approach: Creative Approaches for Video
        Productions   91
    21 Script Writing   95
    22 The Perfect Plan: Storyboard and Shot List Creation   100
    23 Storyboard Examples   105
    24 How to Make a Documentary: Funding, Financing and
        Budgeting   110
    25 Communication: The Foundation of Production   115
    26 Recruiting Talent   119
    27 The Right Place at the Right Time   123
    28 Production Planning   128
    29 Gearing Up for Battle   138

PART III   **PRODUCTION TECHNIQUES**   **143**
    30 How to Make a Video   145
    31 The Divine Proportion: Balancing the Golden Rule   149
    32 Shooting Steady   154
    33 Basic Training: The Nine Classic Camera Moves   159
    34 Video and Photography Light Reflectors   164
    35 Applying Three-Point Lighting   167
    36 Get Real with Practicals   172
    37 Outdoor Cinematography   176
    38 Audio Levels   182
    39 10 Common Audio Mistakes   186
    40 10 Tips for Great Interviews   190
    41 Makeup and Wardrobe   196
    42 How to Make a Documentary   201
    43 Green Screen Directing   215
    44 Making Your Video Look More Like Film   219
    45 Screen Direction   223
    46 Shooting for 3D   228
    47 Optimizing Edit Organization   232
    48 Video Editing for N00bs   237

PART IV   **POST-PRODUCTION TECHNIQUES**   **243**
    49 Editing: It's the Pace, Ace!   245
    50 Editing Effects Software to Make Your Video Sing   249
    51 Easy Tricks to Edit Quickly   253
    52 Color Correction 101   258
    53 Less is More: Editing Titles and Graphics   262
    54 Fixing Audio in Post   266
    55 Recording Sound Effects   270
    56 Sync Sound   274
    57 Simple Compositing   278
    58 Be a Good Scout, Have a Backup Plan   282
    59 Public Access Television   287
    60 As Seen on TV: Citizen Journalism Worthy of Your Local News   292

PART V   **DISTRIBUTION**   **299**
    61 Options for Marketing Your Video   301
    62 Taking it to the Screen   308
    63 It Could Happen: Festivals   313
    64 Video on the Web   319
    65 Compression Software for Web Video   323
    66 Streaming Video, No Longer an Upstream Row   328
    67 Tips to Promote Your Video Online   332
    68 How to Make a Documentary: Distribution   337
    69 What's Legal   343
    70 Jacks of All Trades   349
    71 To DVD or not to DVD?   351

PART VI   **AUTHORING DVDS AND CDS**   **357**
    72 DVD Authoring Buyer's Guide   359
    73 DVD Authoring Freeware: A Guide to Free Tools   364
    74 Authoring Blu-ray Discs   369
    75 DVD/Blu-ray Duplication Services versus Home-Use Duplicators 376
    76 Special Features: DVD Extras   382

        JARGON: A GLOSSARY OF VIDEOGRAPHY TERMS   **387**

        CONTRIBUTING AUTHORS   **408**

        INDEX   **411**

Preface

We live in an age where most every family in America owns a video camera and editing software, even if they never sought out either. Anyone with an internet connection can put their video online where it can be seen by everyone on the planet. The Web has given anyone who wants it access to far more information than any film school alone can provide. The world of video production has entered a golden age. There are no more excuses not to pursue whatever goals you hope to achieve with video. *Videomaker* has been there very step of the way.

In the late 1990s, when the average middle-class American could purchase video editing software to run on the home computer they already owned, it was clear that we were entering a new era of video production. Consumer camcorders were already common, but with non-linear editors entering people's homes, so too was a quality of production previously reserved only for professionals or those willing to spend thousands on dedicated equipment.

Consumer video production stayed at that point for about ten years, as individuals shot SD footage on their home camcorders and edited on their PC or Mac. In the last few years, however, we've seen a surge forward in the process of consumer-level video production. It's a result of computers and cameras getting cheaper and moving into every electronic device in the home.

When *The Blair Witch Project* came out, people were amazed that someone could shoot an entire film that would be released worldwide, on a simple consumer camcorder. Today, an iPhone 5 could easily take better quality video and cost significantly less. The only reason, I believe, that we haven't yet seen a nationally released film shot entirely on a smartphone is simply because an extreme upgrade in picture quality and functionality can be purchased for under $1,000.

The world of video production has never had a lower barrier to entry. With cheap cameras, this book, and the ever-expanding audience on internet, there's no reason not to dive in.

Mike Wilhelm
Executive Editor
Videomaker Magazine

If You are New to Making Video: Welcome!

Matt York
Publisher/Editor of Videomaker Magazine

The craft of making video is an enjoyable one. Whether video production is for you a pastime, a part-time moneymaker or a full-time occupation, I am certain that you will enjoy the experience of creating video. There are many facets to video production. Each brings its own pleasures and frustrations, and each will stretch your abilities, both technical and artistic.

Video is a wonderful communication medium that enables us to express ourselves in ways unlike other media. Television and Web video are pervasive in our society today. The chance to utilize the same medium that the great TV and film producers have used to reach the masses is an incredible privilege. Video is powerful. Video is the closest thing to being there. For conveying information, there is no medium that compares with video. It overwhelms the senses by delivering rich moving images and high-fidelity sound. Having grown up with TV, many of us lack the appreciation for its power. Compared with radio or print, television profoundly enhances the message being conveyed. For example, reading about a battlefield in war can be less powerful than hearing a live radio report from a journalist with sounds of gunfire, tanks, rockets, incoming artillery fire and the emotions from an anguished reporter's voice. Neither compares with video shot on a battlefield.

It is amazing that you can walk into a retail store, make a few purchases in a few minutes and walk out with all of the essential tools for producing video. For less than $500, you can buy a camcorder and a personal computer and suddenly you have the capacity to create video that rivals a television station. Your mobile phone might work just as well for making simple videos. The image and sound quality of a camcorder or a mobile phone is better than broadcast television as viewed on an average TV. The transitions and special effects, available with any low-cost video editing software package, exceed the extravagance of those used on the nightly news.

If you want to share your videos on the internet, all you need is a Web-enabled mobile phone and you can upload directly to one of the many video-sharing sites. Realistically, if you are reading this you have a greater commitment to excellent video, which can only be accomplished with a dedicated camcorder and video editing. While many of the videos on these video-sharing sites are of low quality, there are plenty of people uploading and sharing some wonderfully produced videos. Video sharing is a wonderful new way to reach anyone on the planet that has an internet connection.

There was a time when any message conveyed on a TV screen was perceived as far more credible than if it were conveyed by other media (i.e. print or audio cassette). While that may no longer be as true, video messages are still more convincing to many people.

Once a highly complex pursuit, video editing is now just another software application on a personal computer. We all realize that simply using video editing software doesn't make someone a good TV producer any more than using Microsoft Word makes one a good writer. However, the ability to edit video in your own home or office is so convenient that it enables more people to spend more time developing their skills.

One of the most rewarding experiences in video production is getting an audience to understand your vision. The time between the initial manifestation of your vision and the first screening of the video may be just a few days or several years, but there is no more satisfying (or nerve-wracking) feeling than witnessing an audience's first reaction to your work.

PART I
Video Gear

A guide to essential equipment: what to buy, how it works

1
Cameras Need Lovin' Too: Camera Maintenance and Cleaning

Brandon Pinard

Figure 1-1

As a videographer or photographer, you might have multiple lenses and filters that you lug around wherever you go and change whenever the shot requires their use.

Over time and even with proper storage and care, your gear begins to wear out from use. It is always good to maintain your equipment well, by properly cleaning and storing it before and after you use it.

Body Care

The first part to address in caring for your camera is the largest part of your camera: the body. While the body collects the majority of dust and debris particles from the air, it is a fairly simple process to keep clean. One way is to use compressed air to blow debris from your camera's body. But be careful using this technique, because you can blow debris deeper into areas you are trying to clean.

Another is to use a microfiber cloth or a natural-fiber cloth of some kind to wipe off the excess debris from your camera body. Being cautious, you can continue by very lightly dampening a cleaning cloth and swabbing your camera's body surface, but be very careful around your camera's dials, buttons, lenses, viewfinder and controls. Next, immediately dry all surfaces of your camera with a clean and dry microfiber or natural cloth.

Lens Cap/Hood

Never leave your lens cap off for longer than required or your lens hood open after shooting—ever! This is extremely important, because the lens is the "precious" piece of equipment that also is the most difficult to properly maintain and care for in the long term. It can easily be the first thing to go. That is why the use of lens filters really safeguards your actual lens from the elements.

Filters

Keeping a filter or skylight over your lens is a great way to insure added protection and enhance your images. With a fixed lens camera, however, cleaning your lens can make you nervous, especially if the lens has fingerprints on it, which can happen from time to time and potentially can damage your lens. The oily residue from fingers can spot the touched area to a degree that could lead to permanent fogging. If you never use interchangeable filters, we still recommend at least keeping a fixed clear filter on the lens, it's cheaper to replace than the lens itself.

If your camcorder doesn't have the threads to attach a standard filter to it,

we discovered a new device you might want to check out: magnetic filter holders by Cokin. You have to first attach a lens frame to your camcorder using a special adhesive that comes with the kit. This is permanent, and you never remove it. Then the magnetic adapter attaches to the frame and you slide the filter up and down within the magnetic lens holder. Check the website for your camera's compatibility.

Be forewarned, though, with using any filter, some camcorders have detachable lens hoods, and you might not be able to reattach them over the lens that is sporting a few filters.

Solvent-Based Cleaners

In the past, lens cleaners have contained various harsh and abrasive chemicals that can strip away the protective coating on lenses of all types. Such chemicals include alcohol, ammonia, acetone, silicone, glycerin and chlorine. These are coincidentally bad for your health and are generally things you don't want to come in contact with, especially not on your lenses and camera gear. In our modern era of seemingly unlimited information, high technology and, more recently, sustainability, it seems fitting that, if you spend the money to purchase an HD camera, you should be able to preserve its ability to capture images clearly.

Applying Cleaning Solution

When applying a lens cleaning solution to a lens surface, the first thing to do is to blow off excess dust and debris from the lens surface. A hand-pumped blower made specifically for camera comes with a small brush attached and is a perfect device to add to your camera care kit. The bristles on this special brush are soft enough not to scratch your lens, and the hand-pump blows air softly to blow off most surface dust (see micro-tools.com and magicmicrocloth.com).

Figure 1-2 *A great accessory is a specialty cleaning pen made just for lenses. Besides having a lint-free brush, the pen uses a special carbon-based non-liquid cleaning compound.*

Like the camera body care we mentioned, you can use canned air, but be very careful with it, as you can't control the direction you blow, and it's quite powerful. In the worst case scenario, you can blow the debris off with your mouth, but don't get closer than about four inches, or you will get condensation on your lens, and don't blow so hard that you start spraying your lens. Just use short gusty breaths like you would use to gently help a fire get started without putting it out.

Cleaning Cloths

After you have blown off your lens surface, you want to proceed by wiping your lens clean with a cloth. A microfiber lens cloth is the best choice.

If you do not have access to a lens cloth, then the next best thing is a clean natural fiber like a lint-free strip of cotton fabric. Don't use cotton Q-tip, as it will leave behind more lint than you're removing. Some engineering shops use a device similar to a Q-tip, but it's made of a micro-fiber-like substance and is lint-free.

Once you have your lens cloth in hand, proceed by gently wiping your lens surface in a circular motion. When your lens surface is clear of excess debris, you are ready to use a lens cleaning solution. I recently tested a product called Purosol Optical, which is a completely natural

and non-abrasive lens cleaning solution. I was very impressed with Purosol: it did a great job of cleaning my lenses (of varying types) and is non-solvent-based, so there are no harsh chemicals that strip away protective lens coatings. Purosol is supposed to work in a way that neutralizes the molecular charge of the lens surface. This acts as a repellant for dust and debris particles, for at least a little while. Purosol is one of the few products that are good for cleaning your LCD viewfinder and even plasma TVs.

When applying a lens cleaning solution, don't apply the solution directly to your lens. Rather, apply the solution directly to your cleaning cloth, and then gently wipe the lens surface in a circular motion. Follow this action by using a dry area of your cloth to polish off the solution in the same fashion.

Stay away from solvents in general. Now that natural lens cleaners exist, there is really no reason to keep using solvent-based lens cleaning solutions. If you do not have access to a lens cleaner, then some warm and soapy water will do the job. Always make sure that you completely and immediately dry off all parts of your camera that encounter any liquid.

Guerrilla Cleaning

No matter how much you prepare, plan and obsess about all of the different things that can happen when you are using your camera gear, you will sometime find yourself in a situation when you need to clean your gear off immediately and just don't have your cleaning supplies with you, such as in a rainstorm or dusty environment. Use your best common sense and whatever resources/tools you have available to you to gently resolve the situation. If you have to wipe a lens with some piece of clothing, use the cleanest, softest and/or most natural piece of material that you have available. A used cotton T-shirt or "tightie whities" are the best non-lint cotton fabrics you can grab. Additionally, try to use a fabric that is dry, or you will likely do more damage than good, as you won't be able to successfully capture additional footage through a saturated lens.

Storage

After you go through the cleaning and maintenance part of caring for your camera, put it away safely. Having a secure place to put your camera gear is one of the best ways to properly maintain equipment for as long as possible. The best place is not your desk or closet, but a secure hard-shell camera case with a foam interior that can be custom-molded to your camera. When you store your camera, don't place cleaners or any potentially damaging materials or items in the case with your camera, as a single leak can be catastrophic to your precious equipment. Another option is a simple camera case. A bag with some ample padding will work as a camera case, but there are also numerous varieties of camera bags made specifically for different-sized cameras.

For get-up-and-go shooting, I use a LowePro camera backpack that fits a Digital SLR still camera, lenses and accessories in the bottom section, a mid-sized video camera and accessories in the upper section and a laptop computer in its top section. It is water-resistant (not water-proof), but it really holds a substantial amount of equipment and protects it while

Figure 1-3 *Unlike fixed foam casing, pluck foam can be custom fitted for your camera and extra gear. Cut a slot for your camera, battery, cables, etc., and there's a place for everything.*

it is in immediate use. I still remove my equipment from the backpack and store it properly in a hard case after I use it.

Conclusion

There is no substitute for proper care and maintenance cameras and lenses. Taking the time to clean and properly store your equipment before and after each use will make activities like lens cleaning less arduous and will ultimately result in having your equipment last long enough to be outdated by a newer technology or format. Remember, It is profitable to be a bit obsessive about keeping your camera equipment in the cleanest and best over-all condition possible.

2
CMOS vs CCD

Edward B. Driscoll, Jr.

(a)  (b)

Figures 2-1

The great film directors know that they're really not in the business of photographing actors–they're in the business of recording light. Eventually, by the 1960s and 1970s, they began to capitalize on this, occasionally shooting right into the lights on their sets, which became a trademark for directors such as Stanley Kubrick and Steven Spielberg.

Videography is film cinematography's younger brother, and understanding the role that light plays in videography is the key to understanding the difference between CCDs and CMOS technology.

CCD stands for charge-coupled device; CMOS stands for complimentary metal-oxide semiconductor. These are the chips onto which the light captured by a camcorder's lens is focused. Those signals are processed further inside the camcorder and ultimately the image is recorded to the camcorder's storage medium, whether it's tape, DVD, or an internal or external hard drive. Cameras with multiple image sensors use one chip per light primary color (red, green and blue), and utilize a separate image processor to combine the three signals into a color video image. Newer and cheaper CMOS chips bundle both an image sensor and image processor into a single chip. All CCD designs utilize an image processor that is separate from the actual light-capturing sensor.

The first big difference between the two is that CMOS chips are manufactured much like traditional microchips, whereas CCDs, utilizing technology that dates back to a 1969 invention by Bell Labs, use their own proprietary manufacturing process.

To understand their roles in recording video, it helps to flash back to a century-old technology, the film-based movie camera. On a film camera, once an image passes through its lens and aperture, it records onto a strip of plastic film containing light- and color-sensitive chemicals for later development. On a video camera, a CMOS or CCD image sensor translates the image from the lens to whatever digital medium the particular camcorder uses.

Because of their origins in the computer chip industry, CMOS chips are cheaper to manufacture. But in general, a camcorder equipped with separate CCDs will produce a better quality image with less electronic noise than a single CMOS chip.

Advances in manufacturing technology are reducing the quality differences between the two image sensor types. But before either type of chip can work its magic and electronically capture a picture, the image has to get there. Let's take a few moments to analyze its signal chain.

Let There Be Light

As most videographers know, proper illumination is essential both for aesthetics and to minimize video noise. Whether it's the sun, "God's 10,000,000 kilowatt light," as *Titanic* director James Cameron once dubbed it, or a simple bank of quartz lights, the lighting on your set or location enters the interior of the video camera through the glass of the lens, (or the plastic of the lens, on some lower-grade consumer cameras).

The size of a camcorder's lens impacts its performance. Many of the small consumer-grade camcorders on the floor of your local big-box electronics store have remarkably tiny lenses. This can impact their ability to perform in low-light situations: a larger-diameter lens will capture more light than a smaller lens. The general miniaturization of many consumer camcorders also explains the emphasis on CMOS chips, as CCDs typically consume much more power. Using CMOS helps consumer camcorders use smaller, but longer-lasting batteries, helping to keep the size down.

Once the light moves beyond the glass of the lens, it first hits the camcorder's

Figure 2-3 *The growth of CMOS technology has yielded smaller camcorders with better battery life as compared with models from previous generations but they tend to come equipped with smaller lenses. A larger-diameter lens will capture more light than smaller ones.*

Figure 2-2 *An image sensor is primarily based on a light-sensitive surface that picks up the light focused by the lens.*

aperture, and then its shutter—if it has one. Although a few higher-end CCD camcorders have mechanical shutters just as film cameras do, most consumer camcorders do not. CMOS chips electronically determine exposure length.

Like Having a Fotomat in Your Hand

Once light hits the image sensor, it becomes an analog electrical signal. In a CCD-based camcorder, the signal goes to the image processor, but in a CMOS-based camcorder, the output of the CMOS device is an encoded image, so the image processor is not required. The next stop for the encoded image is the camera's storage medium. Depending upon the sophistication of the camcorder, its image processor also automatically performs a variety of digital processing functions to the image that was passed to it. These can include white balance, image filtering and stabilization, error correction, color transformation and other processes.

The number of pixels on an image sensor impacts its performance in terms of resolution in general, and in more specialized applications, such as low-light shooting. Ultimately, pixel count will increase as the quality—and price—of the camcorder increases. But at least this is something that you can easily compare.

Another area where CCD-based designs provide more flexibility than their CMOS cousins is their ability to control gain. Professional camcorders often have an external gain control switch to adjust the sensitivity of the CCD, to help boost the input or throttle back video noise as appropriate. For typical usage, it's best to adjust the exposure with the aperture and shutter speed rather than the electronic gain control. However, there are times when increased sensitivity—and the inherent increase in noise—is the trade-off to getting a usable shot, particularly in low-light, run-and-gun conditions when the lesser video quality and graininess might be accepted.

The Color-Coordinated Camcorder

Image sensors only detect and record the intensity of the light hitting them, recording the grayscale image; they don't actually record in color themselves. In a single-chip camcorder design, a color filter array sits on top of the image sensor. Somewhere between the surface upon which light hits the image sensor and the encoded output of the image processor, the color is extracted in accordance with the pattern of the tiny color filters. The data stream passes through the codec utilized by the camcorder (such as DV, MPEG-2, MPEG-4 or AVCHD) to be compressed before it's recorded to whatever media the camcorder is using, be it tape, a hard drive, a disc, a memory card, a network connection, etc.

In the case of higher-end camcorders with multiple image sensors, each sensor captures a single primary light color via a prism inside the camera. The prism splits the light entering the camcorder's lens into red, green and blue and then sends those colors off to the matching image sensor, where the intensity of each color is encoded. The need for the three individual sensors, one for each primary color,

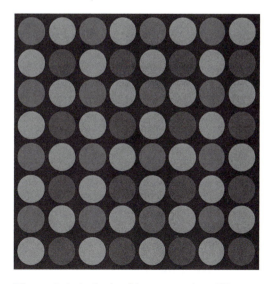

Figure 2-4 *A single-chip camcorder utilizes a filter array to break apart the image into a pattern of red, green and blue samples. This sample is converted to a usable picture by the image processor. (Seen here as shades of grey)*

is yet another reason why 3-chip pro cameras are more expensive than consumer-grade cameras.

Regardless of whether you have a small CMOS-based camcorder with a single image sensor, or a 3-CCD pro unit with a separate and complex high-end image processor, these chips do a whole lot of work that used to be done by many mechanical parts and a lot of chemicals in film-camera days. But they are not without their own problems.

Rolling Shutter, Smearing CCD

No, that's not the name of a rollicking martial arts film, but it does highlight some of the trade-offs of each technology.

To build on our analogy at the beginning of the article, shooting directly into over exposed bright lights with a CCD camera can result in smearing, which often manifests itself as glaringly obvious vertical streaks, very different from the way that lights bloom when photographed using film.

Most CMOS cameras use a rolling electronic shutter to capture an image sequentially in thin rows from top to bottom in the course of a single frame. This is in contrast to the more traditional global shutter of the CCD camera, where the sensor captures an image in its entirety.

The CMOS camera's rolling shutter can impose a different type of distortion: skew. This can cause distortion of the vertical lines in a shot during a quick pan. (Picture a whip pan shot of a New York skyscraper, for an extreme example.) But for those who primarily shoot weddings or news-gathering talking-heads footage, neither of these issues will occur very frequently. However, action-oriented videographers, take heed.

Choosing a Video Camera

Choosing between CMOS and CCD is only one element among many that must be considered when shopping for a new video camera. The size of the lens and whether or not the camcorder accepts interchangeable lenses for wide angle, telephoto, macro and other specialized applications is another. Is the camera equipped with XLR inputs for use with professional mics? Do those XLR inputs provide phantom power for clip-on lavalier mics? How flexible are the camcorder's controls, for those times when you don't wish to run the camera in automatic mode?

As with any professional equipment, from musical instruments to microscopes, poor technique will produce bad results, even if you are using the most expensive camcorder. Conversely, good technique can produce acceptable—sometimes even great—images on even the most inexpensive consumer cameras.

So should you choose CCD over CMOS? We asked Hahn Choi, who is one of the behind-the-camera talents at the streaming HD video web startup PJTV.com (where, in full disclosure, I am an occasional on-air talent). Choi said, "When it comes to quality, my personal opinion is that it doesn't make a difference, because of compression that's being used with most HD cameras. Whether it's HDV or AVCHD, it's still compression, and that'll affect the video quality. With the processing cameras, too, it's tough to say one is better than the other." However, although many higher-end manufacturers, including Red Digital Cinema, are beginning to use CMOS chips, if you can afford it, 3-CCD is the way to go. This is

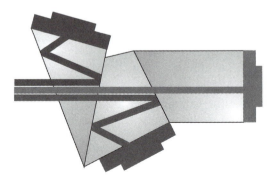

Figure 2-5 *A prism-like structure sends individual bands of the light spectrum to the three designated image sensors in a three-chip design.*

especially true if your material is ultimately designed to make its way to broadcast TV.

But so much material is being shot these days for the web, for video aggregation sites such as YouTube and as blogs and big media websites go multimedia. If that's the case, given the factors Choi mentioned, a good CMOS camcorder will suffice for many purposes.

3
Adjust Shutter Speed for the Best Video Images

Kyle Cassidy

Your camcorder has many manual settings – focus, white balance, aperture – that can make better images, but why would you want to change your shutter speed?

If you're like most people, you probably haven't thought much at all about shutter speeds on your camcorder; in fact, you don't lose any points if you hadn't even considered that your camcorder has different shutter speeds. Most modern

Figure 3-1 Some camcorders have direct button access to the shutter but on many camcorders you'll need to find it in menus.

camcorders do an excellent job of setting an exposure so it doesn't typically come up.

So why then would you even want to set a shutter speed? Well, for a few reasons, but the big one is control. Very often we'll rely on our camera's internal electronics to choose a shutter speed and aperture—it usually does a pretty good job but can be confused by situations that are very dark or very light, such as something backlit by the sun or the inside of a dark room that you want to keep dark in your footage. For this reason you'll sometimes want to tell the camera what settings to use rather than let it choose. Another reason is because you want to shoot at a particular aperture to achieve a certain depth of field. In this chapter we'll take a look at some reasons you'd want to set your shutter speed manually, but first a little bit of background.

How Your Camera Sets Exposure—It's Math (But Not the Difficult Kind)

Your camera is a bit like an hourglass. A certain amount of light needs to hit your camera's sensor in order to make a properly exposed image. This can happen in a number of ways: a lot of light can come in quickly, or a small amount of light can come in slowly. The two ways that you control this are your aperture and your shutter speed (there is a third variable, your "gain", which is essentially telling the camera to multiply the amount of light it has recorded and pretend there's more. Read more on your camcorder's gain setting.) The aperture is a circular iris that can be opened or closed to let more or less light in. (Video cameras have a "virtual aperture" but the concept is the same.) The shutter speed is the length of time light is collected on the sensor.

Let's go back to the days when motion picture cameras were just being invented. The way Thomas Edison's fascinating device works is that a ribbon of light-sensitive film is moved behind a lens which

Figure 3-2 *Like an hourglass, light hits your camera's sensor in a number of ways: a lot of light can come in quickly, or a small amount of light can come in slowly.*

focuses an image on it. In order to keep this from being just a continual blur, there is a little door between the lens and the film. This door called the "shutter" is open only for a brief fraction of a second, an image is frozen on the film, the shutter closes, and the film moves while no light is hitting it, then it opens again for a brief fraction of a second, freezing another slightly different image. These are viewed back the same way—an image is projected on a screen, a shutter closes, the screen goes black, the film moves, the shutter opens and the second image appears. It's like a slide show at 24 frames a second. A phenomenon of our brains known as "persistence of vision" makes us believe we are seeing one image that is moving instead of several still images in rapid succession. The rate at which motion pictures play back has largely remained constant since Thomas Edison invented his first camera in 1891. It was a bit variable at first because it depended on a person turning a crank at a constant speed, tending to be about 16 frames per second, but later it became set in stone. One of the biggest reasons why frame rates haven't changed is the NTSC standard used for broadcast television. This dictates a frame rate of 29.97 frames per second. Which in the days of film meant you couldn't have a shutter speed longer than that and many camcorders have a minimum shutter speed of 1/60th or 1/24th of a second. However, since there is no physical transport—no film that needs to move from one place to another this limitation has become somewhat theoretical—a number of new camcorders have special modes which will allow slower shutter speeds which are then converted to 29.97 fps by repeating the same image over multiple frames of video. Using frame rates lower than 1/30th of a second can create significant blur in moving objects which can, if used appropriately, be a very interesting effect.

Changing Your Shutter Speed to Affect DoF

Until relatively recently, shooting at a wide f-stop didn't necessarily translate into the super shallow depth of field (DoF) we're used to seeing in Hollywood movies. This is because of the relatively small sensor size of consumer video cameras. In the past few years more and more people are shooting HD on digital SLR cameras that provide access to a wide range of 35 mm film lenses with their huge f-stops. This gives a very tangible reason to want to shoot wide open in daylight. Set your lens to the widest aperture possible, then adjust your shutter speed until the image is properly exposed. If you're shooting in brightly lit conditions, you may need to add some neutral density filters to the front of your lens.

Looking Back

Exposure really hasn't changed since the invention of film photography back in the 1800s and, except for the substitution of electronics for chemical and mechanical parts, motion picture photography/videography is essentially the same as well. Settings that used to be made entirely by hand—the aperture and shutter speed as well as the frame rate and film "speed" (now gain) are mostly these days set automatically by your camcorder. But these guesses aren't always correct and a videographer who wants to very specifically affect the look of their footage needs to understand how and when to change these settings.

See for Yourself

Figure 3-3 and 3-4 *Sharp images are the result of a high shutter speed whereas blurred images are the result of a low shutter speed.*

Here's a homework assignment. Enlist the aid of a fast moving assistant—Frisbee-catching dog, rambunctious teenager or local dancer—and videotape them using a variety of shutter speeds. Also try panning across a scene very quickly. If your camcorder allows very low shutter speeds, also try some shots indoors in low light both with motion and static shots. Then when you review your footage, pay special attention to how the images feel to you visually. At what point does a fast or slow shutter speed distract from the action and at what shutter speeds is it most appealing? Try this for a variety of different actions at different speeds.

4
Weighing In on the Tapeless World

John Devcic

Figure 4-1

This chapter looks at the overwhelming positive reasons for a move to tapeless production—however, these would only be half the story.

When it comes to tapeless, many people assume there is no downside. No technology is without a downside. This article will talk about both pros and cons and aims to introduce some of the popular solutions available today. Keep in mind that tapeless is another word for what is known as Digital Asset Management or DAM. If you are on the fence about a move from tapes, this article is the perfect starting point.

Advantages of Tape-Based Productions

Tapes have one big advantage that even today still shine through. Tapes are very durable. Some tape collections can be decades old and still work. CD and DVDs were originally believed to last forever. After a period of time, we began to see CD and DVDs degrade and stop working. They also required certain optimal storage conditions that were rarely met. The one crucial drawback with CD and DVD is simply the all-or-nothing factor. If a CD or DVD is old and is scratched or damaged in some way the data on there is lost, usually for good. A tape on the other hand can be damaged slightly or worse but the undamaged portion can still be played back.

Disadvantages of Tape-Based Productions

Degradation—tape degrades over time sometimes portions of the tape can be so badly degraded that the content is unrecoverable. Depending on how many copies you have this can become a serious issue.

Storage—tapes take up a lot of space and will fill shelves quickly. Tape retrieval from this storage area can be a hassle. Depending upon how well the tapes were labeled it can take a long time to find something you know you have but do not know where it is. A constant updating of the library is essential.

Advantages of Tapeless Production

Stable recordings—if properly taken care of, digital media will not suffer from the same sometimes-bizarre jittery behavior that can often occur when using tapes. To be fair indeed, tapes can be a great way to record, and have been for years. We have all had a tape that may have been brand new and for some reason or another midway through the tape may fail to record something. Of course, this is not brought to your attention until after the shoot when you go back and review the tape.

Reliability—once recorded you can quickly make copies of what you shot on site. Often times once backed up elsewhere, you can reuse the same cards and hard drives over and over again without loss of quality. Digital transfers do not degrade, no matter how many copies of the original are made.

File-based recording—using the file structure is new compared to the old thinking of dumping everything on a few tapes and spending hours going through and logging tapes. Files make indexing and retrieving a file easier. Naming of files is entirely personal and can be quickly changed.

On-site editing—instead of having to wait till after the shoot to edit, you can easily take the files and begin editing

Figure 4-2 and 4-3 Tapeless production makes for easier on-site editing. Simply transfer the files from the card and you're ready to dive in.

them on a laptop using any number of available editing tools. Since editing is completely digital now anyway, you no longer have to wait to import anything you shot from a tape. Being able to edit on-site during a shoot means you can see if you will need to add something and redo the scene while you are still on-site instead of finding out later that you are missing a good cutaway or a shot does not work.

Cost reduction—there are two major costs associated with tapes. First, of course, is the cost of the tapes themselves. Tapes are expensive and you need to buy many of them because you never know how often you will need them. Since you can only really use a tape once for reliable video production that means you need a new tape every time you take your camera out on a shoot. This of course brings on up the question of what to do with all of those tapes that you have only used once. That is the second major cost associated with using tapes. Storage is indeed a cost incurred by anyone who needs to store tapes for future retrieval or use. It is not uncommon for major production facilities to have a large storage area only for the storing of their tape collection. Now you have another cost associated with tapes: the cost of logging and retrieving of content. Tape management can become an unruly and difficult job to say the least.

Media Management and Archiving

Three types of copies—when you deal with media management you really need to start thinking about what you shot in terms of three. Simply put, there are three types you need to always be thinking about:

First is the master copy. The master copy is the one that should never be worked on or edited from. This one is your ultimate copy. I know what you're thinking—there is probably a lot of stuff on your master that you do not need. While it is easy to say that now, you never know exactly when you may need something from the original shoot that you no longer have because you deleted it. The master copy should be backed up to make the second copy and not touched again except for retrieval.

That brings us to the backup copy. The backup copy should be the one you go to when your working copy fails or you over-edited the working copy without backing that copy up. In any case, your backup copy is the one you will keep around during postproduction, referring to it as needs arise. The backup copy is basically a copy of your master but is kept on-site to be worked on if the need arises.

The working copy is the copy of the master or backup that is used for editing purposes. This is the one that can be touched up if need be. This is the last rough copy you have before the finished product. This copy can be worked on immediately after

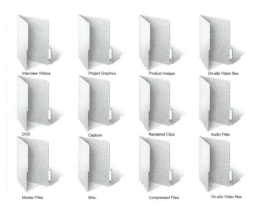

Figure 4-4 and 4-5 *Video servers are much easier to work with as they save you time and can be accessed virtually anywhere. Plus they do not require a ton of physical storage space.*

filming or better yet on-site during a shoot. You have little worry about over editing since you have a backup.

So you have all of this content indexed but what is the best way to manage it?

Entering Stage Left is the Video Server

Think of the video server as one big library filled with all your video. However, this library can be accessed from anywhere in the production facility or anywhere else for that matter thanks to the internet. This computer's only purpose is in the serving up of your media upon request. Now you no longer have to worry about going into the storage area. Instead, you have this video server or digital librarian, if you will, handling and serving your content. There are many advantages to using a video server.

Advantages of Using a Video Server

Your files are easily accessed. The video server saves the changes where you want them. Other computers can be connected to it and access and work on the files. It's not unusual to see a video server in its own room without a monitor or keyboard attached. This is done so no one uses the video server directly but can only access it over the company's intranet.

The video server also handles all of the access and can be set up to automatically save a project to a different location. It saves all current and past projects in files where you specify. You have control over who can access what files and if necessary for how long.

Your files can be located anywhere as long as the video server has access to the files and you have access to those same files.

Archiving

There are many choices for long-term storage of your digital media—here are the most popular:

Hard Drives—hard drives can be enclosed in a computer or can be daisy chained and used as one big hard drive. They can be easier to work with and easier to access data from as compared to other storage media. Rewriting is a cinch and with no loss of quality. Prices for drives are always dropping. They do have their issues. Some hard drives will fail early and eventually they will all fail. Proper care and maintenance is required. Hard drives are not necessarily portable. You really do not want to be carrying around an external hard drive wherever you go. They do make travel sized drives but not with the same storage capacity. Backing up is crucial.

CD/DVDs—the biggest advantage offered is their size. They are small and portable. Their cost is low and they can be purchased in bulk easily. You have to keep in mind that they are fragile. They can be bent and damaged easily. Scratching is an issue. You will also need to store them in a cool dark place. CD and DVDs are not permanent storage solutions. You will need to back these up occasionally or you will find that your data may be gone without warning.

Solid state—this encompasses all solid state devices such as SD cards and hard drives. There are no moving parts that can fail. They are the most durable of the archiving options. They can be mistreated and retain data. When it comes to SD cards, their small size makes them easy to store and transport. Solid state has some drawbacks. The small size of SD cards means they can be lost easily. The other is cost per megabyte. Solid state is still more expensive per megabyte when compared with other archiving options.

Off-site or cloud solutions—one of the best ways to secure your digital media is by backing it up and storing it off-site. Since the internet and faster modems have become the standard, backups can be done in what is known as the cloud. You can purchase space from any number of retailers that will backup your media on their computers in a server farm. You are paying for the space you use. The benefit is

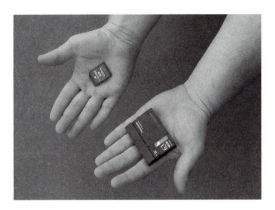

Figure 4-6 *Memory cards take up far less physical space than traditional tapes and can be more durable.*

you do not have to worry about maintaining those storage computers; the people operating the program do that. Often times off-site will go hand in hand with other archiving solutions.

Think about your shoot and what you have recorded in three sections and you will never have to worry about over editing or having to go back for some extra shots. You can record far more then you think you will ever need without worrying about the extra cost of new tapes. Moving from tape to tapeless can be a challenge but one well worth the time and investment. Archiving is the most important challenge in the digital world. But remember, making a backup does not mean you should not check it every year or so to make sure the medium still works—this is, and most likely always will be, quite important to long-term storage.

Size Matters

Size and speed will be your two biggest factors. Regular SDHC cards will have a 32-gigabyte limit. There are newer cards called SDXC cards that can range in size from 32 gigabyte all the way up to 2 terabytes. The cost per megabyte does increase dramatically the bigger the size. You will also want to look at their access speeds. This will tell you how fast the card performs when written to. Choose SDHC cards or if available the newer SDXC cards. When it comes to choosing the manufacturer, stick to recognizable companies. The quality will be better, thus making the cards more reliable.

5
Lens Accessories for Your Camcorder

Bill Davis

Figure 5-1

There's nothing more satisfying than finding just the right thing to give your videos a fresh new look.

Three types of camcorder lens accessories—lens filters, wide-angle lens adapters and telephoto lens adapters—offer you extra flexibility and creativity when you begin to acquire your footage.

Wide Angles

The frustration of not getting everything you want into a shot simply because you can't physically move any farther back is a common one.

Those clever lens accessory makers provide a wide array of add-on lens adaptors designed to let your camera see more of the horizontal and vertical field of view at a given distance. At some point, wide-angle lenses introduce an unacceptable amount of distortion, which manifests itself as a fish-eye view.

Probably the most flexible type in the category is the "zoom-through" wide-angle adapter. As the name implies, this design lets you increase the viewing angle of your lens, but keeps its ability to zoom intact.

Figure 5-2 *There are a variety of high quality wide-angle adapters available at reasonable prices.*

Not all wide-angle lenses are of the zoom-through variety. A standard wide-angle diopter provides a larger viewing field, but at a fixed focal length. Once you put it on the camera, you're restricted to that one wide shot.

Go Long

Tele-extenders do just the opposite. These screw onto the front of your camcorder's lens and expand its long-range zoom capabilities.

A 2× extender affixed to the end of your camcorder lens will let you make objects appear twice as close as they appear without the accessory.

However, with that plus comes a minus. Lens extenders typically restrict the amount of light that reaches your camera's CCD. So, to get a properly exposed picture

with a tele-extender in place, you'll need to arrange for more light to fall on your subject or you'll need to open up your aperture, thereby reducing your depth of field. These long-lens accessories are most useful when used outdoors and in other situations where you have plenty of available light.

Another challenge with tele-extenders is that at your camcorder's widest zoom setting, the barrel of the extender will actually mask a portion of the frame, providing a round window effect instead of a full frame.

With an extreme extender, like a 5× lens, you might only get a full field of view at your camcorder's maximum zoom. And the resulting images will be quite a bit dimmer than your camera would otherwise produce.

Get Close

At the other end of the lens spectrum are macro units designed for closeup work. These attachments allow you to focus your video camera's lens nearly on top of an object. Although most camcorders have fantastic default macro capabilities (just see how close you can get to an object with yours), you can use macro attachments to get extreme close-ups without getting physically close to the object, which in practice allows you to get more light onto your subject.

These accessories are ideal for videotaping coin or stamp collections, and closeup lenses are often just the ticket for copystand work, allowing you to get your camera really close to modest-sized objects so they'll fill the entire video frame.

Lens Filters

The artistic uses of a colored piece of glass (albeit an optical-grade piece of glass) in front of your camera's lens do not begin to cover the sophisticated applications of lens filters. The most simple and inexpensive is a protective filter, which is a clear piece of glass used to guard the expensive optics of your lens. Glass inherently stops potentially damaging UV radiation, so most protective filters also tout their ability to stop UV light; it can't hurt and doesn't cost any more for a UV filter. The next level is a neutral density (ND) filter, which is a gray piece of glass, designed to lower the total amount of light entering the lens without changing its color. This can be useful when you want to open up the aperture for some depth-of-field effects on a bright day. ND filters come in a variety of densities. Another variation on the ND filter is the gradient filter, which you can rotate to diminish the light from the sky for example, allowing you to properly expose two greatly disparate areas of a scene.

Another handy filter for use in the sun is a polarizing filter. It controls reflected light, which comes at the camera in straight, parallel lines. Polarizing filters can reduce glare from water, snow, glass or other non-metal reflective sources and thereby allow you to capture deeper, more saturated colors.

Color correction filters are also available, but camcorders can often do without these filters with careful and intentional manual white balancing techniques. You may find artistic or creative uses for colored filters, however.

Figure 5-3 Star filters and polarizers can be purchased as part of a kit that makes it easy to keep all of your go-to modifiers in one safe place.

Special Effects

Special effects are also a part of the lens accessory toolbox. From special colors, gradient colors, fogs, frosts, stars, multi-image to petroleum jelly, there are many tricks and effects you can perform in-camera without fooling around with capturing and editing your video on a computer. Just remember that the real world doesn't have any levels of Undo.

There is another whole class of lens accessories designed to work with your filters and help you improve your shots in the field.

Matte boxes, special holders that attach to the front of your camcorder, allow you to mount glass or plastic filters such as polarizers and gradient filters to the front of your lens.

These often provide the same capabilities as screw-on lens filters, but by using a matte-box system, you get the benefits of being able to easily use multiple filters for the same shot, and you have the ability to quickly change filters as your shooting environment changes.

So called "French flags" are shades mounted on special flexible arms that can keep the sun from spoiling your shots with unwanted lens flares.

Lens Control

Two other extremely popular lens accessories that come to the camcorder world from the world of broadcast video cameras are remote zoom and focus controllers.

In the pro world, studio kits are extension handles with controls for zoom and focus that let camera operators control their shots via special connectors and gears that manipulate camera settings.

Modern camcorder equivalents use electronic connections (most often the LANC port on your camcorder) to provide some of the same remote-controlled convenience.

If you've ever mounted your camcorder to a jib arm, or tried to use it while your tripod is at its maximum height, you'll understand how useful having remote control of zoom and focus can be.

Wrap it Up

Lens accessories have been around almost as long as the camcorders themselves. And the best of them make our lives easier by providing us with creative options and giving us more control over the images that our camcorders produce. For more information on lens filters and accessories, visit the companies listed below.

Lens Accessory Terms

Zoom-through—a wide-angle lens type that keeps an image in focus through the range of your camcorder's zoom.

Lens speed—the efficiency of a lens to pass light.

Multi-coated—optical coatings put on lens elements to reduce lens flare or other distortions.

Barrel distortion—the effect of the physical length of a lens housing on the image passing through it.

Vignetting—when a lens doesn't pass the full picture and essentially "masks" part of the original image.

Edge distortion—the effect of lens curvature on the edges and corners of a frame.

Fisheye—a type of ultra-wide angle lens providing an extremely wide angle of view at the cost of extreme image distortion.

6
Stabilization: Tools and Techniques

Randal K. West

Figure 6-1

Like most people, you probably began shooting video handheld. After all, when confronted with a camcorder, often your first instinct is to pick it up, hold it to your eye and begin rolling tape. Chances are that your initial handheld footage was pretty shaky too. Sure, shaky shots have their place. Where would MTV and *Blair Witch Project* be without them? However, in the video world, shaky footage makes a statement about your professionalism. In the mind of the viewer, shaky video equals home video. And home video is considered the work of amateurs.

Figure 6-2 *Tripods.*

If you are serious about producing video, take a few moments to get familiar with the options available for camcorder stabilization and smooth movements: namely tripods, dollies, jibs and gliding camera stabilizers. In addition to smoothing out those shaky shots, each type of support will affect the look of a shot. In this chapter, we'll investigate each type of stabilizer, and examine the impact that each will have on the look of your footage.

Tripods

The most common stabilization tool is the tripod. There are many well-made tripods on the market (see the August 2000 issue of *Videomaker* for a complete tripod buyer's guide), and they offer a number of advantages. You get a rock-solid shot, the ability to make smooth pans and tilts, and the ability to shoot for hours without the right side of your body cramping up.

Figure 6-3 *Dollies.*

The "head" of the tripod connects to the legs and holds your camcorder. The camcorder mounting head (fluid is preferred) should have adjustments that will apply a variable amount of drag or resistance to the pan and tilt controls. These drags allow you to adjust the tension on the head so you can complete camcorder moves with a minimum of jittering and jumping. You accomplish any change of position, whether done as a continuing movement or simply for changing the shot for alternative framing or composition, by pivoting the camcorder mount side to side (pan), up and down (tilt) or in some combination.

You will find that raising and lowering the actual height of the camcorder can dramatically change the composition of a shot. Generally, the level of elevation should place the lens at eye level with your talent. If you are having problems in the background, (a plant seeming to grow from someone's head or a reflection from a light source), you can usually alleviate the problem by changing the height of the camcorder. Most adjust from as low as a foot or two from the ground to six feet or more in height.

Dollies

A dolly is simply a device that allows you to roll the camcorder from one position to another. Many of us think of film dollies as large carts that roll on tracks carrying a camera and camera operator.

In video, dollies tend to be smaller and lighter. The standard video dolly (sometimes referred to as a "crab dolly" because of its ability to move quickly in all directions) simply a set of wheels into which a tripod locks.

Some directors will use a dolly move in place of a zoom in or out by moving the camcorder closer or farther away from the subject. We call this "dollying." There is a definite difference in the way the zoom lens, in a wide-angle mode, sees two objects

Figure 6-4 *Jibs.*

separated by 10 feet and the way the lens sees those two subjects in the high-magnification mode. A wide-angle setting makes backgrounds seem larger and farther from the subject. A telephoto setting compresses the apparent distance between subject and background. While a zoom in or out causes a change in perspective, a dolly towards or away from a subject maintains the perspective of the wide-angle or telephoto setting as the camera moves through a scene.

You can experiment with different camcorder-to-source distances and change lens focal length to get the effect you're looking for. One effect to try is to slowly zoom from wide angle to telephoto as you dolly the camera towards your subject.

With a dolly, you can also "truck" the camcorder, or move it laterally. You can use this move to accomplish a change of framing and picture. As the camcorder "trucks left" or "trucks right," it moves sideways but does not pan to the left or right. You might also use this move to follow alongside, or "track" with, a jogger as he runs.

You can watch almost any Hollywood film and spot a dolly move if you pay close attention. A classic instance occurred when Alfred Hitchcock used a zoom in combined with a dolly out in *Vertigo*. This was the first time a director moved the camera away from the subject at the same time the camera zoomed in. This created the illusion of "vertigo" as the background appeared to crash in on the subject.

Steven Spielberg's famous shot in *JAWS* of the sheriff sitting in the lifeguard station and seeing the shark from the beach was a dolly shot. This time, the camera simultaneously dollied-in and zoomed-out.

Jibs and Cranes

The jib is a cost-effective alternative to the camera cranes that Busby Berkeley flew around on while shooting his 1930s dancing extravaganzas like *Dames* or *42nd Street*. The camera crane actually raised both the camera and the operator

Figure 6-5 *Crane shots.*

into the air. For this reason, the crane had to be very large and very heavy.

The Jimmy jib, the professional standard, is a full-sized, remote controlled crane arm designed for motion picture photography. A full-sized Jimmy jib has a crane length of 4 to 28 feet. Standard gym weights make up the counterweight, which balances the weight of the camcorder.

Jibs often sit atop tripods mounted to dollies. Many models of jibs also run on a track to accommodate long, smooth dolly moves. The operator controls pans, tilts, zooms, focus, f-stops and the VTR with buttons, levers and/or a joystick at the weighted end of the jib. Since the jib operator controls both the camcorder and the jib arm, he has the ability to perform arcs, sweeps, cranes, trucks and dollies. A jib allows the operator to position the camera from as low as eight inches to as high as 35 feet.

The jib has brought a much broader range of shots to video. Any time you see a shot where the camera appears to fly over an audience toward the set of a game show, that's a jib shot. When you see an over-the-shoulder shot of a chef in a cooking show, it's most likely a jib shot. When the camera seems to rise above a city street as the hero rides into the sunset on his motorcycle, you guessed it, it's a jib shot.

Gliding Camera Stabilizers

The gliding camera stabilizer, like the well-known Steadicam brand, usually attaches the camcorder to a harness worn by the operator, allowing him to move freely while the camera remains steady. This creates shots that seem as if the camcorder is rolling on a dolly on tracks, or floating through a scene.

The need for the gliding camera stabilizer arose from the need to move a camera into areas that operators could not access with a dolly. Kent Hofmeister operates a gliding camera stabilizer and provided us with an explanation of what a gliding camcorder stabilizer is and how it works. "A gliding camera stabilizer uses Newtonian physics to stabilize the camera. The mass of the camera is enlarged and, in turn, stabilized by mounting it on a post (known as a sled), which has a counterweight at the bottom. This sled is then suspended through a free-floating gimbal (horizontal stabilizing mechanism) at its center of gravity. This is essentially the same principle used by a high-wire walker with the long pole used as a balance mechanism. The camera/sled combination is then hung or suspended on a spring loaded arm."

Smaller units for consumer models use the same principle on a smaller scale. The operator's arm replaces the vest and spring-loaded arm. The operator simply moves the device by grasping a handle attached to the gimbal. The smaller units can be a little trickier to operate than the professional ones, because it takes less force to de-stabilize the system. However, the lighter systems fit into tighter places

Figure 6-6 *Stabilizers.*

and are easier to maneuver than their larger counterparts.

The gliding camera stabilizer provides a cheaper, less time-consuming and more flexible method of creating dolly-style shots. A director can rethink and re-plot an entire camera move without having to relay the tracks. Good Steadicam operators make their work invisible and almost indistinguishable from dolly shots. The use of this sort of device allows the camera to steadily capture shots it simply couldn't before: going up stairs, climbing ladders, riding horses and running, to name a few.

The director can use a gliding camera shot to make dramatic statements or very subtle ones. Action scenes have become much more involving and engrossing since the camera can move so freely through the action. Look at the action sequences in both *Saving Private Ryan* and *Braveheart* and you will see the results of substantial use of gliding camera stabilizers.

Get Moving

There are many ways to stabilize and move your camcorder to get more interesting shots, and it isn't as difficult as you might think. You will be amazed at how quickly you can learn to operate any of this equipment.

I often tell clients, "Television is magic, but some forms of magic cost a little more." Try that with your clients and see if you can get them to splash out for a jib or a gliding camera stabilizer! If you're the director, perhaps it's time to try some of this equipment yourself. The good news is that you can try many of these techniques without a big investment. You probably already have a tripod—you just need to use it. You can create an effective dolly shot with a wheelchair. Jibs and gliding camera stabilizers can be purchased for a few hundred dollars. If you don't want to splash out with a big investment for purchasing stabilization gear, you can often rent production equipment from local vendors. Check around. You might be surprised at what is available.

If you want to add a professional look and feel to your camerawork, consider employing one of the stabilizers mentioned in this chapter, and exercising a bit of creativity. Your viewers will never mistake your camerawork for home video again. Unless, of course, you are shooting a *Blair Witch* spoof.

7
DSLR Workflow Tips: a Pro's Eye View

Mark Holder

Figure 7-1

HDSLR cameras are taking the digital video production world by storm. Cameras like the Canon EOS 5D Mark II video DSLR have large sensors producing gorgeous high definition images with incredibly shallow depths of field and interchangeable lenses.

It's easy to see why the Canon EOS 5D Mark II video camera and others like it have become so popular in such a short period of time. Of course they do have their challenges. Their physical form is not particularly conducive to hand-held work so they must be attached to a tripod or some other stabilizing device. Their audio capabilities as a professional video camera are, well, awful. And many of them leave much to be desired in terms of LCD screen resolution, focusing aids, exposure assistance and more.

Fortunately, for each of these shortcomings there is an answer, even several. And the pros of working with these cameras are great enough that it is often worth the added expense required (for the professional at least) to purchase the extra gear needed to overcome the cons.

Whether you're a weekend shooter or a professional DSLR user, fully equipped and heavily funded with the highest end professional video cameras and gear, or you've just pulled your sub-$1,000 camera and stock lens out of the box, one thing you simply must do, in order to save yourself from a world of potential grief on your next digital video production, is follow a solid, proven, workflow. Here are a few shooting with DSLR tips that might help you accelerate and refine that workflow.

Workflow Worries

In its simplest sense, the term workflow refers to a repeatable sequence of steps performed to get from state A to state B. For our purposes we'll use workflow to describe each of the steps taken from the moment we press *record* on the camera until we close and lock the door on the "archive vault." A workflow is designed to assure optimal efficiency throughout the production and post-production process and to guarantee, to the highest degree possible, the security of the data acquired.

A workflow should be repeatable to ensure that it will become automatic over time for all persons involved. It should also be scalable so it can be adapted to the size of the operation. A simple, one-person, single camera shoot and a fully crewed, multi-camera feature production are vastly different in terms of scale but have two things very much in common: the need to be efficient, and, most importantly, data security.

Time lost due to misplaced, mishandled or lost footage results in a serious reduction in efficiency. But imagine completing a week-long, multi-camera shoot, only to discover in the edit bay that the media card containing the best takes from the best camera angle was inadvertently recorded over because it wasn't handled properly. Perhaps worse, what if this were to happen on a single-camera shoot

with no coverage whatsoever from other angles? If you're out shooting some kids and their skateboard acrobatics at the local skate park, it might not be such a big loss but what if it were your daughter's graduation—or wedding? If a commercial project, how do you explain to your client that you lost the key footage and will have to reshoot? The dog ate my media card probably won't fly any better today than the excuse did in school. The message here is that by following a solid workflow, and following it fanatically, you should never have to face any of these devastatingly nightmarish situations.

Cradle to Grave

Once the record button is pressed, birth is given to an HDSLR digital asset. In its rawest form, it must be protected from corruption and loss. The workflow process is designed to ensure its safe journey throughout gestation, delivery, and finally, taking its place in digital asset heaven—the archive room. It is transferred from camera to card then from card to computer. Here it is cloned; multiple copies to ensure its survival should disaster strike. Once the clones are sent on their respective journeys it's off to post, where it will be cut, rolled, time remapped, color corrected, blended with others and compressed. In this final state, more clones will be produced with some

Figure 7-2 *Labels on cameras and cards will allow for organization among different people and throughout the process.*

being delivered to anxiously awaiting clients and others sent to join their raw, primal brothers in the archive room.

Dangers lurk in every corner and care must be taken to prevent the loss of data. One of the first steps to take is in the area of proper media management. This becomes especially critical on multi-day, multi-camera shoots. A single media card is one thing but trying to manage a dozen or more media cards is another disaster-waiting-to-happen altogether. Someone must be responsible for the proper handling of all media. Not several people—one. Having just one individual in the role of digital media manager will avoid confusion. If you're a one-person show, then it's pretty evident who that person is going to be.

One key task is to develop a naming system that will enable you to keep your media cards and their digital assets straight and intact all the way through the process. Start by labeling your cameras externally with tape: A, B, C, etc. Next, the camera is labeled internally. Place a card in Camera A and take a still shot. Remove the card from the camera and connect it to the computer via a card reader. Find the image you just captured in the card's DCIM sub-folder and rename it using the numbers 0999. Now, the next images captured on this camera will be in the 1000 series. Repeating the process for other cameras, make Camera B the 2000 series, Camera C the 3000 series and so on. When developing a naming scheme, be sure to check your camera's manual for its accepted file format. Set file numbering to continuous to ensure that

file numbers continue in sequence when changing cards rather than starting over with each new card.

When shooting, as cards are filled, remove them from their respective cameras and label them with tape; i.e. the first card out of Camera A is labeled A1; the third card out of Camera C is labeled C3, etc. Once filled and labeled, the cards are placed in a protective case, flipped over, backside up, making it obvious that these have yet to be downloaded onto the computer and copied to backup drives. The case goes to the digital media manager who knows, at a glance, which cards need to be downloaded, and which camera they came from. The media manager loads the cards into the reader and downloads the images to the hard drive(s). Before sending the card back, the media manager renames the DCIM subfolder as DONE so the camera will read it as empty. The tape label is removed and the card is placed back into the protective case, right side up, to show that it is ready to be recorded onto once again, and sent back to the field. When this card is placed in the camera for formatting it will show that there is data on the card. When play is pressed, however, the camera will indicate that no image is present, confirming that the card has indeed been downloaded by the media manager and is OK to format and re-use. Consider protecting your data by making several copies on different hard drives. These drives can then be distributed to the director and editorial. One hard drive should be kept as a backup and the one should go into a vault for safe-keeping.

Figure 7-3 and 7-4 Jarvis shoots both video and photos with HDSLRs. Left: Dasein: the Art of Being is one example of Jarvis' documentaries. Right: Still photo from www.chasejarvis.com.

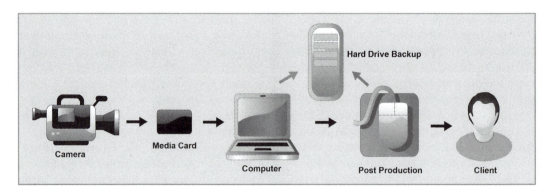

Figure 7-5 *An efficient and safe workflow is critical to your successful DSLR production.*

Chase Jarvis is a well-known, professional DSLR user. He shares his complete workflow on his website, www.chasejarvis.com. Immediately after recording, cards are given to the media manager (also known as the Digital Asset Manager) for ingestion. With the card in the card reader, data is copied simultaneously to two daisy-chained hard drives. In the field, all files are then run through Compressor and output as ProRes 422 files for an even starting point back in the studio.

Each day after shooting the crew returns to base camp where data from the field drive is copied to a 2TB RAID 1 drive. This creates two 1TB drives that are exact copies of one another. Each drive then goes to a different location for safety. If something happens to one, the other is readily available to continue working. Next, initial editing begins with the shots fresh in mind; the best shots are noted now so they can be worked on later.

Back in the studio all data is copied to a server (and backup drive) which runs a 16-drive storage array, set up in such a way that should any single drive fail, the remaining drives contain all the information necessary to restore all the data onto the replacement drive. Chase makes a critical distinction between raw data and worked data. Raw data is untouched; unchanged from its original form and is considered sacred. Any data whose pixels have been manipulated in any way however, is saved separately on the server as Live Work. When raw data comes in, it is saved on the server. Then,

at the workstation, it is manipulated using Photoshop, Final Cut, Compressor or other software, then saved to the "Live Work" folder on the server before final delivery to the client. Both raw data and live data are backed up and stored offsite in a secure location. Additionally, each workstation is also backed up hourly to an external hard drive.

Another important consideration in the plan to protect your data is the medium itself. Paul Hildebrandt, of *Eventide Visuals* in Northern California, highly recommends using fast media cards: 133X or better for Compact Flash memory cards and Class 10 or higher for SD cards. He suggests that you "never go below these speeds" to minimize the possibility of potential data loss. Paul also recommends using card capacities of not less than 16GB as anything less is not really practical for field use. If your situation allows you time to frequently switch out smaller cards then they'll work fine but as a wedding and event videographer he points out how critical it is "to get through a ceremony without switching cards."

Audio "Audities"

It's well known that the audio capabilities of HDSLR cameras are severely lacking. Fortunately there are a number of satisfactory solutions out there. If your camera is equipped with a 1/8-inch microphone jack you could simply plug in an external microphone with the proper connector. If you want to use a professional mic with XLR connectors you'll have to use one of several adapters that are available.

If your camera lacks a microphone jack altogether you can still capture great audio with a quality recorder such as Zoom's H1, H2 or H4 or the recorders by Tascam, Sony or Yamaha, among others. Recording with these devices requires another step in the post production process: synching the audio with the video. You can use the tried-and-true method of using a slate, clapboard or simply clapping your hands loudly in front of the camera but then you're faced with the tedious task of synching audio and video manually. Alternatively, many video producers are turning to PluralEyes software from Singular Software to synch up their HDSLR footage with separately recorded audio.

For the professional, time—and data—is money. Lost data means lost income. For the non-professional, memories fade, and captured images, once lost, can never be replaced. Employing a consistent, secure workflow, from capture to archive, can help prevent these and other mishaps, from ever happening.

RAID Types: Pros and Cons

RAID stands for Redundant Array of Independent Disks and refers to a data storage system utilizing multiple hard drives. There are a number of RAID configurations but three in particular are of use to the video producer.

RAID 1 is a mirrored array meaning that it writes to two discs at the same time, creating two drives that are identical to one another. This arrangement requires only two hard drives and provides complete redundancy; if one drive fails, the other drive continues to house all the data. On the downside, it is slow and results in a loss of half your drive capacity.

RAID 0 is a striped array. In this configuration, data is written to both drives simultaneously but in only one location. This results in very fast write speeds, twice the speed of a single drive, with no loss of drive capacity, but with no redundancy. If one drive dies, everything is lost. This arrangement is useful as scratch discs, such as when editing video, where speed is a plus but the data is temporary and a loss isn't critical.

RAID 5 requires a minimum of three hard drives but in practice can be very large with moderate drive speed results. This arrangement provides complete redundancy while only giving up about 25 percent of total drive capacity. RAID 5 setups require a hardware controller and are expensive but can be built to provide a large, fully redundant storage solution.

8
Shooting with Interchangeable Lenses

John Devcic and the Videomaker *Editors*

Wouldn't it be great if you could get one lens that did everything? One lens that can zoom into a subject from far away, one lens to take those great wide-angle shots, one lens that would make shooting so much easier?

Although there are all-in-one lenses that cover zoom-to-wide angle, unfortunately there's no single lens that covers the whole range well, from wide-angle to telephoto. Thanks to HDSLRs, you can now have the ability to swap out that ordinary lens for a wide-angle or telephoto lens. However, shooting with interchangeable lenses can be daunting and the variety of lenses available can be overwhelming. This feature looks at shooting with the different types of interchangeable lenses while our associated feature *The Mechanics of Interchangeable Lenses: Working with 35mm Adapters and Lenses* looks at how these lenses operate. Another associated feature, *DSLR/HDSLR*

Buyers Guide, looks at the variety of cameras on the market today that give you options to use interchangeable lenses in your video production.

Lenses

Wide-angle—the name is familiar and pretty easy to understand, however it's not always easy to use properly. A wide-angle lens captures a much taller and wider view of the scene than standard or telephoto lenses. A wide-angle lens is a great choice for travel videos for capturing wide vistas or real estate videos when you have to capture an entire room.

Figure 8-1 *The ability to remove a lens from your camcorder and change it to another with vastly different qualities can give your productions an exciting new look.*

Standard fixed-video camera lenses can't always capture wider angles well.

Wide-angle lenses are usually the de facto choice for shooting sweeping landscapes or capturing breathtaking mountain views. While you see them used in travel magazines or shows, a few enterprising videographers and photographers use the wide-angle lens for more then just capturing grand scenes. By physically moving a camera equipped with a wide-angle lens closer to a subject, the image changes drastically, bringing your foreground up close and personal. This makes the subject important and impressive by taking up the majority of the screen's real estate or causing other areas in the scene to appear smaller and less important. Your viewer has no choice but to be grabbed by this type of in-your-face approach. However, using your wide-angle lens in this way requires some caution, since doing so can introduce distortion in facial features, and other objects.

When done properly, a wide-angle shot can be breathtaking. However, like all good composition styles, while wide-angle shots are great for getting a lot of information into a scene, they should be sprinkled in only when needed and for effect.

Telephoto—the telephoto lens is like having a magnifying glass on a scene. You use these lenses to isolate something important in the scene. If you want to get

Figure 8-2 *Bringing a wide-angle lens close to your subject can enhance storytelling elements. However, this technique should be used with great caution as it can quickly introduce image distortion.*

a great shot of that lion's face, but have no interest in being its lunch, you might use a telephoto lens. This way you can be a safe distance away from the lion and still get a great close-up of its face. But you don't have to buy a telephoto lens and use it to only capture something far away. You can also use the telephoto lens to bring some details into sharper focus, adding depth to your scene by also blurring the background which then makes your in-focus subject appear more prominent and important. It is amazing how many interesting details and colors come alive when using a telephoto lens.

Telephoto lenses allow you to create the appearance that many subjects are

Figure 8-3 and 8-4 *Telephoto lenses can distort the sense of space in the frame by squeezing the distances between objects. This effect can be used to make the frame feel more crowded than it is.*

crammed into one picture. Telephoto lenses bring the background closer to your subject, which can distort the perspective a bit, but can make for some really interesting visual images. A great example of adding emphasis to freeway gridlock is to shoot all the cars lined up using a telephoto lens. You're crunching the distance between the cars, making them appear closer to each other illustrating a more dramatic scene. It is important to also realize that the telephoto lens has a very limited area of focus. This is where the camera's autofocus can play havoc with an image. It goes without saying that you shouldn't use auto-focus to assure that your camera is focused properly on what you want and not on what it thinks you want.

Zoom—the all-important zoom. A zoom lens appears similar to a telephoto lens, but it usually allows you to zoom in to get closer to a subject, like a telephoto lens, or zoom out to get a wide shot, like the wide-angle lens. However, this typically comes at the cost of losing light as the image is magnified. Zooming the lens out allows more information into your picture. Zooming in closes in on a subject and makes it that much more important. The zoom lens tends to be a blessing and a curse to most inexperienced videographers. There is a natural tendency to zoom into an image and bring it into focus quickly. While this is good, there is the temptation to use it far too often. Watching a scene that employed shots of a camera zooming in and out can be nauseating and

unpleasant to watch. Your viewers don't want to see how the mechanics of your gear work. They want to see the images of the subject you are showing them. Use the zoom lens with discretion. The pros usually practice good zooming techniques by zooming in or out very slowly, beginning and ending without any movement at all. Focus is important as well. Again, the camera's auto-focus can quickly get in the way of a good zoom, so practice the move in advance, making sure that the focus is set correctly.

Macro—a macro lens is perfect when you need to be close-up on something very small like a bug or detail on a flower. Good use of a macro lens calls for a counter-intuitive setup: you don't need to zoom the lens in for a good macro shot; you just need to get closer to your subject.

Depth of Field Shots

The beauty of recording great depth of field shots is unequaled. Depth of field is the distance between the closest and farthest objects that appear in sharp focus. We've seen depth of field imaging on TV and movies. Soap operas are shows to watch for good examples in depth of field shooting, and rack focus shots. These scenes usually have two or more people in a room engaged in a conversation. As one person is talking, the other person may be in the background. The person talking is in sharp focus and the person in the

Figure 8-5 *A zoom lens with a large aperture will allow you to focus in on your subject, nicely blurring the foreground and background.*

background is soft. The emphasis is on the person talking, because that is where the eye is drawn to and that is where the focus is. However, if the camera operator, or focus-puller, 'racks' the focus to the person in the background, even if the first subject is still talking, the viewer's attention is drawn to the reaction of the person listening. This type of technique is called a shallow depth of field and is used to make sure that the most important subject stands out from the background.

A long or extended depth of field shot means that all of the subjects in the scene are in focus. Movie makers and travel videographers use these shots with great effectiveness when they want to illustrate a sweeping landscape or a busy town square. One easy way to control depth of field is to physically move the camera closer to or farther away from the subject. If you move away from the subject, you will be able to capture a deeper depth of field. On the other hand, by moving in closer, you can create a shallow depth of field.

Different ways to shoot a scene will change the way you want your viewer to perceive it. For example, you want to capture the scene of a lovely park in full seasonal color, using a wide-angle lens. You decide that the subject will be a maple tree in this park. Placing your camera as far back you can then setting your lens as wide as possible, with a high f-stop number, you will capture a deep depth of field shot. Everything will be in focus. But if you zoomed in on that maple tree, and set your f-stop to a very low number, the tree or portions of it would be in focus, and the rest of the park would be blurred giving you a shallow depth of field. Your typical video camera comes with a standard lens making it very difficult, if not almost impossible, to obtain shallow depth of field shots. Depth of field shots can make a stunning addition to all your shoots.

Shooting with interchangeable lenses has an immediate impact on your work. Being able to pick and choose the right tool for the job is a liberating feeling. Having choices can give you the ability to use lenses that let in more light, allowing you to lower the f-stop and get a shallower depth of field. It also allows you to upgrade your optics whenever technology improves, keeping your camera relevant for a longer period of time.

Getting used to shooting with interchangeable lenses comes with practice, patience and determination. No matter what your skill level, you will be instantly rewarded when you begin to swap lenses for the proper occasion. Like all tools, you will need to practice in order to figure out which lens will be the right one for the job, but from family gatherings to commercials to your kids' soccer game, creating interesting depth of field shots using interchangeable lenses is an artistic touch that can be mastered through time and practice.

9
Guide to Buying Camcorder Tripods

Terry O'Rourke

Figure 9-1

The perfect support, or how to spend $625 on a $100 tripod

You just popped a pretty penny for your camera and have little left over for a tripod or other support. So you hope to get by with that cheap dimestore tool until you can upgrade later. Here's how to go from entry-level shooter to pro in four steps:

Step 1

First, buy a cheap tripod at the local department store for, say, fifty bucks. Use it a few times, just to get used to the idea of having a tripod. Then use it a few more times, and make sure you scratch it up pretty well, so you can't return it. Then try out somebody else's nice tripod, so you can get used to using a good one. Then go back to using yours and say to yourself "well, it's good enough." Then go shoot a critical project and have one of the legs fail on you. No real problem—it only slipped a little bit and most of the taping went well.

Step 2

Repeat Step 1, but this time spend a bit more. Let's say you spend $75 and the legs hold up well, only to have the head tip while shooting unattended. No problem, because the legs are pretty good, so you can now go out and get a new head for, say, $100. The only problem is that your tripod doesn't have a removable head.

Step 3

Repeat Step 1, but this time spend a bit more. Let's say you spend $100 this time and the legs hold up well and the head's not too bad. Now you have a nice tripod and the confidence to go out and shoot some really great stuff. With the camera in your bag and tripod on your shoulder, you go out and shoot some distant subject, only to find out that using your zoom at maximum reveals all the flaws your tripod really has to offer. You can't tilt, zoom or pan smoothly at all—and it shows. After some investigating, you realize the head isn't really very good. No problem, because the legs aren't too bad, and this time you can separate the two, so you can now go out and get a new head for, say, $100.

Step 4

OK, now you have a tripod with a pretty good head atop an OK set of legs. But when you stand back and look at it, you realize it's pretty silly, because the head looks way too big for those tiny legs. So you finally break down and buy a good tripod, for, say, $300. You put that other tripod along with the "rest of the story" in your closet.

From Entry to Pro, in One Step

It's a ridiculous thing but it happens all the time: we start out with an "entry-level" item, only to outgrow it several times and finally get what we should have purchased in the first place. So what should we have purchased in the first place? Say you shoot for a theatrical production company and you need to put up two cameras, a stationary camera to cover the entire stage and one to cover individual performers. That means you need at least one tripod, but you would like to shoot the performers with a long focal length, since the production company doesn't want the videographer near the stage. You really need two tripods. But you can't afford two really good tripods, so you have to strike a compromise. This is where you need to understand just what you are going to do with the camera, where you can skimp and where you shouldn't.

The stationary tripod really doesn't do much of anything but stand there and earn you money, but the tripod for the performers is in constant motion, because the performers are in constant motion. The stationary tripod must be steady, but, since you're not really interacting with it, the head can be pretty clumsy. That means it doesn't need to be lightweight and fast to set up and, since you're not panning and zooming, there is no need for a high-quality head. It does need to be steady, because your reputation depends on it. On the other hand, if you are moving around a theatre taping performers during a live performance, that tripod needs to be a really nice unit: lightweight, fast to set up, with a nice head for panning and zooming. As with anything else, you get what you pay for. So let's roll up our sleeves, sharpen our pencils and figure out how to get the most bang for our buck!

Consideration: Tripod Head

The first thing to consider when investigating tripods is whether the head can be separated from the leg-set without the use of farm implements. In other words, whether the components are available separately, because no self-respecting videographer needs to consider any tripod components that are not. The second consideration is the head. This is the "money" part of the system: it can make or break your production. Here is where you show your talent and please your clients, because, as a videographer, you are expected to "render" your ideas visually, and that means nice steady pans, zooms and tilts. Heads come in a variety of shapes and sizes and can cost anywhere from a few dollars to several thousand. Just as you interact with any subject you are taping, you interact with the tripod head. You become "one" with it, learning just how it reacts when you suddenly pan or tilt. You learn exactly how to adjust it for each situation. If you treat it properly, it rewards you with fabulous pans, gives you years of service and pays for itself many times over. So start with the best head you can possibly afford, even if you have to compromise on the leg set.

Size and Weight Matter

When selecting a head, you should consider the weight of the camera you are using. Obviously the heavier the camera, the sturdier the head must be, but, if it's too sturdy and mismatched to your camera, you will find the resistance on the drag settings are just too strong. This results in jerky movements, especially when starting and ending pans and tilts, even when the settings are at minimal. On the other hand, if the head is too small, you will find the head does not control the movements you try with your camera. The key word here is "control." Your tripod head must control the camera with ease and finesse. This leads us to which type of head to search for. Ideally, your first choice would be a true fluid head. This head controls resistance hydraulically with fluid, similar to the hydraulic suspension system on any machine. This system allows for extremely precise control of the resistance and offers the advantage of not overheating the surfaces when you are continuously panning and tilting. It's not like your tripod head is going to catch fire, but, if you select a friction head, it controls by just that: friction. Friction generates heat, and, with long shoots and lots of pans such as you might find on your stage performance, that friction will change the characteristics of your settings. So, if you can live with re-setting the "drag" on your tripod frequently, and you are on a tight budget, any high-quality friction head will do just fine.

Legs!

The third thing to consider is the leg set. The legs determine the weight of your tripod, which is critical if you are going to carry it around. If all specs are equal in the tripods you might consider—such as camera size rating, height fully extended and closed size—the one thing that will clearly differentiate them is price and weight. Tripods are available in either aluminum, carbon fiber, wood or a combination of the three. Generally speaking, the price goes up as the weight goes down, so we can get away with a low-cost, high-quality tripod for our stationary tripod, one with a basic head and sturdy, fairly heavy all-aluminum construction. But for the tripod we carry around, set up and take down, open and close and, frequently, toss around, we need a lightweight one. This one can be all-carbon fiber, which would be the lightest, easiest to set up and by far most expensive. Or you might choose a carbon fiber/aluminum combo material, which would be a nice compromise of price versus weight. Or you might go "old school" and choose a nice wood tripod, as many shooters do. They choose wood because wood tripods are incredibly sturdy, weigh relatively little and absorb vibrations quite nicely. There are basically two styles of folding tripods. The first type has been around for hundreds of years. Its tried-and-true design—sometimes referred to as a "crutch" design—has legs with a two-piece side-by-side arrangement at the top—or yoke—of the tripod and a single-piece tube on the bottom. The lower tube slides between the two top tubes and provides a very sturdy leg. It is quite fast to set up, because there are only two sections, and can be very lightweight. This type of tripod is usually trussed, or secured with chains, straps or bars suspended between the legs.

The lightest and most compact leg-set features single telescoping tubular legs with three sections. Though not as sturdy as the two piece type, it provides the advantage of folding up to a very small package, which comes in handy on shoots that require you to trek long distances. It is a bit slow and noisy to set up, because each leg has three sections, each of which has its own latch, which leaves you with six latches to open and close and six leg sections to extend. Of course, the most important consideration is always cost, and this is where you really can save money. By purchasing the right system in the first place, you won't end up tossing away problem tripods.

A good way to start out is to buy the nicest head you can afford and match that to a lesser set of legs. As you grow as an artist, you can then migrate to a nicer leg-set and end up with a really nice tripod and a back-up leg-set. Once here, you can then buy a sturdy but cost effective head and have two functional tripods, one for stationary shooting and one for the thing that brought you to video in the first place: making fabulous video footage with beautiful pans and zooms!

Figure 9-2 *It is important to match the size of your tripod and head with both the weight of your camcorder and the demands of your projects.*

The Other Support Toys

Now that you have a nice tripod—the "meat and potatoes" camera support in your kit—you might want to consider some specialty items such as jibs, dollies and stabilizers, and don't forget to consider a monopod. Imagine zooming out while you dolly the camera forward! It's usually referred to as a trombone shot or vertigo shot, and the results can be quite claustrophobic for your viewers. Dollies are necessary for a shot like this. Dollies are also nice for pans that require very consistent camera movement that follows or moves about your subject. They usually need a near-perfect surface or a track on which to glide. You can bring along plywood to make a surface. The effects can be quite nice, and the trouble involved in setting a dolly is definitely worth it.

How about a shot that comes from above the subject, slowly rotates around it, then drops in and down for a view from below?

Figure 9-3 *A small jib will lift your shots to new heights (an impress your clients at the same time).*

as much as 25 feet. They can have simple pan heads or elaborate systems that control the camera angle and zoom the lens. Start off with a nice si6-foot one, add to that your sturdy tripod and you can get a shot from 10 feet right down to ground level. Yep, the smaller jibs actually attach to your existing tripod, and the nice thing is that they use standard weights you get from the sporting goods store. Good thing you bought a good tripod right from the start!

Another wonderful support is the tried-and-true monopod. Fast to set up and lightweight, they provide fantastic stability while affording you the freedom of handholding. They also provide a nice "pole" for those times you need to shoot from a high angle, such as over a crowd or some other obstacle.

Final Consideration

Today there are lots of tripods available in many shapes and sizes, with pricing to fit just about any budget. Whether you are a seasoned pro or a budding artist, any one of them will provide options that will allow you to interpret your creative vision, please your clients and give you years of service. It's really up to you how you will unleash the power of these devices, so go out there and express your own POV!

You'll need a jib for that, and they aren't too expensive for even a budding videographer to consider. Jibs come in a variety of sizes, ranging from a four-foot reach to

10
The Right Mic for the Job

Hal Robertson

Figure 10-1

Every shoot is different and while a single camera can work in just about any situation, microphones have more specific roles.

Whether it's recording-studio microphones with a sound mixer, or a run-n-gun field shoot with no other sound equipment, one-size-fits-all doesn't apply here. It's easy to get bogged down in all the types of patterns, electrical connections, shapes and sizes. Then you have to decide if microphone A is really worth it to you. If your eyes are blurry from catalogs, spec sheets and online vendors, let us insert a little clarity in your search for the right microphone.

Environments

For just a bit, let's think about the audio recording equipment required for the Discovery Channel's *Dirty Jobs*. If you've never seen the show, you have to look it up online. Host Mike Rowe and his crew visit a wide variety of locations seeking the dirtiest jobs in America. Waste processing, pig pens, sewage ponds, meat packing, the list of dirty locations numbers in the hundreds. And his audio crew has to be ready for just about anything. In

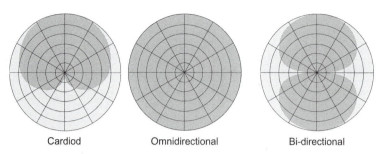

Cardiod   Omnidirectional   Bi-directional

Figure 10-2 *Being aware of the pickup pattern of a mic is important, and should serve to keep you in focus of where sound is being collected.*

addition, they don't work in a studio, so their audio recording equipment has to be portable and pretty much bullet-proof.

Dirty Jobs isn't shy about showing its crew and equipment, including audio production and voice recording gear. Typically, the host and his guests all wear wireless lapel mics and the audio dude also carries a shotgun mic on a boom pole. This is a simple backup strategy. While either type of microphone could work just fine, there's always extra recording equipment in case something bad happens—which it often does.

Having one or more of everything is great, but we can't all afford that. So it's up to you to make the best choice of microphones, given your typical recording environments. Shooting in a controlled studio situation would be a dream for most of us, but we work with what we're given. An outdoor shoot could take place on a busy street corner or in the middle of 200 acres of pasture. An indoor shoot might be in a glass-walled executive office or a warehouse. You just never know.

Another consideration is how many people will be on camera. Do you always shoot talking heads or is there a possibility of another person in the shot? How do you handle three or more people? What about a dozen folks gathered around a conference table? The good news is that there's a microphone (or microphones) for every scenario. Understanding the strong points and how each type of mic works is a great place to start.

Microphone Speak

You've probably seen several terms used when describing microphones. We're going to break them down into simple categories of directional, non-directional and specialty mics.

Directional microphones pick up sound primarily from one end of the device—sort of a point-and-shoot thing. The most common type of directional mic is called "cardioid" for the upside-down heart-shaped pickup pattern. A quick look at the pattern shows that this type of mic favors sound from the front, while still picking up some sound on the sides. Virtually no sound is received at the back of the microphone. This type of pickup pattern helps to reject background noise and accentuate the sounds you want to record, whether that is a voice, music or sound effects.

There are a couple of variants on the cardioid design—specifically, the super-cardioid and hyper-cardioid. Each has a progressively narrower sweet spot while rejecting more sound from the sides of the mic. You'll also notice that as the mics become directionally tighter, they also start to pick up a bit of sound from the rear. The amount is small and shouldn't pose a problem.

The ultimate in directionality is the shotgun microphone. These mics are extremely sensitive toward the front with small bumps of pickup to the side and rear. This means you can either pick up sound from further away or better isolate the sound close up. Because they're so sensitive, they also tend to pick up more

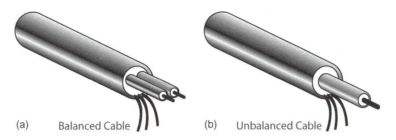

(a)   Balanced Cable   (b)   Unbalanced Cable

Figure 10-3 *Balanced cables are typically thicker and longer than unbalanced cables. Other wires like extension cords and computer cables need to be kept apart from unbalanced cables to avoid interference.*

handling noise. That's why you'll often see them mounted in some type of shock-absorbing device.

Non-directional microphones—also called omnidirectional mics—don't emphasize sound from any direction. In fact, their pickup pattern looks like a ball or sphere around the head of the mic. They're available in hand-held models, but the most common non-directional microphone is a lapel or lavalier mic.

Finally, we come to specialty microphones. There are many variations here, but we'll concentrate on two that a video producer might use from time to time. If you need to cover a large area with a single mic, it's hard to beat a boundary microphone. Boundary mics lie on a flat surface like a wall or floor and pick up sound in a half-sphere pattern. Without getting into a physics lesson, a microphone on or very near a flat surface becomes equally sensitive to all frequencies, 360 degrees around the microphone. This means you'll record anything happening anywhere near the mic.

Another specialty microphone is the bidirectional or figure-8 mic. This mic has a unique dual pickup pattern—much like two omni-directional mics with one on either side of the mic body. One side is out of phase with the other and both patterns are combined into a single connector. There are several audio tricks that can be performed with a mic like this, but a common application is recording two sound sources at the same time. For instance, a voice and an instrument, or a speaker and the audience.

Electrical Ramblings

Of course, microphones are only useful in video if you can attach them to your camera or recorder. Fortunately, there are just a few things to deal with here. First, a microphone is either balanced or unbalanced in its electrical connection. A full discussion is beyond the scope of this article, but it's pretty easy to figure out which is which. Most balanced microphones use a three-pin connector, called an XLR connector. If you look closely, you'll see the pins numbered 1–3 with pin 1 as the ground connection, pin 2 carrying the positive portion of the signal and pin 3 carrying the negative portion. Balanced audio is preferred in the pro audio world because it allows very long cable lengths with little signal loss. This type of connection also naturally rejects radio and electromagnetic interference.

An unbalanced microphone uses only two connections; a ground and the signal. You may see this type of connection on mics designed specifically for consumer and prosumer equipment, since they rarely use balanced audio. Short shotguns, lavalier mics and even wireless mics could have a simple unbalanced audio connection. Normally, these microphones use an

Figure 10-4, 10-5, and 10-6 *From left: shotgun, boundary and lavalier represent very different types of mics and each excels in specific tasks.*

1/8-inch connector. Unbalanced microphones have limited cable lengths and may pick up more electronic noise than balanced models.

Application Notes

Now that you know how they work, it should be easier to choose a microphone based on your shooting application. For instance, many news reporters use handheld cardioid mics while reporting on camera. It's a fast and easy way to get decent sound. If your video needs that sort of immediacy or just the look of news, you can't go wrong with a handheld cardioid, super or hyper-cardioid microphone.

Sit-down interviews are often done with omni-directional lavalier microphones. This gets the mic close to the talent and the non-directional nature helps minimize volume changes as the talent moves his or her head. It's also the mic of choice in public meetings like a church service or seminar, although omni-directional headset mics have become popular in recent years too.

If you're shooting a concert, play or office meeting, a boundary mic is a great place to start. By placing the mic on the floor or table—central to all the key players—you can be confident that you'll pick up everything you need. It provides a more open and slightly distant sound when compared to other mic types, but you can compensate with post processing.

For those just starting out, or needing one mic to do it all, choose a shotgun mic. A nice one will be more expensive than some of your other options, but this microphone type is a workhorse. It can be used overhead for interviews and small groups, as a handheld mic, and for other utility recording like sound effects and voice overs. Whether stand or boompole mounted, a shotgun mic is hard to beat.

Wrapping Up

For the video creator, the right microphone is a key investment in your audio production equipment. It's something you'll take on every shoot and use as often—or more often—than your camera. Picking the right one for your production style gives you the power and flexibility to bring home excellent audio every time, regardless of the location or other circumstances. Choose wisely.

Pick a Mic . . .

. . . any mic. Now, pick two or three more similar mics from different manufacturers. When you hook them up and listen to their output, each will sound different. One mic might be crisp and clean while another is muddy and dark. One mic might be a little thin sounding while another booms with bass. Regardless of pickup pattern, no two mics sound alike and you're going to have to decide which one works best for you and your production style. Before you make a purchase, try to audition several models. This may mean borrowing from friends or visiting a local store, just let your ears be your guide.

11
Cut the Cord

Hal Robertson

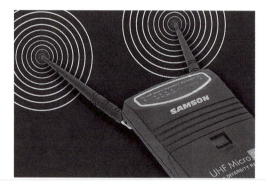

Figure 11-1

A good wired microphone is perfect for reliable high quality audio, but sometimes the wires get in the way.

Wireless mics have been around for ages, but many video creators haven't made the leap for various reasons. The benefits are clear, but with wireless rigs running from $100 to $5,000, it's difficult to decide on a price-to-performance ratio that suits your production style. In addition, there are several obscure terms and features that further confuse the issue. If wireless is in your future but you're unsure which way to go, this month's *Sound Advice* is the perfect place to start.

The Basics

A wireless microphone system is essentially a miniature radio station. First, a microphone is attached to a transmitter. This converts the audio signal into radio waves and is broadcast for a few hundred feet. At the other end is the receiver, which grabs the signal from the air and converts it back into audio for your camera, recording rig or sound system. If this sounds simple, it is, but there are several variables that determine the

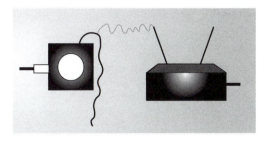

Figure 11-2 *This diagram illustrates the basic components and function of a wireless audio system. In most cases, the transmitter (or body pack) stays with the talent and the receiver connects to the camcorder via a cable with an XLR connector.*

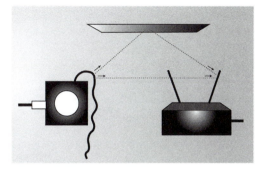

Figure 11-3 *In this diagram the reflected signal reaches the receiver a few milliseconds later creating interference. A diversity receiver can help minimize this type of interference.*

distance and quality of the transmitted signal.

Wireless mics work on specific bands of radio frequency determined by the FCC. At the bottom of the scale is VHF or Very High Frequency. Ironically, this is the lowest band of frequencies assigned to wireless mics. While there are several nice systems in this range, most modern systems have moved to the UHF or Ultra High Frequency band. This band is less crowded and offers better signal penetration through buildings. At the extreme high end, there are 2.4 GHz wireless systems and even all-digital solutions. As a rule of thumb, the higher the frequency, the better the system and the more you'll pay. Fortunately, there is a great deal of competition for your wireless microphone dollars and manufacturers offer better, cheaper systems all the time.

Features Galore

Buzz words abound in the wireless mic world. Reading the specs from two or three manufacturers may cause your eyes to glaze over, but each of these terms has a meaning and they're important to understand.

Diversity is a term used to describe the receiver end of the wireless mic chain. Some manufacturers even call theirs "true" diversity, although there is no such thing as "fake" diversity – just different

ways to implement it. A diversity system has two antennas and two input sections. Before the signal hits the radio portion, a circuit or microprocessor analyzes the signal from both antennas, decides which one is the cleanest, and then routes it to the receiver. This may happen several times a minute, depending on the radio conditions at your location. The bonus is you'll never hear it working and the receiver is making sure you have the best possible signal for your shoot. Don't let terms like "single diversity" or "dual diversity" fool you. A wireless system either has diversity or it doesn't. Diversity is not a must-have feature, but it's good insurance. There are many excellent non-diversity systems on the market.

Selectable frequencies are another nice feature. Back in the old days, your wireless system was on a fixed frequency. That was fine as long as there weren't any other wireless systems at the location. If there were, you could experience anything from fuzzy audio to picking up someone else's microphone. Many of today's systems offer a choice of operating frequencies – anything from two to over 1,000. Basic wireless rigs offer a simple A/B switch on the transmitter and receiver. This gives you two frequency options and provides some basic insurance against intruding signals. Better systems provide four or more frequencies and many allow you to custom tune your system to any available frequency. This is a great option in congested

Figure 11-4 *What makes a diversity receiver (bottom) diverse is that it has two input sections ("R"). Other receivers (top) may have two antennas, but they won't take in two diverse inputs.*

Figure 11-5 *Many receivers and transmitters have small dials that allow the user to select a specific frequency. This will allow you to move off channels that may have more interference than others.*

metropolitan areas, theatres and churches where many signals may live at the same location. The most sophisticated systems actually scan the location and set the frequencies for you based on available bands. This is an expensive option, but can save a great deal of time and grief.

The loud, staticky sound you hear when tuning to a non-existent radio or TV channel is the absence of a strong signal. Wireless mics have these issues too, but there are circuits to deal with it when the signal is lower than the noise. The ability to mute this static sound when signals are weak, yet provide the valuable noise when the signal is strong is called *squelch*. In its simplest form, a squelch control is like a noise gate. When the radio signal goes below a certain threshold, the circuit mutes the noise before it gets out of hand. Basic wireless microphone receivers have a simple knob to set the threshold, but you will still hear some brief noise when a transmitter is shut off or goes out of range. Newer systems use some variety of tone-key squelch. In a tone-key squelch system, the transmitter broadcasts an inaudible pilot tone. The receiver listens for this tone and, as long as it hears

it, keeps the signal path open. If the tone fades or disappears, the circuit closes the signal path before any noise gets through. You may still hear a faint click or pop, but that's all. This is more of a convenience feature, but adds to the professionalism of your setup.

Bells and Whistles

We've discussed wireless microphone essentials, but there are other things that make a system flexible, reliable and easy to use. Status displays offer information about various setting and the condition of your system. Typical items include operating frequency, RF signal and level, audio level, battery life and pilot tone. Fancy receivers even show the status of the transmitter battery and estimate operation time. Most wireless mics use standard alkaline batteries, but some offer rechargeable packs or built-in batteries. Rechargeable batteries are a risk with wireless systems as they always seem to die at the wrong time. What about cabling? Does the wireless system you're considering connect easily to your camera or mixer? If not, check the manufacturer's website for accessory cables and adapters. One last question is the durability of the system. A flimsy plastic case is fine for occasional use, but won't hold up over the long term. In general, wireless system should feel solid with clearly marked buttons and easy battery access.

Hopefully we've demystified the wireless microphone world today. With dozens of manufacturers and hundreds of models to choose from, you've got your work cut out for you. Armed with a fresh look at the wireless scene, now you're ready to cut the cord.

Test Drive

Choosing a wireless microphone is a lot like finding a new car—no two are alike. The mic everyone's raving about may not suit you or your production style. You may not even like the sound quality. The microphone element included in your new wireless rig is critical and most manufacturers have more than one model. If at all possible, borrow or rent a system before the purchase. Use it on a real shoot and scrutinize every aspect of operation and sound before laying down your hard-earned cash. Regardless of the spec sheet or reviews, it's best to try before you buy.

12
Portable Lighting Equipment

Terry O'Rourke

Figure 12-1

The best equipment in the world isn't any good if it's too big or too heavy to take with you on assignment.

It is with this in mind that we are going to learn about a location kit that includes enough equipment to shoot a full-blown production but that can separate into component groups that allow you to trek into parts unknown whether by car, bike, plane, boat or even on foot.

Not Your Average Grab Bag

Consider a portable lighting kit that will be transported to you location in your car. It may include several lights with light stands along with all the support equipment that accompanies it such as power cords and splitters so you can plug in more than one light. You may also have a boom with a counter-weight for overhead lighting and maybe a cart to carry it all so you can look professional because you'll get your gear from your car to your location in one easy trip. Throw in a laptop and monitor and you're good to go.

But what happens if your director gets a sudden wave of creative inspiration and without your knowledge arranges an interview with a "sky view" shot from the catwalk above a factory floor and the only way to get there is by way of a series of ladders? The good news is that the director

Figure 12-2 and 12-3 *A compact light stand will be able to fit more places than large C-Stands. Attaching a portable light can reduce the space it'll take and cut down on cords and sandbags.*

understands that your billing for the job has just increased but the bad news is that all that great gear you brought along is just a bit too big, heavy and cumbersome to carry up the ladders. Perhaps all you brought along is that old metal tripod because you don't like packing your nice carbon tripod on the cart. Or maybe you only packed two 15-pound sandbags and the shot from the catwalk calls for a total of four bags, well . . . the shoot was pretty conventional and you thought you were more than ready . . .

Love–Hate Relationship

This is one of the most frustrating situations you will encounter and as you grow into your career as a videographer you will find that this is quite common. As a professional you are expected to deliver great imagery under all conditions and the better the director, the greater the chances of a situation like this occurring. It's a love-hate relationship. The challenges of a great location can be so rewarding while at the same time drive one to complete hysteria! So let's start with exactly what went wrong with the scenario above.

You came prepared for the location that everybody agreed on but things changed. The operative word here is "changed" and as we all know change is good except when it happens to you. So the first thing one must consider when packing a kit for location is "change." Perhaps the lighting will change, such as the room you are shooting in is on a timer and the lights go out at 6 p.m. and you are shooting until 7 p.m. Or maybe the location with those beautiful blue walls you saw in the photograph are now beige. Perhaps the location photos were taken in another season, and the greenery you were counting on is brown and lifeless. Whatever—It doesn't matter! Everything changes and it's your creative interpretation of each situation that will carry you through and keep the clients coming back for more.

Figure 12-4 and 12-5 *Reflectors are about as portable a light tool as you'll find. Some like the Photoflex MultiDisc have a gold, silver and mixed side and double as scrims.*

Pack Light

When packing a video production lighting kit the first thing to consider is how much you can carry by yourself, without a cart and still be able to light an interview. With this in mind always have two very portable lights as well as an on-camera light available. By very portable, I mean no cords to plug in and preferable a case you can sling over your shoulder. Very portable lights don't weigh much so they require only small light stands and small sand bags or if you're lucky, no sand bags at all. Opting for the battery offering on your portable light will give you versatility here since you eliminate bulky cords and won't be relying on wall sockets or generators. Frequently you are called on to record an interview as the sun sets or the subject has only time for one take which means there is little time to plan a set, find electricity to plug in your lights and set up your camera, all while listening to the director tell you what he or she wants. The obvious advantages of small portable lighting are described above, but there are some drawbacks which include limited power and reach which means you generally need the lights closer to your subject in order to be effective. Smaller lights offer fewer options for modifiers so you must be able to adapt your vision to these limitations.

Manfrotto makes a nifty little light stand (5001B Nano, $62) which would be perfect for the "factory catwalk" situation described earlier because the legs lie flat. This stand, with one battery powered light, such as the Flolight MicroBeam 128 ($299), will allow you to put a back-light on your subject while your on-camera light provides fill. The nice thing about the MicroBeam 128 is how flexible the battery system is. You can use an extra battery from your Sony or Panasonic camera or the standard Li-ion battery. If you have some extra hands at your disposal, have someone hold a reflector and bounce some of the back light onto the subject for some soft fill and you have a good portable solution for a fairly complex situation. If you are the lone worker of the lights, you'll want to set up a stand and arm and attach the reflector with clamps, all the while reminding your subject to resist the urge to move out of the light.

All the lights mentioned so far provide very little power so they must be relatively close to your subject to be effective; it's best to have several so you can place them around the set to light each element separately. Imagine recording an interview on a country porch with the sun setting in the background. Rather than blasting the whole set with one or two powerful lights, why not try setting out several smaller lights and creating individual "splashes of lights" to compliment the shadows you will definitely come across. This is how you adjust your vision to the environment rather than trying to change it. This strategy is good but requires time, setup and experience to perfect.

Let the Environment Speak to You

Perhaps you are frequently rushed and you're just learning about lighting but still want to get a great look each time you work. Once again let the environment tell you what to do. One thing you can always rely on is that there will be at least some light when you shoot and the fastest and most reliable way to harness that light is with reflectors.

Still the favorite tool of both seasoned and beginning videographers, reflectors require no power and are easy to set up. Reflectors are also possibly the most adjustable light you could have—shifting positions as fast as humanly possible. One of my personal favorites is a simple 6 × 4-foot taffeta fabric which gives a similar effect to soft-box lighting but is faster to set up. Even in a fluorescent-lit office a large fabric scrim—if placed correctly, can add some definition to your lighting. By placing it right next to your subject—but just out of camera view—you get a beautiful soft rim light around a person's face and clothing.

What's really nice about soft fabric as a reflector is that if the wind causes it to move slightly, the effect is not usually noticeable in camera whereas shiny reflectors such as silver or gold become completely obvious when they get even slightly moved by the person holding them or a breeze. But don't let that stop you from using them because the shimmery effect they have on a windy day can be used to add some excitement to your work. The precious shimmer of your

reflector might be construed along with a light lens flare or sparkle from a plug-in to become a sign of magic.

Try recording a high-energy interview such as a weather event with the sun behind your subject and use a shiny reflector right next to the camera. Any movement in the reflector will be obvious and can add to the energy of the situation. Shiny reflectors are extremely efficient when compared to soft white reflectors and can be used to create strong specular reflections which soft white cannot possibly achieve, plus they have more "reach" so they don't need as much light to reflect and can be placed further from the subject. It's always good to have both soft and shiny reflectors on any location and since reflectors are lightweight and compact there should be no reason not to have them in your kit.

Suppose you frequently carry only a camcorder and one light. Well, don't let that stop you from thinking outside the box. Instead of mounting the light on top of your camcorder, try holding it off the side and slightly above the camera. You will get a more three-dimensional look in the lighting instead of the usual "on-camera" flat lighting that you see in so many videos. Or how about directing the light onto a wall and using the wall as a big soft reflector? It works, but the light output is greatly reduced so you will need to have your subject close to the wall. This where something like the Bescor LED-60X on-camera light is useful because it has plenty of power for reflecting off walls due to its narrow beam and runs on four AA batteries ($100).

With an understanding of all these lighting strategies, you can approach any event or location with confidence and rest assured that you'll be prepared. Collectively, all the lighting equipment mentioned here makes for a complete location kit that includes enough equipment to light a larger production but the real value is how each component of this kit is small enough to be carried by itself and used separately for lighting just about any small setup you may encounter.

DIY Portable

Figure 12-6

How about "re-purposing" a Coleman Quad LED Lantern to create a cheap lighting kit! Yep, Coleman—yes, the camping company—has a classic lantern style light ($80) that can be split into four separate lights each of which is self-contained and battery powered! Each light has its own little handle which provides a quick way to hang them from just about anything you may find on location. Use them side by side for a bit more power or spread them out for more coverage.

Even a simple hand-held LED flashlight can be an effective way to light an interview as long as you understand that they have a limited angle of coverage. Why not have fun with that limited coverage and use it to your advantage. A flashlight will give a lot of falloff on the edges and that can be very effective for creating a spotlight effect. Don't forget the head-lights on your car. They are very powerful and can be reflected off a building wall to create a very large light source. Just watch *E.T.: The Extra-Terrestrial*!

13
Monitors

Marshal M. Rosenthal

Figure 13-1

From the studio to the field, to the editing suite, what to look for in a production monitor.

Editing video content was radically changed when digital technologies became a mainstay. Rather than physical manipulation, the content can now be manipulated at will in non-destructive ways, thanks to the video being stored digitally. The assortment of video-editing software programs range from extremely technical (for professionals), moderately complex (for prosumers) to extremely simple for the casual/occasional video shooter. Regardless of the program's level of sophistication, the single most important component, other than the computer, is the monitor the video is viewed on. The monitor is crucial for viewing your work and accessing the program's editing functions, and also because the monitor's physical characteristics and display settings can affect how the final video will look when presented.

The advent of the LCD monitor spelled the death of the CRT tube-based models.

Beside the fact that flat-panels are lighter in weight and more energy-conservative, the size of the monitor is no longer the inhibiting factor it was with CRTs. Flat-panel monitors can also increase their size without substantially raising prices, thereby allowing for both higher resolutions and a physically greater viewing area. This works in tandem with computers to further the progress of HD as a common shooting and viewing option.

While a single monitor is part and parcel of today's computing (all-in-one models like Apple's iMacs and HP's new Z1 workstation incorporate the technology and monitor together), having a second monitor is more than just a convenience when it comes to editing video. In fact, the addition of a third monitor is no longer viewed as an exotic option; computers designed to handle only one additional monitor are upgradable through an external device that works through a USB port to provide another monitor with "plug and play" capabilities. Additionally, there are tablet-sized LCD monitors, such as the AOC 16-inch Portable USB, that plug directly into a USB socket on the computer—obviating the need for any 120 V plug.

Watch the View

Computers offer two types of viewing systems when it comes to multiple displays: the first will see use for presentations or use with a projector, one monitor "mirrors" what is on the first (or main) monitor. For editing use, it's the second type of viewing system that is used; i.e. to extend the working area (desktop) from one monitor to the next. In a video-editing setup, this allows menus and windows (whether they contain video or other information) to be placed apart from one another for both convenience and reducing clutter.

Computer monitors used for video editing must match the jack, and the graphic capabilities of the computer's video card in order to function optimally. A monitor with a resolution able to display 1080p HD (1920 × 1080 pixels) will not receive the needed signal strength if the computer can't provide this resolution. Similarly, if the computer only has a VGA output, having a DVI input on the monitor only will have to be worked around with an adapter in order to be successful. Fortunately, the majority of computers and laptops are able to display an HD image. The fact that high-resolution monitors have dropped in price is a welcome change.

Computer Monitor 101

VGA is an analog output that has been in use since the days of the CRT monitors, while DVI provides a digital signal. There are also newer standards, such as DisplayPort, which can be found on some monitors. Monitors typically provide controls for calibrating the image's contrast, brightness, color temperature and other levels—in some cases the calibration is conducted automatically, while in other cases it must be initiated and done by hand. Regardless, it is worth noting that the individual taste of the person viewing the monitor will come into play; for example, a higher contrast being perfectly acceptable to one person while another would disagree.

The monitor's aspect ratio is determined by its physical shape (either 4:3 or 16:9), and must be matched to the proper screen resolution put out by the computer's graphic card. VGA, for example, can begin at a resolution of 640 × 480, but generally climbs higher, for example, into the realm of 800 × 600 (SVGA) or 1024 × 768 (XGA). For example, the PyleHome PLVW10IW is a 10.4-inch flat-panel (4:3 aspect ratio) reminiscent of a touch-screen tablet like the iPad. The LCD is wall-mountable (as is the case with most flat-panel monitors) and provides a resolution of 800 × 640 through a VGA input. An example of a widescreen (16:9) monitor with full 1080p resolution (1920 × 1080) is the 24-inch ViewSonic VA2431wm ($291). A DVI input provides for higher density of pixels on a screen with resolution of 1680 × 1050. This monitor features both VGA and DVI inputs and

Figure 13-2 *Multiple input and throughput types can be essential if you need maximum adaptability in the field.*

automatically adjusts for standard definition, (the built-in stereo speakers can be considered an added perk.)

Another example is the 7-inch SWIT S-1071H (1024 × 600.) It features two HD/SD-SDI inputs, along with HDMI and component, and includes a video flip, Underscan/Overscan switch and 4:3 aspect ratio compatibility.

Computer versus Television

Those whose productions are headed for broadcast no doubt realize that the finished video should be viewed on an NTSC monitor that will accurately display the image as it is seen on conventional TVs. This is only reasonable since variations between what is seen on a computer monitor (whose pixels are square) and a TV (whose pixels are rectangular) can exist, both as subtle or not so subtle differences in the final image.

These types of NTSC monitors can vary in specifications and price but must all have the ability to display a video signal conforming to the TV standard. An example is the studio quality JVC's 24-inch DT-R24L41DU LCD monitor ($3,200). Designed for use in post-production facilities as well as broadcast networks and TV stations, the HD image provides 1:1 monitoring with safe area markers compatible with different aspect ratios. The monitor

has a wealth of inputs and, as expected, embedded technologies for metering the signal as it is viewed.

Those creating videos with less ambitious ends will still need to view how their finished work will look on a TV screen. Most computers can take the addition of a TV tuner card, which, besides providing TV-in capabilities, can output video for display on a conventional HDTV. There are also external video streaming devices (for example, the Warpia StreamHD VE) that only require a USB connection in order to sync with the computer and HDTV. Using a conventional HDTV to view the video before completion will add to the overall work time, but, there really is no other alternative if your viewing is confined to computers and mobile devices. The final video should be as compatible as possible with that of a televised signal in order to provide a consistent display of your final piece of video.

Production Monitors

Video broadcast monitors are useful for television production because they provide a realistic image that represents what is captured without any enhancements or alterations initially.

There are three different types of this kind of monitor; each is designed with different characteristics in order to perform various functions. The first is the "Grade 1" monitor, which provides a visual representation of the image without any masking of defects, such as in camera control and color grading. The second type of production monitor is "Grade 2." This monitor comes with a wider tolerance for the image, and is often used in such situations as control rooms where no editing of the picture is necessary. The final type is the "Grade 3" monitor, which is the one most similar to high-end consumer displays. It is suitable for television production applications where durability and transportability of the unit is as important as its ability to handle such functions as audio production and dialogue dubbing. In addition, these types of production monitors are often used as displays in a studio with an in-house audience.

An example of a "Grade 3" monitor, useful for audio editing, is the Marshall OR-181 ORCHID ($3,000) Desktop Production Monitor. The monitor has an 18.5-inch LCD screen (widescreen, 1366 × 768 resolution), has a rack mount option and includes an assortment of production-based tools, for example, real-time waveform functions, an audio level meter and audio peak alarm. The OR-181 can display as many as 16 audio channels and has an audio channel loss functionality to warn against detected audio errors during monitoring.

Field Monitors and Camera-Mounted Monitors

Shooting on location or in the field is no different from in an indoor space when it comes to needing to view what is being recorded. There are two types of displays that can be used in conjunction with the camera: field monitors and camera-mounted monitors. A field monitor is designed for those on location (other than the camera operator) to see what is being shot, while a camera-mounted monitor "rides" the camera for use primarily by the camera operator. Screen sizes can be a bit more restrictive for camera-mounted monitors, while the division between these and field monitors is generally about seven inches.

Both types of monitors are used not only for simple viewing purposes, but also as an aid to ensure the best image with the least amount of difficulties when the finished work goes to post-production. They both feature industry-standard inputs for use with the commercial cameras available. Additionally, independent batteries often power both types of monitors, although conventional electrical outlets can be employed in some instances.

Prices for field monitors vary, depending on the screen size and features—as an example, the 7-inch LCD Marshall Electronics V-LCD70XP-HDIPT Field Monitor (800 × 480) comes in at $1,100. Besides loop-through capabilities for the HDMI, composite and component inputs (for enabling a second monitor to be connected), the monitor has a 600:1 contrast ratio and an adjustable backlight and DSLR ratio adjustment capabilities. Peaking filter/manual gamma adjustment and four user-configurable front-mounted buttons are also included.

At $900, the ikan VX9e provides a 8.9-inch LCD screen with such features as full color/monochrome, peaking and moveable pixel-to-pixel, and an adjustable threshold clip guide. Inputs for the field monitor's 1024 × 800 resolution (300:1 contrast ratio) can be had through HD-SDI (analog component conversion) as well as HDMI, component and S-Video/composite.

On-camera monitors can also come in an "eyepiece" configuration for viewing directly, for example the Cineroid EVF4Le ($700), which also has a HDMI

Figure 13-3, 13-4, and 13-5 Don't' let their small size fool you. Sure, most field and camcorder-mounted monitors can be stashed in the side pocket of even a small camera case but most also have very sophisticated display features.

loop-through feature. Diopter focus adjustments and other controls are mounted on the unit as well. An example is the Marshall Electronics 5-inch V-LCD50-HDI monitor, which comes with a sun hood. Other useful features are a shoe-mount adapter, HDMI input and front panel controls for brightness, color, contrast and the like. A false color view aids in maintaining a consistent image of what is being seen on the monitor, which has a pixel resolution of 800 × 480 and a contrast ratio of 600:1. Should you wish to switch from a monitor to EVF easily, the SmallHD DP4 EVF gives you the best of both worlds: a standalone 4:3 monitor that converts into an electronic viewfinder ($600). The 16.7 million color LED backlit LCD panel is ruggedly constructed and includes frame guides that work with DSLR signals as well as video, focus assist and peaking filters and moveable 1:1 pixel mapping.

You can't edit what you can't see, and field, desktop and production monitors have played a major role in taking video creation into the modern age. Like any electronic device, they are not a substitute for making choices as to how to edit, but they will let you see the results of those choices you've made.

14
Choosing a Video Switcher

Ed Driscoll

Figure 14-1

Finding the best video switcher that'll go the distance.

Choosing a video switcher is a signifi-cant decision for most video producers. While a video project's cinematography determines what it looks like, it's the video switcher that gives a multiple cam-era shoot its overall professional sheen. Video switchers, also known as video mixers, are particularly essential for a live production. A talented operator can use a switcher to blend individual video cameras on the fly with dissolves, wipes, and other effects, and frequently—but not always, as we'll discuss in a few moments—the sound as well. For a video director, the switcher is practically like a musical instrument, and shot timing and

dissolves are often timed for an almost rhythmic feel that's subliminal, but pal-pable. For someone new to this aspect of video production, the switcher's myriad of knobs, faders, T-bars, inputs and out-puts can appear overwhelming at first. But remember that what's going on with one row, is usually the same with the other rows.

Swiss Army Knives Don't Always Make the Best Weapons

Although a few manufacturers might give you the impression that their switchers

(a)  (b)  (c)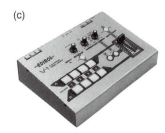

Figure 14-2 *Video switchers come in many shapes and sizes, so be sure to research your needs for special features before you buy.*

can do everything, it's always best to have some idea ahead of time the main type of production you'll be using the unit for. Some units will be more flexible and allow you to work on different types of projects. Others are more limited, but may be perfectly suited for the type of production you make every week.

Are you going to use the switcher at a live performance on location? Then consider a model with its own custom-fitted travel case. Unless the switcher is going to be fitted into a studio control desk and never be transported, buying the case could be well worth the extra cost to protect the delicate circuitry inside. In addition, for those location jobs, you might want to consider, a unit like the Datavideo SE-800, which has its own optional small bank of attachable video monitors.

But if you're working in a studio, then external monitors will give you a better idea what the audience is seeing, and small proprietary monitors become less important.

I/O Silver!

Of course, planning your input and output needs ahead of time is necessary. How many cameras will you need to switch? Are you mixing sound as well? All of these questions should be answered up front.

Most switchers will have a mixture of composite and S-video inputs. Many higher-end switchers will have bayonet-style BNC inputs. Whether these are worth the price depends again on your use: if

you're working in a high-traffic area, a BNC's protection against accidental unplugging is worth the price.

Not all video switchers are set up for audio. Again, ask yourself where the work is going to be done. If you're doing location work, a combined unit may make transport easier. A stand-alone audio mixer will probably have more features, and can provide somewhat better sound quality than combined units. If all-in-one sound and video is valuable to you, make sure the unit has a sufficient quantity of audio inputs and outputs for your needs.

High definition switchers are an even newer beast. Check out a switcher such as Edirol's V-440HD if high def is definitely a high concept requirement.

Check for Effects

Effects are another big consideration. Generally, the greater the cost of the switcher, the greater the number of effects it has built-in, but this isn't always true—with some switchers, you're paying for durability, not a myriad of flashy effects. Typically, video switchers allow for chroma key effects, a variety of wipes and pattern dissolves, and the ability to do titles. Some mixers allow for a variety of chroma colors, others less so.

Some units feature a beats per minute (or "BPM" as all the cool hip-hop guys like to say) display to allow VJs in clubs to sync-up transitions and effects to the beat of the music that's playing. Others also include a MIDI-input, allowing the switcher's effects to be remote-controlled using MIDI (Musical Instrument Digital Interface), which happens to be the common language of electronic musical instruments.

Lower-end machines often lack chroma key, but typically have luminance control for inserting simple titles into a project. These types of low-end mixers also may lack preview outs. But since they typically offer very simple effects, there's little need to preview.

The Focus Enhancements MX-4 is a well-equipped mid-priced switcher capable of producing a host of video effects. An audio mixing feature is also present. In combination audio-video mixers, listen for good audio sync. The MX-4 also includes a T-bar control, which, as we'll discuss in a moment, may be an important feature for you.

The T-Bar Debate

Finally, what many consider to be an important control feature will require some thought. First of all, T-bars are infamous for being bumped if the switcher is in a crowded area. The bar protrudes

in such a way that can be caught on a pants pocket or coat sleeve. A good rule of thumb is to not have any two "bars" together; keep the T-bar away from the martini bar.

Some users, especially when they are doing VJ-style productions, prefer the quicker response of a fader, as opposed to the slow, but more precise feel of a T-bar. In any case, the pacing of an event may determine your choice. Again, it helps to know what types of material the switcher will primarily be used for. Numark's AVM01 streets for less than $1,000, and lacks a T-bar, but is an extremely popular switcher with the VJ set.

So, how to best assimilate this information? You'll benefit the most by knowing your own projects, but leave yourself some room for expansion. See what others are using, and for what purposes. Don't forget to consider the environment in which you'll use it; indoor, outdoor, studio, or travel. Think of wear and tear if you have to set up and tear down often or don't have a dedicated control room. A fair amount of decision-making will go into your purchase, but it'll pay off with a switcher built for your needs.

15
Battery Basics

Michael Fitzer

Figure 15-1

Everyone who has a camcorder has at least one battery. But not all are created equal and knowing which kind of battery and how to best take care of it can be the difference between getting the shot and running to an outlet.

Does this sound familiar? You're running out of daylight but you only have one more shot to grab before you call it a day. There are still two ticks left on your camera's battery indicator and then suddenly everything goes black! A dead battery on your camcorder and no charged spare in your bag means no shot. Knowing more about the type of batteries on the market and how they work will allow you to find the right one for your needs and hopefully keep you from missing that golden moment.

What is this Little Thing?

Everyone knows what a battery is right? OK, before reading on, see if you can come up with a definition for the word. You have 10 seconds. 10 . . . 9 . . . 8 . . .

OK, time's up. Coming up with the correct definition was probably more

Figure 15-2 *Long, continuous run-time, predictable power and rapid refill are three elements that make us anxious for fuel-cell batteries.*

difficult than you thought, right? Put simply, a battery can be any kind of tool that stores energy for later use. However, in this context, the word battery refers to any electrochemical mechanism that uses two electrodes—an anode and a cathode—connected via an electrolyte, which converts chemical energy into electricity.

Eenie, Meenie, Minie, Moe

There are a number of dependable batteries on the market. As for manufacturers, it's difficult to call one better than another. Knowing which type of battery best suits your needs will allow you to make the right choice, at the right price.

When thinking about your next battery purchase, there are three different battery types you will want to consider, NiCd, NiMH, and Li-ion.

- **NiCd**—nickel cadmium is an older cell technology. However, it has a good weight-to-energy ratio and a good service lifetime, which makes it a good choice for portable devices. A drawback to the NiCd battery type is it is well-known for suffering memory effect.

Therefore, it is best to let nickel cadmium batteries completely discharge before recharging.

- "Memory effect," more accurately described as voltage depression, refers to the understanding that when a battery is not completely discharged between recharging cycles, the battery "remembers" the shortened energy cycle and delivers a reduced run time. Voltage depression does not mean your battery has low storage capacity nor will it permanently damage your battery. Fully discharging and then recharging the battery will often correct the problem.

- **NiMH**—nickel metal hydride: is the most common battery type available on today's market. While other cell types are more popular because of their ability to hold a charge, NiMH cells are relatively inexpensive to produce and that low production cost transfers to you, the consumer. While NiMH cell types do experience memory effect, it is not nearly as prevalent in this type as it is in the NiCd batteries. NiMH batteries can also be charged many more times than NiCd batteries.

- **Li-ion**—lithium ion: is one of the most recent advances in battery cell types now on the commercial market. Advances with Li-ion cell types make these batteries lighter than their counterparts, saving users the physical wear-and-tear of transporting and using heavier battery types. Additionally, the Li-ion cell type provides more power and suffers no real problems with memory effect. As for price, advanced engineering costs associated with the lithium ion technology means a much higher cost for you, the consumer.

When used under normal conditions (i.e. no extreme heat, moisture, or excessive physical abuse), any of these cell types will provide you two to three years of dependable operation.

Smart Batteries

So, you've been shooting out in the field for most of the day. You'd like to continue uninterrupted but are unsure about which one of your batteries has the most charge. In the old days you might swap-out batteries on your camera to reveal which one is up to the task. However, many batteries today are now equipped with complex "fuel gauging" technology that allows users to read a built-in lighted meter that indicates how much battery life remains on the current charge.

Batteries that utilize fuel gauges are more expensive than those without, but some consider the increased user friendliness worth the extra cost.

While they are efficient mechanisms, no battery can hold a charge indefinitely. Just like single use batteries, rechargeable batteries, when left unused for long periods, will de-charge on their own. As previously stated, to avoid problems with voltage depression it is best to de-charge and then recharge or "cycle" your battery. You might think that in order to de-charge the battery you have to use it until it quite simply quits or pay more for a battery charger/de-charger (sometimes marketed

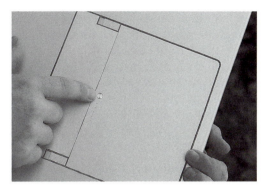

Figure 15-3 *Smart batteries, like the one found on the bottom of the Apple MacBook Pro, will show the user the amount of juice left in the battery.*

as battery conditioners). While those solutions ensure a full de-charge, depending on what you're doing at the time, that former scenario could prove to be rather inconvenient and the latter is more expensive. While it's best to cycle your batteries at least once every month to ensure maximum performance, you do not have to necessarily be using your battery to make sure it de-charges. You can leave it unused for a long period of time and achieve the same results. When you aren't using your batteries, make sure that they have attained a full charge and keep them stored in a cool, dry place.

Alternative Fuel "Sell"

With all the talk about new ways to energize the country, the potential doesn't stop at the car in your driveway. Someday, you may walk into your local retailer and purchase a handy little fuel cell for your home-video camera. In fact, if research is any indication, fuel cells that use methanol as their primary renewable source of energy could be available for portable consumer devices.

While these new sources of energy pack up to 60 percent more energy than the most reliable battery on the consumer market, the chance that they'll immediately replace your standard batteries is slim. Nevertheless, the possibilities are very exciting. When the technology finally comes into play you will no longer replace your battery or have to hunt down an AC outlet to recharge. Instead, your camera (or other portable device) will house a fuel cell capable of accepting a liquid or gaseous "injection" in order to recharge.

Whether you're next battery purchase is driven by need, desire or simply by price, there's a battery on the market that's just right for you. But remember, no matter what type you buy, following the rules of good care will ensure you get the best performance out of your battery.

Spotlight on Batteries and Accessories

- Compact chargers: if you want to charge your batteries but hate packing and unpacking the standard charging plate and AC adapter cord, a number of manufacturers are making compact wall chargers. There's no cumbersome plate and no long cord to manage. Simply snap your batteries into place, flip up the AC plug and let the action happen.

- Conventional AA Approach: some digital cameras can use the conventional AA-size batteries. While very affordable to stock, the standard alkaline batteries are no match for the video world. A couple of zooms, some recording, a playback and "poof" you're out of juice. But there are some rechargeable AA NiMH cells that do well to serve short-term needs. Just make sure you're packing a quality brand and a darn good charger.

16
Recommendations for the Best Video Editing Computer

Douglas Dixon

Figure 16-1

While it's always the situation that "there's never been a better time to get a new computer," this is more true than ever with the completion of the transition to 64-bit computing, widespread support for multi-core CPU (Central Processing Unit) and GPU (Graphics Processing Unit) acceleration, and major boosts in disk interface speeds.

In addition, there's an even broader range of options for configuring a system to your particular needs, not only with dedicated editing workstations and cutting-edge desktop systems, but also with powerful laptops that really can support intensive video work.

Let's look at your options from several perspectives: the system, the trade-offs of cost and performance—processor vs. graphics accelerator, memory vs. hard drives.

The System

The traditional answer for serious video editing is still a dedicated workstation system. These are engineered for performance, often with Xeon processors offering high-performance speed and cores, video acceleration from a professional-grade GPU, integrated high-performance hard drives, and more attention to system integration issues like heat dissipation.

These dedicated editing workstation systems are particularly appropriate for higher-end work such as compositing, effects, and 3D, as well as for working with higher resolutions such as from the cameras from RED.

On the other hand, today's mainstream processors like the Intel Core i5 and i7 can pack a powerful punch in mainstream desktop systems, allowing you to configure a system with impressive specifications while taking advantage of more commodity pricing.

And the power even extends to portable computing, as 64-bit laptop systems with high-end processors and GPUs allow you to take video editing off the desktop and on the road. For complex layered projects, you then can add a fast external disk drive like a RAID (Redundant Array of Independent Disks) storage array to provide the necessary bandwidth for processing multitudes of files.

Configurations

One way to start thinking about configuring your video editing computer is to build up from the minimum requirements of your particular editing software. Products like Adobe Premiere Pro CS5.5, Apple Final Cut Pro X, and Sony Vegas Pro 10 typically recommend at least a 2 GHz multi-core processor (e.g., Intel Core 2 Duo), 2 to 4GB of RAM, a GPU-accelerated graphics card like the NVIDIA GeForce with at least 256MB of internal memory, and a 7200 RPM hard drive for editing compressed video formats or RAID 0 for uncompressed.

That's a good start for even HD editing, but these companies also work with partners to recommend step-up systems for more advanced editing. Apple obviously is happy to offer Macintosh and MacBook systems; Adobe has Dell, HP, and Lenovo as hardware partners; and Sony highlights a selection of certified, pre-configured Supermicro workstations from around $4,000 to $7,000.

If you're doing more intensive editing, you can step up to a mid-range system for improved rendering speeds and real-time playback on the timeline. This might include a next-generation processor like the Core i5, quad cores for better multiprocessing, redoubled memory at 4 to 8GB, a more professional-grade GPU like the NVIDIA Quadro or AMD Radeon HD with more internal memory (512 MB to 1 GB), and higher-performance hard drives at 10,000 RPM/3 Gbps.

Figure 16-2 *When configuring your editing computer, build up from your editing software's minimum system requirements to help it achieve top performance.*

Trade-Off

While you can start with a pre-configured baseline system for your general editing needs, you still can tweak the components to best allocate your purchasing dollars to fit your specific editing projects, particularly the types of video material that you work with and the complexity of your editing timeline.

The key trade-offs for configuring your new video editing computer are the processor for doing the heavy lifting, the graphics accelerator (GPU) for speeding effects, local memory for working directly on sequences, and the disk drive for access to all the media files. The goal is to provide the right combination of hardware to assist your editing software in providing the best editing experience—with real-time playback of layered timelines, instant preview of edits and effects, and background rendering for export while you continue to work.

Your first priority with today's 64-bit software is to bulk up on the local memory to provide more elbow room to directly process sequences. This is particularly useful if you are working with many layers, tweaking a sophisticated effect like stabilization on a short clip, or moving beyond HD to work with film resolutions. More memory also allows you to keep all your applications open and available as you work, to move seamlessly between editing, effects, and rendering as with Adobe Dynamic Link, then bounce over to Photoshop to update a complex layered raw image, or just to check your email.

But if you typically edit native compressed formats like AVCHD (Advanced Video Coding High Definition), or encode your productions to multiple compressed formats, then a faster processor with more cores will help across a wide variety of tasks. This can not only speed up the processing across multiple formats, for example, but also allow you to continue to edit while your files are being compressed and exported in the background.

Or if you tend to have effects-heavy timelines and multiple tracks with

Figure 16-3 *If you work with complex timelines with multiple tracks and numerous effects, a more advanced processor may be needed for real-time previews.*

multiple effects, then look to a more advanced graphics accelerator for real-time previews. The GPU also can help with rendering common formats like AVC (Advanced Video Coding), depending on the available support in your software. Or your favorite third-party effects collections may not be accelerated in this way, and instead would lean more heavily on the processor performance.

Accelerating the Hard Drive

While processor, memory, and GPU all help accelerate local video processing, working efficiently with multiple files and higher resolutions also requires efficiently moving the video frames from and to files on disk. Especially if you tend to composite many layers in your timelines, your hard drive not only needs to have the capacity to store all of your original, edited, and intermediate clips, but also requires the bandwidth to simultaneously deliver the frames from all the files for real-time playback. And again, film resolutions will further push the hard drive requirements.

One developing answer for fast mass storage is the SSD (Solid State Drive), basically memory packaged as a hard drive, and often a good option for the main disk on a laptop system. But good old spinning magnetic disks still provide a much more cost-effective option for very large storage devices, as even portable drives pass 1TB in capacity. The limitation in accessing these drives has been the interface,

particularly the external cabling to attach mass storage to your computer.

The familiar USB 2.0 and FireWire 800 formats offer convenient plug-and play interfaces with 480 and 800 Mbps (megabits per second) transfer rates. eSATA brings the internal SATA interface out of the box to offer another step in improvement, up to 3Gbps for SATA 3G. And then the new USB 3.0 steps up to 5 Gbps, or around ten times faster than USB 2.0.

And now there's Thunderbolt, a new interface championed by Intel and released on new Apple products which provides 10Gb/s rates. Thunderbolt is based on PCI Express technology for data transfer and DisplayPort for displays, so it can be used to daisy-chain multiple high-speed devices without using a hub or switch, including external RAID arrays, video capture devices, and high-resolution displays. You also can connect legacy devices to Thunderbolt using adapters, including DisplayPort, DVI, HDMI, and VGA displays, USB and FireWire peripherals, and Gigabit Ethernet and Fibre Channel networks.

Step Up

So, as usual, there's never been a better time to step up to a new editing computer. The industry has completed the 64-bit transition, so you really can see major improvements in your workflow with the latest 64-bit software running with gigabytes of memory. Software also is taking better advantage of multi-core processors and GPUs for additional acceleration. Even better, all this in-memory performance now is better matched to external disk speeds with new technologies like USB 3.0, eSATA, and Thunderbolt. These even may well be worth waiting for if they're not yet available from your preferred system vendor.

So take the step by starting with a good baseline system, and then make sure to bulk up the right components for your editing needs so you can get the responsiveness that can make editing and experimenting a real joy.

Figure 16-4 *Thunderbolt technology supports bi-directional, high-speed data and display transfers, as well as multiple daisy-chained devices.*

PART II

Production Planning

Every minute spent in planning saves ten in execution. Here's help in getting yourself organized

17
Director's Chair: Secrets of Storytelling

Robert G. Nulph

Figure 17-1

"And Toto, Too?" Say any classic movie line, and everyone knows not only the movie you're referring to, but also which scene and the character who spoke it.

Deep shadows, rustling leaves, the soft tense giggle of children dressed in bright colors and masks making their way past the local cemetery. The headstones throw long dense shadows across the dark fall grass and the children shiver as they rush past the iron fence, casting glances back over their shoulder. Suddenly a giant form looms before them blocking their path.

Thus begins another Halloween tale. Or does it? When planning, ask yourself: "Does the script have the essential elements that make up a good story?"

In light of the season, we'll show you a few examples of how a well-told terror of a storyline is all you need to engross your audience. We will look at how to write a solid story treatment with strong characters and action development in a dramatic arc, following the steps of a great classic of terror.

Fade Up

The movie *The Wizard of Oz* is one of the best examples of storytelling with a

Figure 17-2 *One reason the movie has withstood the test of time is due to its character development with a terrifying "bad guy" and a goody-goody "good guy".*

classic dramatic arc that includes character development, conflicts between good and evil, and challenges that are so well executed that film schools have been taking it apart and examining it frame by frame for decades.

Every good movie begins with a good script. Great acting cannot redeem a bad script, but a good script can make up for a less than stellar cast. A good script comes from a solid treatment written by a writer who takes great care in crafting the story. A treatment is a long synopsis of your story. It focuses on the major characters of the story, both protagonist and antagonist, or more simply put, the good guy and bad guy. The treatment also includes the key plot points and conflicts met by the main characters, and it establishes the emotional undercurrents that run throughout the story.

To begin writing your treatment, you need to remember that every good story has two key ingredients: a character that we care about thrust into a situation or challenge that seems almost insurmountable. The story must have a beginning, middle and an ending. In the beginning, you need to introduce your characters and the world they live in to the audience. As soon as you establish the characters, thrust them into the main situation, problem or challenge they will face for the remainder of the story. Once your characters have met the challenge, solved the major problem or resolved the situation, the story comes to an end.

Figure 17-3 *The roles of a good story's supporting cast are just as important as the main characters. They need to be well-balanced and well-defined.*

However, creating a good story takes a lot of hard work and attention to detail.

Character

The main character in your story must be someone the audience feels some emotional connection with, someone the audience loves or loves to hate. Dorothy, for example, is a sweet innocent farm girl from Kansas who is thrust into extreme turmoil, and we see all of her emotions and feelings unfold as the movie progresses.

You can create strong characters by giving them real human traits, emotions, beliefs and desires. You also need a strong supporting cast for your main character.

Figure 17-4 *As the story builds, give the characters obstacles that they have to overcome, but remember to give your characters (and your audience) some breathing moments between high-tension scenes of conflict, challenge, and despair.*

When you are planning your story, describe your characters both in terms of their physical presence as well as their habits and thoughts. Be as specific as possible. The more you know about your characters, the more likely you will be able to explain how they will react in any given situation and the truer they will ring to the audience. You are creating three-dimensional beings that have to be believable, likable and human. Give them both good and bad traits. Every superhero has a weakness. Every bad guy has at least one good quality. All your characters must also have someone or something that challenges them.

The Situation, Problem or Challenge

After you have established who your characters are, you must throw obstacles in their path and provide conflicts for them to resolve. The main goal or challenge for the lead character should be something that is believable, seemingly insurmountable and perhaps life altering. Tornado, anyone? Well, if that's not enough, let's throw in a wicked witch and flying monkeys blocking your journey home.

Throughout your story, as the characters attempt to meet the challenge, throw more obstacles in their path, and include more conflicts, making it harder to accomplish their goal. Every time they seem to get close, throw them a new challenge. Think of climbing a slippery slope. For every three or four steps up the slope, the characters slide down a few. Following the Yellow Brick Road, Dorothy and friends make it past the enchanted forest, only to be stumped again in the poppy field. Overcoming that, they make their way to the Emerald City, but are barred from entry. Will they ever reach their intended goal?

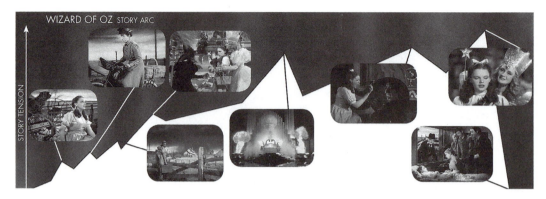

Figure 17-5 Dorothy's adventure begins simply enough with only a scary old lady and a tornado in her way. But the tension rises to her most fearful moment when she's all alone in the witch's castle. The high point is her scene with Glenda, which is happy but tension-packed, when she learns she had the power to go home all along.

When the characters have seemingly run out of options, give them one more boost to meet the challenge, resolve the conflict and accomplish their goal. This is perhaps the trickiest part of writing the story. The climax of the story should be dramatic, unexpected, yet totally believable. If the audience cares about your characters and you have done a good job of stringing them along and keeping them in suspense, the climax of the story should be very rewarding. At this point, let your audience see where the characters will go from here. Whether it is a happy or sad ending, the audience needs a sense of the completion of this chapter in the character's life.

Story and Character Arcs

One way to create a good story and strong character is to use the idea of a character and story arc. Draw an arc and place on it every major growth point or situation met by the characters. The characters and their situation should always be moving forward with each major growth point or challenge noted. As each new challenge is met and the situation intensifies, the arc rises until you meet the ultimate challenge; there is a climax and the problem is resolved, moving the arc down again.

Read through your story and make sure the path of the characters and the challenges they face is continuous, with no breaks in logic or time and with no unnecessary deviations from the main story. You want a few side stories to add to the complexity of the script, but these stories should involve the minor characters and should lead to complications for the main characters but not bog them down and distract the audience. Keep the story flowing at a good pace. Be very aware of time and make sure your characters are always moving forward and that there are no breaks in the timeline that would confuse your audience. This is called continuity, a very important concept in making your story more believable.

Fade Out

Make sure that the goal or need of your main character is clear and that the main conflict is obvious. Ask yourself if you care about what happens to the main characters and does their situation evoke an emotional response? Do you get wrapped up in the characters' situation with a real need to know what happens next? If you have created characters that the audience can care about and provided tense conflict with suspense and a satisfying resolution, you should be able to answer 'yes' to these questions, and you won't need ruby slippers to guide you back home.

Scream Appeal

Scary movies are unique in that they have as their main thrust the desire to scare and surprise the audience. As a director or writer, it is your job to create as much suspense as possible, so that your audience is always on the edge of its seat.

Some ways to do this include making sure you first establish characters the audience will really like and then put them in a situation where conflict surrounds them. Create a really nasty and very powerful demon, ghost, or killer. Add a growing touch of impending doom and increased tension by showing the audience something the main character doesn't know is coming. Fold into the mix a surprise or two with added tension created by a sense of a ticking clock and severe consequences if the time is not met. Wrap it all up in a spooky, deeply shadowed setting and you have the makings of a good suspense movie.

18
Pre-Production Planning: Approaches to Creating a Video Treatment that Works for You

Earl Chessher

Figure 18-1

Even if you are the producer, the shooter, the editor, the distributor and marketing director, taking the time to generate a video treatment will help you present a clearer idea to others and help you stay on track when the time comes to make your production happen.

What's a Video Treatment?

A video treatment is your best effort in defining your project, presenting a clear synopsis of your story, developing your production and organizing its purpose. It is often the first and only chance you have in presenting a commercial project—making a pitch.

It can be as simple as a scratch pad or Post-it note or as complex as a 10-page visual presentation with descriptive and graphical representation that is similar to a storyboard. While not always required, a video treatment is always beneficial to the production in keeping all who are involved focused on the big picture and in minimizing development and production downtime caused by misunderstandings.

There is sometimes a tendency in those generating a video treatment to try to put too much detail regarding the story (storyboard), its characters (screenplay), narrative (script), and camera angles or placement (shot sheet). Keep in mind that while you want to clarify your intended video project and its purpose, its concept and approach, you only want to represent the broader picture. Save the other elements for their specific purposes but know that a video treatment will help you stay focused when the time comes to move forward with your production.

Focus! Focus!

That ring on the camera isn't the only tool important for generating a sharp image. Your video treatment can be the focus ring for your project, keeping you and your production crew, as well as your potential backers, all clearly aware of what you're trying to say and how you want to say it. The more clarity you can give your treatment, the more easily you can keep the interest of those who will help you make your vision happen. Sometimes, something as simple as a Post-it note will serve—at least people working with you and for you won't have to be mind readers. The more time you

take to get your video treatment down on paper, the less time it will take you to get your finished production in the can and on the screen. It will also look a lot more like what you intended instead of taking on a life of its own. But hey, maybe that's what you are working toward—a project that takes a life of its own. Still wouldn't hurt to have that sticky piece of paper on the side of your clipboard.

Step 1: A Sticky Approach

I have two personal favorites when it comes to generating video treatments and one of them is the Post-it note. Those little colored squares are all over my production suite, on my calendar, around the frames of my monitors, on the face of my computer and along the edges of my editing table.

They only look haphazardly placed. Each and every one of them has a specific color and purpose—the light green ones are my current video treatment. We'll save the other colors for another article about production organization. So light green for me, though your colors may vary.

I can get by with one square but my average is six if I take this approach to getting my video treatment down dirty and to the point. A standard square will hold about seven lines—two sentences. What the first sentence tells me is the story line:

Figure 18-2 Post-it notes and index cards can be extremely helpful when it comes to staying organized. Individual colors can each serve different purposes in your production, plus they can be rearranged in the order you desire.

"A university spokesperson takes you around campus, pausing at important locations while telling why this state university system is best-suited for your higher education needs and career plans."

The second sentence tells me this:

"Identify six or more significant locations on campus that best represent the university's programs in academics, sports, and creative arts using a combination walk-and-talk and blocked shots with cutaways of other points for emphasis— elements that will be included in the script and shot sheet."

As simple as it sounds, a video treatment has just been created. And you could have six or so, placed on your clipboard for reference. But you could expand a bit more using index cards.

Step 2: Shuffle the Cards

The advantage to using a dozen or so index cards is that you can not only more clearly define your vision and plan for accomplishing it on video, but you can shift the resulting cards around as one element takes priority over another. And it's easier to use both sides if you want. I personally use only one side because it's easier to reposition elements in my treatment—keeping everything up front.

Generate an overview like "University president Name Here begins his introduction in front of the Pyramid, dwarfed by the structure looming in the background. Use a variety of angles for cuts."

Your second card might say "To emphasize key comments in his presentation, cut the angle and POV to focus on what president Name Here is saying, keeping the Pyramid in the background but smaller."

By the time you've written a dozen or so cards you not only have a presentable short notes-style video treatment for the board, committee or your crew, but can move things around as elements of perceived importance shift in value. This approach also pretty much provides you with the beginnings of a shot sheet and even a storyboard or script.

Step 3: Show and Tell

Video is a visual medium so what better way to approach development of a video treatment than by using comments and visuals. This is my second and most favorite video treatment style. While it is the most complex to generate, a visually focused video treatment is the easiest way to ensure a fully planned approach to your production. It also usually always gives everyone involved a more exact idea of what is intended.

I have, in fact, actually been able to sell my suggested treatment over others who either present off the top of their heads— extemporaneously; from scribbled notes, even Post-its or index cards. Why? Because like video, what I call the show-and-tell video treatment is, uh, visual! The people whom I want to see what I am thinking get to see what I'm thinking.

If I put in the right amount of planning, use good illustrations and have the treatment clear in my mind—and I have because I put in the extra time to become totally familiar with the project and how to best present it to others—I'm making the connection.

Other methods of presentation for video treatments—making the pitch—depend on the audience's ability to visualize. With a video treatment that in fact can serve as your storyboard base, there's not nearly as much explaining to do.

The Post-it and or index card notes you start out with, even scribbled notes on a couple of sheets of paper, provide a good foundation for creation of your show-and-tell video treatment. I have a CD portfolio of art that while some is outdated, much of its content remains useful for illustrating my show-and-tell video treatments. It's called Art Explosion 750,000. I continue to pull usable vector, raster and photographic images from it to create visual references for my video treatments. There are hundreds of available sources for commercial and copyright-free images that can be attained without investing too much money or time. These resources can be found with a simple online search, usually in just a few minutes. They are the

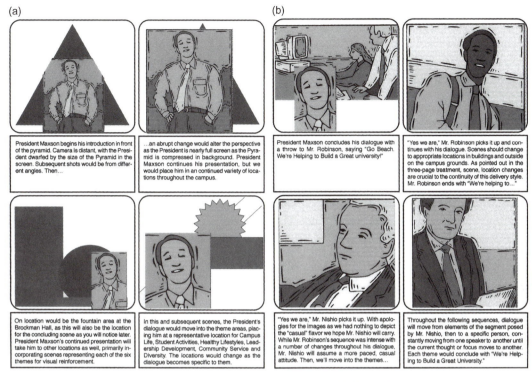

(a)

President Maxson begins his introduction in front of the pyramid. Camera is distant, with the President dwarfed by the size of the Pyramid in the screen. Subsequent shots would be from different angles. Then...

...an abrupt change would alter the perspective as the President is nearly full screen as the Pyramid is compressed in background. President Maxson continues his presentation, but we would place him in a continued variety of locations throughout the campus.

On location would be the fountain area at the Brockman Hall, as this will also be the location for the concluding scene as you will notice later. President Maxson's continued presentation will take him to other locations as well, primarily incorporating scenes representing each of the six themes for visual reinforcement.

In this and subsequent scenes, the President's dialogue would move into the theme areas, placing him at a representative location for Campus Life, Student Activities, Healthy Lifestyles, Leadership Development, Community Service and Diversity. The locations would change as the dialogue becomes specific to them.

(b)

President Maxson concludes his dialogue with a throw to Mr. Robinson, saying "Go Beach. We're Helping to Build a Great university!"

"Yes we are," Mr. Robinson picks it up and continues with his dialogue. Scenes should change to appropriate locations in buildings and outside on the campus grounds. As pointed out in the three-page treatment, scene, location changes are crucial to the continuity of this delivery style. Mr. Robinson ends with "We're helping to..."

"Yes we are," Mr. Nishio picks it up. With apologies for the images as we had nothing to depict the "casual" flavor we hope Mr. Nishio will carry. While Mr. Robinson's sequence was intense with a number of changes throughout his dialogue, Mr. Nishio will assume a more paced, casual attitude. Then, we'll move into the themes...

Throughout the following sequences, dialogue will move from elements of the segment posed by Mr. Nishio, then to a specific person, constantly moving from one speaker to another until the current thought or focus moves to another. Each theme would conclude with "We're Helping to Build a Great University."

Figure 18-3 *Creating a show-and-tell style video treatment will help the prospective client visualize the point you're trying to get across. If you're not an artist, use stock art.*

simplest approach if, like me, you are not an artist.

Using regular typing paper, I create eight or so pages, rarely more than 10, with four visual blocks and four descriptive blocks that adequately represent what I want to see, say, show, capture and create. Though it might take a bit more time, usually no more than a few hours, creating a visual video treatment will cut acquisition time, scripting, storyboarding and shot-sheet generation time by 15 percent.

Keeping High Standards

While there are accepted formats for writing screenplays, for developing storyboards and for presenting shot sheets, as well as acceptable variations, I've

Three Strikes and You're Out!

It seems a video treatment is most common when used in a budgeted or commercial venture. This is not necessarily so. In the chapter, emphasis was placed on using the video treatment for organizing and planning any production—always helpful, never a waste of time.

But what if you have a board, committee or agency that expects you to present something creative, clear and concise? Taking the time to research and develop a video treatment will greatly reduce the need for a pill to calm the nerves, antacid to settle the stomach or a sip of bubbly to smooth the delivery. The video treatment is, in fact, essential to any hope for success. Without one it would be better to not even show up. The good news is that even if you get three strikes you are not yet out. There are things you can do to keep the doors open, even get a call-back.

not identified a carved-in-stone format for a video treatment. In my case, it has been whatever works and as I noted earlier "whatever works" best for me has been the visual or show-and-tell video treatment.

It helps to keep clear and concise in my mind what I want to accomplish and it helps me keep my presentation to others clear as well. When I take the time to do this, everyone involved seems better able to stay in focus. The video treatment is, of course, like most anything else in video production, a work in progress. That is until you see it on the big screen and even then revisions happen. But fewer and less often.

Dress Appropriately

Super casual is best left to those have an image to maintain—a certain adversity to the status quo. This is not us.

- When pitching to a board of directors men should wear a suit and tie and women business attire.
- When pitching to a committee, men can often get by with shirt and tie or casual suit and women non-sports attire, casual business.
- When pitching to the local school board, PTA or church committee the answer is "it depends." Do your homework. If you're on the left coast, business casual or even shirt and no tie might be OK, or not.
- If you find that the group is ultra-conservative and of a suit-and-tie nature— well, as they say—when in Rome . . .

Keep it Sane

You do not want to present or pitch a church committee on the church's 100th anniversary project with the same degree of energy or level of enthusiasm as you would, say for the board of a company that creates first person shooter video games.

On the other hand, you do want to generate some enthusiasm and a controlled level of excitement for virtually any video focusing on a celebratory event. A group of attorneys might want something polished and sophisticated for their founder's 50th anniversary, while the Rotary Club planning committee might want to roll up their sleeves and snap their suspenders a bit.

Know your audience, especially when generating a video treatment for commercial purposes.

Know When to Shut Up

Most of us have a tendency to want to fill the silence. You've prepared your pitch, developed handouts of the show-and-tell video treatment and passed them around. You've introduced yourself and have been invited to "pitch" or "quickly summarize" or "tell us" and have done so smoothly and without hesitation.

That moment of awkward silence that follows doesn't always mean you failed to make your point, pitch a hit or otherwise land the big one. Always, when you have completed your pitch—stop talking. Always wait until somebody running the committee, board, organization or group says something. Asks something.

This is critical, especially when pitching a video treatment to an entertainment group or its agent or CEO. More often than not, if you've hit something, connected in some way, you will be asked if you have anything else. Be prepared. Always have another pitch ready, another video treatment in your briefcase or handouts to pass around for another concept or treatment. It doesn't hurt, in fact, to have a backup video treatment ready even if you knock the first one out of the park.

19
Video Production Scheduling

Laura Martone

Figure 19-1

Every director should have the capacity for spontaneity, the ability to deal with the unexpected during a shoot.

On-the-spot ingenuity, however, is not enough. You'll greatly improve your chance of success—and save time, money and energy to boot—if you use the pre-production phase to craft a detailed plan of attack. If you take the time to create an accurate shot list, consider details like location availability, and fashion a shooting schedule accordingly, your shoot will go much faster and smoother—and your cast, crew and client will thank you for it.

Focus on the Project

No exact formula exists for creating an effective shooting schedule. Every project has different parameters and considerations. For instance, you might need less time to shoot an hour-long corporate video, which consists of interviews and demonstrations in a studio, than you'll need to shoot a 4-minute music video that requires lip-synching and varied locations.

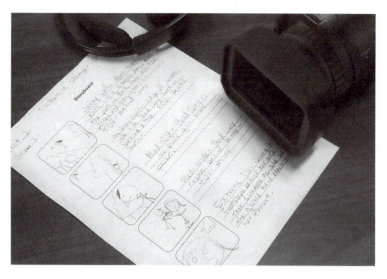

Figure 19-2 *You can use descriptive scripts to explain your needs,
but a storyboard with stick figures that has diagrams, screen
direction, and angles will help the crew visualize each shot.*

So, before plunging into a scheduling frenzy, you must first consider what footage you need in order to complete the project. Based on the client's wishes, the purpose of the video, the intended audience and your own vision, you should prepare a shooting script, with helpful video cues and audio notes. Skip the fancy storyboards and focus instead on crafting a specific shot list—covering everything from establishing shots to cutaways—and, if necessary, a few lighting diagrams to ensure faster setups during the shoot.

This will also help you to determine your equipment needs. For example, if you're shooting a promotional video for a construction company, you might want smooth shots that require a crane or dolly. Conversely, if you're covering a concert from various angles, you'll need multiple cameras, each equipped with a stabilizer.

To figure out how long it could take to shoot your entire script, consider that, on average, one page usually equals one minute on-screen. Of course, the exact timing depends on the exact nature of the project. Dialogue-heavy scenes, for instance, tend to go faster than those filled with action. From here, consider how long it might take to prepare each scene, including lighting, equipment and set arrangement.

To ensure smooth set changes, consider shooting establishing shots first, followed by talent close-ups and cutaways.

The key is to be realistic, not overly ambitious. Though shorter schedules are often less expensive—requiring less money for renting equipment, purchasing food and compensating your cast and crew—it's far better to overestimate how much time you'll need than to rush the production. So, allow some extra room in the schedule, and be honest with your client about your expectations.

Evaluate the Locations

Next, make a list of all necessary locations—from studio sets to outdoor sites. If possible, visit the locations ahead of time and take photographs to reference when planning your shot list and shooting schedule. If that's impossible—due to time constraints or other logistical reasons—contact someone who can provide you with footage, images or helpful details about each locale.

Once you determine what shots you'll need, research the availability of each location and schedule the problematic ones first. For example, if you need to shoot

Figure 19-3 *Take photos of your locations for reference later. Plan to shoot outdoor shots first, so you can work around weather and light. Restaurant or office shots might not be available during business hours, so consider how to create the same warm environment when they're unoccupied.*

inside a bar, you'll probably have to do so earlier in the day, before the place opens to the public. Likewise, you should schedule exterior shots as early as possible, in case the weather turns ugly. Unless you're shooting a corporate video, the opposite is usually true for an office building, which is typically available after regular business hours.

If you're using multiple locations across a wide region, you'll also need to figure out the distance between each location. If possible, you should organize the shooting schedule to allow for the least amount of driving time—by, for instance, combining close locales on the same day. Make sure, too, that you have written permission forms and permits for all locations; it's no fun having to find an alternative site on the day of the shoot.

In addition, try to determine any potential problems that could affect the shoot at each location, such as difficult access,

ambient light and sound, nearby traffic and the availability of parking, restrooms, water and electrical outlets. If necessary, have alternative locations in mind.

Remember the Talent

Whether you're shooting a how-to video about gardening or a documentary about a nonprofit organization, you'll surely have to deal with talent during your shoot. If so, figure out who appears in each shot—and whether there are any scheduling conflicts. As with locations, you don't want to discover that someone's not available on the day of the shoot. This is especially true for children and their guardians, who often follow strict guidelines about their education, shooting conditions and allotted set time.

When creating your shooting schedule, try to plan complicated scenes earlier in the day, before the talent gets fatigued—and don't forget to plan for reasonable breaks, which you can stagger to save time. For example, while the cast breaks for a meal, you can use a smaller crew to shoot cutaways, such as exterior shots or tool close-ups. You must also allow enough time between shoots; even die-hard cast and crew members need their rest.

Strike a Balance

No matter how complicated a shoot seems, it will be infinitely easier if you plan a reasonable shooting schedule beforehand. You'll be far less stressed—and so will your cast, crew and client—if you consider the project scope, location requirements and talent needs before the shoot. It's also a good idea to exhaust troubleshooting concerns ahead of time. For instance, you should have alternative talent and locations in mind—just in case there's a last-minute cancelation or weather concern.

Of course, these aren't the only considerations. Sometimes, you have to schedule around special events, complex stunts, seasonal concerns and other unique issues. No matter how tedious planning might seem, having a plan and effectively communicating it to your cast, crew and client—will ensure that your shoot happens on time and on budget.

20
It's All in the Approach: Creative Approaches for Video Productions

Jim Stinson

Figure 20-1

Some informational programs use gimmicks like butter on popcorn, to hide the bland taste of the subject matter: "Hi! I'm Percy Peatmoss, and we're gonna meet some exciting lichens!" (Suuure, we are!) Though spokespersons like Percy went out with 16 mm projectors, promotional training and educational programs still need what you might call a presentation method.

As the term implies, this is a systematic approach to laying out the content of a program. Mr. Announcer on the sound track, Julia Child behind the cooktop, the talking head in the interview, each of these is a presentation method, deliberately selected because it's well-suited to the program's subject. What are some of these presentation methods and how do you select the right one(s) for your show?

Step right this way, folks; the tour starts here.

When you come right down to it, there're only a few basic presentation methods: documentary, interview, expert presenter and full script. As we look at each method in turn, you should remember that most informational videos still use them in various combinations.

Documentary

A documentary purports to capture and display a subject as it really is, allowing viewers to draw their own conclusions from their impressions of the material. In some programs, they're assisted by narration or commentary, while in others the edited footage appears to speak for itself. (We say "purports" and "appears" because no documentary is a truly passive, neutral pipeline of information. For more on this, see "Liar, Liar!" in the October 2000 issue of *Videomaker* or at www.videomaker.com).

The documentary method works well where you want to convey a free-form impression of your subject. "Beautiful Downtown Burbank, Recreation in Bigfoot County," and "Where your Sales Tax Goes are good subjects for documentary programs."

The most rigorous documentary form (represented by the films of Frederick Wiseman) uses no verbal commentary to organize the presentation and point the message. The entire effect comes from the selection and juxtaposition of shots. To the newbie, this may seem like the easiest form of program ("Hey kids, let's showcase Fillmore High!") but it is in fact, the hardest to do successfully. Without the guidance of voiceovers and titles, the result is often an inexpressive jumble of footage.

That's why many professional documentarians (notably Ken Burns) use multiple voices on the sound track often a mix of narration, dramatized voices and interview quotes. This method is easier because it allows you to comment on the footage as you display it. However, juggling multiple audio sources is a sophisticated process.

For fail-safe simplicity, try mating documentary footage to voice-over narration. By scripting a single stream of commentary, you can control your presentation more precisely.

Interview

Interviews offer ways to get variety into your presentation, especially if you include several people. Interviews are great for subjects that are essentially verbal and require some expert input.

Some topics are difficult to visualize. No matter how many photo albums you have, they don't display family history, but only moments from that history. For the actual narrative, nothing beats Great

Figure 20-2 *Single and Dual Interviews: single interviews—the most popular form in professional TV shows—look spontaneous, but dual interviews are easier to manage.*

Grandmother on the sound track. Other good interview subjects include Our Corporate Five Year Plan (interview with the CEO) and Coping with Depression (interviews with sufferers and therapists). As these examples suggest, interview programs come in several different flavors: single, dual and multiple.

The single interview doesn't look like a Q&A session, but like spontaneous conversation by the subject. The interviewer is never seen or heard, and the questions (dropped on the cutting room floor) are phrased to elicit statements rather than answers ("Tell us about the Boston branch of the family"). Because they omit the overhead of questions, single interviews are the most popular form in professional programs.

However, the dual interview is easier to manage. In this form, viewers can see the interviewer and hear the questions. Furthermore, replies can be free-form in this approach. For example, "Where were you born?" "Cleveland." is fine in a dual interview, but the answer would be meaningless in a single interview. Two-person interviews also offer built-in cutaway material in the form of the interviewer.

A more complex interview form is multiple voice. Using man-on-the-street polls or short sessions with the many people connected with the topic, you weave together a composite audio track that adds richness and variety as well as information. If people you know have some performing ability, you might try dramatized "interviews" with historic figures or people otherwise unavailable. Be cautious, however, because voice-only acting is a highly specialized skill and amateurish results tend to sound embarrassing.

Expert Presenter

If you've watched a David Attenborough nature video ("The vegetation [wheeze] here at 15,000 feet [gasp] is, understandably [rattle] sparse.") then you've seen an expert presenter. This method has many things going for it. First, the expertise of the spokesperson lends authority to the whole enterprise. Second, he or she can often be relied on to flesh out a skeletal content outline by ad-libbing material.

The expert is best in the field whether that field is a studio cooking show kitchen or a construction site or the Sonoran desert. If that isn't possible, you can establish the expert on camera in interview mode and then shift his or her remarks to voiceover narration.

The simplest approach is commentary: the experts react to whatever is presented to them. At its best, this method elicits priceless observations that would never occur to a script writer. At worst, it delivers the DVD prattle of movie directors reacting off-the-cuff to screenings of their films.

One more formal step is the demonstration, anything from a construction project

Figure 20-3 *The expert presenter lends authority to your subject and can ad-lib to expand on outlined program material.*

to a science experiment to a cooking show. A demo is more clearly sequenced (by the steps in the project or recipe) but it still offers ample opportunity for ad-lib expert commentary. A demonstration format works best when the project can be completed at a single place in real-time (except for the 45-minute baking period) and when the personality of the presenter adds interest to the show.

A popular variation seen on home repair, gardening and cooking shows is the dual (and sometimes dueling) expert format pioneered by Siskel and Ebert. This approach combines the virtues of the expert and interview methods, especially if one of the presenters serves as prompter/straight man to the other.

The next level up is a full-fledged lecture, either scripted or ad-lib. Since even the most dynamic expert is still just a talking head, it's good to cut away as much as possible to visuals of the subject matter. In fact, a project like this often starts with the taped lecture; then appropriate visuals are scripted and shot after the fact.

Sometimes, the effect of a lecture can be created by a skillful one-person interview. The questions select and sequence the material, and then drop away, leaving a seamless narrative.

Full Script

An expert isn't necessary when reading narration that's been fully scripted. There are several reasons for going to the trouble of a wall-to-wall script. In some cases, there are issues of legal or technical accuracy. You don't want to misrepresent details of Employee Benefit Packages or Self Administration of Insulin, and the best way to avoid doing so is by writing down (and getting approval for) every image and word.

In training and similar how-to programs, you want the clearest camera angles and the simplest language possible. In highly

Figure 20-4 In some situations, you might want to script the narration for your talent in clear simple language.

controlled situations like this, you'll probably want every sentence written and every setup storyboarded.

A scripted program can use any mixture of presentation forms, including an on-camera spokesperson, a voiceover narrator and superimposed title buildups. You can even use interviews if the questions are closely coordinated with the script. (In real-world situations, the script is often revised after the interviews are completed, in order to bring it into line with whatever was said.)

Full scripts and/or storyboards are almost always prepared for professional commercials, infomercials, video press releases and training programs, for one overwhelming reason: the client. Most people and organizations are reluctant to spend good money unless they can see (or at least think they can see) what they're getting.

As we've seen, the presentation method chosen depends first of all on the nature of the topic. But real-world constraints also play a large role. What if you don't have an expert? Worse, what if you do have an expert who's a droning bore but still wants to be in the program? In situations like this, you need to know the alternative methods available to you and their suitability to your topic. We hope this little survey has helped.

21
Script Writing

Kyle Cassidy

Figure 21-1

Why is scriptwriting important? Using even one other person can waste time on reshoots from poor planning. Even if working alone, you can still save time with a good plan.

"Pay attention!" Bob demanded, waving a donut at us. Next Betsy comes in and shows everyone the microwave and Randy's going to say 'It looks really reliable!' and we'll get a shot from above with the marching band—you know—marching around and playing something, and Betsy, or maybe Gina, yeah, Gina. Gina throws five heads of broccoli into the microwave and says 'and roomy!' and that's when the juggler with the unicycle comes in."

"Juggler?!" cried out Misty, "you never said anything about a juggler!"

"We don't have a juggler?"

"We don't have a juggler!" Misty was nearly in tears, as she was in charge of props and extras. Bob looked puzzled. "I thought I mentioned the juggler. Maybe I didn't. OK, so Betsy'll just say something about how energy efficient it is and we'll call it a day."

"How energy efficient is it?" asked Betsy. Bob's look went from puzzled to worried.

"It's because we didn't have the juggler," Bob said later that night after his sixth Shirley Temple while we all commiserated in the cheapest bar we could find.

"No it's not," I said, "we got fired because we didn't have a script."

"A script?!" Bob set down his glass and motioned to the waitress for another—he was hitting the grenadine pretty hard— "audio ... video ... script ... format ..." he muttered in a seeming daze—then snapping out of it continued, "why would we need a script for a 30-second TV spot! Don't you think I can keep a 30-second spot straight in my head?"

Everyone who has been doing video for any length of time knows that writing is important, though they might not have a formal idea of how to write a video script. We're going to look at making scripts for video productions, from small 30-second spots, to epic dramas; there's something for everyone.

Scripts—how Formal?

While there are very particular formatting demands made for certain types of scripts, they don't necessarily have to be in a particular format with a certain font, indentation or line spacing if you're working by yourself or a small group of friends. As long as you're clear, a script might be as simple as a shot list with notes:

Betsy comes in and shows everyone the microwave.

Bob says "It looks reliable".

Gina microwaves broccoli in it.

Get coverage from multiple angles and closeups.

This might be all you need if you're shooting things on a small scale and don't need approval from anyone before you start. However, the more complex your shoot, the more important a script becomes and the more reasonable it is to format your script the way other writers do.

One reason for very exacting specifications of some scripts is because they're used to gauge the length of a movie where each page of a script averages out to one minute of screen time. This allows producers and directors to gauge the length of a production simply by looking at the size of the script on their desk. Twelve-point Courier News is typically the standard font because of its ubiquity, clarity, and the fact that it's a monospaced rather than proportional font (meaning a capital "M" takes up as much space as a lowercase "i").

Other Types of Scripts

Typically scripts use a screenplay format which looks like a play—people's names, their dialogue, and directions about what's happening. There's another common script format called a "two column" or "A/V" script, which has two columns, one with narration and the second column with a description of what's happening in the video. This might be:

Audio

The mighty moose wanders the mountain-top, looking for food. It remains one of the most memorable sights a lucky tourist will see as the sun sets in the background.

Video

- Start with wide shot of scene.
- Cut to various shots of moose wandering around.
- Closeup of moose's head as he lifts it to look around.

Whichever format works for you, theatrical play, A/V, or a simple outline, scripts have a number of benefits to your production. There are books and websites galore, which will deal with the minutia of formatting just a few clicks away. Let's look at some of the reasons you'd want to use a script and what it'll do for your production.

Scripts help formulate ideas: the writing process helps to get your thoughts down and organize them, looking at the relationship between shots and ideas can often help you see the bigger picture and create a better arc to your story.

Scripts help prevent accidents: scripts make sure that there are no unexpected props or camera angles. If Bob had written a script that included the words "Juggler/unicycle" the production team would have known beforehand that they needed to have one. Likewise if the script calls for a crane shot, or a cake, or lines spoken in French, your team will know that they need props or a dialogue coach; moreover there's a chance to reject it if someone realizes it's unnecessary or too expensive.

Scripts show that you're serious: the video industry is very competitive and you're often dealing with people who have very limited time to make decisions and have many production companies to choose from. Your packaging, website, and script are all things that can show how serious a player you are at a glance. Turning in a polished and properly formatted script when the other guy shows up with some Post-it notes stuck on his sleeve will show the client who's willing to spend the time and attention their production needs.

Scripts help communication and streamline revision: After your client gets your script, it's easy for them to comment on specifics and to shape your production long before you get to the set, they can get a concrete handle on your ideas and the way you want to present them. On professional productions with lots of script changes, new pages will be printed in different colors; for instance the first revision might have white pages with changes on them, then are replaced by pink pages, the next round of changes may come on blue pages, etc. So everyone will know that their script is or isn't current based on the color pages they have. For this reason it's a good idea to put your script in a three-ring binder rather than stapling it.

Scripts help multiple people work on a project: Often, videos are made by people who don't live near one another, or who are working on other projects before the shoot—having a script that can be sent to everyone will let you hear from your lead actress that she's afraid of heights and will need a stunt double for the water tower scene; from your property master that the bonfire you have in scene six will need a permit from the fire marshal; and will let other people comment on pace, dialogue or other things that are important to them.

I don't need a script, I'm just shooting my kid's birthday party! Even the seemingly most disorganized of shoots can benefit from a script. When shooting something like a birthday party, having a script beforehand that spells out not what people will say, but things you want to get and what order you want to get them in—this can be extremely helpful. A script for a birthday party might look something like this:

- Exterior setup shots of house.
- Titles: Junior's Tenth Birthday, January 11, 2012
- Video montage of photos of all of Junior's previous birthdays.
- Mom in front of the house, she says "Welcome to Junior's birthday party! We're at the Baxter household and we have a swell day planned!"
- Baking the cake: have grandma tell the story of her cake recipe, closeups of cake being made and going in the oven.
- Wrapping presents: have mom tell the story of how much Junior wanted a bow and arrow while she wraps it, have her speculate on what Junior will say when he opens it.
- Interview with Junior: ask him what he wants; have him talk about each of the friends he's invited.

- Interviews with friends: ask name, age, how they met Junior and what they like best about him.
- Games: get medium and wide shots, get shots out the window of the third floor showing the whole croquet setup and hedge maze.
- The cake—bringing the cake out, follow grandma from kitchen.
- Pan the table before the candles are blown out; get medium shots of faces. Shot from across the table as Junior blows out candles, shoot second camera on wide shot of room.

- Two cameras during unwrapping, wide shot of room and closeup of Junior's face.
- Recap—after guests have left, ask Junior how his day was, have him tell a story about grandma, ask which presents he likes the best, ask what kind of party he'd like the next year.

That's a pretty elaborate video for a kid's birthday party, but this kind of road map helps plan your shots, sets the story that you're going to tell, and makes sure you'll have all the coverage you'll need to edit a great video together.

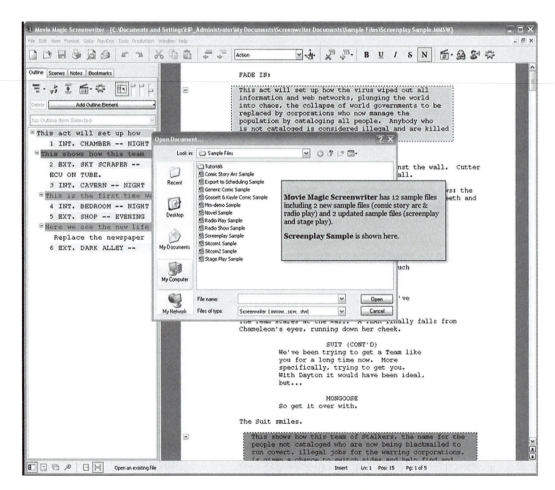

Figure 21-2 *Programs like Movie Magic are software packages that are designed for script writing. Highlighting shot location, formatting dialogue or narration and sample scripts are some of the possible features.*

Scriptwriting Software

The internet is littered with scriptwriting software and they've been around for a while. In 1983, the Write Brothers, Stephen and Christopher, released the first scriptwriting software, Scriptor which has been sold several times over the years. Their current software, Movie Magic, shares the stage with other applications like Final Draft and ScreenForge as well as a number of free and not-free templates for Microsoft Word and OpenOffice. A few minutes on Google can help you find the right one, or you can make your own by setting up paragraph styles in your favorite word-processing program.

Conclusion

Having a script helps you not only get your ideas down clearly, but helps get input from other people before everyone is on the set and things start to get too expensive. It's a very important tool for general preparedness, even when your plan is as simple as "show up and see what happens."

Your homework assignment is to look at some scripts online or from the library—take a look at formatting and organization, see how the dialogue, description and camera positions have been described, use what you've learned in your next production, and let us know how it goes in the *Videomaker* forums!

22
The Perfect Plan: Storyboard and Shot List Creation

Julia Camenisch

Figure 22-1

Script creation is a task that requires lots of time, work and planning. In fact, planning is probably the heart and soul of the production. The proper planning and legwork must be accomplished or even the best script will fall flat on its face.

Figure 22-2 *Storyboards help you visualize your film and determine what shots you need before you ever set foot on set.*

There are many aspects to pre-production planning, but we're just going to focus on two of them here: the storyboard and the shot list. If you're working on a small production, then you might get to do everything yourself! If you have much of a budget, then some of this planning can be done in conjunction with other members of your crew.

In Living Color

Your first planning tool, the storyboard, is essentially a comic book of your production. It covers all the major shots, angles and action involved in the script. Think of it as shooting your movie on paper instead of to tape or digital file. Shot by shot, you draw out the script and decide how to visually compose each scene.

Why is this so important? Because now you know how your shots work together. No jump cuts or bad angles to surprise you in the edit bay. You are also assured that you have adequate coverage of each scene. Storyboarding allows you to maximize both your time and your resources when on set—and that amounts to saving money. The storyboard helps bring out ideas and find trouble spots in your scenes.

There are many options available for storyboard creation. In its simplest form, you can draw one with stick figures on a notepad. Perfect for a quick and dirty board that gets the job done. Another option is advanced storyboarding software, which can create an animated 3D previsualization that almost feels like a movie itself. This fits the bill when there's a client involved that you want to impress. And if money is no object, you can hire a storyboard artist, just like Hollywood directors do.

Figure 22-3 *Storyboards are a timeline of events from start to finish. They help maximize both your time and resources on set. Storyboards also help find errors and trouble spots in your scenes. The more detail and time you put into the storyboard, the easier it will be shooting your production.*

Sketchin' Away

Before you begin the storyboard, study your shooting locations in detail. You might even bring a camera and snapshots of potential angles. This type of scouting work will give you a better idea of how to compose the shots on paper. The camera is also a great tool for creating a basic storyboard. Bring a friend or two along as talent and use your camera to capture all the angles and positions. Load the pictures into a PowerPoint presentation and then play the presentation to see how it all flows.

To create a storyboard on paper, put two rows of boxes on the page with ample space above and below each row for making notes. Make sure your boxes are roughly the same aspect ratio you're planning to shoot with. Have lots of copies of your blank boards—you don't want to run out! With your script in hand, sketch each scene, using multiple boxes to capture all your intended shot angles. Critically examine the finished product, looking for gaps in shot coverage or problematic setups. And don't forget to use a pencil so you can easily erase and redraw.

While your storyboard isn't expected to be a work of art, there are a few standard conventions that will make it more understandable to others. Indicate a zoom or dolly in the frame by putting a floating box around the telephoto position. Use arrows pointing in or out to indicate the zoom direction. Use single arrows to communicate movement. Show the direction of a pan or tilt by drawing the beginning and ending in two separate frames, then putting an arrow and a directional notation to make the action clear, i.e., "pan right".

As you pan right use the space around each frame to make notes on camera action ("Tilt up") or script notes ("Lucy dances around the car"). Also keep a notepad off to the side where you keep track of needed gear, sound effects, props, make-up, special effects—basically anything and everything needed to pull off the scene should be included in those notes.

Previsualization software takes your planning to the next level. By creating 3D worlds and models to inhabit them, you're able to see the way those notes you made on camera and actor staging play out. There are two great benefits to this type of storyboard. One—as previously mentioned, it makes for an effective client presentation. They can easily grasp how your concept will really work. Two—it can help you better visualize complex sequences that are hard to draw on paper.

Writing It Out

When you're finished with the storyboard, move on to planning your shooting strategy. The scenes in your script may each call for multiple camera angles. If you are filming with a single camera, shooting these in linear order is probably not the best choice . . . unless you enjoy constantly changing your camera and lighting setup. Instead, squeeze all

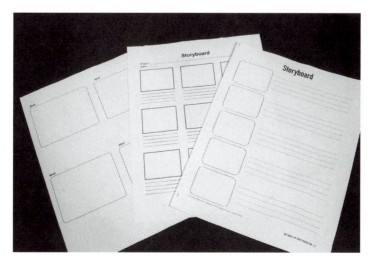

Figure 22-4 *There are several different formats of storyboards to choose from. Choose the format you're the most comfortable with.*

you can from each setup by making use of another indispensable planning tool, the shot list.

In a nutshell, the shot list groups similar shots together so that you have an efficient shooting schedule. Prepare the list by looking through a scene's storyboard and noting which frames can be captured during the same setup. Write them together on the list. Then use your list as a guide, and check off shots as they're captured. You'll protect yourself from overlooking an important close-up or establishing wide-shot.

Another benefit of the shot list is in creating a schedule. You can get a rough picture of how much time it will take to capture a scene as you plan out the various setups. It also allows the crew to easily follow along with what's needed next. For example, by looking at the list, they can see that there are only two shots left in this setup, so it's time to begin preparing for the next setup.

The Art of Practice

If you don't have experience with storyboarding and shot lists, then give yourself a practice run. Watch a scene from a movie, TV show or commercial. Keep your remote next to you, and pause every few seconds to make note of the camera angle changes, screen action and even what gear might have been used in the scene. Then pull out your storyboard paper and draw a few minutes of the scene.

Working from your practice storyboard, write out screen action and camera movement notes. Then create a shot list based on the storyboard. It's a lot of work, but it can help you get your mind around all the planning that needs to be done before your production can get off the ground.

Lighting, camera work, editing—they're all good skills to learn. But don't forget the skill of planning. At the end of the day, it's an investment of time and energy that's just as important as your technical prowess.

23
Storyboard Examples

Kyle Cassidy

Figure 23-1

Getting your story's vision from your brain to the table is hard, so let's look at what storyboarding is, along with some useful movie storyboard examples and tricks from the pros.

What is Storyboarding, and Why is it Useful?

On big video productions there may be as many as 100 people on set at once, which means that every second a director spends stroking his chin and wondering about where the camera ought to be placed he's paying 100 people to stand around and watch him. This is something that motivates a film's backers to make sure that there are no moments during shooting when everybody who's getting paid to work isn't working. One of the ways that directors, producers, art designers, and directors of photography make sure that everything is worked out before the cast and crew actually get to the set and minimize standing-around time is to use storyboards.

Storyboards are typically a sort of comic book style illustration of the entire movie, or sometimes just difficult scenes in a movie, including camera angles and the motion of actors through the sets. Lots of storyboard excerpts have made their way onto the internet; Google can help you track down many of them. Spectacularly popular movies, such as *Star Wars* or Akira Kurosawa's war epic *Ran*, may have their storyboards published as books. Many other movies will show some of the storyboards in the special features section of the DVD—often with side-by-side comparisons of the original storyboards and the final film. Lots of storyboarding tips and storyboard examples can be seen on line on websites like YouTube. There's also a plethora of writing about storyboarding in this history of Hollywood. One very famous champion of the storyboard is Alfred Hitchcock. Rita Riggs, the costume designer for *Psycho*, discusses the director's affectation

Figure 23-2 *The progression of action in a scene can be described by key events in a narrative storyboard. This provides a general template for shot distance, perspective, and any major actions that need to occur.*

for extensive storyboarding in Stephen Rebello's book, *Alfred Hitchcock and the Making of Psycho*, saying: "The real difference working with Hitchcock and his circle was that you had an entire, cohesive picture laid out before you on storyboards. He truly used storyboards to convey his ideas and desires to all his different craftsmen. You knew every angle in the picture, so there was not a lot of time wasted talking an item to death. We also didn't have to waste time worrying about things like shoes, for instance, because we knew he wasn't going to show them in the shot."

Other directors, such as the award-winning filmmaker and documentarian Werner Herzog, find storyboards constraining and an impediment to the free flow of creativity—Herzog is quoted as saying "storyboards remain the instruments of cowards who do not trust in their own imagination and who are slaves of a matrix . . ."

Whatever your ultimate opinion of their usefulness, storyboards are part of the cinematic vocabulary.

Types of Storyboards

Not all storyboards are meticulously drawn cartoon frames worthy of publication. Some are a lot less involved and others can be much more involved. Let's look at a few common varieties.

Narrative Only

Narrative only storyboards are perfect for people who can't draw, don't have the money to hire a storyboard artist, or who aren't risking a whole lot in having people stand around their set for a few minutes while they figure out where they want the

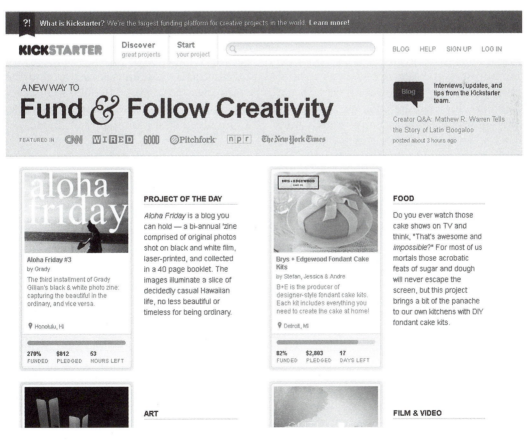

Figure 23-3 *Kickstarter is a website dedicated to fostering creativity, and is one avenue where storyboards may be a deciding factor of whether your project gets funded or not.*

camera—which is probably most of us. It's common that the director, the videographer and the talent live far enough apart that physical meetings aren't practical and who come together on a weekend to bang out a final product. You might not need a great deal of detail. You might just send out a narrative storyboard like this:

- Medium shot, Janet reaches in her purse for her keys.
- Closeup of doorknob from slightly above doorknob height and to the right, the door is already slightly ajar!
- Closeup of Janet looking worried from low angle.
- Closeup of Janet's hand pushing open the door.
- Medium shot, over Janet's shoulder as she looks into the room.
- Medium shot, reverse, Janet looking through the open door, she enters.

Basic Panels

Basic panels are a step up from narrative-only storyboards. As well as a brief description, they'll have a very basic drawing which can help camera operators and lighting designers know in advance exactly what the director is looking for. These can be in the "slightly above stick-figure" range.

Scene Cards

Scene cards are like basic panels, but more elaborate—the drawing usually takes up one entire side of the card with a description written on the back. If you're looking on eBay for scene cards, you'll find something completely different. In the early days of cinema, a "scene card" usually referred to a still from a completed film with a description or caption on the back or underneath—a lot like the collectible bubble gum trading cards popular in the 1960s, 1970s, and 1980s. Collectors' scene cards became superfluous when it became easy to own an actual copy of the movie. This seems a little sad.

Animatic Storyboard

To make an animatic storyboard you can scan sketches, use photographs you've taken, or even tear images out of magazines, put them into your favorite video editing software and add narration or music. The idea of an animatic storyboard is often just to get the idea or feel of your project across.

Many of us tend to think of ourselves as "not the sort of people who will ever have the need or the opportunity to approach financial backers" and because of this don't think too deeply about things like storyboards. One great example of a successful use of storyboarding was Christopher Salmon's animatic storyboard for an adaptation of Neil Gaiman's short story *The Price*. Salmon drew still images from an animation he wanted to produce and uploaded it to kickstarter.com—a crowd source funding website. Enchanted by his narration and still images, 2,001 different backers around the world invested almost $162,000 in his venture spurred along by the author who also got involved after seeing the storyboards.

3D pre-visualization

If you're trying to prise millions out of potential backers or explain a complicated escape sequence involving Bruce Willis, 40 explosions, and a hedge maze, you may want to create a 3D walkthrough of your scene or movie before you start working on it. Using storyboard software like FrameForge's Previz Studio 3, you can show virtual camera angles and scaled sets to your backers before they plunk down their cash. The 3D will allow you to see the relationships between your actors, your scenery and your camera. This can be an enormous help if you want to see how adding additional lights to a scene may change the shadows or light characters moving from one place to another.

Storyboarding software

There's lots of storyboard software, along the gamut from freeware to relatively expensive software that can help you put your story together—freeware like Atomic Learning's StoryBoard Pro to Six Mile Creek System's Springboard Storyboard which retails for about $40, to PowerProduction Software's StoryBoard Quick which starts at $300 and finally to powerful tools like FrameForge's Previz Studio whose full featured software ranges between $400 and $900 and will allow you to add things like multiple light sources and even output in 3D. But remember, video production isn't about equipment as much as it is good stories—Hitchcock did it on index cards.

Conclusion

While it may seem at first glance that only big Hollywood productions can benefit from storyboarding, it's often true that much smaller projects can run much more smoothly from pre-planning camera placement and framing. Frequently, in a world connected by the internet; directors, camera operators and talent separated by long physical distances can still work together. The more planning you do ahead of time, the easier things will be in the very limited amount of time you may have together.

Today's directors and creatives may think that they have no interaction with producers, in the traditional sense of the word, but crowd sourcing has given everyone with an internet connection the opportunity to raise money to make a video. The better prepared you are going in, the more money you're likely to raise—this was true of Orson Welles, and it's true now.

For more information, there are a number of books about making storyboards, which you can find on Amazon.com. There are also a number of collections of storyboard art such as *The Unseen Art of Hollywood: A Retrospective of Film Storyboards* compiled by storyboard artist Trever Goring who has storyboarded films such as Watchmen, *The Italian Job*, and *The Lion, The Witch, and the Wardrobe.*

Next time you find yourself planning for a large, complex production, consider adding storyboards to see if they can improve your workflow. And when you're flipping through the special features section of the next DVD you rent, be sure to check if there are examples.

24
How to Make a Documentary: Funding, Financing and Budgeting

Morgan Parr

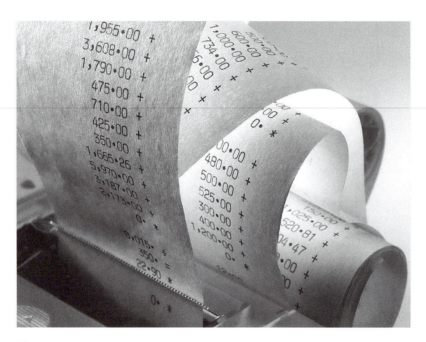

Figure 24-1

Why are you making a documentary? In other words, who do you want to see it? As with every step of filmmaking, you have to ask yourself, "Who is my audience? How do I reach them? How do I impress them/hold their attention long enough to get them to the credits?" It's easy to say I am going to make a documentary on Antarctica and its going to air on the Travel Channel. Making that video and actually having it aired, anywhere, is a much bigger challenge.

The True Cost of Filmmaking

If your dream is to have a piece on PBS, the Public Broadcasting Service, will you need to employ an online editor and what will that cost you? If your dream is to compete for an Oscar in the feature-length documentary category, does the Academy of Motion Picture Arts and Sciences require that your film run in a movie theatre and for the final print to be in celluloid? You need to know these requirements and you need to know what they will cost you.

The answers to these questions can be found from our friend the internet. But even if your aspirations are more humble, your doc will cost money to produce. Tape stock, hard drives, gear you don't own

Figure 24-2 *Michael Wiese Books' website www.MWP.com offers tons of information regarding producing films; from budgeting, to film agreements, even pitching your movie and anything in between to help you get your production rolling.*

Figure 24-3 *Stay away from producing your whole film on credit, as the chances you're going to make it back are against you. There are several funding options available for you.*

(e.g. lavalier mics, lighting gear), unique accessories for your camera, (e.g. protective raincoat, wide-angle lens), compensating those who help you, (if only with a meal if you are not paying them), travel costs, stock footage, music rights . . . the list goes on and on. Even if you are a Jedi master of the low budget, you will eventually incur costs. So we need to plan every step of our production. We need to know what each step will cost and we need to figure out a way to fund it.

The Budget

Before we start kicking the wall yelling, "Show me the money!" like Jerry Maguire (Tom Cruise in *Jerry Maguire*, 1996), we're going to need to put some numbers to paper. Why bother? There are a number of reasons. It helps you pre-plan and understand what you are going into, helps others understand the cost of financing your work and it shows funders that you know what you are doing. Depending on your needs, your budget might be half a page long typed into a word-processed document or it can take the form of a 40-page, itemized spreadsheet. If you are asking your mother for money, the first model

may suffice. If you are applying for an ITVS (Independent Television Service) grant, you'd better use the latter.

How to Make Them Part With Their Cash

Here is a question for you. Will you give me $60,000? (If the answer is yes, please contact *Videomaker* immediately and ask them where you can send me the check.) Chances are you answered, "no." Or at least you were hesitant and questions popped into your head such as, "Will I get the money back?" Is the subject of the film something I believe in?" Or simply, "What's in it for me?" Getting any amount of money out of anyone is a challenge, and it should be. Why is an individual or organization going to empty their wallet or bank account to give their hard-earned money to you? Put yourself in their shoes.

You can ask your Uncle Jerry for the money. After all, he is loaded. But put yourself in his loafers. Why would he do this? Or you could write a letter to multi-million dollar corporation and ask them for money. But what is in it for them? Let's look at a few funding models that have actually worked.

Blood Sweat and Tears, Not Plastic

Here is some concrete advice I can give you with confidence: don't fund your whole documentary on a credit card. The odds of making money on your video, even when the interest rates were closer to something reasonable, are and were very much against you. Let's look at some other ways to raise money.

Get Creative

I had the good fortune of "employing" one of the Bay Area's best film fundraisers to be an independent study advisor as part of my graduate degree in filmmaking. I'll never forget one of the first things she said to me. I was hoping to apply and receive grant money to fund my ultra-low budget documentary, and after looking at my proposal and budget she asked, "Would it be easier and quicker to save this amount by flipping burgers for minimum wage than to put in all the time and effort it would require to secure these grants?" Truthfully, I hadn't thought of that.

Carry a Grant

There are countless grants in the United States and around the world waiting to find a project. Let me repeat that another way: there is money out there trying to find you! This is true, but getting this funding will take work. Here is the deal in a nutshell. Though it is possible to get a 'personal' grant, there is exponentially more money for 501 (c)(3) tax-exempt, charitable organizations. What in the name of Ken Burns is a 501 (c)(3)? To the Internal Revenue Service, it's an organization that can accept money and give the donor a tax exemption, simply speaking. This stimulates giving.

The Fiscal Sponsor Directory, can help you find a 501 (c)(3) who, if they accept your project, will charge a "handling fee," usually around 5 to 15 percent, to act as

Figure 24-4 Shaking the Money Tree *gives filmmakers the full story on how to get grants and donations from individuals, foundations, and government agencies. A great book for anyone serious about getting his or her film funded.*

your fiscal sponsor. Now, if Uncle Jerry or Microsoft wants to give money, they can receive a tax deduction for their charity. And better, it opens the door for a plethora of grants.

Next comes — you got it — "show me the money." A good place to start your search for a grant is the Foundation Center. They have offices with helpful librarians in many of the big cities, but their website is a robust tool as well. Like we stated earlier, this is a work intensive route, but if you need a good amount of money, this is one way to get it.

An invaluable bible for all things fundraising is Morrie Warshawski's "Shaking the Money Tree: The Art of Getting Grants and Donations for Film and Video." Now in its third edition, the sub-$30 book will be well worth the investment.

Chase the Money

Documentaries cost money to make, whether it is $5.00 for a Mini DV tape or airfare for your ten-person crew to Antarctica. There are a number of ways to get that money, all of which are going to take some time and effort. But most things that are worthy don't come easy. So before you roll camera, you most likely will need to crunch some numbers and put together some form of information package to sell your documentary idea.

Funding gets easier as you build your body of work, assuming it is of decent quality or better. Individuals or organizations are more willing to part with, invest, or loan their cash if they have confidence that you can actually finish a documentary and get it seen. Start small. Enter and win a short film festival (there are some festivals that will only take a film that is one-minute or less). Enter competitions such as those found on tripfilms.com or poptent.net, where top filmmakers actually make money. Or compete in one of these 24-hour type film challenges and win (*CinemaSports*, *48 Hour Film Challenge*, *Filmarica Challenge* or *Film Racing*).

25
Communication: The Foundation of Production

Randal K. West

(a) (b)

Figure 25-1

I once directed an infomercial to sell jewelry during the holiday season.
The script writer thought it would be cute to have a scene with our model
and a baby reindeer. The logistics and cost of a deer were substantial, so
I requested that the writer turn the deer into a rabbit. Three days before
the shoot the prop manager left a message for me asking what color
rabbit I wanted. I emailed back and said, "Something with mixed colors
would be cute." The property manager said she couldn't find a mixed-
color rabbit. She did say that she could have one custom painted, but
that was going to bang my budget pretty hard. At this point, I decided
I needed to pick up the phone and actually speak with her. It was then
that I discovered that she was trying to get a Volkswagen Rabbit.

The most important thing a director has to do is communicate. The director must find ways to consistently communicate to everyone who participates in the project, including the producer, client, the designers, crew and talent. I had a director tell me a concept for a solid and original project, but when the project was completed, the concept was just not there. Asking around revealed that the crew and the talent never understood the concept and so the director's vision never found its way into the end-product.

Concept Proposal

As soon as you have an understanding of the scope and complexity of a project, you should write up a concept proposal. A concept proposal details the components of the project in plain English. It should include:

Title—the title is important, but it only has to be a preliminary title and often changes later.

Figure 25-2 *Will you record me? A concept proposal details the component on the project in plain language.*

Objective—the project objective states the goals for the project. Even if the project is as simple as shooting a high school reunion, explicitly stating the objectives might reveal that you will need to not only shoot footage of the reunion, but that you will need to interview the participants and collect archive materials (like a yearbook) as well.

Summary—this should be a description of the proposed show elements and how they are to function. For example, "Documentary style with B-roll" or "Talking heads with host and expert."

Talent requirements—a short list of the required talent, including age, gender and a brief description of each person, as well as what they are required to do. Do you need talent that can act? Will there be any speaking roles? Will you need any extras to be in the background?

Proposed length—you will need to know a precise total running time up front, even if the timeline is not set in stone. You will also eventually need a detailed timeline, but for now, a simple schedule that details major events such as when the script needs to be ready, proposed shooting dates, posting dates and when the video will be delivered.

Design elements—this section will detail the artistic feel of the project. For example: "We will shoot this in a loose-camera documentary style which will feel and seem very real. The director will be invisible and the talent will not answer questions or talk to the camera." This important section lets you communicate your vision and immediate stylistic desires.

Resources required—this is where you state your vision for the scope of shooting. For example, explicitly state that your project is to be shot entirely in "Practical homes" (actual locations) or if it will require a studio set. The more detailed you are in this section, the better off you'll be later. Include the proposed crew, equipment requirements, whether needed items are available or need to be purchased or rented, locations and any travel needs.

Proposed budget—now you should be ready to estimate a simple budget. Break your budget down into pre-production, production and post-production, talent and travel line items.

The Production Meeting

The next step is to call a production meeting with all the major players: the director of photography, sound engineer, camera operator, prop manager, art director and anyone else who will be making creative decisions during the project. The production meeting gives you a chance to communicate your concept proposal to your team.

The Outline

If the project doesn't involve actual written dialogue, then an outline may be all that you need. A project outline breaks the production into isolated segments and defines exactly what to shoot within the segment, including examples of some of the desired content, approximate times for each segment, and the segment objective.

If the project is a high school reunion, the outline might include a segment where the partygoers are seen arriving at the reunion and greeting each other for the first time in a long while. The outline would specify approximately how long the camera crew should stay at that location and how long the edited and finished segment should run. The outline would also detail whether the shots are to be B-roll, video-only footage for a musical montage or if they require audio as well. If you only need audio as a reference or if background music (or narration) will cover it, then the microphone on the camera might work just fine. You can note this as "wild" sound or ambient sound in your outline. If you need high-quality sound, specify that as well, so your camera operator can prepare properly.

The Script

A script is often the best choice for a project that involves written dialogue. A standard television script is formatted with a column on one side of the page that describes the visuals and a column on the other side of the page that designates who is talking and then states the dialogue. One side should contain the description of the shot: "Hostess walks out the front door of the house and walks into a one-shot as she addresses the camera", or a

Figure 25-3 *Syncing up—the production meeting gives you a chance to communicate your concept proposal to your team.*

Figure 25-4 *The script—a script is often the best choice for a project that involves written dialogue.*

thumbnail sketch. The other side indicates what she says.

Shooting Schedule

Finally, you need to break the project into a strict shooting schedule, indicating the order in which you intend to shoot the project. Since the actual shoot will involve the most coordination and the most people, a well-planned shooting schedule is critical.

If the entire project takes place in the same environment, you may choose to shoot it chronologically, but usually you shoot by location. This will require shooting scenes out of order, so you need to communicate to your actors what you will be shooting and when.

Too Much? Too Soon?

If all this communicating seems more complicated than it is worth, just take it a few steps at a time. I know a director who publishes notes after every meeting or phone conversation, summarizing the "action steps" from each meeting. You need to find your own comfort level regarding how much written and verbal communication works for you.

Communication is the single most important element a director brings to a project. If you have a brilliant idea, but cannot successfully communicate your vision, you may end up with a custom-painted compact car instead of a furry little friend at your shoot.

26
Recruiting Talent

Tad Rose

Figure 26-1

Talent matters. Be it on or off screen, good performers can help take your project to the next level. Therefore, it is well worth the time for any producer to find ways of attracting the best talent available.

Sometimes casting is as simple as twisting your kid brother's arm, but most productions require considerable attention to the process of recruiting. Consider a request from the local school district for you to produce an orientation video. The goal is to prepare freshmen for the high school experience and to promote a safer school environment by presenting students with a variety of conflict resolution strategies. Such a project may well require talent in the form of a host for on-camera interviews, a narrator to communicate important facts and statistics, teachers and counselors for expert commentary and actors to dramatize campus conflicts. Each role requires a particular skill and the right casting choices.

Figure 26-2 *Local theater troupes, college drama departments, high schools, comedy clubs and community groups are all excellent sources of talent.*

Determine Your Needs

A script or detailed outline is essential for determining your talent requirements. From it, you can then prepare a cast list. This list should include all significant speaking and non-speaking roles, as well as a brief description of what each role requires. For example, should the host be an adult or a teenager, male or female, clean cut or rugged? If you have a clear idea what you're looking for, it will be easier to find it.

Once you've identified your needs, you're ready to start recruiting talent. It's up to you (and your budget) whether you cast professionals, amateurs or your own mother (like director Martin Scorsese), but it's important to find the best available candidate for the role. Remember that while a Hollywood cast may be beyond your budget, professional quality performances needn't be. Talent grows everywhere.

Sources of Talent

Local theater troupes, college drama departments, churches, high schools, comedy clubs and community groups are all excellent sources of talent. To tap them, contact the person in charge, explain your

project, and ask if they can recommend anyone. Maybe they know the perfect candidate. If not, perhaps they'll allow you to post a flier announcing your audition. If you do post fliers, make sure you do it at least a couple of weeks ahead of any auditions and be sure to provide adequate information, including the type of production, roles being cast and contact number. You can also place an ad in the local paper or on an internet bulletin board. In addition, of course, tell all your friends. Cast your net wide and you are more likely to find the talent you're after.

Auditions

There's no hard and fast rule about auditioning. Some producers have all candidates show up at the same time (cattle call), others schedule individual appointments. You could simply ask candidates to send in a demo reel. I know of one producer looking for voice over talent who even had candidates call and leave their audition on his answering machine. However, if you are serious about finding the right talent, it's best to arrange face-to-face auditions and use the tapes and other demos as screeners.

Most producers provide candidates with audition materials. This can be actual dialog or narration from your script or material from another source that will allow you to evaluate their abilities. You can also allow the actors to use their own audition piece. This isn't really recommended, however, since their choice may have little relation to your project and their polished performance will not give you an idea of what it is like to work with this person on the set.

If you cannot provide candidates with audition material in advance, give them a few minutes to prepare before you put them in the hot seat. Cold readings (auditions without prior exposure to the material) rarely reveal the range and ability of your candidates.

Allow about 15 to 20 minutes per audition with five-minute breaks in between. This will give you adequate time to interview the candidates and jot down any notes between auditions. Make sure you ask about their background and experience. Show interest and be positive: This will relax your candidate and result in a better performance. It's also a good idea to record the entire audition. This will give you the chance to review the candidates later and evaluate their strengths and weaknesses on camera.

Be sure you explain what the role entails, including the number of shooting days and any compensation your are able to offer. Don't be discouraged if your budget doesn't allow you to pay your talent. Many aspiring performers will be happy to work for nothing more than a credit and a copy of the finished piece for their portfolio. Nevertheless, if you can pay a token sum, you should. It recognizes the contribution your actors are making and encourages them to take a professional approach to the project.

Evaluating Talent

For our hypothetical video, we need both an on-screen host and a voice over artist to do narration. The requirements for each are different. For the host, you must consider both appearance and vocal quality, but it is strictly vocal characteristics (such as volume, diction, rate, pitch, tone and timbre) that matter in narration, since that performer will never be seen.

Casting is subjective. The goal is to match the role with the best available talent and

Figure 26-3 *Recorded auditions—it's a good idea to record the entire audition. This will give you the chance to review the candidates later and evaluate their strengths and weaknesses on camera.*

that's not always easy. Many factors besides ability will influence your final choices. Determining the availability of your talent is a pragmatic, but important, consideration. Someone may be perfect to host the program, but if she is only available Sunday evenings after six, you will probably have to keep looking. It's also a good idea to gauge the motivation of your prospects as well, especially if they are working "for credit" ("volunteers"). Enthusiastic, paid performers will be more likely to show up on time and ready to perform, than those you've had to beg and cajole.

For acting roles, you may want to consider typecasting. Unless you've discovered a young Brando or De Niro, it's easier for actors to play characters with traits and characteristics close to their own. If the kid who mows your lawn has a bit of an attitude, maybe he would be perfect to play the bully in your conflict dramatization. Casting close to type will often result in performances that are more natural, especially from inexperienced actors.

Getting the Best Performance

No matter whom you cast, whether best friend or a complete stranger, it is up to you to get the best performances possible. The ability to elicit good performances is the mark of a truly skilled director.

It's not easy. Approaches range from the autocratic to the collaborative. However, in my experience working with both novice and veteran performers alike, I have found one thing improves performances every time: encouragement. Pointing out what was good about a given take before suggesting ways to improve it, will build a feeling of confidence and security in your actors. If they know you have confidence in them, their work may lift your production to an entirely new level.

Summary

Be willing to look outside your immediate circle of friends to find the best available talent for your project. List your casting requirements, then audition to find the right person for each part. Be prepared to provide clear, concise direction to your performers. Create a positive, collaborative atmosphere on the set. And, of course, never forget to provide lunch.

Actors Need to Know

Who—what type of person is the character? What are the traits you're looking for?

What—what will you provide? What compensation will there be, if any? Will they be required to supply wardrobe and make-up? What about lunch?

When—when will the shooting take place? How long will shoots last?

Where—where is the location of the shoot? If necessary, provide written directions and maps. Don't lose a shooting day because someone got lost.

Why—why are you producing this video? Explain what you hope to achieve and why the actors would want to be involved.

How—how do you want the talent to dress, to speak, to move? Give direction in simple, straightforward terms.

27
The Right Place at the Right Time

James Williams

Figure 27-1

Scouting locations ahead of time is a great way to avoid last-minute surprises and big headaches on the day of your shoot.

Consider this: a scene in your short film takes place in a coffee shop. You know you could never pass off your living room as the local java joint, so you decide to shoot that scene on location. It's time to hit the road and find the right spot. There are several elements to keep in mind:

Identify Your Power Source

Power outlets are essential for lights, batteries or other equipment. For such important elements, these power sources are easily overlooked. As you scout the location, ask yourself:

- Are there enough outlets that work?
- Are outlets close enough to where you'll set up lights and camera? If not, how many extension cords will you need?
- Are the outlets grounded?
- Can the location handle the wattage of all of your equipment without tripping a breaker?

If you plan to use a generator, make sure you can place it far enough away that it won't cause audio issues or create a safety hazard. For an event video, plugging into an outlet may not be an option, When scouting, look for out-of-the-way outlets for recharging a spare battery.

Evaluate Lighting Conditions

OK, so you find a coffee bar that has the exact look and feel you want. As you gaze around, you notice several large windows. Break out your tape measure, because you'll probably need to give these windows some attention.

Figure 27-2 *Mixed lighting can be a major problem on location. Having control temperature blue (CTB) will help spread more daylight temperature light onto the scene.*

Combining outdoor sunlight with indoor, tungsten lights can create a look that's either too blue or too orange when viewed through a video camera, particularly when human skin tones are involved.

The reason is that each light source has a unique color temperature that the camera readily picks up. It looks OK to the human eye, because our brain compensates for the color differences, but the camera simply cannot. The result is that the outdoor light looks blue and the indoor light looks orange through the viewfinder. White balancing won't always solve the problem.

The solution is to choose which lighting temperature you'd like as your primary light source, then eliminate or add filters to the other source, so all light in the room has the same color temperature.

Fluorescent lights cast a greenish hue, so most videographers turn fluorescents off altogether or swap the fluorescent bulbs with specialty bulbs that give off the desired color temperature.

As you consider your lighting situation, some questions to ask are:

- Are you using the windows as a light source?
- What are the dimensions of the windows, in case filters (gels) or other light-blocking materials are needed?
- Where are the controls to turn off the overhead lights?
- If you're swapping out fluorescent bulbs, what sizes are the replacements?

Anticipate Audio Problems

Few locations are completely devoid of noise. Scouting your location in advance allows you to hear how quiet the room really is.

Stop walking. Close your eyes and listen. It turns out the room is noisier than you thought. Rumbling softly overhead is a huge AC vent. An espresso machine sputters behind the counter. A telephone rings in the next room. Traffic noise leaks in from the street.

Figure 27-4 *Your shooting schedule and the day-to-day business of the location may have some conflicts. Ask the owner in advance if you should expect any after-hours business or deliveries.*

Figure 27-3 *Store owners have to have their refrigerators up and running. You can reduce noise using sound blankets. Brings lots of them.*

Catching these sounds now allows you to make adjustments. Ask yourself:

- Can you turn off, unplug or cover up any unwanted sources of noise?
- Where is the quietest spot, and is that a good place to shoot the scene?

Bring a mic and headphones to hear how the room sounds to the camera. Check wireless mics for electrical interference or static from nearby equipment or radio towers. Can't get a clean signal? Consider a wired lavalier or shotgun mic.

Consider the Time and Day of the Week

Most places, especially public places, look and sound different at different times of day or night. A side room may be completely quiet at 5pm on Saturday but noisy as a roadhouse Wednesday after work. Sunlight that was soft and indirect at 9am may be extremely harsh and blazing into the room by 3pm.

Some things to consider are:

- How might ambient light changes affect your plans or need for filters?
- How might changing traffic patterns, such as rush hour or sporting events, affect your audio?
- Will any other people occupy the same location while you're shooting? How disruptive will their presence be?

Consider what aspects of the location will change with the day of the week. If you're shooting on a Tuesday morning, you'll want to know ahead of time that Tuesday mornings are when the delivery guy comes. Nobody wants to pause their production every few minutes so delivery dollies can be rolled through the set.

Visit your locations at the same time and same weekday that you'll be doing your shoot. If that's not possible, ask someone familiar with the area what to expect at the time you plan to be there. Most people don't think in terms of poor audio or other hurdles that can hold up a production. A cleaning crew vacuuming before the place opens might not seem like a big deal to the owner, but it's enough to bring your production to a halt. Tailor your questions accordingly.

Getting the Logistics

Location scouting for video shoots and event videos is a great time to assess shot angles, camera setups and any logistical considerations. Bring a camcorder along to preview your shot list or record details of the space.

Some other useful observations you might want to make are:

- Where's the best place to unload equipment and store unused gear?
- If you'll need to rearrange the room, what extra equipment or personnel will be required to do so safely?

Get Permission

Once you've found the ideal location for your shoot, you'll need permission to shoot there. Many folks are OK with letting you use their property for your productions, as long as they know exactly what you're doing and how long it will take.

Figure 27-5 *Don't forget the location and talent releases. Always have more than you need, just in case something unexpected happens. It's best to have everyone sign before you shoot.*

When you are asking permission, it's always a good idea to:

- Be polite!
- Be upfront and honest about crew size and time requirements.
- Explain that they will get exposure for the location and it will be noted in the credits.

Make sure that the person who is granting you permission to do the shoot signs a release form, even if you have had a verbal OK. That release form will come in handy if anyone questions your right to be there on the day of the shoot or anytime after that.

If you're shooting in a public space, check well in advance whether a permit is required. Permit requests can often take more time to process than you anticipate, and, without the right paperwork, you may find your production shut down before you even get started.

What to Bring on your Scouting Trip

Before you walk out the door to scout locations, you'll want to bring a few key items with you. Make sure you have a notebook and pen to write down contact information, draw diagrams and record measurements. You'll also want a measuring tape to determine window sizes, room widths and the distance from outlets to where you think you'll be setting up. Bring a still camera to snap photos of the room, so you can check the details later on. Better yet, take a camcorder, so you can frame out potential shots as well. Plug in a mic and headphones, and listen to what the room sounds like on tape.

Prior to Your Shoot

Make sure you get permission to use the location, and get a signed release form to prove it. If shooting on public property, check that no special permits are required to shoot there. Finally, check in with your location contact a few days prior to the shoot, just to make sure everything is still in order.

Checklist for your Shoot

Aside from the gear you'll be using for the shoot, you'll want to have the following on the day of your production:

- Names and phone numbers of your location contacts, just in case any questions should arise.
- Any reference notes you took while scouting that location, especially if those notes include where to find power switches and other directions.
- Any release forms and special permits you'll need.

28
Production Planning

Jim Stinson

Figure 28-1

The worst cause of video disasters is bad planning—not just during the pre-production phase, but right through to the end of post-production. Professionals don't just make plans; they implement them and then they follow through on them.

When you plan like a pro, you:

- Plan the shoot in pre-production.
- Shoot the plan in production.
- Edit the planned shoot in post-production.

This sustained planning and follow-through is essential to delivering a quality video on time and on budget.

Plan the Shoot!

The planning aspect of video creation is so often overlooked that we've broken it down into three sections for each phase of production. We'll start with planning the shoot in pre-production. Of course, pre-production is nothing but planning, from first concept to final schedule.

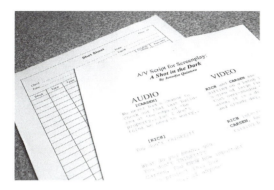

Figure 28-2 *A good script and a well-planned shot list are two of the most important planning documents needed for any serious production.*

Figure 28-3 *A storyboard is a useful tool for visualizing complex action and/or special effects sequences.*

Here, though, we are focusing specifically on developing plans that you can, indeed, shoot and then edit. We'll look at scripting, casting, staffing, scouting, and budgeting.

We'll also look at a new planning area: special effects. In other words, pre-production planning relates to editing as well as shooting.

First, The Script

Though writing itself isn't planning, the resulting script is the basis for every single decision you'll make in prepping production. Without a complete script, you can't cast the program, design its look, determine the crew and equipment needed, list the locations or sets, budget the production, or set a schedule.

No, an outline isn't good enough, even if it's 50 pages long. Only a true script is specific enough for planning. How about a storyboard? Storyboard sequences with complex action and/or special effects work to visualize the layout of the video, but use a written script for production planning.

For nonfiction programs, a two-column "A/V" (Audio and Video) formatted script will include complete narration and essential audio in the left column and visuals in the right one. Fiction films use the classic screenplay format. The bottom line is this:

when you get to production, you can't shoot the plan unless you've planned the shoot in detail.

Special Effects

People think that special effects are compositing and computer graphics that belong in post-production. However, the most convincing effects are fully planned in pre-production so that location, composite, and CG work can be seamlessly integrated by implementing the detailed plan. That's why you have to develop your special effects fully even before you scout locations and budget props.

For example, take a spectacular head-on car crash. To achieve the actual impact, you'll have the cars drive toward and past each other, maybe two feet apart for safety, shooting the master with a long telephoto to conceal the gap between them. In post, you plan to speed up the collision shot and then conceal the fact that they miss each other by filling the screen with a well-timed CG fireball over the live action.

So far so good, but the secret of any effect lies in selling it with supporting shots. To make sure you get them, you need to plan high-speed shots of the individual cars, closeups of the drivers, and maybe a shot across the hood of one car after the crash, as one victim struggles out the door. You plan to put one side of the car up on blocks to tilt it and to increase the tilt by canting the camera off-level the opposite direction. (Note to DP: choose a vague background that won't reveal the Dutch angle shot, and throw a flickering "fire light" on the windshield, door, and struggling victim.) In post, composite a raging fire effect in the foreground to complete the gag. Every part of this must be planned, right down to the cinder blocks and the fire effect.

The moral is, you can't just say, "Oh we'll do the car crash in post." Only through detailed planning both before and during the shoot can you deliver the raw materials needed to create a classy effect.

Figure 28-4 *Scouting locations ahead of time can help you avoid a wide range of production problems.*

have to improvise a fix on the spot. That seldom works very well.

People, Places, and Feedback

Even the biggest Hollywood productions are planned and developed by successive approximation: the script describes the requirements; the planners come as close as possible to meeting them; then the script is adjusted to eliminate the resources that were unobtainable and maximize those that were.

This is always true with casting actors. Suppose, for instance, the script demands a beautiful, enticing, evil stepmother; but the closest actress you can find is a frumpy, heavyset person who would look silly vamping around on screen. Happens all the time. So you do some fast script revisions to create a frumpy, heavyset evil stepmother. By planning to fit the circumstances, you save both the actress and the show from embarrassment.

Or take locations. If you can't find anyplace resembling the dungeon where the evil stepmother imprisons the heroine, you have three choices: remove the dungeon part, create it as a CG virtual set (if you have the resources), or just chain the lady up in a storeroom or something.

Again, if you plan these adjustments before production begins, you can still shoot the plan; but if you haven't invested in the planning, you're going to arrive at an unconvincing "dungeon" location and

The All-Powerful Schedule

In reality, budgeting and scheduling are two halves of a circle. Scheduling brings the right cast members, crew, and equipment to the right location at the right time, crucial if you're paying people by the hour or day and just as important if folks are donating their time.

With good planning, you can also save big bucks (that's where scheduling and budgeting play tag with each other). For instance, if that antique fire engine rents for $200 a day, you'll want to schedule all its scenes back-to-back so you can return it as soon as possible.

Oh, and how is it going to get to your location? I once rented an antique vehicle without knowing it didn't really run. At the last minute, I had to put out expensive, unbudgeted bucks for a day's use of a platform-bed tow truck.

This is also true for anything else that's time-sensitive. With meticulous planning, you'll always have the correct cast list at the proper place with the required equipment and props, all ready to shoot. Without planning, everyone ends up standing around, and that's not good.

And if it rains or something else goes wrong? A planning pro will have a contingency plan: a way to shoot something

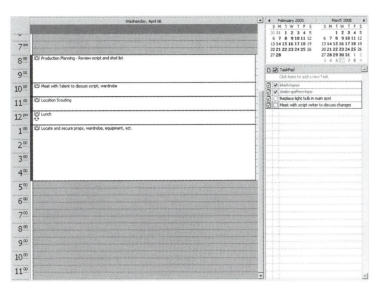

Figure 28-5 *Scheduling programs like Microsoft's Outlook can greatly help you set up a schedule for your production, and easily share with others.*

else until you can resume the original schedule.

Money, Money, Money

Professional production accountants must keep tiny altars to the spirit of Murphy, on which they burn symbolic dollar bills, because on a shoot, anything that can possibly go wrong will go wrong. Corollary #1: everything that goes wrong costs money.

Everything. It goes without saying that good production planners budget the show line-item by line-item, right down to cold cream for the makeup department. Then they run an eagle eye over every aspect of production. Does one character throw a vase at another? How many takes might that require, and how many replacement vases? Does one sequence call for actual snow? What will the weather be like and how many days might be lost while waiting for the fluffy stuff to start falling?

Obviously, every production is different. If you're taping the CEO's speech in her office, you're probably very safe. If you're covering whale migrations from the subjects' POV, good luck.

Since you don't have unlimited funds, you can't just say, "well, whatever it takes." You have to cast a cold planner's eye over every script page to spot every place that could run over budget. Then you add a contingency fee for protection.

Then you double it, and pray.

That's it for creating a production plan. Next, we'll see how that plan structures the actual shoot so that you can end up editing the show you started out to make.

Shoot the Plan!

Plan the shoot, shoot the plan, edit the planned shoot.

That's the mantra we introduced earlier. Talk about obvious! Not so fast. If that deceptively simple rule were routinely followed Hollywood epics would never overrun their schedules and amateur productions would never look embarrassing (assuming they didn't crash and burn before completion). So let's review reasons for staying on-plan, gremlins that attack production plans, and ways to protect yourself against disasters, both serial and parallel.

Figure 28-6 *Having every shot on paper will help coordinate your production team.*

Figure 28-7 *What might seem like a minor change in wardrobe can quickly turn into a large out-of-control, chain reaction avalanche that could bury your production. You did such a great job planning, now do a great job of following it.*

The underlying concept is that crucial decisions are made in pre-production planning that will affect everything that follows, all the way through to the end of post-production. A good planner keeps that long timeline in mind, the way a good chess player thinks many moves ahead.

Stick to the Plan

Sticking to a plan no matter what seems sort of, well, retentive; but there are several reasons for resisting changes or at least studying them very carefully before making them.

First, remember the law of unintended consequences. Even small productions are complicated organisms with many interdependent parts. If you decide to shoot, say, scene 22 instead of scheduled scene 14, the cast, location, and time of day might be fine—but what about the actor's distinctive Grateful Dead shirt, which got all muddy in scene 13 but has to be clean again for scene 22? Thinking fast, you run it through a Laundromat during lunch break. Uh-huh, but when you go to scene 14 later that shirt has to be dirty again—with exactly the same stain pattern as before it was washed.

So things start to domino. Cleverly, you have the actor play scene 14 without the shirt, adding a line like, "Boy, I hope I can get that shirt clean; it's an heirloom." Right away, you've handed the editor two problems. Since the action is continuous across scenes 13 and 14, the character has

no off-screen time in which to take off the shirt. Major jump cut. Also, the added line tells viewers that the shirt's valuable, which is totally irrelevant to the story and distracting from the point of the scene.

You're already thinking of 50 things at once, under time and money pressure to move, move, move! If you must make alterations, take the time you need to think them through. The second moral is that post-production is very demanding. Once you wrap production, it's expensive and often impossible to re-open the shoot for vital pieces that are missing or mismatched to other pieces.

The Enemies of Planning

The first big foe of systematic shooting is good ol' Murphy's Law in all its many forms. Things go wrong; stuff happens; you have to roll with the punches.

Outdoors, time and weather are huge factors. Obviously, you can't shoot if it's pouring rain, and even if it hasn't started yet, the light in that sullen overcast before the storm doesn't match yesterday's sunshine. As for time, an equipment malfunction held up the shoot until yesterday's pearly dawn turned into high noon.

Whether outdoors or in, personnel are always a problem, especially when they're

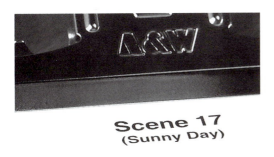

Figure 28-8 and 28-9 *The script says the scene takes place on a sunny day and it's pouring out. Instead of re-working the script, you should have a "plan B', (and maybe a "plan C"), for when the inevitable Murphy's Law occurs.*

not getting paid to show up on time and keep working all day. You might limp along without a certain crew member, but if the performer isn't there, the show doesn't go on.

Inanimate objects are just as bad. People bring the wrong wardrobe; props are missing, equipment malfunctions. When you arrive at the gym where you got permission to shoot the "hurricane disaster relief center" you find it's been decorated for the Senior Prom.

Above and beyond Murphy, there's another threat to shooting as planned: your own creativity. You show up at the vacant lot to find that there's a carnival set up there. Wow, what visuals! What production values! Thinking fast, you replace half your planned setups to exploit the unexpected dividend. Or maybe it's just a brainstorm on the set: hey! why not do it this way instead? Either way, you risk omitting stuff the editor will need and adding stuff that doesn't belong in your program.

Cover Your Caboose

No shoot is ever completed exactly as planned, but you can minimize the risks by following a few vital procedures.

First, always have Plan B ready. If weather might be a problem, identify indoor scenes with the same cast and have the locations, costumes, and props

Figure 28-10 *The people who make six-digits plus making movies view their "dailies" at the end of each day and so should you. Just make sure you don't accidentally leave the record head in the middle of a scene and record over your work.*

standing by. If performers are flaky about showing up, know where to find them and how to shoot around them in the meantime. The trick is to identify the vulnerable parts of your plan in advance and have alternatives ready to go.

Second, learn how to adjust plan A. Understand that a simple thing like a dirty shirt can ripple all the way to post-production. Take the time and care to work out all the implications of proposed changes.

Next, know when to quit. Nothing is more frustrating than doing all the work of getting a day's shoot together and launched, then sending everyone home again. Your instinct is to say, OK, let's call Fred and Wilma and see if they can go over to the church and shoot their stuff today,

Figure 28-11 *It's important to not only shoot with a plan, but also edit with a plan. Always keep a script within arm's reach.*

and try to rent that '57 Chevy, oh, and phone the church sexton, and . . . Uh-uh. This kind of desperate improvisation may keep your crew busy, but the results will be hasty and undercooked. You have to develop the good judgment to know when you're licked for now so that you can live to fight another day.

Finally, review your footage, preferably before you wrap at any one location, but at least at the end of every shooting day. In even the most professional production, you're going to find stuff that's inadequate, wrong, or just plain missing. Before matters go any further, make the notes you need to get pickup shots, to retake bad stuff, to re-think and re-stage sequences that plain don't work. Then plan the reshoot as meticulously as you planned the original. When post-production starts, you'll bless yourself.

Next, edit the shoot you planned.

Edit The Plan!

Post-production is supposed to fulfill the promise of pre-production (the script) and production (the shoot). Editing, they tell you, pulls everything together and delivers the program envisioned by the producer, director, and sponsor.

As usual, reality falls short of theory, because editors almost never get exactly

the raw material they expected, and they don't always shape it as well as they might. Earlier we talked about planning the shoot and then shooting the plan. Let's wrap it up here by seeing how to carry planning forward into post-production.

In a nutshell, you work as hard as you can to complete the original vision, and, where that's impossible, to make the best program you can with what you've got. To do this, you need to systematically evaluate and deal with your raw material and then systematically mold it throughout post-production. In both cases, "systematically" implies that you're doing some planning of your own.

In the best production setups, the editor is in on the shoot, evaluating each day's footage and providing feedback to the director to ensure that he can edit the show to the original plan. Too often, however, the editor joins the process after shooting wraps and is presented with a done deal: here's the stuff, now.

Planning for Post

First off, a good editor is not an auteur (a director who is believed to be the major creative force): Your job is not to express your own vision, but to carry out the vision of the writer, director, producer, or whoever it is that presides over the production. With that in mind, you should take your very first step even before you start screening footage: you should discover (or recollect) what the original plan was—what the program was supposed to be. Typically, that means reviewing the concept with the producers or, at the very least, closely re-reading the script. Only when you have the original concept freshly in mind can you start dealing with the footage.

Build a program. This is the real-world situation we'll talk about here.

The obvious next step is to review all the raw material, constantly comparing it to the program concept. First and foremost, did they shoot all the material needed? (You'd be surprised how often

Figure 28-12 *Make sure producers acquired all the planned video and audio by checking the footage against the shot list and marking where you need pickup shots or changes.*

they didn't.) Does the footage they did shoot do its job? Are the establishing shots and closeups and inserts taken of the right stuff from the right setups? Is the technical quality uniformly up to par?

And don't forget the audio. Is the production sound good quality (or even usable)? Did they record background tracks, ambient sound, and wild sound? Have they planned the music to use and how to use it, or are they leaving that to you?

After a thorough review of the raw material (and a yellow pad bristling with notes) you're ready to plan your post-production strategy. First of all, what absolutely has to be shot (if overlooked) or re-shot (if loused up)? For example, your documentary on glass blowing covers the whole process of making a vase, from molten glass to finished . . . Whoops! The beauty shot of the completed work is badly lit and out of focus. Try as you might, you can't think of a way to drop the poor shot and edit around it because it's the whole point of the program. So it has to be re-shot.

And as long as they have to send a crew back out, what other shots can you improve? What missing angles could be picked up? (Which is why they're called "pickup shots.")

Sooner or later, you'll run up against a wall: you can't get more coverage of the master glass blower because she promptly retired and left for Maui. Now your strategy shifts to developing Plan B. Studying

the footage you discover two things: Several shots (some with multiple takes) in which her body blocks the furnace opening, so you can't quite see what she's doing. Inserts of her assistant's bare hands and arms that look similar to hers.

Gotcha! Plan B is to support shots of the blocked furnace door with narration explaining what she's doing (even though she was doing something else) and shoot the missing inserts with the assistant's hands and arms subbing for the Master's. In summary, then, you evaluate your raw materials, reshoot where it's feasible, and plan workarounds where it's not.

With plans A and B implemented, you do your best to create the finished program as originally envisioned.

Planning the Edit

With your post-production strategy worked out, you're ready to turn the raw footage into a work of genius. Here too, you need a systematic plan, though admittedly, the plan is much the same for most editing jobs.

The problem with digital post is that it encourages you to do everything at once: find the shots, assemble the sequence, trim to length, build the tracks, add CGs and graphics, repeat with the next sequence, and so-on. Completing one sequence at a time, you're more likely to end up with a bunch of individually fine pieces that refuse to fit smoothly together. Instead, it's generally (though not always) better to work vertically instead of horizontally: go through the entire show, doing one job—building just one layer—at a time. Here's how it works:

First, break out and catalog all your footage at once. Why? I can't tell you how many times I've plugged a hole in one sequence by remembering a shot I could steal from a different one. You need a mental inventory of all your footage before you start.

Then begin assembling your show, sequence-by-sequence, to be sure, but without worrying about fine-tuning. Once you've previewed the result, you'll have a good feel for the way the program's coming together.

Figure 28-13 and 28-14 *A plentiful supply of cutaways will save an editor's . . . reputation. If you can get to the production crew before they shoot, request cutaways.*

Now do your tuning, trimming shot lengths, adjusting cut points, pulling whole shots that turn out to be superfluous. By working the whole program at once, you keep a feel for its rhythm and pace.

So far, you've had just the production track, if any. Now it's time to pull things together with audio, layering ambient and background tracks, adding sound effects, timing narration, selecting and adding music.

Finally, you're ready to begin adding CGs and graphics: transitions, titles, and the like. Again, seeing the show as a whole will help you keep them consistent.

And don't forget the DVD (which will almost certainly be your release format). As you polish the show, start looking for the material to repeat as backgrounds for your disc's main and sub menus.

So, do your strategic post-production planning by evaluating your materials and deciding exactly what you want to do with them; then do your tactical planning by working through the editing process one careful layer at a time.

How Detailed a Script?

Whether scripting in the A/V or screenplay formats, you do not—in fact, should not—specify camera angles and individual shots. For instance, if the story calls for a character to window-shop along a street, it's enough to write Marcie walks down Main Street, looking in shop windows, pausing at some, then moving on. Half-way along, she spots something in a window. It is the statue of a black falcon. Surprised, she gets her courage up and enters the store.

Notice how the paragraphing suggests a rough breakdown of the scene content, but without trying to do the director's job. Any director worthy of the title will know how to distribute that action among appropriate setups. On the other hand, the production manager can learn enough from the description to schedule the "Marcie" actor and plan for a small town street, an antiques or pawnshop, and a Maltese Falcon prop. In short, the script is detailed enough for planning, without being too restrictive.

Your Key Collaborators

You know you've reached the big leagues when you can have three key people beside you throughout the shoot.

Script supervisor—if the script is the basis for the shooting plan, the script supervisor is the guardian of that script. Did you get the closeup? Do you have the insert of the pistol in the drawer? Did you overlap the wide shot and the medium shot enough to provide good edit points? A good script supervisor will catch every problem and let you know. No matter how creative you're being or what else you're thinking about, listen to continuity!

Production manager—a good production manager knows who is available, which locations are open, and when the rented '57 Chevy is coming. If you have to change the plan in real time, the production manager can figure out a workable alternative. Never make changes in the plan without consulting the person who is directly responsible for it.

Editor—continuity can tell you if you have full coverage and matched action; but only the editor can cut things together in his or her head and predict whether the result will be effective. When allowed the luxury, I like to have the editor on the set, making sure the shooting plan is being followed—and that it was a good plan to begin with.

29
Gearing Up for Battle

Michael Reff

Figure 29-1

Before you grab your gear and hop on your trusty steed, you need advance preparation to successfully ride off into battle.

As any good knight will tell you, having the right weapons for the right fight is as important as the battle itself. Not having the right equipment, or having the right equipment but not having it in working order, can destroy you. Possibly worse, it can destroy your reputation.

One way to prevent these errors is by preparing a gear grid: a list of the client's needs before every shoot. This standardized gear grid should contain all of the usual and essential items that you take on every production as well as a section for the custom items that are unique to that particular job. Let's break the standardized portion of the grid down. Your essentials consist of equipment that never changes. It could be key words to remind you to check certain items too. The hard core, "Can you make pictures or not?" type of list. Before I go charging off on my steed into battle, I review a gear grid that looks something like this:

Video Gear

- **Batteries**

Charge the batteries— prepare them the night before and check them again before walking out of the door. Always carry extras and the charger.

Figure 29-2 *All shooters who have to work on location should have a minimum of three batteries. Three chargers would be nice as well, but not as important, as batteries can rotate on the charger on the day of the shoot.*

Figure 29-3 *Check all your gear: lugging a tripod without the camera mount plate can ruin the shoot if you're on a tight schedule.*

• **Camera**

Power it up— check all the major functions: zoom, white balance, black balance if you have one, iris and focus. (Be sure to check the Auto functions as well if you plan on using them.) Power it down—OK, I know it is simple but come on, who hasn't at least once been in a hurry and grabbed the camera only to arrive at the location with a dead battery on the camera?

Tip: preset your white balance, before you leave, for general lighting conditions of your first location (indoor or outdoor). That way, you can hit the ground running and at least your settings will be in the ballpark, should you forget.

• **Tapes**

Pre-label tapes— now is a good time to do this. It will save you time later when you're crunched for time.

Tip: try putting the type of the camera you used on the label along with the camera operator's name. This is always helpful if there are equipment breakdowns or reoccurring video problems. It also reminds the client who you are so you can have them repeat business. Load and record on a tape—Once you have checked all the switches, record 30 seconds of bars and tone and then several seconds of live video on each tape. Bars and tone are the unifying factor, a sort of master key that enables all tapes to be set up for the

same color and audio levels. The live portion of your recording should contain flesh tone and some movement. This will show you that colors look good and that no hidden switches have been thrown. Since what you see is what you get, it's better to know now, then later.

• **Tripod**

Check for your camera mount quick release— got it? Good. Without it, your tripod is useless.

Audio gear

• **Microphones**

Wireless
Handheld

Test each mic through the camera—by testing through the camera you can be sure that you have all the parts necessary and working when you get there. Also, be sure that you have fresh batteries and listen through a good set of headphones. Because what you hear is what you'll get *and* . . . it's better to know now, rather than later.

• **Mixer**

If you use one, be sure you have the correct batteries for it and use the mixer when hooking up to your camera. However, you decide to set up your gear, now is the time to make all the parts fit and run together.

Figure 29-4 *Always take the time in pre-production to check your audio gear. Also be sure to bring extra batteries and cables.*

- **Headphones**

This is an essential item on any shoot. When you are running your audio tests, be sure to listen for any distortion or audio that drops out which could lead to major problems down the road. Recheck the setup again. If there are any problems, fix them now. Composing shots in the heat of battle is hard enough, without the added distraction of deciphering audio problems.

- **Boom**

If you have someone to operate your boom, bring it. Even if you don't, you can often rig a C-stand to hold your boom if your talent happens to be stationary (or just moving around in a small area).

Lighting

- **Light kit**

List each piece of lighting equipment separately—another article could be written on what to have in your light kit. Needless to say, until such time that you have it grouped into a case or bag, listing your equipment will help you remember it. Carry extra lamps—not having a spare could end your entire shoot.

- **Extension cables**

Bring at least one per light—carry a multi-plug power strip too. In a crunch you can bundle your smaller electrical items on the same cord.

Tip: pack a small bag with emergency items, such as ground lifters—electrical adapters that go from three prong to two prong, light socket adapter—pull a light bulb, then screw in a power outlet. A three-way adapter turns any extension into three outlets. These are just few suggestions; we'll save a thorough look at what should be in an E-bag for a later chapter.

Custom space

You have your essentials together, so it's time to start thinking about items in your custom space. What makes this shoot different? Will it be indoors, or outdoors? Does it look like sun, or rain? Do you have a long way to travel with your gear? Is the shoot fast moving, or stationary on a tripod? Visualize your entire production from start to finish. The most professional way, if you have the time, is to do a scout of the location before the shoot, or carefully research it, so you will know exactly what you need. Special items like reflectors, rain covers, extra wireless mics, long cables, backdrops, battery lights, carts and extra lights all need to be noted here. As you become more comfortable with your gear grid, this custom space will turn you from a forgetful lowly squire to a 'got it on the ball' professional knight.

Contacts and Directions

It goes without saying that every shoot has a contact, even if it's the janitor who opens the door for you. Before the shoot, you should know who is in charge and his or her phone numbers. A backup contact is also a good idea. You never know when a personality conflict will happen. (And you thought I was going to say because the other person couldn't be reached.) Directions and timing are also very important to examine before you depart. An individual's directions may not always be accurate and he or she might not have taken the rush hour into consideration.

Figure 29-5 *Include in your contact list: the location person to meet, equipment vendors, nearby hospitals, food stores, and after hours and weekend contact numbers.*

Tip: I have found a GPS mapping system is worth its weight in gold. If nothing else, when you start having doubts about their "clear directions" it will give you great peace of mind.

Tip: locate local businesses and emergency contacts; print out their address, phone number and business hours and stick them in your camera bag. Radio Shack, hardware stores, pharmacies, hospitals, etc.

Ready for Battle

OK, your steed is loaded, your armor checked. The last thing a good knight must do is . . . recheck! That's right, stand by your steed . . . er . . . vehicle and mark off your entire gear grid again. Physically confirm that everything on your list is, in fact in your car, not on the coffee table or sitting next to your computer. Be sure to check off both your essential list and any of your custom items, if you need to have any for your particular shoot.

Certainly, it may seem a bit redundant, but there have probably been many times where you're sure you were ready, and you showed up with a wooden shield when it turns out you should have brought a metal shield to fight the fire-breathing dragon, instead. If you're unprepared, somebody's going to get burned. Don't let it be you.

PART III
Production Techniques

Tips for capturing the highest quality video and sound

30
How to Make a Video

Kyle Cassidy

Figure 30-1

So you've got a video camera! Perhaps you went out and bought one specifically or perhaps you've discovered that the fancy DSLR you have shoots video. Either way, video is a great way to tell stories, stay in touch with friends, and get information from one place to another. The better your video, the more effective it will be at doing what you want. We're going to look at the basic steps necessary to make a video. We'll look at things like how to make a storyboard, finding video editing tutorials, and some cinematography techniques to make your production shine.

Preparation

The first thing to do is decide on what type of video you want to make. Start small with a project you know you can finish, and aim for something under five minutes. The techniques you use for this will always be applicable to larger projects. Your video can be fiction (either a story of your own invention, or an adaptation of an existing work, or even a dramatization of an event in your family history) or it can be non-fiction—a "how to" video demonstrating something like a baton twirling trick or changing a car tire, or it can be of an event, a wedding, baptism, or sports match.

Figure 30-2 *Lenses can give you different fields of view. A wide-angle lens will show more of the surroundings. A telephoto will magnify and show less and a zoom lens can do both.*

Once you've come up with your idea, you can make a storyboard, which is usually a series of drawings showing camera angles, framing and movement, and used as a visual map for the shots you'll make during production. This is a really good idea if you're making a multi-million dollar Hollywood blockbuster. You don't want Bruce Willis and a 40-person crew standing around twiddling their thumbs while you figure out where you want the camera. On smaller productions, some directors will storyboard completely in their heads, but most will do it simply by writing down an outline that may look like this:

1. Wide aerial shot of Snake River Canyon.

2. Daredevil Bob, voiceover: "Snake River Canyon, the one thing that Evel Knievel couldn't jump."

3. Wide shot of Daredevil Bob standing next to his mondo rocket-cycle.

4. Daredevil Bob: "Today I plan to succeed where Evel failed. After achieving a speed of 900 miles per hour in my mondo rocket-cycle, I'll hit this ramp."

5. Medium shot, pans across ramp, Daredevil Bob voiceover: ". . . and be launched over the 1,300 foot gorge to land in a pile of old mattresses on the west side."

6. Medium shot of Daredevil Bob jumping from a ladder onto a pile of dirty mattresses.

More useful often in small productions is to simply have a "shot list" which is a list of all the angles and sequences you want to have before you get to the editing room. A shot list for Daredevil Bob's jump might look like this:

• Medium shot of Daredevil Bob giving his intro speech.

• Closeup of Daredevil Bob giving his intro speech.

• Wide shot of the mondo rocket-cycle.

• Closeup pans across the rocket-cycle.

• Wide shots of Snake River Canyon.

• Wide shots of the ramp.

• View over the edge of the canyon.

• Medium shot of mattresses.

• Wide shot of Bob jumping into mattresses.

As you can see, the shot list is just a broad reminder of what to shoot when you're in the field. For short projects this should be plenty.

Articles on basic composition will help you in framing your shots which is important in making things look nice and keeping your viewers entertained.

After you've got a general idea of what you want, you may need to find a location and you may need to find some talent. This doesn't mean that you have no talent now—talent is what you call the person in front of the cameras (regardless of whether or not they have any). If you're making a video about Daredevil Bob's historic jump, you've got your talent and you've got your location, but what if you're doing a video about how to change the side mirror on a 1965 Ford Mustang? You'll need someone who's capable of doing it, and you'll need a place to do it. Here's where you take into consideration things like "out of all my friends, who has the best lit, cleanest, most spacious garage?" and "out of all my friends, who's the most likely to do well on camera and to be able to explain and carry out this task?" The people who end up on TV aren't necessarily the best at what they do, rather they're the best on TV doing what they do.

Your Camera

A camera is only a sealed box that allows you to control the amount of light that gets in to hit a photosensitive microchip. There are really only three important controls on a camera. Two of them control the amount of light that gets in; your "aperture" controls how much light goes through the lens and your "shutter speed" controls how long the shutter is open and thus the amount of time this light is hitting the sensor. The third, "focus", controls the amount of your image which is in sharp focus. Most modern video cameras have a "program" mode that will have the camera set all of these. On your first videos, go ahead and let the camera make these decisions, as your explore various cinematography techniques like shallow depth of field and fast or slow shutter speeds. Later,

Figure 30-3 *There are many ways to edit video today. Whether you're using a Mac, a PC, a smartphone or a tablet, one goal remains the same: trim your raw footage down to something watchable.*

you'll want to take the camera off program and experiment with manual control.

The lens on your camera is either a "fixed" or "zoom" lens. A fixed lens can only show one field of view while a zoom lens can cover a range of angles from wide to telephoto, and the range depends on the exact lens. There are benefits to each of these.

Your camera doesn't have to have any of these fancy controls though—you can make a video and find video editing software for lots of smart phones. The world of video production has come a long way in the past 15 years.

Quiet On The Set!

Your camera probably has a built in microphone which records audio synched with your video image. This is convenient, but not the best option for a number of reasons. The biggest reason is that the microphone is in one place and your talent may be in several places, meaning that audio from one will be louder than audio from others. Eventually, you'll want to get some off-camera microphones, but in the meantime, be aware of the distance from your camera of all the audio you're recording. Also, remind people to turn off their cell phones and anything else that might make background noise, like the air conditioner. (Now is the time when you begin to suffer for your art.)

It's also likely that your camera has something called "automatic gain control" which is the camera's way of dealing with audio sources from a wide variety of distances. It will attempt to boost the signal of quiet things and limit the level of loud things. Like any automatic setting on your camera, this comes with mixed results. Eventually you'll want to control the audio gain manually.

Lights!

Many a great video has been ruined by bad lighting. This can either be direct, overhead sunlight giving everyone heavily shadowed eye sockets, or it can be green-hued fluorescents that make everybody look like the recently undead. (Or a bunch of other horrible things that can go wrong with lighting . . .)

Luckily, natural (sun) light is very good light if properly treated and abundant for a good portion of the day. The three most typical types of light used in video production are "key", "fill" and "back" or "hair" lighting.

You can often get away with a single source of light if it's broad enough and soft enough. A large window to one side of your subject will provide flattering light, as will shaded daylight. You can also use some guerrilla lighting options such as halogen work lamps bounced off walls or ceilings.

Figure 30-4 *Placing your talent next to a large window is a viable lighting solution that can provide a soft and broad light. This type of lighting is simple to achieve and can be flattering to your talent's features.*

Editing: Connecting the Dots for a Fluid Scene

Nobody wants to see all of your raw footage, so after you've shot your footage you need to edit it down into something that people will watch. (One other option is to edit "in camera" meaning you shoot everything in order and use everything you shoot. This made more sense when people were recording onto linear tape and editing systems were expensive and difficult to use.)

There are many types of video editing software available for every computer platform (including smart phones), and free ones that are part of your computer's operating system including iMovie for the Macintosh and Movie Maker for Windows Live (Microsoft's Movie Maker is no longer installed by default, you can download it from the Microsoft website).

When beginning to learn to edit, it's best to stick with cuts: Editing systems have lots of "transitions"—ways to move from one shot to another, things like page turns and star wipes—these are best avoided. Most professional editors stick with cuts and the occasional cross-fade.

Adding titles to the beginning and ending of your production can help make it look professional and set your scene ("Brad's Birthday Party" or "Vacation in Roswell"). Titles can either be on a solid background or can be superimposed over live action.

Conclusion

Keep your first videos simple. Make them projects not too daunting that you can't finish them in a weekend. There are a plethora of *Videomaker* articles available online that go over in detail all of the key elements of how to make a video. Once your video is complete, you can learn how to distribute your video electronically, so that friends and family can see it.

31
The Divine Proportion: Balancing the Golden Rule

James Williams

Figure 31-1 and 31-2

Nature created it; visual artists follow it. From sea-shells and leaves to flower petals, and yes, a Gecko's tail, using aesthetically-pleasing framing creatively draws your viewer into your shot composition.

A cold breeze blows across the relic hunter's face as she approaches the stone tomb. She inches closer as her torchlight dances across the darkened church walls. She reaches out to the stone door—and the torch flame suddenly goes out. Total blackness. The director yells "Cut!" The lights come back on as everyone prepares for the next scene.

As the editor, you review the video replay of the take, and it immediately strikes you that something doesn't feel right about the shot. The lighting is fine, the acting is solid and the audio is spot on. Then it hits you. The framing of the shot is off, and that's what feels unbalanced.

It's All in What You See

Whether dealing with ancient subject matter or the dozens of soccer goals your kid scores this season, how you frame your shots is crucially important to how your video will look.

Poorly-framed shots not only leave much of the important visual information out of the picture, but they can also subtly—or not so subtly—create unwelcome tension for the viewer. That's fine if it's a horror flick, but it's not so great if it's your kid's fifth birthday.

Composing your shot is also an act of artistic expression. There's power in pictures. Giving some forethought to how to frame your shot allows you to convey any number of emotions, from fear to peaceful tranquility.

An Age-Old Question

For hundreds—if not thousands—of years, visual artists have been studying how best to frame their subjects and exactly where to plant the focus of their compositions. While there are no definitive rules about how to frame your shots, there are certainly tried and true guidelines that are well worth looking at.

The Divine Proportion

In 1202, an Italian mathematician known as Fibonacci published a book introducing to Western mathematics the numeric symbols we use today. In the same text, he also introduced a series of numbers, known today as the Fibonacci Sequence (see Figure 31-1). The first number of the sequence is 0, the second number is 1, and each subsequent number is equal to the sum of the previous two numbers of the sequence itself.

What makes this sequence so special is that eventually, no matter what two numbers you start with, the sequence will settle into a ratio of 1:1.618, also known as the Divine Proportion (see Figure 31-2). Curiously, these numbers and ratio show up throughout nature, from the measurements of the chambered nautilus shell to the number of spirals on a pinecone.

The idea behind using the Divine Proportion to frame your shots is that, since it's found throughout nature, it therefore lends itself to creating intrinsically beautiful compositions.

The formula to create a template using the Divine Proportion is fairly technical, so for our purpose, we will illustrate it graphically (see Figure 31-3). Each rectangle is half the size of the previous one, tightening up to where the supposed sweet spot lies.

This ratio shows up in architecture, paintings, photography and musical compositions. Leonardo da Vinci supposedly used it in many of his classic paintings and sketches, including the *Mona Lisa* and the *Vitruvian Man*. Salvador Dali used it in his portrayal of *The Last Supper*. And perhaps, now, you can get creative and use it in your masterpiece as well.

One interesting aspect of the Divine Proportion is that many visual artists naturally place the focus of their compositions in the sweet spot, seemingly without knowing it. In many cases, we'll never know whether some of the great artists

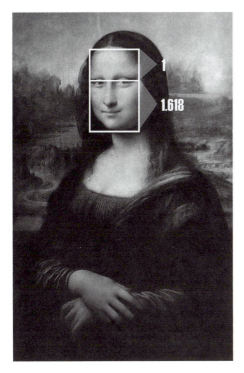

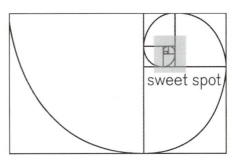

Figure 31-3 and 31-4 *The rule of thirds is based on vertical and horizontal lines that intersect within the Fibonacci Spiral. In art and science, these lines are found in many places.*

Figure 31-5 *An object of interest residing at the intersection of a vertical and horizontal third should be in focus (left). If it is not, in can create an unbalanced look (right).*

used these measurements intentionally or if the placement just felt right to them.

The Rule of Thirds

You won't need an advanced degree in mathematics to sketch out the Rule of Thirds. You simply divide your frame into nine compartments, using two equally-spaced vertical lines and two equally-spaced horizontal lines. Those lines will intersect in four places. Those are the sweet spots, and that's where you'll want to place the focus of your composition.

Figure 31-6 *Look room is additional space given to the composition, depending upon which way the talent is looking or the direction the talent's body is facing.*

Using the Rule of Thirds allows your subject room to breathe. Human subjects will sit comfortably in the frame, without feeling crowded by the edges of the image.

The horizontal and vertical lines are also good guides to use when breaking up the composition with skylines, waterlines, walls, highways and other straight-line images.

The Subject of Your Focus

When you first glance at a composition, your eyes will automatically try to extract meaning from the image. There's usually a focal point that draws your gaze and stands out—a sunset, a drag race, a surfer at the water's edge. The subject is what the composition is ultimately about. It's the main object you'd use to describe the composition to someone else. With people, the focus is usually the eyes. In action shots, it can be the center of the activity.

Exceptions to the Rule

Once you have a good handle on the rules, you can think about breaking them. Ignoring these compositional guidelines

is a trick you can employ to convey tension in the shot when the situation calls for it.

In general, a subject talking on screen is speaking across the frame with a fair amount of breathing room in front. If you want to immediately create tension, you can take away the breathing room and have your subject speak directly into the edge of the frame.

This technique instantly creates tension, because the subject appears suffocated. It also denies the viewer valuable information about what or whom the subject is addressing off-frame.

The Eyes Have It

You'll notice that the Rule of Thirds doesn't line up exactly with the Divine Proportion. But when you compare them against each other, it's clear there isn't a huge difference between the two. Seeing where the sweet spots lie in both formulas does offer some good insight into how to compose your shots. Given that all art is ultimately subjective, you'll need to come to your own conclusions as to what placement works best for you.

Knowing how to create a well-balanced composition is an important tool for every videographer. Like anything worth doing, it takes practice. Eventually, you'll find yourself gravitating towards well-composed shots that accentuate, rather than distract from, the interesting or emotional aspects of your subject matter. That said, your shots may look terrific, despite ignoring the guidelines. It's all in the eyes of the beholder. If you think your shot compositions could use some help, these guidelines are an excellent place to start.

32
Shooting Steady

Robert G. Nulph

Figure 32-1

Shooting steady video is perhaps one of the most fundamental skills of good video production. If your camera isn't steady, your shots will be difficult to watch (unless you provide a healthy dose of seasick pills). In this chapter, we will take a look at various ways you can shoot good solid video every time, no matter the subject or the situation. We'll start out with the fundamentals of shooting handheld video and move towards more sophisticated electronically-aided methods for keeping your video smooth and steady.

Shooting Fundamentals

Shooting handheld video is perhaps the most difficult way to capture images on tape. No matter how steady you think you are, even your breathing can make the camera move and shake. If you find yourself in a situation where you must shoot handheld, there are a few things to keep in mind.

One of the most important things to remember about camcorders and their lenses is that zooming emphasizes movement. The closer you zoom, the more your movement is magnified. Because of this, when you are shooting handheld video, you should get as physically close to your subject as you possibly can and zoom out as far (wide) as the camcorder's lens will allow. This will give you the steadiest shot possible.

The second step towards good handheld shots is maintaining good posture. Keep your back straight; legs shoulder width apart; knees slightly bent and your elbows close to your body. If you are handholding a small camcorder with an LCD screen, hold the camera with both hands in front of your body, elbows tucked into your sides. If shooting from the shoulder, tuck your elbow into your side and use your right hand and arm for support, while your left hand controls the focus and iris.

If you have to move while actively shooting, do so slowly and as smoothly as possible, keeping your subject composed well in the shot and maintaining good solid posture throughout the entire move.

The World Around You

If you find yourself in a situation where you don't have a tripod, any solid surface can act as a camera platform. You can set your camera on a rock, fence post or parked car, or lean up against a tree or the edge of a building. Use a table or chair to steady your shot. If shooting on the beach, lay some plastic down and steady the camera on the sand, or set the camera up on the steps of the lifeguard tower.

Figure 32-2 *Rock stable—if you find yourself in a situation where you don't have a tripod, any solid surface can act as a camera platform. Set your camera on a rock, fence post or parked car, or lean up against a tree or the edge of a building.*

When using a solid platform to shoot from, you will most likely have to tilt the camera to get the best shot. Once again, objects around you might be useful: credit cards, cardboard, newspapers, pencils, even gum wrappers can be used to stabilize your shot. Once you compose your shot, press the record button and take your hands away.

Tripods

Every videographer should own a good tripod. A tripod lets you shoot solid, steady video with little effort. There are, however some things you need to keep in mind when using a tripod. Always set your tripod and camera up so that one of the three legs is pointing towards your subject. This will create a space for you to stand in between the other two legs. If you know you are going to pan in one particular direction a lot, point the front leg of the tripod halfway between the farthest left and farthest right your subject will move so you won't have to walk around or step over one of the back legs.

When adjusting the height of your tripod, use your subject as your guide, instead of setting it at a level that makes you feel comfortable. Set your tripod up so that the camera, when completely horizontal, is pointing at the neck of your subject. Unfortunately, this might mean that you will find yourself in some uncomfortable shooting positions, but that's a small price to pay for better-looking video.

If you do not have to move the shot and the subject will not be moving, lock down the tripod, press the record button and let go. If you do need to move, position yourself with the camcorder so that you are as solid and comfortable as possible and slowly move in the direction you have planned. Always plan and rehearse camera movements before making them.

Monopods

A monopod is like a hiking stick with a camera mount at the top. Monopods are primarily still-camera tools, but can be quite handy when you must be mobile and you still need to shoot steady video. You will often see camera operators on the sidelines at football games or other sporting events using monopods. The monopod is lighter and more manageable than a tripod. While the monopod prevents vertical movement of the camcorder, it does nothing to prevent the horizontal or tilting movement.

Flying Supports

If you have a little extra cash in your pocket, you might want to check out one of the many types of flying camera supports on the market. These handheld counterbalanced supports allow you to move freely while shooting and produce gliding, shake-free

Figure 32-3 *Required equipment—every videographer should own a good tripod. A tripod lets you shoot solid, steady video with little effort.*

Figure 32-4 *Fly right! Handheld counterbalanced supports allow you to move freely while shooting and produce gliding, shakefree video.*

video. The most famous flying camera support is the Steadicam and the brand name has become a shorthand for the entire class of products. Beyond simple handheld devices, you can get complex vests and harnesses that will help you hold the camera during long shoots. The professional gliding camera stabilizers are so smooth you can barely tell the camera is not sitting on a tripod. One note of caution: if you are considering buying one, try it out first to see if it will work with your camcorder.

You can create a flying camera support of sorts by mounting your camcorder onto your tripod or monopod and lifting it off the ground, using the weight of the legs to act as a counterbalance for the camcorder to keep it upright. This will not produce anything close to the results you'd get from a precisely engineered and finely balanced flying camcorder support, but you may be pleasantly surprised at the look of the shots.

Image Stabilization

Image stabilization is the video engineer's gift to amateur videographers. Your

Figure 32-5 *Oversized CCD—electronic image stabilization can reduce the overall number of pixels on the CCD that are used to capture an image. This can result in a general softening of the picture.*

camcorder's built-in image stabilizer seeks to smooth out handheld video, minimizing camera shake. Image stabilizers are found in most camcorders today. There are two types: electronic and optical. Optical is generally better, and is typically found on higher-end camcorders. Although they can be quite handy if you find yourself in a situation where you must shoot handheld, they do have a couple of limitations. First, electronic image stabilization can reduce the overall number of pixels on the CCD that are used to capture an image. This can result in a general softening of the picture. Second, when the stabilizer is used during a pan, the smooth pan might jump slightly from one point to the next as the stabilizer tries to correct your intentional movement. Still, image stabilization, both electronic and optical, can be a shotsaver when shooting handheld.

Keep It Steady

There are times to move the camera and times to hold it still, but, unless you are trying to create an earthquake effect, there are seldom times when shaky video is good video.

Time is of the Essence!

You should never handhold shots that demand rock solid video. Long interviews, cutaways of objects with vertical or horizontal surfaces, and steady landscapes should never be handheld. Moving subjects, shots with camera movement already built into them, such as pans and tilts and shots where the camera physically moves from one place to another can easily be handheld. Always plan your movement and move steadily and in one direction.

33
Basic Training: The Nine Classic Camera Moves

Brian Schaller

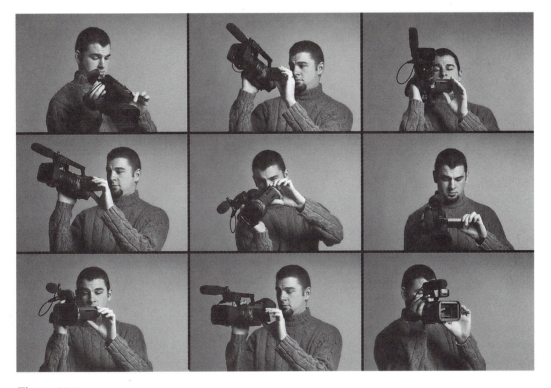

Figure 33-1

Professional videographers usually follow this one rule of thumb: when it comes to camera movement, it must be motivated. "Because it looks cool", is usually not a valid reason for using tricky camera moves. Instead, you can use camera moves to change the viewer's perspective making what you shoot look bigger, smaller, or even scarier. You should use camera movement to tell your story better and to enhance the viewer's experience.

We'll break it down movement by movement so you will know how to execute each shot and why you might use it. We've also divided the chapter into three easy to follow sections:

- Mounted camera creates the move.

- Camera and operator or devices move together.

- Only the camera lens moves.

Mounted Camera Creates the Move

Pan

How: move the camera horizontally left or right. Ideally, you should use a tripod for a smooth effect. To be a great "panner," practice the shot several times at several speeds before you feel comfortable with it.

Why: to follow a subject or show the distance between two objects. Pan shots also work great for panoramic views such as a shot from a mountaintop to the valley below.

Rule: always start on a still shot, began the pan, and finish on a still shot. Practice first. Look at the scene as the pan reaches the middle portion between the beginning and end of the scene. If there is nothing worth seeing, then the pan isn't worth shooting.

Tilt

How: moving the camera up or down without raising its position.

Why: like panning, to follow a subject or to show the top and bottom of a stationary object. With a tilt, you can also show how high something is. For example, a slow tilt up a giant sequoia tree shows its grandness and enormity.

Figure 33-2 *Before shooting a pan, practice it a few times until it looks just right.*

Figure 33-3 *Tilts are useful for emphasizing the height of a tall object, like a redwood tree or a skyscraper.*

Here's a good tip. In general, when you tilt up and shoot an object or a person they look larger and thicker. The subject looks smaller and thinner when you tilt down.

Rule: always start on a still shot, begin the tilt, and finish on a still shot. Practice first. Look at the scene as the tilt reaches the middle portion between top and bottom of the tilt. If there is nothing worth seeing, then the tilt isn't worth shooting.

Pedestal

How: not tilting, but physically moving the height of the camera up or down, usually on a tripod.

Why: you pedestal the camera up or down to get the proper height you prefer. If you want to get "eye to eye" with a six-foot-six basketball player, you would pedestal up. While shooting a flower or a small child, you would pedestal down to their level.

Camera and Operator or Devices Move Together

Dolly

How: the camera is set on tracks or wheels and moved towards or back from a subject. A dolly is also a noun, describing a train track contraption used for a dolly (verb) shot or a device attached to a tripod. A wheelchair, because it has large wheels, rolls smoothly, and has a seat for a videographer, works quite well as a dolly, but you can also use a rolling cart or even a skateboard.

Why: to follow an object smoothly to get a unique perspective. In some movies, directors combine the dolly and a zoom shot for a real sense of doom. To do this, the camera lens zooms into the subject at the same time as the camera physically dollies out, and the person in the shot remains the same size, but the background appears to move. It's difficult to master smoothly, but done right, the shot conveys a real sense of tension and feeling of vertigo.

Floating Stabilizer Device

How: the device straps to the photographer and the camera is mounted by a series of metal joints controlled by gyroscopes. These machines are quite complicated and a real Steadicam can cost several thousand dollars. But you can buy an inexpensive alternative that uses counterweights to get a Steadicam-like effect.

Why: to follow an object through twists and turns. Although the dolly is great, its movements are limited. With the stabilizer, you can follow someone through hallways, doors and around rooms.

Crane or Boom

How: this works and looks similar to a construction crane. It is used for high sweeping shots or to follow the action of your subject.

Why: gives a bird's eye view. It looks as if the camera is swooping down from above. Movie directors use this for street scenes so they can shoot from above the crowd and the traffic, and then move down to eye level.

Handheld

How: you hold the camera without tripod, monopod or other device. Professional

Figure 33-4 *Crane shoots require extensive equipment and a lot of finesse, but when done right can add a lot of production value to a video.*

cameras are large and rest on the user's shoulders. This balances the camera and keeps shaking to a minimum. Because of their size, most consumer cameras can't rest on your shoulder, so you'll need a few tips to shoot steady well-executed hand-held shots.

Why: due to the spontaneity of the action, many news crews and most documentaries use hand-held shooting techniques. Sometimes, it is used in TV shows and movies. Notice that in horror or action movies they often use handheld shots when something bad is about to happen.

Rule: when shooting handheld, do not zoom in! The more you zoom in, the shakier the shot gets. It is better to move closer to your subject and shoot with as wide of a setting as you can. Handheld is best when you are shooting someone or something that is moving. It looks very bad when shooting landscapes, buildings, or stationary objects.

Only the Camera Lens Moves

Zoom

How: you press a lever or rocker to zoom in or out. This lever controls the lens mechanism inside the camera. Usually, the harder you press on the lever the quicker the zoom. Some camcorders have only one zoom speed whereas others allow you to zoom manually by turning a ring on the lens. A zoom lens gives you the option of having both telephoto and wide-angle lens in one camera. You use the telephoto lens when you zoom in, bringing objects closer to you. There is less visible area around your subject, and distant objects are compressed. Zooming the lens out gives you the wide-angle shot and more of your subject and surrounding areas are visible. Depth perception is also changed, and the size and distance between objects is more pronounced.

Why: to bring objects at a distance closer to the lens, or to show size and perspective.

Rule: continuous zooming in and out is annoying to viewers. Don't zoom while shooting unless the scene calls for it. Use a tripod if you zoom. Start on a still shot, then zoom smoothly, and end your zoom on a still shot. Practice first. Look at the scene as the zoom reaches the middle portion between the closeup and wide angle. If there is nothing worth seeing, then the zoom isn't worth shooting.

Rack Focus

How: focus on one object, like an actor's face, and have everything behind him out of focus. Then adjust the focus so his face becomes blurred and the actress behind him becomes clear. In this movement, you are changing the focal length so that one subject will go out of focus while the other comes into focus. The two subjects must be at a correct distance from each other and from the camera for this shot to work.

Why: you are actually making a transition similar to an edit by constructing two distinct shots. You often see the rack focus in dramas and soap operas, changing focus from one actor's face to another during their conversation or tense moments.

Rule: use a tripod. A rack focus looks bad if the camera is shaky.

Get Out and Play!

Now that you have learned the basic anatomy of camera movement, remember this: the best and most versatile shots of all are the standard wide, medium and close-up stationary shots. However, a well-executed camera movement is the icing on the video-cake. They add style, feeling and depth to a project. Although we have given you several reasons why you would use each camera movement, these are certainly not the only motivations for moving the camera. Like any artist, you can invent your own reasons for using camera movements. Play around. Experiment.

Be an artist. And watch movies, TV and even commercials with the sound off, to see how the camera movement plays out. You'll quickly see how one shot motivates the next and you may begin to predict the next shot or the following sequence. Eventually, with minimum effort, you may be on par with the pros.

34
Video and Photography Light Reflectors

Terry O'Rourke

Figure 34-1

So, you're thinking about going green with your life. Perhaps a car with better fuel economy, and outfitting your home with energy-efficient lighting and even installing solar. Well, why not consider green technology with your video lighting as well? What's that you say? How am I going to get green video lighting equipment—and besides how much energy does lighting a set consume anyway? Cost savings and even altruistic motives aren't the only reasons to go green; the inconvenience of running around plugging in lights is a compelling reason to consider green lighting. Not just some Johnny-come-lately "green fad" we've all been hearing and reading about, green lighting has been around for decades.

Multitude of Light Reflector Choices

Cardboard flats or basic foam core video light reflectors covered in simple paper or foil were the first "high tech," green lighting supplements to arrive on the scene. Due to their popularity, the market eventually became flooded with such things as collapsible sheets of pure white fabric, and reflective materials that you could manually clip around a frame. As the demand for these video and photography light reflectors increased, so did their quality.

Today, there are hundreds of video and photography light reflectors available ranging from simple white reflective

Figure 34-2 *A reflector, a white card and the sun are all you need to get what is essentially three-point lighting outside.*

fabrics designed to wrap around specially designed collapsible frames, to specialized rigid boards covered in highly reflective materials which are available in various colors. There are plastic tubing-style frames that can be snapped together to make a nearly seamless wall of video and photography light reflectors limited only by how many you have in your kit.

By far, the most popular design today is a system whereby a reflective fabric is sewn to a flexible spring steel frame that quickly folds into itself and can be stowed in a soft flat case several times smaller than the light reflector itself. These are offered in many styles, including shoot-through materials that can be used as a scrim and also provide a nice reflective surface if no lights are available. You can also find reversible frames wrapped in reflective synthetic silver on one side and gold on the other; perfect for those times where you want to carry both styles, but are limited by space. Alternatively, choose one with silver on one side and white on the other, and add to that one in gold/white and you are ready for anything.

Using Video and Photography Light Reflectors Outdoors

Any lighting style starts with a key light, and unless you are working on a special lighting type, you will likely require some fill light and probably would benefit from a "rim" or hair light as well. So how does a reflector fit in? Well, the best way to answer that is to let your situation tell you.

Always start with your key light, which, if outdoors could be the direct sun: direct sunlight bouncing off a wall or full shade, sometimes referred to as "north light." With your subject facing the sun the light is shining right into your subject's eyes creating harsh shadows. You could try strategically placing a reflector to one side of your subject, and reflect it back into your subject's face, thus creating fill, but you'd probably end up with a squinty-looking video. Or you could turn your subject around, facing north or away from the sun (north light), and let the sunlight from behind your subject make a nice rim light on their hair and shoulders. One well-placed large white reflector in front of your subject could then bounce some of that sunlight back into your subject and produce some nice soft fill light.

This example is a nice soft look, but there's no real key light. Try using two video light reflectors: one smaller soft white reflector close to your subject for your key, and one larger soft white reflector farther away for your fill. Mix it up a bit and use a sliver reflector for your key or try a large gold reflector for a warmer-looking fill. There's really no end to the ways you can reflect sunlight back into your subject, because it's such a strong light source. If you don't like where the sun is coming from, you can even get a large acrylic glass mirror, completely redirect the sunlight, and then use all your video and photography reflectors as described above.

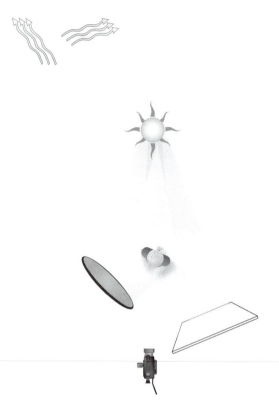

Figure 34-3 *This is an alternative arrangement that works great during the magic hour, when the sun is low on the horizon.*

Using Video Light Reflectors Indoors

If you are indoors, you become limited to what's available. Try looking for a window and use that as your key. You would then bring in a large reflector exactly opposite that window for fill and create a nice soft fill for "window light". While you're there, try boom-mounting a gold reflector just above and behind your subject to capture some of that nice window light and reflect it back for a little hair light. White balance your camera to the window light, then bring in a large gold reflector as your fill to create a beautiful warm room light mixed with that cool window light. Move it just behind your subject while still allowing some of it to fill the front, and you get a wonderful warm rim around the full length of your subject. To add more glow to the effect,

try two large gold video light reflectors and create a wall of warm light for a dramatic fireplace light!

Save the Power Bills, Think Green

Green video lighting sounds silly, doesn't it? However, if you think about just how easy it is to unfold and set a reflector or two, you will then realize how liberating it is to be truly "off the grid". And to know you can shoot great video just about anywhere without the need to search around for electricity allows you to find something else in your videos. And think about it: working without video lights has a certain esthetic, quietness that creates a calm inviting set and really helps to bring out your subject's true personality.

35
Applying Three-Point Lighting

Robert G. Nulph

Some folks consider it a tired cliché, but it's important to know how to set three-point lighting, so you can work within or without this classic lighting style.

We are often told, "you have to know the rules before you can break them!" In the case of lighting, the rule for good lighting involves the use of three-point lighting. In this chapter, we will provide pictures and diagrams that will give you the rules you need to produce good lighting in simple situations. Once you master three-point lighting, you will be ready to move on to creating realistic quality lighting for your video productions.

Key, Fill, and Back

The key light is the main source of light in a scene. You place the key light in front or to the side of the subject,

depending on the situation. The more dramatic the light needs to be, the further to the side you should place the light. Usually you place the key light at a 45-degree angle above the subject and 45-degrees to her side (see Figure 35-1). If the light is correctly placed, it will create a shadow that pleasantly slants down the side of the subject's neck as well as the side of her nose, giving her a three-dimensional look.

The role of the fill light is to fill in the shadows created by the key light. The fill light also gives the image a sense of time, place, mood and drama. The fill tells the viewer the brightness of the location where you are shooting. To prevent secondary shadows, it is best to place the fill

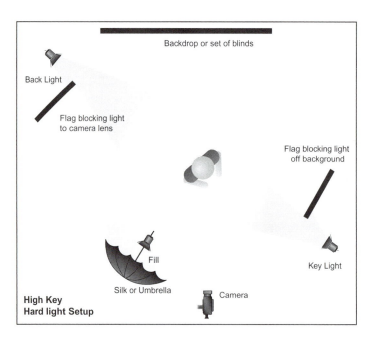

Backdrop or set of blinds

Back Light

Flag blocking light
to camera lens

Flag blocking light
off background

Fill

Key Light

Silk or Umbrella   Camera
High Key
Hard light Setup

Figure 35-1 *This is a classic three-point lighting setup with the key light being a high, hard light. A high hard key will give you a more dramatic, high-contrast look.*

light in front of the subject and closer to the camera lens than the key. This light should always be some degree less bright than the key and, as described below, is best if it is a soft light.

The back light is essential to three-point lighting in that it separates the subject from the background. To set up a good back light, place the light behind the subject and opposite the main light source (key light). The back light should be set 45-degrees above the subject so that its light falls on the back of the subject's head and the top of the shoulders. Use more back light for black, brunettes and less for blondes.

When you put all three lights together, it should create a very pleasant and natural looking three-dimensional image.

High Key Versus Low Key

If the fill light approaches the intensity of the key light, the contrast is reduced and is often called high key lighting. You would use this type of lighting if you did not need to create a dramatic mood or just wanted a low contrast scene.

If the fill is a great deal less intense than the key light, the lighting is called low key lighting. You would use this type of lighting for dramatic scenes, scenes shot to look like night time or dramatic interviews. To set up this type of lighting, place the key light further to the side of the subject to reduce the intensity or eliminate the fill light (see Figure 35-3).

Hard Versus Soft Light

The quality of light can be either hard or soft. Hard lighting comes from small lighting instruments that create hard-edged shadows. You can create soft light by making your lights bigger by diffusing their light with large silks, umbrellas, or softboxes. You would use hard light to create intense dramatic lighting with sharp-edged shadows. However, if you want your subject to look soft and smooth, use a soft light setup.

You can also use soft lighting for both high and low key lighting. You will find a lot of high key soft lighting used in interviews and news shows. You place the

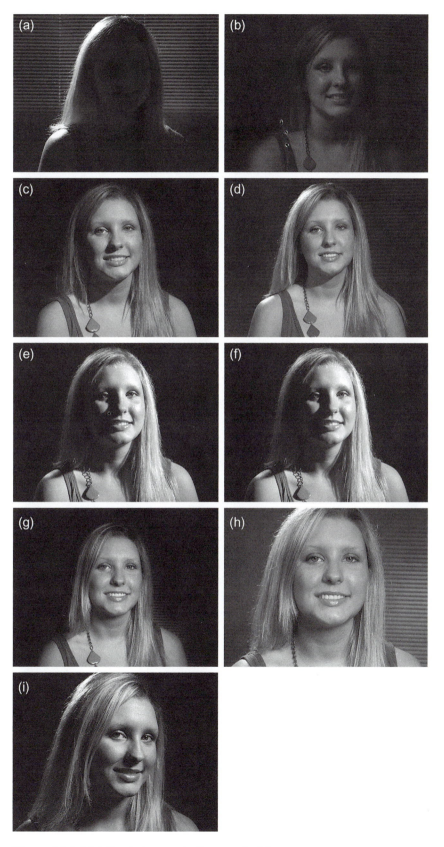

Figure 35-2 *Lighting helps create the mood of the scene.*

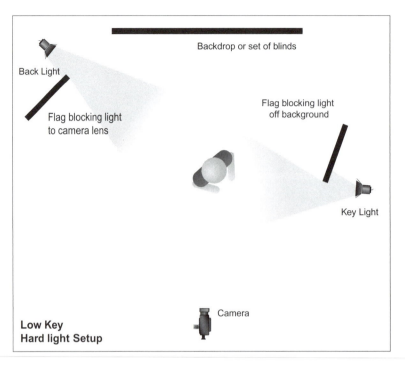

Figure 35-3 *Without a fill light, a hard key light can cast a high contrast and harsh shadows. Keeping the light low and directly in front of your talent will minimize the effect.*

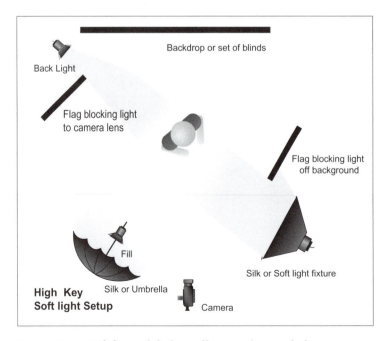

Figure 35-4 *High key soft lights will cast soft, even light on your subject. Soft boxes or umbrellas are a perfect tool for this effect.*

lights in basically the same places as the hard light high key setup in Figure 35-1. However, it can also be used to create soft and dramatic shots using a low key setup by eliminating the fill light and moving the soft light more to the side of the subject.

Mastering It All

Whatever your lighting situation, always ask yourself, "What are the quality and position of the main light source?" Place your key light so that it best approximates the look of that major light source. The fill determines the level of the ambient light in the scene and the back light, which is as intense as the key light, completes the setup.

Now you know the rules . . . you are ready to break them.

36
Get Real with Practicals

Terry O'Rourke

Figure 36-1

I'm kind of a control freak when it comes to production. I don't like to be late and I don't usually allow the existing lighting in any environment control how I will shoot. I arrive at all of my assignments early and with lots of equipment. It's nice to be early so I can scope out the situation and decide how I want things to look. This strategy gives me plenty of time to plan for compromises because it's inevitable that something or someone will not work out. It also allows for time to lay out all my gear: the lights and stands, the extension cords, the sandbags, the tripods and so on. I have several production carts, each of which is designed to compliment each other. One cart is self contained and can carry several lights and all the ancillary grip equipment they require as well as the computer, a note pad, my phone and a place to put several cups of coffee. I can do most shoots with just this cart. Another cart is designed to carry more lights and stands, booms, sand bags and lots of "other stuff." When I have both of these carts out I have a feeling of control, or you might even say "power" because there's nothing I can't do with all this stuff, given enough muscle, time and room to put it all out.

As a videographer, I usually look at a room and try to figure out the easiest way to light the set while maintaining a natural look. That usually means working with the ambient light and supplementing it with lights from a kit.

Cart-full of Goodies

Sometimes things don't work out as you would hope. Perhaps a room you are working in has a nice big north-facing window and your vision is to use that window as your key light and fill in the shadows with your light. Your director, however, has this wonderful vintage table lamp and decides to go with an evening living-room look with the table lamp as your key light and as a focal point of the set. Welcome to the world of practicals and the art of integrating existing light fixtures and windows into your set.

This is where all that equipment comes in handy because frequently what looks great to a director looks hideous to your camcorder. The only way to correct this discrepancy is to match the ambient light of your set plus the light output of practicals to the dynamic range of your camera while making everything look like the practicals are doing all the work!

Shade It

In the scenario described above we have a large window providing lots of light and a small table lamp providing very little light and a cart full of goodies. The director wants the room to appear as an evening scene with your subject sitting at the table and the lamp is part of the scene. That window can become your master if you allow it to, so the first thing to do is knock that light down to match the output of the table lamp. If your director is agreeable, the easiest way to do this is to close the drapes, shutters, shades or whatever window covering the room may have.

If your director is determined to leave the window exposed for a dark blue early

Figure 36-2 *A wide variety of gels, neutral density filters and fabrics are available for controlling light from outside windows. Gels may be preferred because once applied, they are invisible, plus they can be stacked for increased ND value.*

evening look, or if you're really ambitious, you can place a neutral density window filter on the glass. You can get 60-inch wide rolls of plastic filter material in daylight balance or 3200k balance. It's available in several densities so you can choose which one is best for your lighting situation. Rosco supplies products called Cinegel. The Cinegel Rosco N.3 material is daylight balanced and has a 1-stop value. The N.6 has a 2-stop value and the N.9 has a 3-stop value. They also have similar products in the Roscosun Cinegel line that correct daylight to 3200k which are perfect for integrating tungsten practicals such as the above mentioned table lamp into your production. This is by far the best way to handle any window lighting situation and as such gives the most predictable results.

There are alternatives to plastic gels that include fabrics such as Rosco Black Scrim, which is also available in wide rolls. This fabric material has a 2-stop value. This material is easier to handle but isn't always invisible and can move in the wind as you tape, which will show up in your video as blurry motion. Unlike plastic gels, which can be stacked for more neutral density value, fabrics can not be stacked or they will create moiré, which will also show up in your video.

Lighting the Light

Now that we have the window brought down to reasonable levels, we can light the room. We have decided that the lamp is an integral part of our set so it must look properly exposed and the set must appear as though this lamp is the only light in the room.

The next step would be to light the room with the correct exposure to match the exposure in the window, which in this case would be dark, blue evening exposure. What you are doing is setting the camcorder to a proper setting that will allow the window to be exposed for a dark, blue window and bringing up the light in the room to give you the correct overall exposure. The reason we put the NDs (neutral density) in is to reduce the overall exposure of the window to more closely match the output of the lamp. But, if you put the lamp where you want it without lighting the room, the rest of your set will be under exposed because table lamps don't have enough light output to light a room for video. Your subject might be properly exposed because they are close to the lamp but the light fall-off will be too drastic to reach much beyond your subject. We will get to the lamp a bit later but for right now it's best to forget the exposure of the lamp and light the room so it looks properly exposed relative to the window.

Bouncing off the Walls

Remember the room is an evening set, so it would be a bit dark but not so much that there are no details. There are a lot of ways to do this, but the easiest way is to put up several light heads and bounce them off the walls and ceiling. Be sure they are behind your camcorder with no spill-over into your set because if any direct light from them is in your view, it

Figure 36-3 *To bring up the overall light values in a room, try bouncing light off the walls and ceiling, taking care to avoid spill onto the set.*

will look staged. You can experiment by moving them around and you can try different power settings until you get the look you want. This is where barn-doors in your kit are absolutely necessary.

You can also add other practicals to your set if your bounce lights are too harsh or bright. Try turning down the bounce lights and turning up your practicals. The best way to "turn up" practicals is to bring several extra light bulbs ranging from 25 watts to 250 watts. You can also use dimmer switches on lamps that plug directly into standard wall plugs. You plug the dimmer into the wall and plug the lamp into the dimmer. I find these at the local hardware store and carry a lot of them.

Now that the room matches the window it's time to bring in the star of the show . . . that vintage table lamp that needed all the attention! Put it on the table and take a look. If it's too dark or too light, use one of your extra bulbs or adjust the output with your wall dimmer to match the set and start taping!

Setting Up the "Spill"

But wait! You didn't think we were really done did you? All we did was light

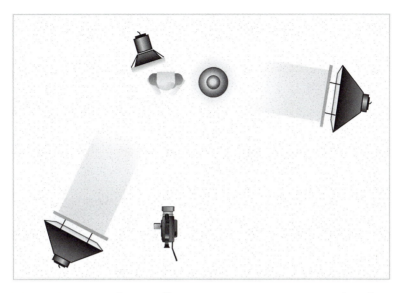

Figure 36-4 *Once the overall room exposure is correct, complete the illusion of a nice soft evening look with a blue rim light overhead and a warmly gelled fill and key lights.*

the set and that lamp. Unless the real star is the lamp you still have the subject to light. If you did everything right, that should be pretty easy because the room lighting has been set up to closely match the level that your kit provides, so all you have to do is light your subject the way you normally would, but with a few subtle differences. Since the room set has an evening look and the subject is near a dark blue window you might try a blue rim light just above and behind your subject. And if you rely on the table lamp for light on your subject, it might be a bit harsh so try a medium soft box with a warming gel for a key light. Put it just behind the table lamp so it doesn't

show and it will soften the light from the table lamp. This is where dimmable lighting comes in handy because you need to adjust all these lights to match each other. Throw in a fill from just behind the camera and you have a nice soft evening look that was created in broad daylight.

The techniques discussed here will separate you from the rest of the pack and once you truly master these strategies there is no stopping you or your creativity, so don't be afraid to experiment, fail and try again because integrating practicals in your production can be daunting. It takes practice and experience but it's well worth the effort!

37
Outdoor Cinematography

Jeanne Rawlings

Figure 37-1

There is nothing quite like lovely, outdoor cinematography. Bringing it to the screen requires that you retool your perfect vision to serve the eye of the camera.

Outdoor cinematography is a challenge because the camera does not adjust for contrast as smoothly as the human eye. Consider the subtle adjustment your eye makes while watching a waterfall and noticing the fish in the swirling shadows. The problems of contrast simply don't exist for humans. That's why many videographers don't even place their eye to the viewfinder when putting together outdoor cinematography. Amateurs don't notice contrast problems, but professionals do. Pros in outdoor videography always compose and light for the camera's eye.

A Problem You Don't See

Lighting guides explain technical issues, and that's the easy part. Outdoor videography challenges that range from sunlight drilling down on a subject to tinted rays bouncing off a painted wall are largely solved with white-balance controls and a light metering system. But real skill is in intuiting how to see like a camera. Remember that the greatest editing software can't compensate for compositions ruined by poorly-conceived contrast ranges. The way to navigate this landmine is to practice four steps: scout big, reframe for contrast, light right and be prepared.

Step 1: Scout Big

Lighting the great outdoors means isolating its immensity by time and space. You can do this only by scouting your location. Bring your camera, find and frame your setups and travel close to the shoot date. Outdoor videography technicalities are secondary to the unknown site itself and the weather changes that add

adrenalin to the mix. Understand the nature of light sources. That means timing the movement of the sun and shadows, finding electrical plugs or measuring football stadium halogens. Your confidence from the scout will motivate your crew. Even more, it will reassure the talent and client that your shots will look their best.

Outdoor videography lighting is akin to camping, and you must approach it with the same patience and respect. Scouting gives you an instant read on what is happening with seasonal sun angles, in particular. At certain times of year, the sun is moving very quickly from day to day. You can determine backup plans, workable sheltered areas, exterior elements critical for lighting that tricks the viewer and contrast ranges ahead of time. Tomorrow the sun may or may not shine, so always find electric sources for lights and load limits, how much extension cord you need and how many battery-powered lights you should bring as main or backup sources. Unless you're conjuring a remake of last year's blizzard, the weather must be workable.

Bear in mind that, while professional outdoor videography lighting requires equipment, at the heart of it are the

Figure 37-2 *The best way to plan for the exact light condition you'll have outdoors is to scout your location in advance at the same time of day you'll be shooting. Take a close look through the eyepiece to gauge the scene's contrast.*

electricians, gaffers and grips who are experienced in outdoor light. Practicing teaches you to watch that dropping sun and tree shadow that is creeping onto the scrim or reflector.

Workarounds for unforeseeable problems on location, such as audio noise off-screen in a scene that has perfect light, might mean changing location—but consider the time required for breaking up and setting up again. By scouting, you know beforehand whether to shoot the scene wide and dub in dialogue later or to drop dialogue altogether. Prioritize lighting, shooting and schedules to make the hard choice of letting some things go in order to get the well-lit action you need.

Step 2: Reframe With Contrast in Mind

One principle of shooting outdoors is set in stone. As soon as you lift the camera to your eye, you should find the optimum contrast range between all elements in the shot. Ask yourself how you might reframe or light your subject to compensate for an overly-bright background. Practice without an impending shoot.

On an artistic note, you should decide how exposure affects your story. If you are going for drama, then high contrast in the frame is good. But bear in mind that wide exposure ranges must work intimately with composition—for instance, the audience must recognize that the blown-out background is intentional.

Consider the rules of contrast between subject and background as they apply to clothing, as well. Be aware of the floating head syndrome, the result of a light-skinned subject in a dark shirt on a dark background or a dark-skinned person in a white shirt with a light background. For color choices, know that, if you want your movie to have a mood of heightened reality, then bright colors and vivid color ranges may work. But keep in mind that most video does not adjust to certain color and luminance qualities within a frame. For example, a green tree, if lit properly and in the near- to mid-background, will dominate even a properly-exposed fleshtone subject and create aberrations in the lighter subject image. Understanding composition, contrast, light and video avoids surprises in the editing room.

Step 3: Three-Point Sunshine

As odd as it may seem, the elements of three-point studio lighting apply in the field. While reflectors and lights pop your image and render three dimensions to the screen, Mother Nature dictates much of what you decide when setting up a shot outdoors.

That great ball in the sky now fills in for the studio's key, fill and backlight. In the role of key light, the sun classically fits the definition when you use a reflector to target it exactly where you need it. Keep in mind that reflectors are easy to move, and their bounced sunlight is a softer light. Also remember that the size of the source determines the softness of a light—the bigger the reflector, the softer the light. Morning and late afternoon are best angles to contour shadows when working with sunlight as your key. As the sun moves, the color of the light also changes. Maintain lighting continuity, and consider shooting a sequence over the course of several days.

Similarly, reflect the sun as a rim light—or back or hair light—to separate your subject from the background. Create this third-dimension illusion with a second reflector throwing light onto the back of the subject. Get creative, and pull a white vehicle just off-screen to mask sounds and wind, to reflect the light or to act as a huge light stand!

The industry refers to raccoon eye light for poorly-scheduled filming during midday that creates harsh shadows in eye sockets. If you must shoot during these hours, reflectors are critical for redirecting the light and creating good key light effects. Problems still may arise when the talent is squinting to avoid sunburned eyes.

In the studio, a flood usually throws the fill light to increase overall exposure.

Figure 37-3 *Our subject in a dark shirt with a dark background gives him a "floating head" appearance. Try to allow for contrast between your subject and background by having him wear a shirt with a tone similar to his flesh tone. The reverse applies to dark-skinned subjects with a light background.*

Figure 37-4 *The sun at high noon is like a big light directly over your subject's head. His foreground and eyebrows will still cast shadows, losing details in his eyes. Using a reflector bounces a bit of light under his eyes to bring them out of the shadows.*

Figure 37-5 *Sunlight can be too harsh, causing extreme shadows and bright peaks. Filtering the sunlight through a simple sheet of diffusion softens the entire image, allowing features to stand out while still giving your subject depth and shadowing. It also keeps squinting at a minimum.*

Outdoors, the sun fills this role perfectly by always casting a wide illumination. But the purpose of fills is to soften the harsh shadows of the key light, and, unless there are clouds, you will need to diffuse that hard sunlight fill by one of two methods: reflecting or diffusing.

Reflectors come in a range of varieties, from art-store purchases of white core board to photography-store flexible reflectors. With many sizes, colors and price ranges, the deciding choice may be how you plan to hold them: the trick to reflecting light is keeping the material steady in the wind. Beware of rippling fabric reflectors, which create a wavy light or core boards that blow out of position.

Diffusing sunlight can be a challenge. It means putting a scrim, or gauze, high and far away to keep out of the shot. Remember that the sun is moving, so find a place where a building or tree line won't interfere before you're ready to shoot.

Depending on the sun's angle and intensity, you can use single or doubled sheets or cotton muslin to diffuse the sun. Be ready for building moveable frames on your set. There are professional diffusers, light stands and arms for this specific purpose. Remember to rent or make sand bags for stability, whether the wind is a factor or not.

The quick solution to a bright day is simply to find a tree to act as a natural diffuser. Be aware that your fill, the sun, is moving. You have worked hard to control even lighting, so watch for it piercing through leaves, which can happen in seconds.

If you need to shoot with the sun behind the subject, place a reflector in front of the subject to increase the light in the shadows. Always be aware of lens flare unless you intentionally want it, and flag a shadow across your lens with a reflector. Watch closely for the sneaking edge of the reflector, which is another good reason to use tools to hold flags rather than bystanders with weakening arms. In even tougher scenes, when you must shoot the subject from below, and you are literally shooting into the sky, a diffuser on the brightly-lit subject itself works well.

Step 4: Light Kit Care

Track hours on your bulb-life, and have spares. Clothespins are critical for pinning diffusers. Even the ordinary elements must be protected like eggs. For starter kits, consider 12 items: manual light reflector, mid-to-large whiteboard, poles and clamps to stabilize it, plus external extension cords, traditional lights, extra bulbs, diffusers and gels, as well as a battery-powered light, gaffer tape and sand bags. That's a dozen in a nutshell. There will be more.

Remember that your battery-powered light will not cast far and works as a spot light, unless you have the option of using a white ceiling or reflector to bounce and soften it. Battery management is a real concern. If you're in a shadow area and it's hard to bounce sun into the subject, use a portable light and blue gels to match the temperature of the sun. If you are buying one, consider paying more for movable arms, gels, bulb life, sturdiness, weight and flexibility of use.

Summary: Seeing with New Eyes

Shooting in the great outdoors brings gold to your video production. After all, the viewer is sitting in a dark room, and nothing beats the allure of travel. Similarly, the performance of onscreen talent is often enlivened by being outdoors. But the importance of learning the four steps of outdoor lighting is that it gives you confidence. Like camping, if you bring the right gear, protect it and know when and how to use it, your crew, cast and client will appreciate your methodical approach to the whims of nature. While they may be distracted or overwhelmed, they will recognize that you're not seeing what they see. Your eye is set to see in a new way: adjusted to the lens of your camera.

Lights for Nights

High contrast is the definition of outdoor night scenes; the trick is to keep blacks rich and mid-tones exposed for detail. If you're working at night, scouting pays big rewards when you locate potential light sources within the shot. Keep in mind that wide-angle compositions open your iris and let more light into the camera. Of course, you can't always shoot wide, and thus you will get better images if you find ambient streetlight to bring up the background levels.

It's more practical and very realistic to create pools of light that mimic true night-time light. Gels can simulate sources and stimulate mood. Consider blue gel for the moon or colored tints to simulate emergency vehicles. Finally, avoid using video gain to increase your exposure, because it desaturates colors and increases tape noise. After all, you are simulating night! Remember, making the picture seem brighter destroys blacks and adds a haze, or noise, if you boost the signal with the gain control. If you must use it, don't go beyond +3 dB gain.

Whether you have electric outlets or need battery-powered illumination, remember that any light can be used in multiple ways. Take your three-point lighting principles into the field. Reflectors bounce a single key light and thus become the fill, if they're big enough. Frontal lighting is never a natural look, so turn your camera-mounted lights toward a reflector. But if you want the reality-TV or live newscast look, you're in luck with the headlight-on-the-camera position.

38
Audio Levels

Hal Robertson

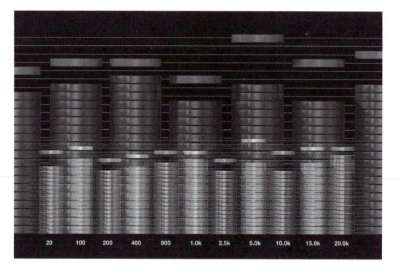

Figure 38-1

The popularity of HDSLRs, GoPros and other compact video cameras come with a new surge of interest in audio recording. Since many of these cameras record meager audio at best, it's become common to go the extra mile and record audio on another device such as a portable recorder or computer. With new gear comes new questions and this renewed focus on audio may have a few people scratching their heads about proper audio levels, monitoring and mixing. Good audio practices are important whether you use professional editing software or just record audio for YouTube.

By the Numbers

Audio recording equipment and software comes with its fair share of numbers and letters. Measurements are usually in decibels—abbreviated dB—but there are different reference levels, depending on your gear and where you are in the signal chain. You've probably seen the label 0 dB on home recording equipment, a cheap audio mixer or your music editing software, but 0 dB can be measured in different ways.

For instance, if you found an old analog audio recorder, it would probably have one of those retro needle-style meters. And, sure enough, there's 0 dB on the scale. But, depending on whether that recorder is consumer or professional, 0 dB could be one of two actual signal levels. On consumer gear, it references a .775 volt signal while the professional level is referenced to 1 volt. Now, a quarter of a volt may not seem like much, but in the audio world, it's pretty big—14 decibels big. If you suddenly added or subtracted 14 decibels from your audio signal, you'd notice it.

Back in analog times, we recorded on magnetic tape and could push the recording level past the 0 dB setting on a regular basis without any serious consequences. In fact, many recording engineers did just that to achieve "tape compression"—a mild overloading of the recording that usually provided a nice sound. This technique pushed the limits of the recorder and medium, but in the controlled circumstance of a studio, it was a calculated risk. If you'd like to hear an extreme example of analog tape overload, just listen to Led Zeppelin's "Whole Lotta Love." Around the four-minute mark, you'll hear a pre-echo of Robert Plant's voice just before he sings. This wasn't done in post. His voice was recorded so strong on the tape that the signal actually magnetized other tape layers below it on the reel.

Digital Days

Of course, today we record digital audio and it comes with its own set of rules. Digital audio has a hard ceiling that is measured as 0dBFS or 0dB full scale. Once you hit that level, there's nowhere else to go. Think of it this way. Let's assume we're recording in 16-bit resolution. That means that each digital sample is 16 digits long. At any given time,

any of those digits can be a one or a zero. When all 16 become ones, you can't add any more. That is 0dBFS. When you push the audio level beyond that point, digital clipping occurs. This produces nasty distortion that effectively ruins your recording during the clipping.

To avoid digital clipping, it's good practice to keep your recording levels well below the ceiling. A common setting is −10dBFS. This gives you some headroom for inevitable peaks and still keeps the signal loud enough to avoid noise. It's not exactly intuitive at first, but by standardizing on this level, you'll record consistently clean audio that is easy to work with in post.

As an added safety measure, dig through the audio menu of your camera or digital recorder. Many devices include a signal limiter of some kind. Normally, you want to record audio without any kind of processing—reserving that for post—but applying a limiter can save the day from time to time. Limiters only work when the signal reaches a certain level—usually 0dBFS. Any incoming signal level above that point is lowered to eliminate clipping. Most built-in limiters don't sound as good as their post-processing cousins, but they're only working on extreme levels and won't affect normal audio. A lower average recording level and a safety limiter is a powerful combination.

Back in the Suite

The term edit suite used to mean a dedicated space for editing audio and video. Things are a little fuzzier these days. An edit suite might be a laptop in the front seat of your car or a desk in the corner of a bedroom. In the corporate environment, your editing computer might be primarily used for word processing and spreadsheets. In any of these situations, audio monitoring is a secondary concern. However, if you have the convenience of a dedicated editing space, a proper audio monitoring setup is essential.

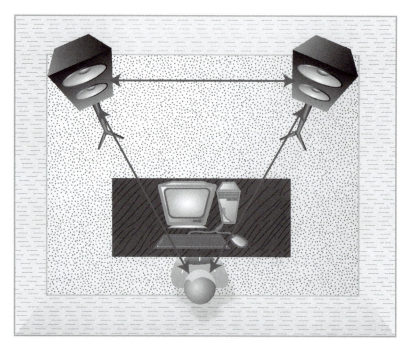

Figure 38-2 *Speakers in your edit suite should be set up away from walls and oriented toward your mix station, providing the best possible monitoring.*

A real edit suite would be set up much like a recording studio, with acoustic treatment, specialty speakers and equalizers to match the speakers to the room. But you can still get good results without spending a boatload of cash. If we rule out $20 media speakers from your local office supply store, or the freebies that came with your desktop, pretty much anything else could work. Your main criterion is trustworthy sound; something that sounds good with familiar material and won't wear you out after extended listening sessions. If possible, mount your speakers on stands, away from walls. This minimizes audio reflections and gives you a more accurate audio image. Stereo speakers should be set up in a triangle—with equal spacing between the speakers and your mix position. Whether you mix your audio using speakers or headphones, use conservative volume levels and compare your mix to "real" television shows.

This is a great reality check. Finally, if you can route your video mix to a TV, listen on those speakers too. Yes, they sound terrible, but this is how most people watch video. If your mix sounds good on the monitors in your edit suite and ordinary TV speakers, you have created a great mix.

And the Answer Is . . .

A lot of people have spent a great deal of time and money defining how loud is too loud. These standards are primarily for delivery—either through acoustic output or electronic measurement. But the concept carries all the way through the production process—from acquisition to final product. If you can keep your capture levels lower, monitor properly and deliver a product that plays well on all systems, you've pretty much answered the question already.

The CALM Act

In the past year, the FCC has implemented the Commercial Advertisement Loudness Mitigation or CALM Act. To boil it down, the CALM Act basically says that audio in commercials can't be any louder than the audio during normal programming. Television stations and cable operators are responsible for ensuring compliance. So you can still make your commercials as loud as you want, but the broadcaster has equipment in place that will turn it down to meet the new rules. Better to create your content with more realistic levels and preserve the quality of the mix.

39
10 Common Audio Mistakes

Hal Robertson

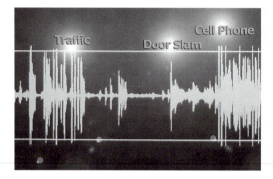

Figure 39-1

Let's be honest here. We've all botched an audio recording from time to time. It happens. While you can't be ready for every possible situation, you can avoid some of the more obvious problems. This issue, we're reviewing the 10 most common audio mistakes and how to fix them before they happen.

Recording with AGC

Automatic Gain Control, or AGC, is the nemesis of every video shooter. AGC is a special circuit that monitors the incoming audio level, decides what is too loud and too soft, and adjusts the recording level accordingly. What's wrong with that? AGC isn't very smart and works in real time. It can't predict what will happen next and only reacts to volume changes as they occur. This means that loud sounds will suddenly get softer while quiet sounds get cranked up until the noise is unbearable. If your camera has a manual audio level setting, use it. If not, you have to pay close attention to the recording to minimize the effects of AGC.

Background Noise Problems

Virtually every location has some background noise; there's just no way around it. While some background noise occurs

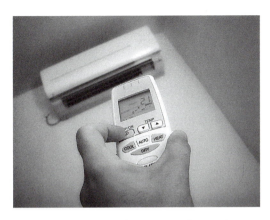

Figure 39-2 *Air conditioning units produce severe background noise that can ruin your audio. Try to turn off the unit 5 to 10 minutes before recording to avoid getting that constant "hum" that will ruin your otherwise pristine sound.*

naturally—traffic, birds, bugs and weather—many sounds can be controlled. For instance, refrigerators and freezers are usually easy to unplug. They'll stay cool long enough for your shoot and you won't have to worry about their compressors kicking in. Air conditioning systems make lots of noise too but, if it's not too hot or cold, you can turn them off temporarily. Don't forget to silence the cell phones and turn off the background music. Sometimes, the simplest way to eliminate background noise is to simply shut the door.

Wind Noise

Savvy outdoor shooters know that wind is the enemy. While foam windscreens are available for most microphones, a light breeze is about all they're good for. Any stronger wind and your audio will be ruined with rumbling noise similar to thunder or an earthquake. Fortunately, the fix is simple—a fur windscreen. Also available for most microphones, a fur windscreen can block much stiffer winds and salvage an otherwise impossible shoot. If you need to improvise a fur windscreen quickly, visit your local fabric or crafts store. Look through their

selection of craft fur and get a piece large enough to wrap around your microphone. A couple of ponytail holders and you've got a temporary windscreen that will minimize most wind noises.

Not Using Headphones

You're still not monitoring your recordings with headphones? Seriously? If your camera has a headphone jack, it's time to find a pair of headphones, leave them in your camera bag and use them on every shoot. While a nice pair of full, over-the-ear headphones is preferred, anything is better than nothing. This means your MP3 player earbuds can do double-duty in your shooting setup. With headphones, you'll hear hum and buzz, wind noise, catch shorts in cables, dead batteries and other audio problems before they're permanently recorded. Unfortunately, not every camera has a headphone jack. In these cases, try monitoring through a mixer or simply do a test recording and check it before the shoot.

Picking the Wrong Microphone

Imagine a crazy, urban skateboard video with a bluegrass soundtrack. It's just wrong and everyone knows it. The same can be true of your microphone choices. The choice of a mic is determined by situations that arise during the shoot or simply what you have on hand. It's hard to go wrong with a good shotgun mic in your bag. They work for interviews, dialogue, handheld use and even effects recording. If you're using other types of microphones, make sure they suit the situation. This simple step will improve both the visual and audio portion of your video.

Relying on the Built-in Mic

There are times when the built-in microphone is the right choice, but we're talking about birthday parties and vacations, not a production for a client. In those instances, you need to plug in an external microphone. Camera-handling noise, tape drives, zoom and focus motors all transmit sound directly into the built-in mic. Whether wired or wireless, an external microphone gets the pickup closer to the source and eliminates all the noises associated with your camera. Of course, not all cameras include a microphone jack. That's why portable recorders have gained popularity lately. It's an extra piece of gear, but for the results, they're worth investigating.

Picking Up Hum and Buzz

Many of the tools we use to make video also make noise that sneaks into the audio path. Power supplies, computer monitors and even lights all generate electromagnetic radiation. When your camera, audio recorder or audio cables are near these things, it's easy for hum and buzz to creep into the signal. To minimize or eliminate the noise, make sure your audio equipment and cabling is as far away from these noise makers as possible. If you can't keep the cables apart, try crossing them at 90 degree angles. Distance is important, too. Parallel cables separated by even a few inches can make a huge difference in hum and buzz pickup. Whatever you do, don't tape the power cables and your mic cables together. Bad idea.

Recording Levels

There's not much worse in the audio world than an overloaded digital recording. Sending too much signal to your camera or recording device results in nasty digital distortion and there's no way to eliminate it after it's recorded. At the other end of the scale, too little signal level on your recording makes it noisy. When you bring the level up in post, the noise may be too much to bear. Monitor your recording levels closely to get a good, healthy signal into the recorder. This will eliminate distortion and noise and make your editing job much easier.

Mic vs. Line Levels

Microphones put out a very small signal level. The mic preamp in your camcorder amplifies the signal to a level that's perfect for recording. If you plug a line level device—CD player, mixer, electronic keyboard, etc.—into the same mic jack, it amplifies that too, which can overload

Figure 39-3 *An all-round great microphone to have in your kit is a shotgun mic which works well in all types of situations.*

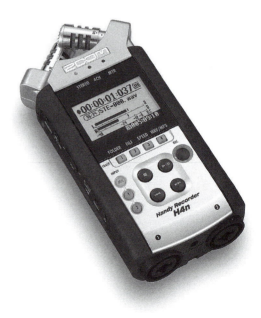

Figure 39-4 *A portable recorder like the Zoom H4n is worth its weight in gold and it's a good idea to have one on hand in your audio kit.*

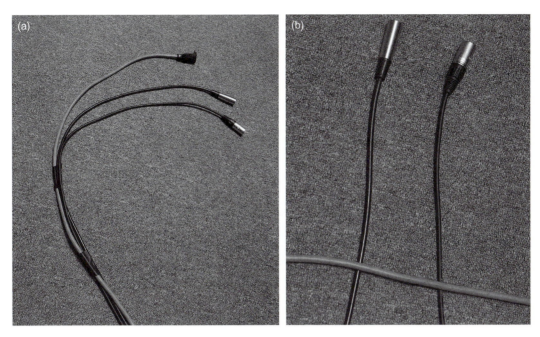

Figure 39-5 *Power cables often interfere with and distort the signal carried over audio cables. In order to avoid this, run the cables at 90 degree angles.*

the recorder. Make sure you keep your mic and line level signals sorted out and only attach them to the appropriate connections. If your camcorder has a mic/line switch or menu setting, learn how to use it. If you're using a mixer, send the proper level to your camera. You'll get nice, clean audio and make your post efforts easier.

Other Audio Foibles

The dictionary defines 'foible' as a slight flaw, defect or weakness. In the audio world there are times when things are close, but not quite right. For instance, you chose the right microphone but your positioning isn't quite right, making the audio muddy or indistinct. You've got strong audio levels, but they're just a little too strong, resulting in momentary distortion in your recording. Or, you minimized most of the background noise or hum, but it's still audible on the video. All of these foibles are avoided with some simple attention to detail before and during the shoot. Double check everything before you hit the record button and reduce the chance of these foibles during your next shoot.

Audio Options

We've mentioned it before, but the new handheld flash-based audio recorders are quickly becoming the new standard in audio gathering. The reasons are simple. They're small, run on batteries and record to flash memory. In addition, they offer options your camera might not have, like microphone and headphone jacks. Most have AGC and manual level control along with mic and line level inputs. Some even record surround sound. This is an excellent way to buy a serious audio upgrade for very little cash.

40
10 Tips for Great Interviews

Earl Chessher

Figure 40-1

There are many interview approaches and styles. Are you looking for a hardcore journalistic approach or something less intense? Will you casually guide interviewees or follow a defined path? Video interview techniques will vary depending on project intent and focus and interviewee personalities.

Whatever your intent, it's important to pay attention to the basics before moving on to interview sessions. Interview techniques are as diverse as the questions you ask your interviewees.

Don't become so involved during preparation and set up with the technical aspects that you overlook the needs of your interviewees. It's possible to have the perfect setup yet wind up with a bust.

These interview techniques and tips will help you avoid that.

Plan Your Interview Approach

Interview techniques and decisions you should consider:

- Using one camera or two?

- Shooting a one person production or with a crew?

- Interviewing free style with open-ended questions?

- Recording the question-and-response or response only?

- Capturing single or multiple takes for each question/response?

- Using an interview style of a person on the street, in a formal studio setting, or a casual/business home or office location?

- Making your interview style provocative, to get the real story or casual and informative?

- Shooting one-on-one with a single interviewee or several simultaneously?

Time Isn't Always on Your Side

Time is a crucial, even critical, factor when it comes to what needs to be done

Figure 40-2 *Time often isn't on your side, so as soon as possible, pack your camera case. A checklist and checking batteries and functionality can sure help here too.*

before and during interviews. It's impossible to avoid every delay and problem, but give yourself as much time as is realistically and economically feasible to get the interviews you need.

Take time to check and prepare equipment before you think about shooting interviews. Sure, that goes without saying, but too often too many video producers take equipment and batteries for granted. Given the opportunity, this stuff will let you down. Don't show up for interviews and discover your mic is missing, batteries are dead or you left your notes on the kitchen counter.

Preparing the Interviewee

Having jammed up on interview techniques and tips, you're ready to put them to work. You've made notes to help guide the interviewees.

The first thing to do is prepare your interviewees so they know what to expect and what is expected of them. Good interview techniques include content and visuals. Discuss the topic focus and interview process with your subjects. Know your topic and your interviewees.

Time is the measure. Focus tightly on questions and anticipated responses. You should plan with an open schedule and plenty of time to allow for wandering off-script or even an extended session for extra content.

Put Them at Ease

It's hard to conduct positive interviews if you appear too aggressive. Some interviewers have been at this for a long time. Their reputations precede them. If you've developed interview techniques for hardcore, gritty interview style, your interviewees may arrive with defensive attitudes or chips on their collective shoulders. On the other hand you and your subjects may have had very little exposure, experience or notoriety. Either way, most interviewers will discuss the purpose of their session with their subjects.

Except in a person-on-the-street interview, you should know the general questions you intend to ask and discuss them in a pre-production session. It's a better idea to prepare well in advance, providing your subjects with notes and question sheets prior to scheduled interviews.

Stay courteous, genuine and personable. Exuding an air of antagonism or judgmental attitude at the start is a sure way to sabotage your interviews. Essentially, regardless of your programming, interview style or provocative content or intent, being nice will put your interview subject at ease.

Using a Stand-in During Setup

Setting up prior to your interviewee's arrival is a good approach but that isn't always possible. Maybe you're conducting impromptu interviews on the sidewalk or in a public place. There's not much planning you can do during a run-and-gun session or reality-show style production.

With studio, office or controlled location interviews it's great to have assigned help, with crew acting as stand-ins while setting up lights and audio while you prepare your interviewees. Good interview techniques work hand-in-hand with most directing tips, as interviews are often as much a performance as entertainment productions.

When They Look Great, or Not

Always advise your subjects regarding desired physical grooming, proper colors and what to wear. Of course if you're interviewing any person-on-the-street or sabotage-style interview, you're going to go with what you get. But if you're interviewing an authority on the benefits of higher education, you're not going to suggest wearing what he or she had on after mowing the lawn.

Occasionally you'll have to make do when, regardless of suggestions, interviewees show up not looking or dressing as desired. In a studio it is often good to have a few casual jackets in different sizes to hide the T-shirt and jeans combo, or sweaters, scarves and other clothing accessories to dress up or down for the right look in an emergency.

Use angle, posture and powder for ways to approach improvements. People want to look their best as a rule. Rarely will they be offended if you genuinely focus on making that happen.

How Did I Do? May I See It?

Other interview techniques and tips should always be what to do when your subjects want to see the results or themselves on the monitor. There's a broad range of possible reactions to being told no, you can't. As a rule you don't want this to happen for reasons ranging from poor eye contact or angle as they watch themselves on the monitor, to being second-guessed by subjects regarding how they look, sound or perceive themselves.

Talk about this prior to interviews. Explain about the eyes-on-the-monitor syndrome or time and scheduling restraints making it difficult to evaluate each and every session. Mileage will vary

Figure 40-3 Having an assortment of outerwear and accessories will help your talent look great, because his or her favorite green striped shirt may be inappropriate for green screen or produce a moire pattern.

based on who's paying for the production or the program's purpose and intent. Vanity can also rear its perplexing head. Verbal encouragement and reassurances can help avoid potential problems. "Great session! Looking good!" Sounds sappy and spurious; sometimes calmly stating, "That's exactly what I wanted," without exclamation points, will suffice.

When the Producer Wears All the Hats

Producers that wear all the hats: interviewer, shooter, grip, lighting, audio; face unique challenges. Again, time is key. Schedule additional time that is required for doing it all single-handedly.

Discuss sessions in advance. Share the Q&A sheet and anticipated responses ahead of time. Set up early. Be ready to move into interviews quickly. Keep downtime to a minimum by being ready and pushing the agenda with confidence. Let nothing interfere with your primary objective: great interview sessions with quality audio and video.

A Little Help's a Big Help

It helps if you can afford or acquire a volunteer crew. One additional body makes a big difference, someone to handle setup while you prepare interviewees saves time. Time is money. Getting more done in less time by bringing in crew for audio and video reduces risk of fatigue or overrunning the clock. Crewing up isn't always a matter of money. It's often a matter of friends, family, wannabes or networking with other video producers.

A Well-known Secret

Shooting video is usually exciting. Preparing to shoot video often isn't. Editing video is fun for most of us, preparing to edit usually isn't. The catch to having fun with all this video stuff, including recording interviews, is—it takes preparation. This is the part of what we do that most of us wish would go away!

An underlying theme of many *Videomaker* articles is managing your time by being prepared and informed. This strongly applies to acquiring great interviews instead of mediocre or disastrous ones. See the associated sidebar, "All-Time Greatest Interviews" for some interesting study sources. You don't get great interviews by being a run-and-gun videographer operating on serendipity with large doses of luck. The impulse to get to the fun stuff is huge but take some time to prepare yourself. Solid video interview techniques will put you on top of your game.

All-Time Greatest Interviews

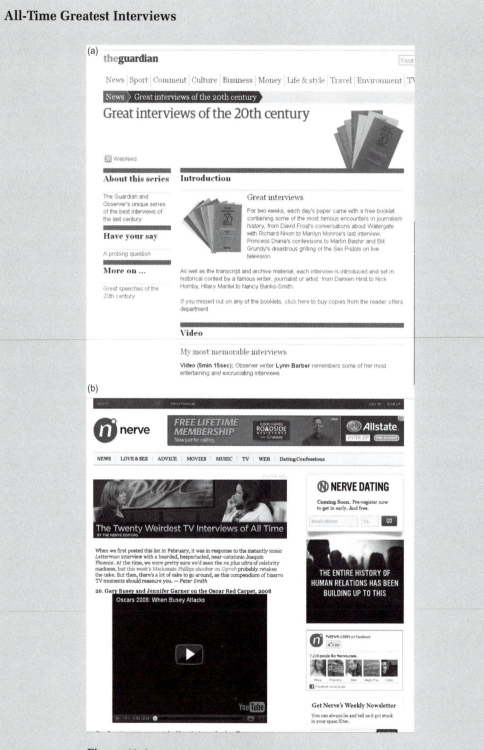

Figure 40-4

When researching to study interview techniques you don't have to go very far on Google to discover the *Guardian* website and its great interviews of the twentieth century.

In the top spot you'll find Richard Nixon interviewed by David Frost followed by Diana, Princess of Wales interviewed by Martin Bashir, John Lennon interviewed by Jann S.

Wenner, Marlon Brando interviewed by Truman Capote and Dennis Potter interviewed by Melvyn Bragg.

Others on the list include Francis Bacon, Marilyn Monroe, Malcolm X, Adolf Hitler, F. Scott Fitzgerald, Margaret Thatcher, Fidel Castro, Mae West and what the *Guardian* calls Bill Grundy's disastrous grilling of the Sex Pistols on live television.

On the other side of TV interviews is the "Twenty Weirdest TV Interviews of All Time" compiled by Nerve.com editors featuring some interviews that went seriously wrong.

Among the TV personalities often noted for their interview successes or disasters are David Letterman, Conan O'Brien, Dick Cavett, Tom Snyder, Jim Rome, Oprah Winfrey and of course Barbara Walters.

Interviews in this "Twenty Weirdest" include Russell Tyrone Jones, Andy Kaufman, Jerry Lawler, James Brown, Adam West and Farrah Fawcett, along with Tom Cruise, Crispin Glover, Whitney Houston, Paula Abdul and Mike Tyson.

Finally, Toli Galanis, a New York University journalism graduate on quora.com, names C-SPAN's Brian Lamb "best in class" citing Lamb's talent for "staying out of the interview process, as it should be" and suggesting, "If you study his methods, you will mostly notice questions devoid of inflection, frame, presupposition or agenda—a rare thing." Galanis also mentions Richard Heffner from "The Open Mind" with more than 50 years in public television and Real Sports with Bryant Gumbel, suggesting that these interviewers are worth studying.

A whole world of interviewing history, techniques, styles, with class and with crass is available for video producers who want to pump up their video interview techniques.

41
Makeup and Wardrobe

Bill Davis

Figure 41-1

I remember watching an interview on television that featured a world famous supermodel. During the interview, she said something that surprised me. "I sure wish I looked like that." The picture she was talking about was a major magazine cover featuring her. She went on to explain that the picture was the result of hours of careful work by a team of professionals including both wardrobe and makeup stylists.

It reminded me that no matter how good someone looks naturally, there are "tricks of the trade," that can help make them look even better. In that spirit, let's take a close look at wardrobe and makeup — two of the most overlooked elements that can enhance the look of your videos.

Figure 41-2 *Wardrobe worries: Always be aware of the wardrobe in which your talent is dressed. Traditionally, deep reds don't hold up well in video. Even as technology improves, reds have a tendency to bleed. Also, tight patterns can make your viewers seasick with the moiré effect. Blue tones have a pleasant lighting quality while details are completely lost in solid black.*

Dress for Success

In movies, academy awards are given out for doing an excellent job of finding or creating precisely the right clothes for the cast of a movie. For most of us, costuming for our videos is nowhere near that difficult. In fact, in most cases we just shoot whatever our "actors" happen to show up wearing.

But if you want your videos to be as good as they can possibly be, you should never leave any important element to chance. And wardrobe is certainly no exception.

After all, the clothing your actors wear can have a big effect on the technical quality of your video. Remember that your camera is a light-gathering device. Depending on the amount of light that strikes the image sensor, the iris will need to open or closed to achieve the proper exposure. This technical truth means that the wardrobe you choose can literally change what your camera needs for a good exposure.

Think about it. If the actor is wearing a pure white T-shirt, that shirt is reflecting the maximum amount of light back into the camera lens. Confronted with this bright subject, the iris closes. Everything else in the scene gets correspondingly darker, the background, the foreground and, even worse, the very face of your subject. This will particularly problematic if your subject has dark skin. When the iris is adjusted to expose the white shirt, everything else in the shot becomes darker, and dark colored items may become lost in blackness, including your subject's face. All this is simply because the major element in the scene, the talent's T-shirt is white.

And, of course, the opposite is true. Put a light-skinned talent in a navy blue or black shirt, adjust the exposure for the dark shirt, and white objects will be over exposed and blown out. For these reasons, it's best to put your talent in clothing that falls in the medium range of brightness and hue. Pastel colors work particularly well in video. As do medium grays and blues since the light reflecting qualities of shades such as these help you establish a good exposure.

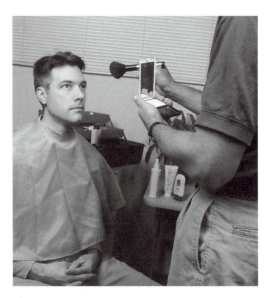

Figure 41-3 *Touch ups—you can see the makeup on a person in regular lighting. However, when they're under the lights, it's nearly invisible, with the effect of warming skin tones and highlighting facial features.*

Check Out Checks

The relative brightness of your cast's wardrobe isn't the only factor that can help or hurt your video. Some kinds of clothing patterns look just terrible on video. Thin spaced lines or small repetitive patterns can cause a distracting moiré pattern to appear in your shots. Moiré areas are where the picture seems to crawl or vibrate with a rainbow-like pattern. If you see moiré develop while you're shooting, you can often get rid of it by either zooming in or out. But if you need to zoom back later, the problem will re-occur. Clothing can also have an effect on how the audience perceives your subject. If a person is supposed to be a successful businessman and he's on screen wearing a poorly-cut, ill-fitting or out-of-style suit, you'll have a hard time convincing your audience to take his business advice seriously.

Just Make it Up

A large percentage of the population (typically women) wear makeup every day. Professional directors wouldn't dream of shooting screen actors without makeup. In the professional realm, not wearing makeup is just not an option. So it's surprising that more videographers don't use this valuable tool to enhance the look of people appearing in their videos.

Most of the time the natural look is best, and very little makeup is necessary. The goal is merely to minimize distracting elements such as skin blemishes and provide your talent with a smooth, healthy look. While every drug store carries hundreds of shades of makeup, you might be surprised to learn that many of these tones are decidedly video unfriendly.

If you've been making videos for any length of time, you already know that what the camera sees is often very different from what is perceived by the

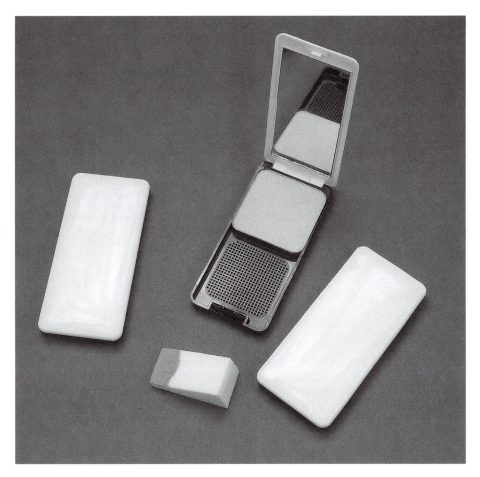

Figure 41-4 *Safety first! One area that's particularly important to understand when applying makeup is sanitation. Since makeup tools are commonly used in sensitive areas such as around the eyes, it's quite possible to spread germs and even infections if the same application tool is used for more than one subject. There are plenty of safe and inexpensive ways to keep things sanitary. Disposable makeup sponges are readily available in any drug store. Always think safety first, and make "one tool equals one person" a rule you live by.*

human eye. According to Mary Wright, a Phoenix-based professional makeup artist who's plied her trade for a gamut of celebrities including Michael Jordan, Annette Funicello, and even Scary Spice, the pros go to great lengths to carefully match the makeup they use with the kind of lighting that will be in use.

"Some types of light that look fine to the eye, can look greenish, golden or reddish to a camera. Makeup can work the same way. By applying makeup with the wrong base tones, you can conceivably make a shot that looks good to the naked eye look very wrong on camera," she said.

Avoid makeup that incorporates green hues if you'll be working under fluorescent lights. If you're shooting outdoors and have white balanced your camera for daylight and are using a lamp—which is more golden—to provide fill light, makeup with strong yellow tones can make talent look ill and jaundiced. For these reasons, professionals typically use specially formulated video and film makeup that avoids color tones that can cause on-camera problems.

Makeup Basics

Along with establishing a smooth foundation, you need to consider whether your
talent has any serious cosmetic flaws. If
someone has a distracting facial blemish
there are concealers available that can
diminish or even eliminate the appearance of these visual challenges from
showing up on screen. It's important
to match these cosmetics with the subject's skin tones. Fortunately there are
literally thousands of shades of makeup
allowing for a good match with the natural complexion of nearly any subject
you're likely to videotape. Professional
makeup artists carry a bewildering array
of makeup shades to match the wide
array of skin tones that are reflected in
our diverse society, but for the beginner,
a few neutral shades that compliment the
likely complexions of your cast members
or interview subjects should be fine.

Along with the makeup itself, you'll
need the tools with which to properly
apply it. Small sponges, soft brushes for
powder, and fine brushes for work around
the eyes are all tools that every makeup kit
will typically contain. So too are plenty
of tissues and makeup removal products
to help clean up after you yell, "That's a
wrap!"

Going beyond these basics and using
makeup to create highlights, shadows and
colors and to help enhance, diminish and
define facial features is beyond the scope
of this chapter. However, spending some
time learning the basics of video-friendly
wardrobe and practicing the application
of on-screen makeup, you will be prepared when it's time to turn your camcorder toward a person who needs to look
their best.

Figure 41-5 *Executive makeup: in many
cases, the most difficult subjects for makeup
will be male corporate executives, industry
leaders and other men in significant positions.
For them, using makeup might be perceived
as "phony" or less than masculine. When you
find yourself in this situation, communication
and tact are critical. First, it's important
to help them understand why makeup is
important. Calmly explain that hot video
lights can make people perspire and that
leads to an unsightly condition that a little
light powder can help avoid. If they still
object, remind them that people associate
perspiration with nerves and nervousness with
dishonesty. That usually does the trick. Once
they agree to use makeup, it's critical to apply
it quickly, efficiently and professionally. If at
all possible, leave the office or set and apply
the makeup somewhere privately. Avoid the
possibility of making an executive feel foolish
in front of his or her staff by having them
watch during a makeup application.*

42
How to Make a Documentary

Randal K. West

Few other communication forms have the power to reveal a unique perspective, capture imagination and even motivate change. We break down the process of how to make a documentary into three parts so you can discover how to move your story from dreaming your documentary concept, fulfilling the dream and sharing your vision through distribution.

To Dream a Possible Dream

Walk onto the working set of any television production studio and almost every person on the crew has a documentary they are shopping around, getting ready to shoot, or trying to fund. Why? Because everyone from the director of photography to the key grip has a story to tell, they feel compelled to share their stories with a larger audience.

True, the percentage of would be documentary filmmakers is potentially greater within the film/television community than among antique car salesmen, but there are many people from all walks of life who want to share their story or a significant piece of history through documentary filmmaking. In today's world dominated by high tech gizmos and reality TV, documentaries have never been more popular and the equipment to shoot and edit them more accessible and inexpensive.

Is Your Story Compelling?

The founder of our agency and I were approached one day by a reasonably well-known and respected individual in our community. He wanted to pitch a documentary idea to us for possible

Figure 42-1

production by our company. The man went on to explain that although he still seemed to exist as a "regular" guy in our community, since his divorce he had lost everything and was living between his car and an abandoned building. We asked many questions, but despite his having managed to hide his status from the rest of the community, there just wasn't a strong enough plot line to hang a documentary on. We felt horrible for the guy but there was no universal truth, no significant lesson to be learned that we felt warranted filming a documentary.

Two months later a woman named Patti Miller came to my office and described how 40 years ago as a Drake University junior, she had traveled to Mississippi to participate in the Freedom Summer, in order to help African Americans sign up to vote. Patti, "a lily-white Iowa girl" was fundamentally affected by her experience, an experience shared by others who had participated. She pointed out that the fortieth anniversary of Freedom Summer was approaching and many of the volunteers were now in their fifties and sixties. Patti's story was a part of history that could easily start to slip away and the 40-year anniversary presented a seminal opportunity to share the story. The story moved me, and my crew and I headed to the South to start filming. Patti's story had universal appeal and importance. We decided that we would tell this story of national racism, politically controlled hatred, and the individuals who fought oppression, through the very personal eyes of one Iowa undergraduate female, alone and out of her home state for the first time in her life.

Tell Me a Story

What's your story? Is it universally applicable? Is it simply a slice of life anecdote, but very funny or very profound? Would someone who doesn't know you care or benefit from becoming aware of your story? Is it a scholarly piece addressing an issue or topic discovered through research and others should be made aware of? Could others benefit by seeing the world through your eyes, watching you follow a particular person or group of people around as they do what they do? If you can find a way to turn your personal experience into a universally shared or recognized experience, you have the foundation for building a documentary. At this point, identify your eventual audience and keep them in mind as your documentary morphs toward its final form.

Putting it Together, Bit by Bit

So, you've got your story, now what? Old fashioned as it may seem, try to get all the elements of your story written down in simple outline form using 3 × 5 index cards. Keep it loose and put each element on one 3 × 5 card so you can shuffle and re-shuffle them. Lay your story out and look at it. Examine all your possible elements. (Of course, you can do this with a computer too, but the index cards work well for sorting out thoughts and ideas.)

If you have old 8 mm film from your youth, log it and list it as an element. Do you have old photos or access to old newspaper articles? Who are the people you want to interview and what subject mater will they cover? Record every element and every topic on a card and separate the cards with only one topic or element per card. Lay them out in an order that makes sense to you and use this to create your first outline. Keep these cards! You will use them over and over again.

Dramatic Structure

Every story needs three things, a beginning, middle, and end. You must define where these points exist in your story. Does your story have a great hook that will involve the audience from the outset and

Figure 42-2 You may not have used index cards since grade school, but they are a great tool to help you and your creative team pre-visualize the project.

Figure 42-3 How will your finished piece look or how do you hope it will look? Storyboards or large sketches will further help you communicate with your crew to assure everything proceeds as smooth as possible once the camera starts rolling.

hold them? Is it most effective when told chronologically or should it jump around in time? Will your story be narrated? Will you write the narration, or will the subjects you interview tell the entire story in their own words? Will it be a combination? You must discover what is most dramatic and engaging about your story and tell it in a way that highlights those points.

Tone and Treatment

How do you want your story heard? Do you want to create a formal documentary with voice-over narration and drops to interviews and B-roll, or do you want to do a Cinéma Vérité piece where the camera seems to just exist as it captures everything around it? Many documentaries

these days have the raw reality look of the "Cops" TV show with handheld cameras loosely carried on shoulders. Other documentaries use guerilla tactics; they surprise people by simply shoving a microphone in their face. Michael Moore is famous for this.

An Emotional Center

Regardless of your choice of treatment or subject matter, almost every documentary needs an emotional center. The audience needs someone or a group of "someones" to care about. A message or idea is not enough. The characters in your documentary will carry your plotline as strongly as your storyline. Very few documentaries based solely on intellectualism succeed. Give your documentary some heart and some emotion. Give us someone to root for.

Formulating a Plan

As soon as you have determined the structure and treatment of your documentary, you are ready to take your outline and create a projected timeline and budget. In order to create a budget you must decide the format in which you want to shoot your project. Will you shoot film or video? What type? How often will you need sound? Will you be lighting with instruments or will you be shooting in available light? How many days and in how many locations will you need to shoot? How big a crew and how much equipment will you need? How long and with what means will you edit?

After you answer these questions, you will be in the best position to get close to a bid for creating your project.

Go Find Some Funding

Collect your outline, timeline, bid and distribution plan (distribution will be fully covered in part three of this series but it must be fully fleshed out in your pre-production planning if you wish to raise funds from someone other than your parents or credit cards). Create a printed proposal using these elements to pass for your fund-raising efforts to support your project. Documentary film budgets can run the gamut from low-budget to multi-million dollar ventures, but many make it on a very limited amount of hard capital. Documentary filmmakers as a group are notoriously successful at getting "sweat equity" from people who volunteer their equipment and their expertise for a stock in

Figure 42-4 *A detailed budget is an extremely important part of your pre-production planning. You don't want to be halfway through your project to realize the funding is depleted. Factor in every possible expenditure and then add a 1% contingency.*

the project. There will always be some hard costs though, and if you are not in a position to cover them yourself you should see an attorney and get help setting up a simple system that will enable you to accept funds on behalf of your not for profit project. Some filmmakers seek financial support by asking existing non-profit organizations to sponsor their project, then take in the funds, and allocate them back to the filmmaker.

Figure 42-5

Fulfillment of the Dream

Considered an art form by many, documentary video production has its own special challenges and rewards. In this part of this story on how to make a documentary, we'll explore how to plan your approach, find your subject and begin the process of bringing your vision to fruition.

Once you've chosen your topic for your documentary, you still have many choices facing you. How do you want to approach your subject? Will your documentary seem to have a passive feel? Will the story be told by the people who are interviewed as the story comes out in their own way, or will an aggressive interviewer (e.g., Michael Moore) drive the interviews, or will you mix interviews with written narration to be delivered in voice-over? Will your documentary be a balanced view of an issue where both sides are equally and fairly explored? What criteria should help you make these decisions?

Point of View

Whose story is it really? You can choose to not have a "voice" in your documentary and make it "news" style and as impartial as possible, or you can choose the individual or group that is most affected by your story and let it be

their story. This doesn't mean you can't explore both sides of an issue; it just means that you are going to put a real face on one side of the issue and allow them to personalize the story. A compelling documentary should not only be factually correct, but it should be engaging and emotionally compelling. You can also personalize both sides of a story. We have said for years in the advertising business, "don't just sell the steak, sell the sizzle." Find the sizzle in your story, because that is what is going to eventually get you distribution, and remember that even a personal story should have some universal appeal.

Sound Issues

Never take sound for granted. Nothing ruins a video that is shot on a budget quicker than bad sound. I always fight to get a sound person who is solely responsible for sound, because it is that important to me. If we truly can't have the extra body, I will listen for sound as I direct, as I don't feel a camera operator can split his attention well enough to both shoot and listen effectively at the same time. That said, there have been times when I have both shot and monitored sound; you just increase your percentage chance of having a problem. Use a lapel mic on the person you are interviewing and if possible put a pole mic on the other channel right out of your shot. Blending these

Figure 42-6 *Sound matters. Pay attention to your setup, and shoot on location for great emotional reactions.*

two microphones together in post will give you a rounder and fuller sound. If you only have access to one mic, make sure the sound is as pristine as possible. Listen to the room before you shoot and turn off air changers if you can. Also take the time to record room tone (everyone sitting in the room making no noise for 30 seconds) or outside ambient sound, as this will help your editor remove background noise in post.

Shooting

If you don't know the camera well, you can probably survive mostly on factory settings. You do want to be aware of the iris setting and watch for backlight that becomes overwhelming. Always white balance every time you change locations. When in doubt, keep your shots simple and clean. As you gain confidence you can shoot "walk and talks," but when you're just starting out, find a safe, pretty environment to shoot.

Conducting Interviews

I rarely have a subject speak directly to the camera. Unless they are doing a direct

appeal to the people watching the video, they should not speak directly to the lens. Sit directly next to the lens, either to the left or right with your eyes at the same height as the lens, and have them speak directly to you. Don't feel like you have to just jump right into the subject of the interview. If you don't know them, spend some time getting acquainted. Ask about what they like to do. Find out who they are and then lead them into the subject you want. The cheapest component of your project is the videotape, so let it roll. This is a technique to make them feel more at home in front of the camera, but sometimes you also discover gems you didn't think you'd find. Also, listen! Don't be so wrapped up in the questions that you have planned to ask that you don't listen to what is actually being said. Ask unscripted follow-up questions and closely explore their reactions. Let them control some of the content of your interview. Be very open to finding a surprise and letting it blossom into something wonderful.

B-roll

Keep track of everything your interviewer says and keep in mind possible B-roll shots that could highlight this dialogue. A-roll is when the camera is on the subject and the words are coming out of their mouths. B-roll is footage without sound that is shot to break up the talking head portions of an interview and is inserted in place of the talking head during the postproduction process.

Documentaries rely on old pictures or licensed stock footage many times, but those elements can be expensive even for smaller projects and the licensing can limit how and where you can show the finished piece. Reenactments are a way to create footage that can help fill the needs of the project. If you are doing a piece about the 1960s, you can find old civic buildings that

Figure 42-7 *Shoot plenty of cutaways and angles. Your B-roll shots will be invaluable for insertion over your interview audio.*

still look as if they are in the 1960s. Go to someone's attic or to a thrift store, locate appropriate wardrobe, and create your own footage. You can pull this footage into sepia tones or make it black and white in post. You can blend this created footage with the old photos you can find and it will give the piece a sense of movement.

Discovery in the Moment

If your documentary is taking a person back to an event or a moment that changed his/her life, if you can afford it, don't just talk about it but go there. Shoot the first time they see this place after so many years and let them just describe what and how they feel. If there is a significant person who helped them at one time, don't just talk about it. Shoot them meeting again, and get the energy of that exact moment.

Finding your Vision

Every documentary should begin as a blank sheet of paper or a canvas to paint upon. What colors you use and what format should come from a combination of you as an artist and the content of your story. Content should always dictate form, but you are in this equation as well and it will be your passion that drives this project. Five filmmakers could attempt the same topic for a documentary and each would most likely create a piece that only resembles the others by subject matter and that is as it should be. Find what excites you, then find your own means to express it.

Figure 42-8 *Go back to the location where pivotal events happened within your story to give your audience some additional perspective.*

Share the Dream

You found the "story" that needed to be told, you scraped together enough funding to shoot and post it and now you have an end product that you and your small circle of best friends think is great. But now what? Our final look at making your documentary shows you several ways of getting your story seen by the masses.

Festivals are one of the first places you should look to get your project noticed. Start by building lists of potential places to show your film and group these into at least two categories: festivals that are well known and often lead to distribution, and festivals that are grouped by production type or topic (i.e., an all female film festival if your work was all done by women, or a film festival that celebrates stories from the South for documentary about Freedom Summer in Mississippi). Most festivals will charge admission and you need to count this as a loss even if your film doesn't make the selection cut.

Your Own Backyard

Look locally. There are at least 15 film festivals each year here in Iowa that feature projects created within the state. Contact your state (or even county) Film Commission to get a list of all the local film festivals. If you can, speak with someone in the film office and tell him or her about your film. Their job is to promote films produced in state, so allow them to offer their suggestions for local distribution and attention. (This *Videomaker* forums page lists US Film Offices by state, is a good place to start: www.videomaker.com/community/forums/topic/us-film-offices-by-state.)

Public Television

Accessibility to public television will vary greatly from state to state and even regionally. Iowa, for example, has a very developed public television programming department that is very accommodating in terms of providing information and support for our documentaries. They even offered seed monies for one of our projects, but we decided to self-fund and maintain complete rights until the project was completed. They did, however, refer us to ITVS (Independent Television Service), which is a service that assists filmmakers and showcases independent producers.

Figure 42-9

Unfortunately, much of what you have heard about the state of public television is probably true. They still seek first-quality programming and though open to documentaries, they are no longer the land of "milk and money." Public television has become quite dependent upon grant and gift monies to support project funding.

Cable Distribution and Television Syndication

What cable outlet or broadcast channel is the best possible match for your project? As more and more channels become available, the appeal of each channel becomes more selective and niche oriented. Many cable channels run a high level of documentary programming and much of it is tied to a very specific topic (E Entertainment, Style, the History Channel, Bravo). Some cable channels are connected to entire cable networks. The Discovery Channel is a flagship cable station connected to 14 other cable channels including Animal Planet, The Learning Channel, the Travel Channel, and FitTV. If you contact the Discovery Channel distribution office they can send you the required forms for submission and will help move your material to the proper cable outlet.

The internet

The internet is exploding with showcase opportunities. Many websites allow for very extensive streaming video. Does your project relate to or help clarify some aspect of someone else's website? Could a portion of your documentary play on their website via streaming video and then be offered for purchase? Do you have your own website where you can sell your end product? If not, and your documentary is one that people might purchase if they knew it existed, you probably should be selling it through a website. Make sure the site is clean and simple and has a shopping cart that allows others to purchase your documentary in a variety of either downloadable formats or DVD.

Vidcasting

Vidcasting (also known as video podcasting, vodcasting, and other names) is different from streaming. It is a method of transmitting up to broadcast quality video via an RSS feed (Really Simple Syndication) to a computer. This method of video sharing provides a low-cost, broad and immediate marketplace for video distribution by enabling users to

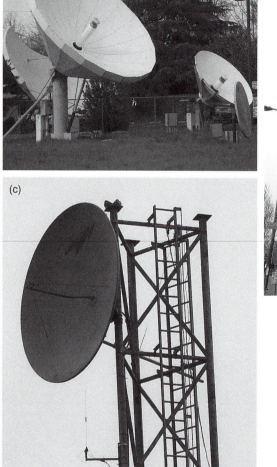

Figure 42-10 *A satellite uplink sends video to a satellite; a microwave dish sends video to a TV transmitter and movie theatres send video straight to the viewer.*

receive continuous, high quality updates directly to their personal computer. Independent producers and filmmakers can benefit greatly from this technology as it enables them to cut out the middleman and make their videos instantly accessible to a wide audience at TV broadcast quality.

Independent filmmaking especially documentary filmmaking is by nature a challenging area of video production and finding a viable distributor presents a special challenge all of its own. If you are new to the documentary arena, this is an opportunity for others to see examples of your work and for your exposure to networking and marketing opportunities. If you are ready to start selling or marketing your work, you can create a sample or a trailer of your documentary and encourage those

Figure 42-11 *A well-designed website may be the best tool available to get your project in front of thousands of eyes across the globe.*

who see your sample to go to your website to purchase the entire piece.

Educational Video

An internet search for educational videos will bring up a substantial list of catalogs and services that specialize in videos and documentaries appropriate for classroom and educational purposes. If your documentary qualifies as a possible option in one of these catalogs, it would certainly be worth a study-guide for your documentary if they request one.

Finding Funds for Distribution

Fundraising to help find distribution outlets and marketing opportunities for your project is different from looking for "seed" money. You already have a relatively finished end product and now you simply need help finding ways to get people to see it. In our small town, there are many known businesses that routinely give to special projects. The cost of underwriting the marketing for your documentary will probably not be that much more expensive than underwriting a good-sized event for your town or for an organization.

Take your outline, your budget and a one-page synopsis of your project which includes not only your subject matter but why your "subject matters," along with possible areas for distribution to the meeting. If you can create a short 3–4 minute DVD that can function as a sample reel of your documentary, it can be a very motivating portion of your pitch. Take a portable DVD player to the meeting just in case. Have a detailed marketing plan for your project that shows all the festivals you plan to enter, all the ways you want to present your documentary, and the costs for this exposure.

You don't need a formal business plan at this point, unless you are truly attempting to raise a substantial amount of money. If that is the case you will need to create a formal business plan that includes projections for how the money will be returned to those who invest. Many documentary filmmakers have been very successful at raising dollars in support of their endeavor while promising no more than a credit listed at the start and finish of the documentary. PBS won't allow much more than a simple acknowledgement of support. You do however need to know how you plan to accept the funds if an individual or a company offers them to you. If PBS partners with us on one of our projects, anyone wishing to donate to the project designates the funds as a gift or

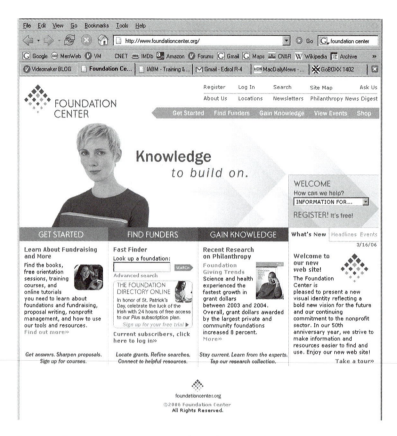

Figure 42-12 *Organizations such as the Foundation Center can assist video producers with fundraising right from the internet. (www.foundationcenter.org).*

grant to Iowa PBS. PBS then re-allocates the funds back to the project. Sometimes the organization which functions as the "pass-through" will charge a "processing" percentage to cover their time and effort.

Last Thoughts

We have now traveled the full course of documentary filmmaking. We have discussed finding a subject, defining your style, the technical requirements for bringing that vision to video, and how to market that video to a group of people. Like any artist or craftsman, you are now equipped with the necessary tools of your trade. We look forward to one day hearing some breathless documentary filmmakers at the Academy Awards stating how an article in *Videomaker* helped get them started. Hey, we can dream too, you know!

Budgeting

Once you have made the initial choices about your documentary you will need to create a budget that reflects accurate estimates of the costs involved. First estimate how many days of shooting it will take to film your documentary. Divide the total into days when you will record sound and days when you will just shoot images. In the industry, they call this type of film/video budgeting as defining your "Day of Days." Create a proposed set of crew costs for both types of days. Even if your crew is volunteer, you will still need to consider food, travel and ancillary costs. Next create a list of equipment for each type of day and project any "real" or "hard" costs. Determine if you will have to rent support equipment, (sound, lights, etc.,) and get estimates for this equipment that you can put in your budget. Will you have to get permits or insurance to shoot in any of your locations? Include these and any projected expendables such as videotape, in your projected budget.

If you plan to use much of your own equipment (camera, editing system) and these will not constitute "hard" costs in your budget, create an "in-kind" contribution section of the budget that demonstrates the savings created by your "sweat-equity" (volunteered hours), and owned equipment. This is helpful when soliciting contributions to cover the remaining "hard costs" because potential investors can see exactly where you allocate their contributions. Create a post-production budget and be sure to include both editing time and costs for licensing stock footage, existing film footage, photos or music.

Video/film budget templates exist on the internet that can help you create your budget. Just be sure to eliminate any line items that don't apply to your project.

Why Doc?

Documentary filmmaking is the art of telling real stories in imaginative, entertaining, and insightful ways. A documentary can retell an old story with a new twist, or present a never before heard of issue, person, place, or event that has universal appeal. It can be fair and impartial, presenting both sides of a split issue, or pure propaganda. A documentary provides its audience with an intimate look into the lives and worlds of the people and places captured therein. There are documentaries that explore major historical events and ancient civilizations, documentaries that take us from the bottom of the ocean to the top of Mt. Everest, works that can show us the lives of a local quilting group, or teach us to ride the most powerful and impressive ocean waves. Documentary filmmaking is about finding a subject that you are passionate about and using the medium of video/film to share that passion with a larger audience. The key to finding a good subject for your documentary is starting with a personal experience or opinion that you know is shared or opposed by others, and finding a way to educate your audience about that subject in an entertaining and thought-provoking way.

Release Me

Devising an effective paper trail for your project is not the most fun you'll ever have as a documentary filmmaker, but it is an essential step for avoiding potentially costly legal suits. It doesn't matter if everyone appearing in your documentary is a friend or family member, but you should still have them sign a simple release allowing you to use their name and likeness at no charge to you. I have witnessed too many cases where someone who was fine with being shot initially, but insisted later upon edits or complete removal from the finished product. The way to protect yourself is to get a release before you shoot them.

I hereby consent and authorize the use of my name and likeness, which may appear in any film, videotape, or still photograph released by, (you and your address), in connection with the distribution of an as yet untitled documentary (the documentary).

I hereby authorize (you) and/or their assignees to use, reproduce, sell, exhibit, broadcast and distribute any promotional materials containing my name and likeness for the purpose of the documentary.

> I hereby waive any right to inspect or approve the finished videotape, soundtrack or advertising copy, or printed matter that may be used in connection therewith or to the eventual use that it might be applied.

You will need each individual to state whether they are over or under 18 or 21 years of age, depending upon the legal age of adulthood in your state. If they are under that age, you will need to have a parent or legal guardian undersign the release. They should provide you with their name, address, date of birth, and signature and you should have a witness present at the signing. Some producers also state directly in the release that there is "none nor will there ever be any recompense for this recording" if that is in fact the case. I realize that this sounds a little like over-kill but these kinds of releases aren't often read before the shoot, but they may save your project farther down the road.

43
Green Screen Directing

Marshal M. Rosenthal

Figure 43-1

With the advent of YouTube and inexpensive HD camcorders, pretty much anyone who wants to be a movie director can be one. But for the aspiring Spielberg or Cameron producers who wish to beef up their vids, well, using a green screen is hard to discount. The idea of being able to create a background of your choosing—be that a pastoral scene, the Eiffel Tower or an asteroid in outer space—is hard to beat. And, surprisingly, easier to do today than ever before.

A "green screen" at its most basic is a surface wide enough to replace the background of your video. The color green, which is used for the simple reason that it is the least likely to appear in human skin tones, gets "stripped out" in digital post-production (assuming it is human beings that will appear before the screen). Once an expensive process, it is now almost commonplace to do on pretty much any desktop or laptop computer that has video editing software running with a green screen component. The desired background is then placed into position and voilà—you're in France—or walking on the surface of the moon.

Interestingly enough, there was a time when the green screen work was many times more complicated than the shooting process. Due to digital computer technology, the roles have been reversed. If you are going to direct a movie which will be using green screen, the time spent properly executing the shooting can be much more involved than at the digital end. Not to mention it being a lot easier to avoid problems while shooting that otherwise will involve ridiculously long post-production sessions to fix—if they can be fixed at all. "Directing for green screen" might as well be a category rather than just "directing," because it does require a different mindset that would be the case where the background is real. What must be considered and applied in order to direct for green screen are staring right at you and involve more than just knowing what the background is going to be once the video editing program takes over.

Lighting

Those who think you just set up a few lights and you're done need to think again: in a real sense you must "direct" the lighting so it will apply correctly to the green screen environment. Lighting plays a major part in how well lit a scene will be of course, but it also can provide touchstones that blow the green screen "effect" you are trying to create right out

Figure 43-2 *Light the green screen and subject separately to avoid spill from the green screen. Then light the subject properly to match the desired background. This ensures the green screen will be lit evenly in order to pull a great key.*

of the water (or computer, in this case). Classic lighting schemes, such as applying a main light from one side towards the actors at a 45 degree angle while a much weaker one is at the other side, can cause shadows to fall on the green screen. While these shadows may be able to be eliminated in post-production, a simpler and less time-intensive solution is to manage the actors far enough away from the green screen so that the shadows are too weak to register.

By this same token, you can also more acutely angle the lighting—throwing the shadows away from the green screen. Of course the more acute the angle, the more shadow there will be on the actor. This can be used to good effect in a scene but, as a general rule, should be avoided (unless the actor's faces aren't worth seeing all that much).

The color temperature of the lighting can also negatively impact your "green screening." Fluorescent lights have a tinge to them that must be corrected in post-production, adding another layer of time to the production. Daylight attuned fluorescent bulbs are the way to go if fluorescent lighting can not be avoided; daylight-attuned incandescent bulbs being the best solution due to their being less costly and easier to handle. Regardless, using lighting which is not balanced for daylight will only add to your problems—and avoiding those problems is always good advice.

One thing to remember is that there are different types of lighting schemes, each having their own unique advantages and disadvantages, But whether you are a proponent of full frontal lighting, side lighting, edge lighting or any other variant (including that of illuminating the top of the actor's head for greater separation from the background), don't lose sight of what the lighting on the background you will add later will look like. Sure computer programs can do amazing things when necessary, but it's much easier to light the shadows on an actor's face to match the shadows on the background that is already being readied in the computer rather than having to do it the other way around. And obviously if you're shooting a night scene, you must match the general ambience the viewer expects in such a situation while still balancing the need to provide a discernible image.

Screen Light

In all of this, we've yet to address the issues of lighting the green screen itself: which you must do. Thinking of the screen as an actor doesn't hurt because most of the rules applying to actors being lit, such as intensity of the light and color temperature, apply to the green screen. Where it differs is that you must strive for a uniform lighting scheme to illuminate the green screen—avoiding hot spots by having more light on one side than the other. The idea is to light the surface of the green screen so that there is no sheen—just an overall, well-lit surface. This will provide the best route for post-production work.

Color vs. Green Screen

It should be evident that a color that is similar to that of the green screen (which, by

the way and horror-of-horrors, doesn't actually have to be green) will behave exactly the same as the green screen does, be it a prop, piece of clothing, jewelry or whatnot. While this can be problematic—and in the case of Popeye the Sailor, even catastrophic if Bluto should appear and Popeye has to pull out his green can of spinach—all that is required here is some careful planning to avoid it becoming an issue. Of course testing everything that goes in front of the green screen goes without saying: a few minutes performing a video recording that can then be used in the video editing/green screen program that is going to handle the post production will alleviate your fears—or provide a needed early warning.

Blocking

Proper positioning, or "blocking" of the "actors" who will be performing in front

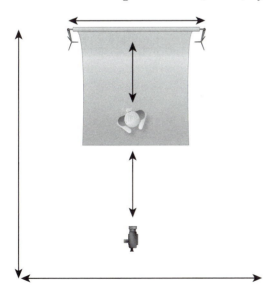

Figure 43-3 *One of the tricks to getting great results with a green screen is separating your subject from the background. Allow yourself plenty of room to position your subject 6–9 feet from the green screen.*

Figure 43-4 *Be sure to mark off areas where the talent should stand to avoid falling off the green screen. A simple piece of tape or chalk will do the job.*

of the green screen is vital; important as regards their position relative to the green screen, but even more vital should they not be "static" but moving during the shooting. The most vital necessities for effective blocking can be condensed into the following:

Being Aware of the Green Screen

The actor needs to be aware of the physical limits of the green screen behind him/her. While this should be less problematic when not moving, even simple hand movements can break the boundaries of the green screen and cause disconcertion in the image being shot. A simple marking on the floor (chalk or strip of tape) can be used to line up with one of the legs of the actor, keeping him/her in a proper position relative to and safely within the confines of the green screen.

Hitting the Marks

Movement can occur in front of a green screen, providing that the actor has a firm understanding of his/her position relative to the green screen's spatial confines—which isn't confined to just side-to-side movements, but also front to back. In simple terms, this means that there are lateral boundaries on both sides of the actor's "space" in which he/she must not exit so as to remain with the green screen's confines as well as front/back boundaries the actor must also be aware of.

Actor Versus Green Screen Perspective

The perspective between the actor and the "background" that will be added later must be considered also. These front-to-back boundaries can be a bit tricky since, unlike moving from side to side, moving forward, away from, or backwards towards the green screen can betray the fact that the perspective does not change as it does in real life. Careful planning (and pre-testing) is the best solution here.

We Don't Need No Stinkin' Green Screen

Who says it has to be a "screen" anyway? Maybe you want to use one of those fluid stabilizers that let you move fluidly during shooting (can you believe they're being made for iPhones, even?). Doing a 360-degree spin around an actor becomes easier—but then you'd lose the green screen, right? Wrong—as a director it's your job to think outside the green screen box—or panel in this case—so what's to stop you from wrapping green screen—like material around the person and having the video shot from inside? Or creating oddly shaped green screens that suit your purpose? Nothing!

Green screen shooting—like any good video idea—is limited only by your imagination.

44
Making Your Video Look More Like Film

Kyle Cassidy

Figure 44-1

I've noticed that while watching the "Coming Attractions" previews on DVDs, anything that looks like it was shot on video automatically gets bumped down on my "have to see this" list. Why is that? Growing up, as I did, in the age where home video technology first became available, I was both fascinated and put off by it. On the one hand it meant that anybody could now make movies, but on the other, they all looked very different from what was coming out of Hollywood—they looked cheap. Over the years, video technology has improved dramatically from the old VHS camcorders with their low resolution and low dynamic range. Today, even the most inexpensive HD camcorders are capable of producing very good images. But there's still something subconscious that makes many people prefer the look of film.

Differences Between Film and Video

When we look at something and think "shot on video" what is it that we're noticing? The differences between film and video used to be a lot greater—specifically in terms of the much greater dynamic range and resolution that film could capture. Over the past few years, these have largely gone away and, in many ways, digital may actually be superior to film (though we can leave that

Figure 44-2 *35 mm film captures more information at higher resolutions than most video camcorder sensors, essentially producing higher-quality images, which has an impact on depth of field, dynamic range and low-light sensitivity.*

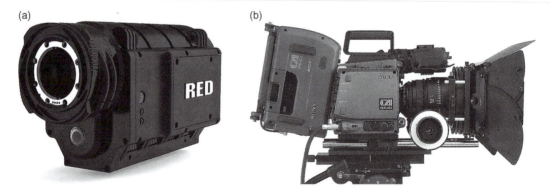

Figure 44-3 *The Red One and Sony's CineAlta line of camcorders are commonly used on most high-end digital films and they both produce amazing images and boast high resolution capabilities.*

battle to the *Videomaker* forum). What remains, though, is that most consumer camcorders have a very small CCD compared to the 35 mm sensor which might have as much as seven times the surface area—this has a very real impact on the depth of field, dynamic range, and the camera's low-light sensitivity.

Blockbusters Shot on Video

Film has a lot of unenviable qualities— first, it's expensive. Remember how much it cost to buy and develop a roll of 35 mm film? In a movie camera, that's one second. Multiply that by two hours, multiple takes, positives made from your negatives and even the most miserly shooting will cost you thousands and thousands of dollars. Film's second big drawback is that you can't see it right away. You don't know if your shot was in focus, what was going on in the background, any number of things that would make you want to re-shoot a scene. For these reasons, Hollywood has been very interested in figuring out how to shoot on video.

Commercially successful movies like *Benjamin Button*, *Star Wars* episodes 2 and 3 and *Collateral* were shot digitally and in 2009, Anthony Dod Mantle won a "best cinematographer" Oscar for *Slumdog Millionare* which was made up of 60 percent digital video. For the most part, these movies are using ultra high-end cameras, like the Sony CineAlta line of camcorders or the Red One which will set you back $17,500 for the body alone, but other successful movies, like *Open Water*, were shot on prosumer equipment and put through filters to make it look more film like.

Making it Look Like Film

So what can you do with your consumer or prosumer video camera to achieve the look of film? Here's a look at some software, hardware, and techniques.

Shoot in 24p

Film is shot at 24 frames per second, but video is typically shot at 29.97 frames per second. The reasoning behind all of this is arcane, but our eyes have gotten used to seeing "film" at 24 frames a second. Most HD camcorders today have an option for shooting 24 frames, progressive ("progressive" means one solid frame rather than the two interlaced fields we're used to with NTSC). Blu-ray as well as most HDTVs will support 24p playback, as will your computer.

Set Your Shutter Angle to 180 Degrees

"Shutter angle," a holdover from film cameras, has to do with how long the light is hitting the film and how much motion blur there is when things are moving across the screen. Many camcorders today have an option for shutter angle. Setting this to 1/48 with a frame rate of 24 best approximates the look of a film camera.

Use a 35 mm Lens Adapter

Anybody with a DSLR and an inexpensive 50 mm f/1.8 lens can take images with very shallow depth of field, allowing you to blur out the background and concentrate on your subject. However, given the very tiny size of the CCD on consumer video cameras, your depth of field might be a dozen feet or more.

Companies like LetusDirect (letusdirect.com) and P+S Technik (pstechnik.de) make devices that will allow you to attach 35 mm lenses to your camcorder and get the shallow depth of field often associated with 35 mm film productions. They get past the small size of the CCD by projecting the image onto a screen about the size of a 35 mm piece of film and actually videotape the image from that screen. It's a bit like sitting in a movie theatre videotaping the screen, but it actually works.

Filters (the Physical Kind)

Tiffen makes a series of filters they sell called "The Film Look Kit" for making video look more film like. They work by slightly reducing the contrast and sharpness. You could also use a slight diffusion filter which will soften the image a bit.

Filters (the Digital Kind)

Companies like Boris FX (borisfx.com) Red Giant (redgiantsoftware.com), BigFX (bigfx.com), and Nattress Productions (nattress.com) sell plug-in filters for your editing software that give a variety of "film looks" from old and scratchy, to things like adding subtle grain and reproducing different developing techniques, to color grading. You can find many before and after examples of these filters on YouTube.com by searching for the name of the filter.

There are even apps for the iPhone like "Hollywood FX Video Maker" that will make video captured by your cell phone look more "film like".

Light it Like a Movie

One of the first tipoffs to a low-quality production is skimping on the lighting. This doesn't necessarily mean not spending money on the lighting, but using lighting that's unrealistic in an uninteresting way.

I worked on a shot-on-video movie for two days in 2006. We were shooting a scene that takes place in an office and the director had borrowed an office which looked—very office-like. The first thing he did was have production assistants remove all the pictures from the walls and everything from the desk. Then he lit it with a giant bright light that threw razor sharp shadows against the bare wall. It looked like an empty room with a desk lit by a super bright bare bulb—because that's what it was. In real life, nobody would light their office with a giant bare bulb. Had there been a real lighting expert on the set, they would have come up with a way to make sure the room was bright enough to be captured by the camera, but lit believably.

Pay attention to lighting while watching movies and if you're not a lighting expert yourself, call in some help before you start your own production. If your town doesn't have a film and video group, you can try websites like Craigslist (craigslist.com) to meet other people interested in video production.

Figure 44-4 *Stabilizing your shots will give you professional-looking footage.*

Stabilize your Camera

While the jerky handheld camera is in style now, using a camera stabilizer will smooth out your handheld movements and add an air of professionalism to your production. Steadicam (steadicam.com) was the first camera stabilizing system, but today they're made by lots of companies like Manfrotto (manfrotto.com) and Camera Motion Research (camotionllc.com) in a broad range of prices.

Conclusion

Video is no longer film's poor-quality cousin, though the two can still look distinctly different. We've been trained over the years to think that film looks more "professional" and for that reason there are a number of tools available to make video look more like film. Some of these are digital and some are physical, but one of the most important is the mindset—shoot your video professionally, carefully, and with attention to detail, just like any Oscar-winning cinematographer would do.

45
Screen Direction

Robert G. Nulph

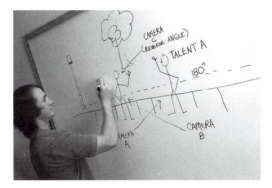

Figure 45-1

Screen direction is perhaps one of the most confusing yet easily remedied problems in directing a video production.

We are often tempted to place our cameras so that we get the cool background behind our talent as they move through the landscape. However, sometimes when we move the camera, we inadvertently change the direction the talent is looking. In this column, we will take a look at the 180-degree rule, continuity, cutting on action, camera and talent movement and basic blocking. Never again will you have to resort to the age-old trick of reversing the image because the talent is looking in the wrong direction.

The 180-degree Rule

Some call it the "Motion Vector Line," some call it the "Sagittal Plane Rule," and still others call it the "line of action." But most in the film world know it as the 180 rule. What is it? It is the rule that will always serve you well to make sure your talent is always looking or moving in the right direction on the screen. It works like this. If you have two people talking or an object moving in a specific direction, draw an imaginary line through them in the direction they are looking (see Figure 45-1).

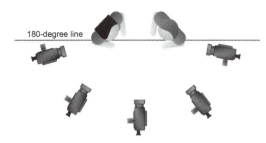

Figure 45-2 Whenever you move the camera for cutaway shots, as long as you stay on the same side of the 180-degree line, you will never break screen direction continuity.

By making sure your camera never leaves the 180 degrees of space on the one side of the line, you can be sure your subject will always be looking or moving in the same screen direction. If you are taping a conversation between two people, make sure the camera never crosses the imaginary line that runs through them. If you stay on the same side, your talent will always be looking towards each other. If, however, you cross the 180 line, they will both be looking in the same direction (see Figure 45-2).

When shooting a parade, a race, a chase or any other movement that has a specific direction, always make sure your cameras stay on the same side of the action. If you decide to shoot the basketball game from the home side of the court, all of your cameras have to be on that side so that you don't have the players making baskets in their opponent's goals. The only way around this is to make sure you put a graphic on the screen that says "reverse angle." If you are taping a car chase, decide if you want to shoot the chase from the passenger or driver's side of the cars and do not deviate from that plan, no matter how cool the background looks at various locations. The instant you decide to switch sides, the cars will no longer be chasing each other; they will be crashing into each other or running away from each other! Not a good outcome to the chase! If you are taping an actor chasing another, decide if you want to tape from the left or right side and again, stick to it. Just imagine how hard it would have been for the

cowboys to catch the cows if you shot the cowboys from their left side and the cows on the right. They would eventually meet in China!

The 180 rule can be very confusing sometimes because, when we tape actors and other talent, they are often in motion. Just keep in mind that the camera has to stay on the same side when focusing on two people, and you will be OK. To move the 180 line, you have to physically move the camera during the shot so that the audience recognizes the change in position. You can also shoot a direction-neutral shot where the talent looks directly into the camera or, in the case of a car chase, the car comes right at the camera (see Figure 46-3).

Continuity

One of the reasons the 180 rule is so important is that it gives you a sense of continuity. Your audience must always feel like they are watching a moment in time that unfolds in a continuous direction. Thus the idea of continuity: maintaining a sense that time, distance and objects continue through time in a logical way. If the car was moving from the left to right side of the screen and was rushing away from a following police car, you wouldn't suddenly show it moving from the right to left unless it was planning on ramming the police car! You must be consistent to maintain this idea of a continuous time.

Cutting on Action

Cutting on action is one of the best ways to maintain the feeling of movement through time and maintaining screen direction and continuity. When editing, it is always best to cut as the talent does something—not as they are getting ready to do something or have already finished the action. If they are sitting, make the cut as they are on their way down, not while they are still standing. Cutting on the action will also hide the cut because the movement

Figure 2

Camera C
Reverse Angle

Camera B

Camera A

180° Line

Camera A and B are
on the same side of
the continuity (180)
line. Camera C is
across the line.

Camera A

Camera B

Camera angles A
and B keep screen
direction continuity.
Camera C with B
breaks continuity.

Camera C

Camera B

Figure 45-3

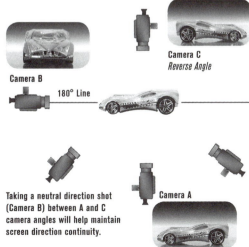

Camera B

Camera C
Reverse Angle

180° Line

Taking a neutral direction shot
(Camera B) between A and C
camera angles will help maintain
screen direction continuity.

Camera A

Figure 45-4

of your talent will distract the viewer from the hard cut. Cutting on action also lets you do a very interesting thing called a parallel cut. This is a cut between two similar actions yet involves two different subjects in two different places. For instance, say your subject is a boyfriend going to meet his girlfriend. He walks through a door; she gets into an elevator. You shoot him from the left and her from the right to give the feeling that they are moving towards each other. Cutting as he opens his door and her elevator door closes gives you two similar actions and speeds the action along. The 180 rule, screen direction and cutting on action work together to bring these two together!

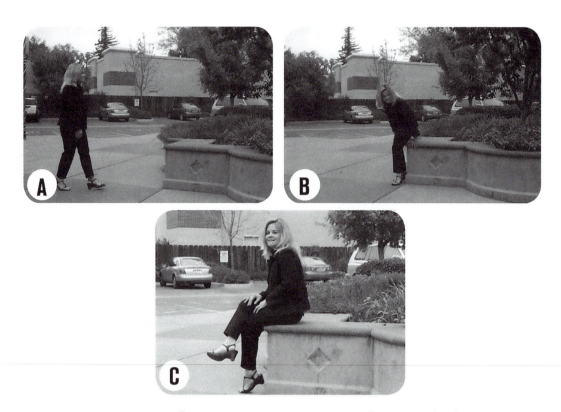

Figure 45-5 *Frame A: You call, "Action." Frame B: Here's your edit point in the shot. Frame C: Edit in the new close-up shot.*

Camera and Talent Movement and Blocking

Blocking is the term used to describe how the director moves his cameras and actors during a scene. Sometimes it is a very sophisticated dance, especially if you are using dollies or Steadicams. When you block your actors and cameras, you must always keep in mind the 180 rule and screen direction. Build a sense of the acting space in your audience's mind and maintain that space. If a door is to the actors' right when the scene begins, it should always be to their right unless they turn around. This may seem like a simple thing to do, but if you move the camera to the opposite side of their 180 line, the door will suddenly be on their left. Use an establishing shot at the beginning of a scene to help place the location of the actors in the audience's mind, and then maintain that orientation by always maintaining screen direction. If an actor

moves, make sure you see the movement in at least a medium shot, so that you can see the background change and see that there is a change in orientation. This can be a bit confusing. For example, say you have an actor coming down a flight of stairs. You shoot him from the top of the stairs from his right side as he begins to descend, but you then shoot from the left side as he got to the bottom, because you liked the background that was on his right side. He would suddenly change direction in the editing suite. Make sure when you block your camera and actors that the camera operator knows what side of the actors the camera should stay on, unless the action changes direction and the actor at some point comes right at the camera or moves directly away. However, you can always move the camera around the subject over the course of the same shot, giving your audience an opportunity to readjust to the new space that you have just created.

Final Direction

To maintain screen direction, talent movement and camera blocking; moving at an angle toward or away from the camera is much better than moving from side to side in front of the camera. Television is a two-dimensional medium, and it is always your job as a director to help create the feeling of a three-dimensional space by moving onto and out of the screen.

Your stories will flow much better and make significantly more sense to your audience when you control and maintain screen direction.

Go West, Young man!

This mantra was often repeated in the days of the expansion west towards California. When you set up your shots and the action is supposed to go in a very specific direction, such as the movement west, make sure you keep in mind the screen direction of your subjects. If you want them to move towards the west, you have to tape them so that they are moving from the right to left side of the screen. All the maps in the world have the west on the left side. Think of the screen as a map. If the subject says they have to go west, they move to the left; east, they move to the right side of the screen. If they are watching a sunset, they should be looking off to screen left; sunrise, screen right.

46
Shooting for 3D

Tony Bruno

Figure 46-1

No matter the movie at the multiplex, chances are you'll be offered the chance to see it while wearing big funky glasses that would have looked really hip back when bellbottoms were in style. With that much exposure, it's only a matter of time before a client will ask the question, "Can this be delivered in 3D?" Not so surprisingly, the answer to that question is, "Yes." Just like any other new technology, though, there are some new terms and rules that have to be learned to deliver the best video possible.

Simple to Pick Up, Difficult to Master

One of the most dangerous things about shooting in 3D is that it's deceptively easy. After all, anybody can strap two video cameras side-by-side and shoot some test footage. Then load the output into a non-linear editor, slap a red filter over the left camera's output, and a cyan filter over the right camera's output,

render and voilà! A cheap pair of paper 3D glasses and a computer monitor is all that's needed to enjoy the newly-minted 3D video. Unfortunately, it doesn't look that good. The world looks like it's a tiny model, or worse, gigantic? Meanwhile everything in the foreground seems to float in space, while the background elements rest on the screen. What went wrong?

Back to School

Answering these questions involves learning a bit of new vocabulary and a couple of new techniques. Oh, and not a little bit of patience. There are two terms that any 3D videographer needs to know: interocular distance and convergence.

Interocular Distance

Try this experiment. Grab a ruler and measure the distance from the center of your left eye to the center of your right eye. The number will probably be pretty close to 2.5". This separation between eyes is known as the interocular distance, and it is, in part, why we see the world in three dimensions.

In order for your footage to best simulate what viewers would see with their own eyes, it's important to match the human interocular distance as closely as possible. This means that the distance between the centers of your camera lenses should be approximately 2.5".

Ignoring the interocular distance can result in some surprising and even unpleasant effects. Move the cameras too far apart, and the world will look like it's been miniaturized. Move them too close together, and suddenly the smallest object appears gigantic. 2.5"—learn it; live it; love it.

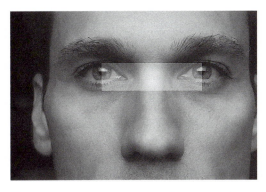

Figure 46-2 *The interocular distance is the distance between camera lenses. The ideal distance is 2.5", similar to the distance between the irises in our eyes.*

Convergence

Now that you've got this interocular distance thing down, you decide to shoot some piece of test footage. You take your son and daughter out to a scenic overlook and frame a nice 3D shot. You place your son close to the lenses, your daughter further back, while in the distance you have a mountain range to complete the shot.

After your post-production and rendering work, you pop on your glasses to check out your handiwork. Unfortunately, things are still not right. The depth in the shot is all wrong. Your son and your daughter both appear to float off the screen, while the mountains in the distance appear to be on the screen itself. What gives?

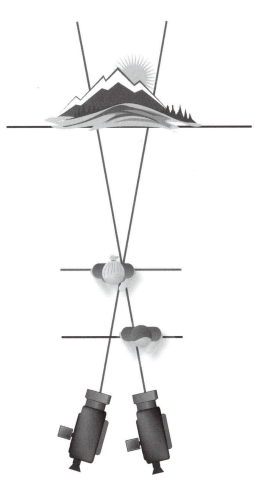

Figure 46-3 *The point of convergence is where both lenses are focused to meet, known as the convergence place.*

The reason is that both of your lenses are aimed straight forward. This parallel focus plane results in objects of infinite distance (the mountain range) appearing to be on the screen, while all other closer objects (your son and daughter) seem to pop off the screen into space. In order to get more depth to the shot, both cameras have to be rotated slightly inward. This converges the main image plane, and provides more 3D data to the camera.

To get the best effect, the image planes for both cameras need to be centered on the subject that is intended to appear to be on the screen during 3D playback. Objects closer to the lenses than the image plane will appear to come off the screen, while objects in the distance will appear to be behind the screen. With this new knowledge, you take your kids back to the same spot, and frame it as before, but with the cameras converged on your daughter. Result? Your son, being close to the lens, pops off the screen, while your daughter appears to rest on the surface of your display. Finally, the mountains rest comfortably behind the surface of the screen.

The Devil is in the Details

Given the added complexity of any 3D shoot, planning becomes even more critical than normal. There are, however, some pre-production steps you can take to ease the whole process:

- 3D Location scouting—shoot 3D stills of the locations in your film using a pair of digital still cameras. What better time to work out the best convergence angles for your shots than in pre-production?

- 3D storyboards—as helpful as 3D location images are, a 3D storyboard— created in part from the 3D location images—will be an enormous boon for the entire project. Getting the most impact from your 3D landscape can be planned in this way far before the first shot is lit.

- 3D pre-visualization—once the 3D storyboards are locked, bring them into your non-linear editor and produce a timed, 3D pre-viz cut of your project. Once rendered, you can not only judge the flow of the project better, but you can also show it to your clients, ensuring that they are happy with the intended use of 3D.

Unlearn what You have Learned

So you've got your cameras set, your 3D storyboards put together, and you've even cut a 3D pre-viz video. Why, then, does the whole thing still seem off? The 3D is disorienting; the images still seem somewhat flat, and for some reason the project is harder to follow than a normal 2D video. What's wrong? The problem is that, no matter how many years you've spent behind the camera, shooting in 3D is a new experience. Rules that work well in 2D actually hurt 3D projects.

To better get acclimatize to the process, here are some simple rules to help you get started:

1. Put some "D" into your 3D shots: make sure that all of your shots have real depth. Good foreground, midground and background information, while important in normal cinematography, is critical in 3D shots. Oh, and if you get the urge to have a sharp pokey thing fly straight at the camera to scare the audience, do yourself a favor: Don't. It didn't work in 1955, and it doesn't work now.

2. Cut back: 3D information takes longer to process in the human brain than 2D images. To allow for that, consider the following for your shots and edits:
   - No fast camera moves.
   - Avoid jump cuts.
   - Don't hit audiences with any sudden changes in the depth-of-field from shot-to-shot.
   - Slow down the pace of editing.

3. No zoom-zoom: nothing is worse than 3D elements that look like they are

Figure 46-4 *Creating depth is extremely important when composing 3D shots, more so than in 2D. Depth will help sell the 3D experience and make it more enjoyable for your audience.*

cardboard cutouts pasted at different distances away from the camera. Using zoom lenses during 3D shoots can cause this effect. Save yourself the headache. Don't use zoom lenses on 3D projects.

4. Wide open: with the added complexity of the interocular distance and convergence, focus becomes not merely another checklist item, but a genuine nuisance. Simplify your project by using wide-angle lenses and focusing to infinity. It might not be as artsy as a shot with lovely depth of field, but you'll avoid a few more gray hairs in the process.

World of Tomorrow

With 3D entering the home market, the argument about whether it is just a passing fad or not is rapidly becoming moot. Though it's a difficult to master medium, it's better to learn its strengths and foibles now, when time is still a luxury, rather than later, when it's a short-deadlined necessity.

47
Optimizing Edit Organization

Peter Zunitch

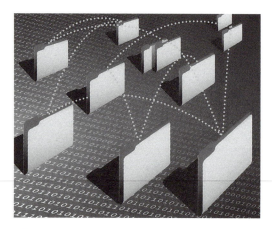

Figure 47-1

Organization is the key to a speedy, efficient and enjoyable edit. You know it; I know it. Every click, every drag of the mouse wastes time, and you certainly don't need to constantly waste your time and your client's money searching for a clip that should be at your fingertips. The time you waste hunting for footage is better spent tweaking and experimenting creatively. Proper labeling and placement of your material means you'll be able to retrieve it quicker. Knowing where a clip is at any given moment lets you achieve great speed and meet deadlines others will perceive as impossible. So let's dispense with every extra mouse click. Let's cut out the needless hunting. Let's minimize every repetitive gesture. Let's talk organization.

Establishing a Routine

I have three tips I want to impress upon you with this chapter that will make your post-production life easier. The first, and most obvious is that you should be ordering every aspect of your business from the top down in a similar fashion. Ideally you want every project laid out identically, every type of material in the same place in every project, and every clip named and referenced in a like-minded

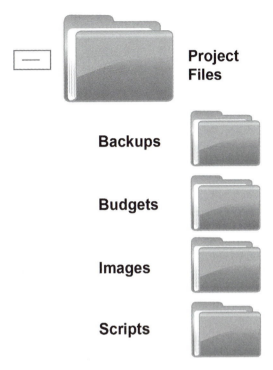

Project Files

Backups

Budgets

Images

Scripts

Figure 47-2 *Using the same folder structure for every project can help save time.*

fashion. This way, you can always draw on material from previous edits at a moment's notice, and will be able to recall exact tapes or clips even if you don't remember any of the specific information about it.

We all know that every editing project has more attributes to it than just footage. This is where organization must start. Before I create a project in my edit system, I create a supporting folder on my desktop. I like to label it the same as the project name, with a "_files" extension at the end. Everything from scripts to image files, budgets to backups is put inside this folder. Anything relating to this project that does not come from a source tape is kept here. This way, if I ever need to recreate the project in the future, I need only copy that one folder back to my desktop.

Beyond the A to Z

The second trick is going to sound rather overboard at first, but stick with me. As you'll see later, when combined with the

above it will come in handy over and over again.

So we all know editing programs allow you to sort everything alphabetically. In fact, they do this by default. However, it is a convenient, but limited organizing philosophy and you should know how to circumvent it. Why should you have to scan through to the middle of your bins to find, say, your "media" bin if it's the one you open and close most often? But how can you move it without renaming it?

Your computer assigns a numerical value to each letter of the alphabet. When you ask it to sort, it simply looks for the lowest number and lists that item first. What you may not know is that the symbols on a keyboard all have values assigned to them as well. Further, some have lower values than the letter "A", and others have higher values than "Z". The tilde for example, (~) is a symbol I often use to make any entry jump to the bottom of an ordered list. It also has the added benefit of making the entry stand out from everything around it.

Be warned that your system will not allow every symbol to be used. The question mark for example is a reserved character on most platforms (used for searching) and you will likely not be allowed to use it in a bin, folder or project name. You should experiment to find the symbols that work for you.

The Details of Being Generic

The third device you should consider employing concerns how we handle the common material that we incorporate into multiple jobs. If you do a lot of similar projects, then chances are you have a pool of generic material you draw from often. Establish a project strictly for this material. If you have different types of generic material, consider multiple generic projects. Here's a good place to use that tilde key. Let's say you have a pool of royalty free or buyout music. Create a project titled ~Music. Log and load all your songs in there. Then when you need something in your current edit, simply copy the clips you're considering.

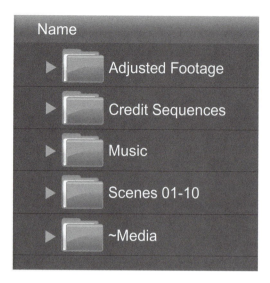

Figure 47-3 *Alphabetically organizing your folders can put frequently used items out of reach. Adding character like the tilde at the front of a folder title can bump folders up or down on the list.*

So what will this extra effort get you? First, you'll have your catalog of music at your fingertips, searchable by any means you see fit. You won't have to go searching piles of CDs for the right disc, and countless tracks for the right song. Second, each time you use the song, you won't have to re-edit it. (Use the "add marker" tool to remember common looping points.) Third, you'll be able to separate your generic clips from your project-specific clips in the media tool. Thus when editing is done, you can sort by project and delete only the media captured in your current project, while being assured that you won't be deleting your music. Finally, if you ever have to re-create your edit, your music will still be in the sequence and properly mixed.

This grouping system should be employed for generic images as well. On my desktop is another folder containing any image I might use in multiple projects, like backgrounds, borders, and company logos.

A Well-Ordered Project

Let's explore how to organize bins and folders within a single project. You should keep all of your edited sequences

in one place. The name should be obvious, "EDITS" or "SEQUENCES". Establish a method of calling attention to your vital folders. In this case, I've used all caps. It will stay that way until the project is done and I am ready to master. Then I will make it mixed case, and make a new bin called "~FINAL OUTPUT." This new bin will contain only the timelines directly involved in mastering to the final medium(s). Any old timelines, and/or backups will remain in the (now named) "EDITS" bin.

My next favorite bin is the "working" or "scrap" bin. This bin holds all my effects templates, sub-clips that I use for mixdowns, pre-builds and one-off titles. This bin can fill up quick and tends to get messy, but since most of the items in here are only needed temporarily it's OK. Resist the urge to sort such a bin by anything other than creation date/time. You'll be able to find the previous effect much better by the things around it than by its name, especially when you will inevitably end up with 10 items all labeled "Title". Speaking of . . . When you have an effect or title template you know you'll be using often, don't be afraid to give it a unique name.

The next few bins are specifically for sorting material by source type. In any given project, I may use "Photos", "Stills" and "Graphics" bins to take care of all non-moving images. Typically the latter is used for computer-generated text, backgrounds, frames, etc. The former holds headshots, and the middle contains any other real life photos or sketches of people places and things. Typically I don't need all of them for every edit, and will often combine all still material into one bin. It all depends on the project.

Organizing your Audio Files and Footage

Next, audio. Typically I have a "Music and VO" bin, containing ADR, narration, background music and sound effects. Again, these may get split up if the project calls for intensive use of them. The music of

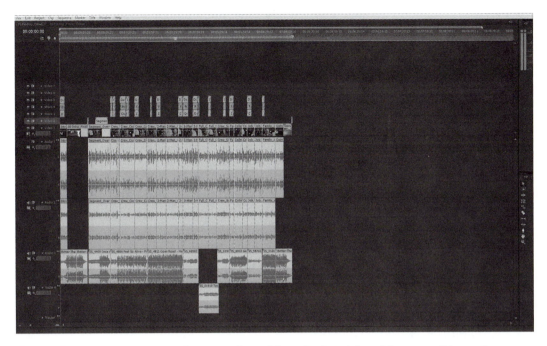

Figure 47-4 *You can save time by using the "add marker" tool found in your editing software.*

course will be reference clips I've selected and copied over from my generic music project and the stills are all imported from the project_files folder on the desktop.

The layout of your source video bins will undoubtedly be influenced by what type of projects you typically edit. Typically you'll want to break them down either by location, subject, or scene. Tag them with buzzwords that remind you of the contents, as labeling only by scene number and take alone will usually mean nothing without rifling through the script. I also recommend making separate bins for your generic B-roll, and for your project specific footage. Consider names like "^ Broll", "^ Cemetery" and "^ Host Stand-ups". Notice too that we're using a new symbol here, called an "up caret", to keep all our source bins together.

Well we're down to individual clips. Symbols at this level become rather redundant, so instead, we're going to use a keyword first to help group clips together when sorting. I'll then follow it with a hyphen, or underscore to separate it from the rest of the description. This is followed with framing, the typical description of the subject, and relevant development in the shot.

"Tim—MS, Ghost steps in behind him. Zoom in." Dialogue covered is a good fallback when the action isn't distinguishing: "Table—WS Come on, you hardly . . . it's my mother'". As a general rule of thumb, if your clip description is more than half a screen long, you're packing too much into a single clip, and should consider splitting the footage into smaller chunks.

Order—a condition when things are in methodical or harmonious arrangement

The key to efficiency is consistency. Have a plan and stick to it. Combine this with the ergonomics of language and symbols. Remember, too, that the edit system is made for organization beyond alphabetizing. Utilize the columns provided to annotate framing, scene and take, etc. This information in conjunction with a standardized workflow will allow you to manipulate your material by any criteria you desire, and minimizing search time. In the end, organization ensures a faster, and thus more profitable edit session, creating a better final product and a happier client.

Case Study

I once worked at an edit house whose bread and butter was making convention videos. We typically had need for generic shots of the expo floor, an audience, lecturers, parties and the like. Often we'd borrow one of these generic shots from another venue, making sure there were no logos in sight. It made sense then to take all footage from every convention, log it in a similar fashion, and store it in an archive project of its own. We ultimately ended up with two separate projects that acted as source libraries for all the other edits.

Project 1 had a folder for every organization, and a bin for each year's convention footage within it. The clips in each bin would be labeled first by a one-word location ("Expo", "Keynote", "Party", etc.). Then, if the clip contained an organization logo I had to look out for, I'd place a plus sign, so I could find branding when I needed it. Following that would be a short description. The end result would be that I could find a shot I needed by association, year, event function, or action.

Project 2 held one bin for each city to hold a convention. These held only the footage we had of the city and its attractions. Using this method, we could grab footage from any association, and copy them with footage from any city into a new project to edit from.

A Word on Workspace

Laying out a proper workspace is also a key to improved efficiency. If your edit system lets you move bins and buttons around, do it. Optimizing position minimizes strain. Typically you don't need to access the EDITS bin unless you're making a new timeline or reverting to an old one. Therefore make the window rather small on your screen and place it far from the timeline. On the other hand, place the scraps and media bins close to your preview window, allowing for quick drags and drops. Also, don't be afraid to move around the on-screen buttons, or even re-map keyboard commands. There's undoubtedly a command you use often that isn't even mapped to the keyboard.

48
Video Editing for N00bs

Mark Montgomery

Figure 48-1

So you're the techie at your place of work and at home. You get called in to help the boss set up new equipment at work and you're the one getting calls at home about what camera Aunt Linda should buy. It's a fact of life. You're the one people depend on to do the technical tasks and with it comes the assumed responsibility of video work too. Corporate slideshows, presentations, junior's little league game and so many more projects are sitting on your desk waiting to get done. We can help you get started on the path to becoming a better video editor with these simple hints.

Don't be Afraid to Ask for What You Need

If you're just starting your journey, you're going to need to be prepared. A full-sized keyboard with a numeric keypad is a must. Keyboard shortcuts are an editor's best friend.

Make sure you have plenty of hard drive space. It would be wise to have an external USB 2.0 hard drive handy. Get the most storage space money can buy. Lastly, a second monitor makes your workspace much more functional. Make sure to check if your computer can support a second monitor before you make this purchase.

Figure 48-2 *Adobe Premiere Elements and Apple's Final Cut Express are both great editing applications for beginning editors to grow into.*

Software is key, but as you're starting off, sometimes it's best to work your way up. Most free solutions, like Microsoft Movie Maker and Apple's iMovie, are great for beginners as they don't have a lot of features that can be more of a distraction to the editor in training. If you want a more options and control in your editing environment, take a closer look at Adobe Premiere Elements or Apple's Final Cut Express. They are well worth the money as they can be real time savers and do a lot of what any editor (new or experienced) would need to do.

Techniques: Keep It Organized

Projects pile up quickly and video files all look the same when they're just sitting in a folder. Naming conventions for files and folders become quite handy for a busy video editor. We organize our file structure by project, one folder with a descriptive name. For example, you're creating a video for the local after-school program's annual fundraiser, so you label a new folder called "Boys and Girls Club Fundraiser 2011" and that should clearly

explain what will be in this folder. Then, you can put a few more generic folders into this folder, like a Video folder, Music folder, Photo folder. Just a little bit of work will keep you organized and help you find what you're looking for. It will also make it easy to back up your work.

Techniques: Keep It Simple

Video projects big and small should start with a clear storyline (if it's a narrative) or an objective if it's a corporate presentation or something similar. Developing good storyline for narrative films is truly a fine art and outside of the scope of this chapter. But an objective for your video can be very simple and useful in saving yourself time and energy. A good objective should keep the audience in mind. Who will be watching your video? What do you want them to do as a result of viewing your video? Now ask yourself what is the most critical thing you can show them in your video to reach this outcome? There's your objective. Now it's time to get to work.

The building blocks of any video start with A/B editing. The primary action

Figure 48-3 *A/B editing is a great way to carry along the story by giving your viewer a visual context and keep their attention span by separating long, drawn-out shots with more descriptive footage.*

of the video is considered your A-roll and the secondary, supportive visuals are considered B-roll. Let's use an example to illustrate this example. You're producing a birthday video for your 3-year-old nephew. You have a video clip of your nephew telling the viewers what he received for his birthday. He describes in short detail, (he's 3, remember), that he got a red tricycle. The clip is rather informal, with you behind the camera asking the questions and prompting your nephew. It takes you a good 15 seconds to get the details out of the birthday boy. A 15-second clip is a little long to run by most video editing standards, but you can't omit this crucial first-hand account of the birthday. This is A-roll, a crucial part of your video. So you drop in the A-roll into the timeline and try to remedy the lengthy 15-second description of the birthday present. This is where B-roll comes in. Looking through your video footage, you find a clip of your

nephew as he unboxes the new tricycle. Ah ha! Now we got a clip related to the first clip. We could just throw this in the timeline after the first clip, but better yet we should cut about 5 seconds into the video clip while preserving the audio from the first clip. In this way, the viewer continues to hear the boy describe his new tricycle while we see the action itself unfold. This is a much more powerful edit giving the viewer the visual context of what your nephew is describing on camera.

The trick with these edits is to think critically about what your audience needs to know (back to our objective) and then think how many different ways we can support that with visuals. The other trick is making sure that you (or whoever is working the camera) takes plenty of B-roll shots. Think of any professional wedding videographer; they are B-roll freaks. A wedding has so many different elements that comprise the entire day: not only the participants of the event, but the cake, the guest book, the church, the flower petals left by the flower girl, the table settings, etcetera, etcetera. All these elements must be recorded as they will be used later to build the bride and groom's story. Plenty of B-roll is a must.

Techniques: Compressing Time and Pacing

The wonderful thing about being a video editor is that we have a lot of flexibility on how we will tell our story. We can unfold our story chronologically, or skip around in time. We can take an hour-long baseball game and edit it down to a riveting 60 seconds. Manipulating time is critical in producing compelling videos. The best of the best find clever ways to move the audience along the story as quickly as possible without losing them to confusion or without letting key moments pass too quickly. We can take a look at some examples to see how we can better manipulate time in our videos.

Start thinking of a video clip or a shot as a single idea. Put multiple shots together and you can start to put scenes together. Multiple actions in multiple shots can go together quite nicely as one thought. For example, your sister is having a baby and she wants you to put together a family video. The big day arrives and you've got 14 hours of footage (long labor, it was her first child). Now, she'd be more likely to watch a 14-hour video of her delivery, but most of her friends have realistic schedules and booking a showing at that length won't do. So, you rely on our objective to focus our attention on the most important parts to the video.

You have a video clip of the original phone message your sister left as she urgently tried to get hold of you to let you know the baby is coming. That's good place to start. Next clip is a short clip of the hospital waiting room where the extended family patiently awaits. Next shot a close-up of the clock in the hospital and you dissolve to your next sequence of your sister talking about her childhood and what her

expectations are as a new mother. This was an interview you set up weeks ago and you're using B-roll of childhood photos. This sequence goes on for 30 seconds or so and you dissolve back to the hospital break room where soon-to-be grandpa is getting a cup of coffee. He looks down at his watch and says bluntly "It's been five hours." Now dissolve back to your next sequence with your sister's husband talking about his childhood. And, then we'll dissolve back to the hospital again, perhaps this time with some more "waiting for it to happen" moments. The big idea here is that we don't have to show things in a linear progression. Neither do we need to think literally for each action. A phone message can provide enough context to quickly move to the hospital location without confusing the viewer. That saves us a lot of time relating less interesting details, like how you actually got there. It doesn't really matter. What matters is that the day came and you showed up (unless, of course the story of how you got there is riveting). Who knew the new parents arrived in a hot air balloon? That might be more interesting.

Pacing is a tricky subject but there are some basic rules to pacing your edits in a video. Scenes where fast action is important (a big play at home plate) will have the pace of the edits around 3 seconds per shot. That means every 3 seconds the viewer sees a new shot. Scenes where the pacing is slow (like a funeral) will have the pace of the edits around 5 to 7 seconds or more. These are general rules, and you can break them if you have good reason.

For beginning editors, a great trick to keeping a good pace to your edits is to lay down a bed of music that has a beat at the same tempo of your desired pacing. With the music in place, you can start making your edits on the "hits" of the musical tempo. More advance video editing software has markers on the timeline that you can use to visually mark where these musical "hits" fall. Once the video is edited, you can delete the music track and your secret is gone. The best editors use this technique, not only because it's useful, but often times because the final video will feature music with a similar tempo.

Credit Roll

Lastly, make sure you give yourself credit for your hard work (and whoever else pitched in). Take pride in the work you do and don't be afraid to share it with your video editing peers. YouTube is a great way to get your work seen. You should also consider Vimeo.com which houses a great deal of professional videos created by people who truly love the craft of film-making. Now, go forth and make video, contribute your videos, share them with us and make note of what you learn. It's a great time in history to be a video editor.

PART IV
Post-production Techniques

How to edit all that footage you've got "in the can" with precision and style

49
Editing: It's the Pace, Ace!

Bill Davis

Figure 49-1

OK—I admit it, I have a problem. I walk fast. I don't know why, I just do. If I get out of the car at the same time as my wife and son, I'm almost always inside the store before they are. And my 10-year-old is usually trailing far behind my wife, particularly if there's any interesting junk in the parking lot along his path.

I bring up this example to illustrate that while the goal is the same—walking from the car to the store—for all of us, the pace at which each of us prefers to accomplish this task is vastly different. And so it is with our videos. Each video we make and each scene within the overall work, has its own pace, whether we recognize that fact or not.

The pace of MTV-style music videos is so fast that they can be hard to follow. At the other end of the scale is a new parent watching a tape of their newborn child in the cradle. In the first instance, the audience craves change and action. In the second, the content on the screen is so personally fulfilling that the viewer can gaze for minutes at a time at a nearly unchanging scene—and be perfectly content to watch and dream.

So each video has a pace that fits the content. And both paces are right for the needs of the video. But when the pace of a video feels wrong, what can you do to change it?

Changing Time

The simplest answer is if the pace is too slow, you can add more cuts and more media to watch, hear or judge in a given period of time. If things are moving too fast for your audience to grasp, eliminate some clips and stay with a shot longer. (Of course you'll need source material that allows you to do this.)

The timeline in Figure 49-2a shows a 30-second segment of a video taken at a local car show. Each of the shots is a 10-second slow pan, wide shot of a car. The cars themselves are interesting, but the pacing of the video as it's currently cut will be somewhat boring. Each shot has similar framing, similar length and similar move. While they do a decent job of showing the car, this approach will likely appeal only to a real car buff with an appreciation for the subject.

In Figure 49-2b, we've radically changed the pacing of the same 30-second segment by varying the views of each car within the same period. Now, instead of static shots or long, slow pans, we have an establishing shot of each car, followed by medium and closeup shots of some of the details that make the cars so special. We cut to these frequently and quickly. The first edit provides three basic shots and leaves the viewer plenty of time to think about the subject. The second directs the viewer's attention to details that are special about the vehicle. The average viewer will likely watch the second edit with much more interest, simply because their eyes are being directed to details that keep the experience fresh and shifting. The length and overall timing of the video remains the same, but the pacing of the video is faster.

Pacing Starts at the Shoot

If you come back from your car show shoot with nothing but three static shots

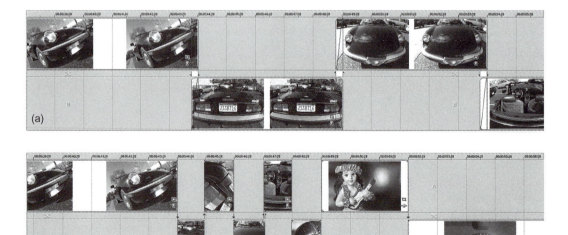

Figure 49-2 *Slower pacing can bore your audience, while more cuts can add interest and excitement.*

of the cars, your options are going to be severely limited. Faster pacing usually requires good coverage, which means shooting a variety of shots and angles of your subject. Ultra wide and ultra closeup, high angle and low, reflections, details, shots with and without people or other objects that can show the relative size and shape of your subject, some or all of these can help you provide good coverage in addition to your basic scenes.

Another example of the element of pacing is action within a scene. Instead of simply a shot of a door handle, the videographer can stage the shot with a hand reaching out to open the car door. Even if the door handle shot is actually longer than a static shot of the handle, the action helps keep the pacing up because the audience remains engaged by watching the action of the hand.

Adding the action helps the editor transition from an outside view to details on the inside. It also brings a human element into the video and allows the viewer to better imagine going for a ride. Scenes with action are, by their nature, faster paced than scenes of static imagery.

The Right Pace

So how do you determine what type of pacing is best for your project? Generally speaking, the younger the audience, the faster the pace they can comfortably tolerate. But that's a generalization and like all generalizations, it's as false as it is true.

The movie *Titanic* was a huge hit with adolescent girls. While it was an action movie on its surface, the scenes that attracted that particular audience were the love scenes between Leonardo DiCaprio and Kate Winslet, and not the fast-paced action sequences. The lesson is that if you give an audience content it wants to see, they'll stay happy when you linger a bit on scenes. If the core material is less intrinsically interesting, it's often wise to keep the video pace moving, so you don't risk putting your audience to sleep.

Wrapping Things Up

The overall pace of information that people in our society are used to consuming continues to accelerate. We're a nation of remote-control channel changers, radio station button bashers and Web-clicking multi-taskers.

So when we sit down to watch a video, our brains are ready to receive data at a heavy pace. That doesn't mean that the only right pace for presenting visual information is with an MTV pace.

Like that shot of the baby in the cradle mentioned earlier in this chapter, sometimes the material on the screen will make all the connection with the audience that you need. When that happens, it's no error to linger over your shots and give your audience the time they need to not just look at, but to think about the material being presented.

Figure 49-3 *Close-ups add intensity, even for inanimate objects, when well-paced.*

Find the Clock

Each scene you shoot has its own internal clock. A shot of speeding freeway traffic clearly has a quicker clock than a shot of a horse and buggy meandering down a country lane. You have the power to quicken or slow your shots simply by virtue of your camera work. If you're shooting a landscape scene with a bridge on the right and a lighthouse on the left, you have an abundance of choices about how to shoot those elements, each with its own pacing.

You can go wide and do a static shot showing both. You can do static shots of each individual scene and cut between them. You can also elect to start on one and pan to the other. That pan can be anything from slow and stately, to a whip-pan where the scenery between the two is blurred. The choice you make will go a long way to determining the overall pace of your presentation of the images to your audience. Or why not shoot it each way and decide later? That's good coverage. And good coverage makes for good programs.

What Did You Really Think?

Most people are reluctant to criticize the work of others. We're polite to a fault. Sometimes you have to dig comments out of people, particularly about subtle things like your work's pacing. If your goal is to really discover if your work is really "on target" you have to learn to risk criticism and find out what others really think.

So the next time you're sitting at your edit system and you suspect that a piece of your timeline isn't paced just right, find someone who hasn't been staring at the material for a week. Show them the piece in question, and ask them what they really think.

50
Editing Effects Software to Make Your Video Sing

Michael Fitzer

Figure 50-1

While dissolves and fades that are inherent to just about any editing software on the market and will never go out of style, the power and accessibility of certain special effects software products on the market have enabled professionals of all types to add real eye-popping effects to otherwise marginal productions. In this chapter we'll cover the vast options for effects software designed to work side-by-side with many of those editing programs so popular in the field of post-production and how to choose the software package that best suits your needs.

What's Your Level?

While we all would like to be able to create a future generation of super robots to fly around in our next video, let's be realistic. The software and hardware used to generate such special effects software are built for high-level pros. The operative word here is "pros." The right software is a must, but without an appropriately skilled operator, understanding the software as well as how to operate it, can be a real struggle.

Now don't take that as an insult. The people that create the stuff of dreams in your favorite movies have all worked for years to perfect their craft. They're experts in their field. However, that doesn't mean you can't find the right software package for you and become an expert in making it work. With that in mind, take heart in the fact that creating and/or incorporating stunning visual effects into your work has never been easier. In fact, effects companies across the globe have turned much of their attention to the prosumer market, ensuring that their software is turnkey and seamless, fitting almost every conceivable platform. Let's not forget to mention a surging cost effectiveness. No longer do you have to pay tens-of-thousands of dollars to create your own high-level effects or hire an expensive digital flame artist to bring your vision to life. Whether you're a beginner, intermediate or an expert in the field of digital compositing, there's effects software built just for you.

More in Common Than You May Think

Here's the good news . . . Almost all special effects software packages operate using similar features like keyframing, drag-and-drop selection, low-resolution preview modes, preset menus, online tutorials, cross-platform functionality, an intuitive interface and more. While the pathway to get to such features is different depending on the software you're using, the basic concepts are the same. For instance, executing effects over time using keyframes is a fairly universal concept. You set an "in" and you set an "out," just as you would on an editing timeline. You can adjust the effect level between the ins and outs by setting more keyframes. It's just that simple. Tell the software to keep an effect up for 10 seconds then slowly fade it away in 3 seconds and all it takes is a few keyframes.

Features like menu presets allow you to manipulate existing effects presets, adding your own flare to a particular effect and then save that preset so you can reuse it time and time again. Additionally,

Sapphire Visual Effects

OVERVIEW	**Sapphire**
Sapphire Effects	**Coming Soon:** Sapphire Version 6 is currently scheduled to be released around the end of September 2011. Get a Sneak Peek!
PLATFORMS:	Sapphire streamlines your workflow, increases the productivity of your team, and frees up your time to be more innovative.
Adobe	
Apple	
Autodesk	
Avid	
Nuke	
Other OFX	
Sony Vegas	

Sapphire visual effects software helped Old Spice get the look. (Image courtesy of The Mill.)

Figure 50-2 *You may not have Ra Lewis as talent in your video, but Sapphire's visual effects give you the same tools as those used in high-end commercials. It's knowing how to use them; that's the key to creating visuals that capture your audience*

Knoll Light Factory 2.7

HIGHLIGHTS   VIDEO TUTORIALS

Figure 50-3 *Recognize this flare? You can add unmistakable feel to your video with effects that simply inspire awe.*

several software companies such as Red Giant, Digital Juice, and GenArts have created effects plug-ins that work across multiple platforms. Take the GenArts Sapphire software, for example. It allows users to create everything realistic: flashbulb effects and gun muzzle flashes to caustics used to create realistic water and several sizzling transitions. GenArts has designed Sapphire to work with Adobe's After Effects, Apple's Final Cut Pro, Avid's Media Composer, Symphony, Xpress, and Sony's Vegas, The Foundry's Nuke, Autodesk's Maya and more.

Options

If you're under the impression that you can simply Google "special effects software" and find a nearly infinite pool of choices . . . then you're under the right impression. In fact, that particular search might reveal more than 37.5 million! Since that's a great number of results,

hopefully the following information will help you narrow that daunting search quite a bit.

First, our hint is to stay away from the free downloads. While the price point sounds nice, the functionality of many of the freebie plug-ins is rather disappointing, not to mention potentially dangerous to your operating system. However, many of the more robust developers will allow you to try free demos or trials of their popular plug-ins. For instance, Red Giant's Knoll Light Factory is a dynamic motion graphics plug-in, which allows users to choose from dozens of designer preset flares, flashes and glows or create your own. By simply logging onto their website you can navigate your way to a free trial version of this or any of their other popular plug-ins including Trapcode Particular and Magic Bullet Suite. The only drawback here is that once you apply and render a clip using the trial download, your clip will render with a company watermark or a giant "X" across the clip. Sorry . . . no freebies here. The whole point

Figure 50-4 *Many software programs will provide presets that can give you something to build from. Through trial and error, you'll see what combinations of brightness, color and size will work for your videos.*

of a trial download is to allow you to test the software's features and limitations and hopefully get you interested enough to buy.

Be aware though; Red Giant and GenArts both serve up some powerful plug-ins which do take some time to master. These programs are deep, which makes them well worth the price. You can download Red Giant's Knoll Light Factory 2.7 for $400 or their bundled Magic Bullet Suite 11.1 for $800, which supplies a ton of firepower, allowing you to de-interlace footage, manipulate skin tone, push stops, and more.

GenArts' Sapphire pushes the price envelope a bit more, coming in at $1,700, but some would argue the strengths of the plug-in is worth the price. But not all GenArts plug-ins come in at a higher price point. For instance, its award-winning particleIllusion is a robust tool, which allows users to create amazing effects from a list of more than 3,000 presets, and it comes in at a palatable $299. The drawback here is that if you're someone who likes to house all of his or her effects plug-ins within your editing platform you're out of luck. ParticleIllusion works only as a stand-alone program or within Adobe After Effects.

As mentioned, Red Giant and GenArts plug-ins are deep and powerful tools. While intuitive in many ways, they do take a while to learn and thus are geared more toward the intermediate and expert users. However, there is a developer that provides a wide array of effects geared more toward the beginner. Digital Juice offers editors a massive library of preset effects and animations (not to mention stock footage and sound libraries) for anyone interested in applying a quick effect to their next video project. Animation bundles range anywhere from under $100 to $300 and more but the tools are easy to use and designed by pros with an eye toward efficiency. Digital Juice also acts as a third-party retailer for many software developers including Red Giant.

Now Get to Work

Hopefully, we've taken some of the confusion or even fear out of the ever-expanding world of digital effects. Whether you're an aspiring animator, an effects guru or simply an editor who wants to add a little spice to your next project, there's a plug-in or pre-designed software package built just for you. So take your time to do a little research. Try out some of the free trials and see what works best for your needs and skill level. Most of all—have fun doing what you love to do because nowadays, the possibilities for what you can bring to life on screen are almost limitless.

Marrying Effects

In this ever-expanding world of video special effects it may be enough to create your glowing particle or apply your preset alpha channeled animation and walk away, allowing the effect to do the work and "wow" the audience. However, if you want to take your effects to the next level without spending a ton of cash, consider combining effects. That's right . . . arrange a little marriage between two of your favorite effects and give your next project a push. Try working an effect of your own design into an animated preset. Whip some smoke around an animated arrow or add some flashing lights to the animated background of a large city. It only takes a little effort and it might be just the right direction to get your creative juices flowing.

51
Easy Tricks to Edit Quickly

Mark Montgomery

Figure 51-1

Editing shortcuts are essential for a productive editing workflow. Beginning video editors should begin training their editing behaviors around these shortcuts before adopting any inefficient habits. Let's take a look at the most common editing shortcuts to help you learn new ways to save yourself time and energy on your editing projects.

The Shot List

When we talk about editing shortcuts, we often think of keyboard shortcuts. Well, we'll get there, but the first and by far one of the most magical of shortcuts is a good, old fashioned shot list. Although a lot of the difficult work is done while shooting, a detailed shot list is really for the benefit of making the editor's chore easier.

In the early days of filmmaking, clapboards were used to mark the beginning of a shot so that the editor of the film strip could visually identify different

Figure 51-2 *Keeping a shot list will save you lots of time when capturing your footage. Most software allows you to enter in timecodes that will go directly to desired shots for capturing.*

shots, even different takes. To this day it's still used and in digital filmmaking, a clapboard can also keep record of the timecode.

Timecode is a data stream that synchronizes each frame of the digital signal so that computers can refer to frames of video in the proper order. When you edit video, each clip has its own timecode and most clips from video cameras have continuous time code. This means that if you record 60 minutes of video, even as you stop and start recording, the timecode is recorded without starting over at the beginning value (00:00:00:00, hours: minutes: seconds: frames). All this data is especially handy to an editor if the camera operator or an assistant keeps record of the starting and stopping timecode for every shot and records notes regarding scene, shot, take and the resulting quality of the particular take. In this way, the editor receives a list of shots, the corresponding timecode and whether or not the take was a good or bad take. Lucky you, the video has already been edited, at least on paper.

Not everyone can make shot lists on the field, especially if you're the only crew member or the content of your video does not allow you to start and stop the camera. Even then, you may be able to find a few seconds here and there to jot down timecode at key moments. For example, when shooting a wedding video, I'd often memorize a few good moments and write them down later when I had a second to stop. Let's say you're shooting the photo session of a wedding and the cute 4-year-old nephew of the bride tugs at her dress to tell her she looks like a princess. Money shot. Make a quick mental note of the timecode. You'll write that down when you move onto the next scene of the event.

Shot lists are much more practical in controlled environments where multiple takes of varying quality are recorded to the camera. In some cases, as you get better with your filmmaking eye, you might find yourself only taking the shots marked as "good" to your workstation and leaving the others on tape (or whatever media you shoot with).

With the shot list handy at your workstation, you can go to your Log and Capture tool in your editing software and enter the timecode for the shots you want to import from your tape (for other recording media, your technique may differ). With all the numbers punched in and logged, (it's really just a data entry job at this point), you can tell your computer to go fetch just the shots you've logged into your software. Now go grab a sandwich, finish that movie you fell asleep watching last night and when you get back to your workstation, all your clips will be imported and ready for you to edit. How's that for a shortcut?

There will be no more wading through hours and hours of footage looking for that one shot that's stuck in your head but lost somewhere in the day's events. Use shots lists, as much as you can. It might even be wise to have an assistant who will take care of it for you. And, keep the shot list with your tape; you'll never know when you'll need it again, or when a good take was as good as you thought in the first place.

Tapeless Made Easy

Now, for those of you using SDHC cards, P2 cards and other memory-based media, your workflow is little different from tape in regards to the capturing process. Since the video data is stored already as a file (in fact, you likely have a bunch of different files from when you stopped and started the camera), capturing video isn't necessary, but you can still log your shots and use the timecode to organize these shots for you before you start laying out your edit on the timeline. Often times, you'll also need to do some transcoding with this type of media, so it nearly takes the computer as much time minute-per-minute as tape media. But, so long as the computer is doing the heavy lifting, you can wander away from the computer and find something else to do. Another nice thing to do with these cameras, since the files are already broken into start/stop points, is to use an old-fashioned clapboard with scene/shot/take information on it. That way you can visually check the shot and take numbers and compare to your shot list quickly.

Keyboard Shortcuts Worth More Than a Dime a Dozen

Most editing software suites have keyboard shortcuts and the most common functions are usually standard shortcuts across all types of editing software. These are the shortcuts we're going to cover as you'll use them time and time again.

More In and Out (Not the Hamburger)

Once you've got your media into your bin and ready for editing (you used your shot list, right?), usually your first major task is to trim the "fat" of the clips. The extra seconds you recorded before and after the action actually took place need to be deleted before the clip can run in your program. As you preview your clip, you get to specify the "In" point and "Out" point of each clip. The "In" point is the "Start Here" point for the video clip. When specified, your software remembers that you marked this point on that frame of the clip, and that's where it should start playing. The "Out" point as you can imagine, is the "End Here" point where the editing software will tell itself to stop playing the video of that clip at that exact frame.

As you play back video in your preview monitor (usually, you can just double click any video from your bin to play it back) you can press the 'I' key on your keyboard to mark the frame the playback head is at as the "In" point. Then, when playback head moves further down the clip and it's time that the clip ends for the program, press the 'O' key and the video clip now has an "Out" point. These points are usually visible on the playback timeline for each video clip as little markers. You can usually click and drag the markers back and forth to set the markers to

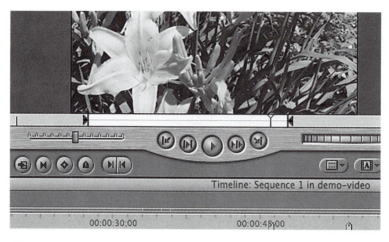

Figure 51-3 *Setting in and out points is crucial when editing. Knowing the right key commands will dramatically speed up your workflow.*

different points of your video clip. Many times your clips will need some fine tuning to get the "In" and "Out" points just where you want them and that's where these next shortcuts come into handy.

Traveling Through Time

The next most common editing shortcuts are the space bar and the 'J', 'K', and 'L' keys. These four work together as a team to move the playhead in your preview monitor in forward (realtime), fast-forward, reverse, fast-reverse and pause position. Go ahead and load up a video in your preview monitor and press the space bar. The video plays in realtime. Now, press the 'K' key. The 'K' key will pause the playhead whenever it's moving (forward or backward). Press the 'K' key again and the video is un-paused and playing again. With the video playing, press the 'J' key. Now the video moves in reverse. Press the 'K' key to pause, then the 'L' key to move it forward. That's the basics of moving the playhead forward and backwards and pausing. These keys allow you to cue up video to the important sections, but you'll also want to use the Right Arrow and Left Arrow keys to move the playhead one frame at a time for real precision.

Now, if your main goal is to trim the fat from your clips, you can easily navigate to the "In" and "Out" points without having to cumbersomely click and drag these points to their ideal locations. By the way, these points can be set multiple times. For example, if you set an out point then discover that the clip doesn't end until two seconds later, simply play the video and hit the 'O' key once again. You'll see the "Out" point snap into its new location.

On Your Marks

Another great tool that will save you a good deal of "where did that go" time is markers. Most professional video editing suites have this tool that allows you to place a marker anywhere on the program timeline. In fact, you can set as many markers as you'd like or need. For example, after you've completed your rough cut, you may want to run through the program quickly and set markers wherever you need a lower third for your talent. Any time you need to make a note, the marker places a visual reminder locked at a specific time on the timeline so that you don't have to scrub your timeline for five minutes looking for that one spot. The actual shortcut keys may differ between software suites. For Final Cut Pro, it's the 'M' key.

More to Explore

These are the most fundamental shortcuts for beginning video editors that will allow you to simplify some of the most repetitive tasks, whether you're importing your media or trimming up a clip. Make sure to also spend time learning more shortcuts. Just about every common task has a keyboard shortcut and if you learn them early on you'll naturally adopt these techniques. Getting in the habit of using these will save you a great deal of time, not to mention that you'll also impress your clients as you wield your video edits with a few clicks of a button. Happy editing!

52
Color Correction 101

Morgan Paar

Figure 52-1

A few simple steps can save an improperly-shot scene or improve one that is less than brilliant.

Don't let the interface of the Color Corrector 3-Way window intimidate you (OK, some of us editors were intimidated by this less-than-intuitive window). Keep in mind that, even though this chapter will show you a few simple techniques, this color-correction tool and others are quite robust, and some editors make healthy incomes concentrating on this fix-it-in-post endeavor.

Let's start with some tools that will help greatly. The first is an NTSC monitor. Though we are aware that many editors work without this essential tool, due to its hefty sticker price (some over $10,000!), we really cannot see the true colors that viewers experience on a television set from our computer monitors. A consumer television set is better than no outside monitoring of the picture, but a true NTSC monitor is best. If you are sure your finished piece will live only on the internet, no monitor is necessary. But if you are making DVDs of your final project (which are usually viewed on television sets), or the Discovery Channel calls and wants to use your piece on air, it's a good idea to view your project through a non-computer monitor before output.

The other two tools we will use won't cost you anything extra if your editing software has them built in. They are two of the four video scopes: the waveform monitor and the vectorscope. We will admit that these highly technical-looking scopes intimidated some of us at first viewing, but learning the basics of how to read them to assist in altering light and color will greatly improve our images.

The video scopes give us invaluable information on color and brightness within a single clip and even help us correct white-balance problems originating in production. They will also quickly tell us if our image is not "broadcast safe," enabling us to bring it within the safe zone with our color corrector.

Invention of the Wheel

Sir Isaac Newton gets credit for developing the color wheel as we know it, with the primary additive colors red, green and blue and the secondary colors magenta, yellow and cyan, formed by overlapping primary colors. The center of a color wheel has no color or is white. As you travel away from the center, colors become more saturated.

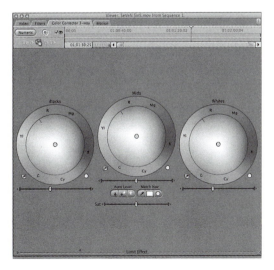

Figure 52-2 *In your editing software, adjusting color via a 3-way filter tweaks black levels, mid-tones, and white levels. It can enhance contrast as well as warm up or cool down an image.*

Two Color Wheels

Please notice that we are talking about with the Color Corrector 3-Way filter in this exercise. There is another tool called simply the Color Corrector. We use the 3-way for "primary color correction," which incorporates the manipulation of the overall color balance of the entire image.

Getting to Work

Many higher-end editing programs will have a "color correction" layout that you can find under the Window pull-down menu. Most modern editing programs will let you work with most of your color correction in real time, that is, if your processor is fast enough and you have a decent amount of RAM.

You can find the Color Corrector 3-Way in your Video Filters folder; usually you'll locate it under Color Correction.

The 3-way has a visual interface as well as a numeric interface. We find it easier to work in the visual interface.

Most Color Corrector 3-Way visual interfaces show three color wheels with luminance sliders beneath them, along with other controls, including an eyedropper. In primary color correction, we suggest you concentrate on image contrast first, then work on color balance. The eye is more sensitive to changes in contrast than to differences in color, so this is the best place to start. We use a work flow that starts with setting the black levels, then moving on to the white levels and ending with adjustments to the mid-tone levels.

Start with Luminance

By moving the black level luminance slider, you affect the overall depth of the black levels in the image. By looking at the waveform monitor, you can see if your black level values are above 0 percent, or what is known as Black, and move the black level slider to the left.

If you keep moving that slider to the left, bringing your black level values down to the 0 percent luminance line in the monitor, you will start to "crush your black levels." For example, if you can see detail of dark hair, you can crush the black level of the image by sliding the luminance to the left. The tonal range in the dark hair that gave visual details in the shadow area are "crushed" into all black, eliminating the shadow detail.

Make sure you check the levels for the entire clip and not just one frame of the image. Changes in the action will cause changes in the luminance levels.

If your white level values go over 100 percent luminance, into Super White, your image is not broadcast-safe (look at your waveform monitor to see if there are any dots above 100 percent). You can slide the luminance slider under the white level color wheel until you see the values for white levels drop below 100 percent into network safe range.

Finally, we want to alter the mid-tones, which will affect the overall exposure of the clip. This slider affects mostly skin tone or middle gray in most shooting situations of a properly-exposed image. If someone's face looks too bright or too dark, the Mids slider could bring them back into normal exposure. Every color corrector that we have used has an on/off check box that will enable you to view your changes and the originally-shot clip with the click of a button.

When color-correcting a certain clip, look at the top of the Viewer window, where you can find the name of the clip, to make sure that you are working on the correct clip. It is easy to think that you are working on one clip, while you're really adjusting the color of another clip. You should also know that adjusting any one wheel (or tonal level) also adjusts others. For example, though you adjust mostly the darker parts of the image when you move the black-level luminance slider, you also adjust white levels and mid-tones a bit. The same is true with the other two wheels. This keeps more realistic gradations, but it means you may need to

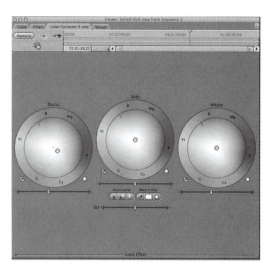

Figure 52-3 *Subtle adjustments give the most pleasing results. The indicator on the black level wheel is nudged towards blue. This cools down our blacks.*

make slight adjustments on the other two wheels when you are drastically changing one wheel.

You will want most color correction to be subtle, unless you are going for a very stylized look. Various keyboard commands or use of a mouse with a scroll wheel can help you fine-tune a look. Check your user's manual, as these effects differ in various editing programs.

Next We Adjust Color

Use color balancing to remove or intensify a colorcast in a scene. The vectorscope will be your friend here. If you look to the center of each of the color balance wheels—the black levels, midtones and white levels—you will see a small, gray, circular object called the Balance Indicator. By clicking and dragging this small circle towards the outer part of any wheel, you will see that you can adjust the hue that corresponds with each of these tonal levels respectively, to the color you move the indicator towards.

This control works in small increments, so small movements might be difficult to notice. Again, the on/off check box will

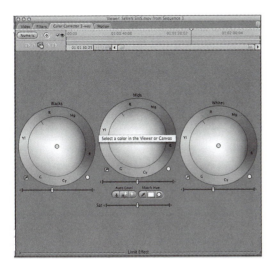

Figure 52-4 *You can adjust poor white balance with the eye dropper.*

help you see the changes you have made. It may seem as if you aren't changing the tint or shade much, but unclick that box, and you can easily see your changes. Again, you want this to be subtle, so move in baby steps and continually check against the original or against an image you are trying to match. The more you drag that gray dot to the perimeter of the circle, the more saturated the hue that affects the tonal range becomes.

Many color wheels have a reset button on the lower right of the wheel. Just like focusing a camera, you move in and out, more extreme and then less, until it looks right. If you are not happy with current changes, just reset to eliminate all changes and start again. Note that adjusting the mid-tones color balance wheel has the greatest overall affect on the image. This is because the mid-tones are the majority of your color information in a typical image that is exposed properly.

On the color wheel, each primary color is opposite its secondary color. These opposite colors on the wheel are complementary colors. If you drag towards one color, the color on the opposite side of the wheel lessens. For example, if you move towards red, you intensify red while reducing the cyan values in the image.

Quick White-Balance Correction

There is a quick trick for simply correcting an image with improper white balance. Click on the eye-dropper under the mid-color wheel, and then click on an object in your clip that should be white. This tells the filter to adjust the overall image in a way that makes this object white, thus adjusting the improper balance of the whole image. See, not too intimidating.

You've Graduated from Color Correction 101

Master these few basic color correction steps, and you are well on your way in the art of color correction. This is just the beginning of what you can accomplish with the robust Color Correction 3-Way tool.

53

Less is More: Editing Titles and Graphics

Mark Montgomery

Figure 53-1 *From beginning to end, your graphics should be consistent to each other and match the style of your video's genre.*

Creating professional titles and graphics in your video production is no easy feat. As an editor, you can often be burdened for hours creating titles that match the aesthetic of your video production.

Most common video editing applications come with built-in text and graphic generators, while more professional solutions allow you to do 3D objects, lighting and particle emitters. With all these whiz-bang features, however, what really matters most is keeping it simple.

A terrific example of the "less is more" philosophy is the opening title of the hit TV show *Lost*. Picture a black, empty background with white, 3D text that says "Lost," moving from far-away and out of focus as it gently twists in space toward the viewer. It briefly sharpens into focus as it continues to swirl forward. Meanwhile a bed of ghostly noises plays in the background. It's visually quite simple: black background, white text and simple motion. But, it says a lot about the kind of show you're about to see. It's haunting; it's disorienting; it's everything that is the main character of the show: a mysterious island with a mind of its own.

Where the Danger Lurks

Many designers (usually the ones with the most tools) tend to make a muck of their titles and graphics, adding layer upon layer of shapes, setting them to motion in every which way they can go, and pouring every color onto the canvas. Their poor viewers and their eyes—how do they manage? Seriously, how do they manage to extract the meaning of titles and graphics that are poorly thought out and executed. The trick for any editor is to be aware of the context and meaning of their editing decisions, down to what kind of font to use.

Choosing a Typeface

Typeface is the fancy word designers use for what the majority of us refer to as

Figure 53-2 *Busy backgrounds can compete with your titles. Since this can make it hard for the viewer to know what to look at, keeping your background graphics simple or out of focus may be the best option for readability.*

fonts. Since we're talking about titles and graphics, I'll continue to wear my designer cap and refer to typefaces from here on out. Many designers make a living from creating typefaces, believe it or not. In fact, typefaces are intellectual property just like the original videos you create. A professionally designed typeface could cost you anywhere from $20–$120 a license. Just wanted to warn you, in case you should be planning your next video budget for a client who's in need of a professional look. Many savvy video creators have learned that there are quite a few royalty-free typefaces out there, but use them at your own risk. A good font is well laid out with the spacing between letters carefully considered. I highly recommend taking a look at professionally designed typeface, just to get a sense of the quality and variety that is available.

A good typeface can say a lot about your production. For example, if you're editing a 30-second spot for a classy restaurant, you'll want a typeface that is elegant, sophisticated and yet easy to read. For example, you would never use the Comic Sans typeface. You could spend a good hour or so cycling through the standard typefaces on your computer and still come up empty-handed (and, please, don't even think about Papyrus, the most overused, overrated typeface on the planet). Do some shopping around. I visit fontshop.com quite frequently. There are probably hundreds of other places to look

Figure 53-3 *Avoid using inappropriate or over-used typefaces like Comic Sans or Papyrus. Instead, search out new typefaces that can be purchased online. There are hundreds to choose from, which can give your titles a fresh new look.*

for good typefaces. They can save you a great deal of time because you won't have to rely on cheap editing tricks to make the titles and graphics look good.

Watch Out for Too Much Detail

Video is rather unforgiving when it comes to typefaces that have too many small details. Typically, serifs are bad. A serif is the ornate design along the tails or heads of individual letters. Not all serifs are bad, just the ones that are so small in detail that they make the letters look like they're flickering. When a small serif gets caught between two video pixels it can flicker between the two. It's an unfortunate distraction to the viewer. So, choose a typeface that has cleaner or thicker lines.

Text on the Move

Choosing a typeface that speaks to the aesthetics of your video and conveys its meaning will get you off to a great start. For the TV show *Lost*, you could say the typeface was a little more than a start and that its movement carried it the rest of the way. The twisting, swirling "Lost" gave the viewer a disorienting feeling, which really sets them up nicely for the entire show.

Now, back to our classy restaurant example, how can we use movement to convey sophistication? Maybe we have the restaurant name move across the screen ever so slightly left to right. It could look as if it were gracefully gliding across. With the right

Figure 53-4 *Due to their size, the serifs can spell trouble for your titles. To keep your titles looking sharp, use a sans serif typeface, or a typeface consisting of thicker serifs.*

typeface, this would be a very elegant movement. And simple too! Two keyframes to mark you positions and you're done. Well, nearly. Add a gentle fade in and fade out and you're done with your title. How easy.

Laying the Foundation with Graphics

Graphics can mean quite a few things, from complicated 3D environments to simple background images. For most of us, we just need something in the background and, unfortunately, we don't have the time or budget to make 3D models and spin objects all around the frame. But, again, I remind you to think about the meaning of your actions as an editor.

Considering the *Lost* example once more I always thought it was odd that the background was black. It almost seemed like a lost opportunity (pun intended). I would not be surprised if the editors had several versions with different backgrounds, perhaps a few options that conveyed more meaning. Yet, the background was an empty black. Most importantly, it was abstract.

The key to creating good, complimentary graphics to your title is making them abstract so that the viewer is not distracted by them, while also trying to reinforce the meaning. With the variety of objects at play, it's all about context. Imagine once again, the classy restaurant example. What kind of background would convey sophistication and elegance. What can fall behind our gliding title that will reinforce the meaning. I would think that a still photograph of blurry lights would be a nice touch. You can take a photograph of Christmas lights at a great distance with a long lens and deliberately take the lights out of focus, softening the points of light. You could even add colored gels to add a nice color effect. Probably warm reds or oranges would be a good fit.

A Few More Tricks

After you've built your composition of titles and graphics you may want to consider these few tricks before finalizing your video. De-interlacing your video can help reduce the flickering that can appear with serifs or other fine-detailed graphics. Most video editing applications have filters that you can apply to video, text, graphics and photographs that will de-interlace your video. Consider doing that for all your text sequences.

You may also find that titles and graphics with very sharp edges are prone to flicker on-screen as well. Occasionally, I've tried adding a slight Gaussian blur (no more than .2 in the Gaussian blur settings) and found that it can help minimize this effect.

Titles and graphics can be overwhelming for many of us. When in doubt, don't hesitate to seek help from professionals. Even many print graphic designers can help in the video world. And most importantly, remember that less is more. There are many interesting templates that can automate all sorts of fancy text and graphical effects, but always ask yourself what the meaning of it is. Don't leave that question up to your viewers, as that's a sure sign that you've left them confused. Unless, of course, you're *Lost* and you're making a point of that.

54
Fixing Audio in Post

Hal Robertson

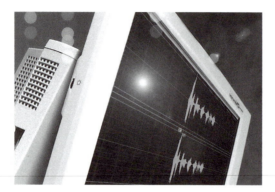

Figure 54-1

Most editors grind their teeth when someone says, "don't worry we'll fix it in post," but fixing it in post are where audio tricks shine.

We've lectured for years on the benefits of proper audio gathering and getting it right at the shoot. Obviously, this makes things easier, cleaner and more professional sounding when you begin to edit the footage. But for whatever reason, it seems that something always happens to mar your perfect audio recording. It may be a simple little thing or some unforeseen catastrophe, but someday, it's inevitable, you're going to have to fix something in post. You can relax because today's audio editing tools—and even video tools—offer virtually everything you need to repair those unfortunate audio accidents, and these tools can help you enhance the audio even more.

Options Galore

Fixing audio in post used to be a nightmare. Just imagine all the equipment it took back in the golden age of television. Video was recorded and edited on tape, so all the audio processing took place in real time with real hardware processors. Need some equalization? Hook up a box. Need some dynamics control? Hook up another box. And don't forget, many of

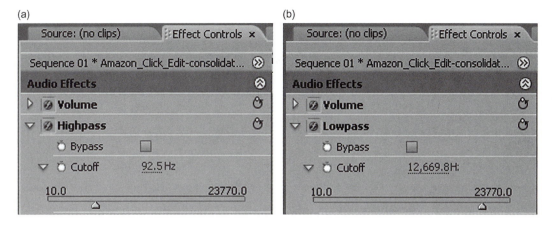

Figure 54-2 *High-pass and low-pass filters can help eliminate specific spectrums of unwanted noise from your audio. By setting the cutoff, you can subtract all frequencies above or below the cutoff point, while allowing the remaining frequencies to pass through.*

those boxes were expensive. Of course, today all our audio processing and cleanup takes place inside the computer. Adding a virtual processor can be as simple as dragging something onto the timeline. If you don't get what you want the first time, just back up and try again with different settings. If you need a processor that's not included in your editor, just download one from the internet—many times they're even free.

The majority of audio repair tools fall into just two categories. First are the filters. These include high-pass, low-pass, band pass and general purpose equalization. Filters affect the tonal quality of your recording and usually serve to add or subtract some portion or portions of the audio spectrum from your audio track. Next on the list are dynamics processors. Compressors, limiters and expanders all fit this category. Dynamics processors generally alter the difference between loud and soft portions of the soundtrack. It's most common to reduce the dynamic range of a recording in post to gain clarity and even out volume levels.

Another popular audio tool is digital noise reduction. By sampling a section of only noise, you tell the noise reduction processor what to remove from your recording. This is a powerful tool that has the potential to rescue noisy recordings and significantly reduce hiss without affecting the quality of sound. Other tools such as de-essers and enhancers operate using a combination of filtering, dynamics control and other techniques. Regardless of the tool or tools you're using, the goal is the same: clean up that audio track.

Working Inside the Editing Program

The most effective audio repair tool you have available isn't a signal processor at all; it's the cut tool. With clean cuts you can eliminate many of the noises that pop up during the shoot. For interviews, a tight cut gets rid of all the shuffling, bumping, umms and ahhs that drove you crazy in the first place. In an action scene, you may be able to cut before the noisy motorcycle drove by or just before someone behind the camera tripped over a light stand. In addition, you have the power to decide which take requires the least repairs after the fact. The cut tool is your first line of defense.

Of course, cuts alone won't fix everything, but it's a good place to start. Once you have an edit you're happy with, it's time to clean up the leftovers. Another good non-processor cleanup tool is the use of volume envelopes. Envelopes are drawn on the audio track which creates automated mutes for the tracks. This works especially well on dialogue when you plan to cover

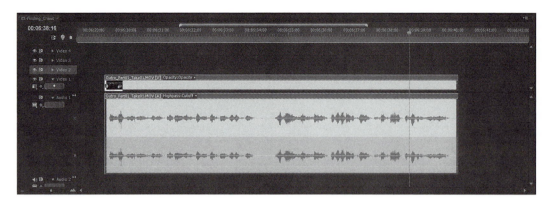

Figure 54-3 *Envelopes allow you to create automated mutes for your tracks. However, if you don't have audio to fill the gaps you have created, you may want to consider another approach.*

the gaps with room tone, music or sound effects. Otherwise, you may have to resort to other techniques. When working on a dialogue track, start with a high-pass filter. By setting the cutoff frequency around 100 Hz or so, you effectively eliminate any audio below that point. That includes rumbles from wind and mechanical noise. Removing this portion of the audio spectrum makes a cleaner track for any additional processing you do.

If you have volume-level issues, consider using an audio compressor. Start with a 2:1 ratio and listen closely to the effect. You should hear a leveling of audio levels—soft sounds become a little louder and loud sounds don't get so loud. It's easy to over-do this effect, so listen to the bare audio track when you make changes to minimize over processing of the sound. Another volume trick is placing a hard limiter on the master output. Sometimes called a brick-wall limiter, this processor puts a lid on the audio volume and keeps any audio spikes under control. This ensures a distortion-free final audio track that won't overload playback systems downstream.

Export and Process

If your editing program offers little in the way of audio cleaning tools, consider exporting the finished audio track and fixing it in a separate audio-only program. This option provides all the audio processing power you'll need. Inside a Digital Audio Workstation or DAW, you can clean and polish audio tracks with a variety of tools. In addition to the standard filters, your DAW offers graphic and/or parametric equalizers to eliminate harshness, get rid of audio mud and brighten tracks. You will likely have access to a spectrum analyzer, too, which provides visual animation of your audio and helps pinpoint areas that need further attention.

In addition to the digital noise reduction we mentioned earlier, most DAWs offer a plug-in architecture, allowing you to include any compatible audio processor you like. Whether paid or free, there are hundreds—maybe thousands—of general purpose and specialty audio processors available today. Using one or more of these, you can widen or narrow the stereo width of your audio, add audio effects like echo and reverb or make your audio sound like it's coming from an over-driven bullhorn. The only limits are your imagination, patience and ability to find useful plug-ins on the internet.

Mr. Fix-It

In a perfect world, we'd all record flawless audio in-camera the first time and editing would be a breeze. Keep

(a) 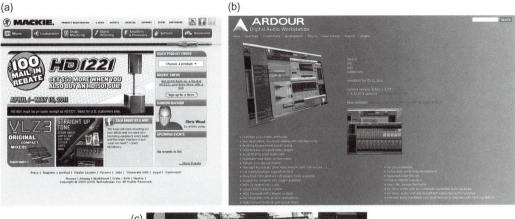 (b)

(c)

Figure 54-4 *There is a multitude of audio processors available today. From general purpose, to specialty audio processors, the sky's the limit to what you can do in terms of enhancing your audio through plug-ins and programs.*

dreaming. It's a cruel world out there for the video producer and it would be easy to let a lot of audio errors go. Nobody will notice, right? Maybe not on YouTube, but if you're creating video for paying clients or for your business, it's worth the time and effort to fix the audio. The nice thing is, whether you do it in your editing program or your DAW, the tools are there if you're willing to invest the time.

Change in the Wind

The Audio for Video landscape is changing. DSLRs have had a large impact on audio gathering techniques and many producers record their audio on separate recorders. In post, you may have to combine a shotgun mic track recorded in the camera with one or more tracks from pocket recorders on talent. The editors' challenge is unifying these sound sources to create a seamless end product. It's certainly more complicated that it used to be, but this is where things are going. Get friendly with the workflow and your audio processors—you're going to need them.

55
Recording Sound Effects

Hal Robertson

Figure 55-1

Movies with true organic sounds, imagined futuristic electronic audio, and even the everyday noises around us, aren't complete without good sound effects.

The spacecraft has crashed into a swamp and as Luke and his droid inspect their new environment, a landscape of sounds surrounds them. Strange noises come from everywhere. Unseen creatures from above and below the water each leave their sonic fingerprints on the scene. Unless you've been living in a cave for the past 25 years or so, you've seen and heard this scene from *The Empire Strikes Back*. Watching the movie, it's easy to believe it's all real, even though the swamp was manufactured on a sound-stage and the environmental sounds were gathered from around the globe. The sound effects sell the scene and connect the viewer to the action. And you don't need a *Star Wars* budget to spice up your productions with sound effects. All you need is a little effort, creativity and some patience. Let's get started.

Think About It

The term "sound effects" or SFX covers a broad range of noises, including ambience, one-shots, human, electronic and mechanical sounds. With our digital editing tools, we can also repurpose sounds by shifting, reversing and other forms of manipulation. You may be wondering why we should go to the trouble of recording our own sound effects when there are so many good libraries out there. It's a fair question. When you have a tight deadline or need a sound that lives on the other side of the world, sound effects libraries are the perfect choice. But sometimes, a project needs a specific atmosphere or sound that isn't in the library. It's also quicker and easier to record the actual sound during the shoot instead of digging through a set of 250,000 sound effects.

Depending on the sounds you want to capture, you can use almost any microphone, from the built-in stereo mic on your camera to a fancy shotgun model. The built-in option carries an upside and a downside—you can record in stereo, but you'll have to live with any mechanical noise produced by the camcorder. If you're recording busy sounds like traffic or running water, the extra noise won't be an issue. For quieter settings, you may need another option. One of those options is a portable MiniDisc recorder or other field audio recorder. These small wonders record in stereo or mono at CD quality and will work for hours on a single battery. Just make sure it has a microphone input! If you prefer to use your camera, simply hook it up like you would for a video shoot, grab a pair of headphones and forget about the pictures. When you're finished recording, capture through FireWire and delete the video part of the media or select capture settings that capture only the audio.

Audio Safari

Scene 27 in our movie has the main characters, Bob and Rhonda, discussing recent events at the edge of the woods. After a heated argument, Rhonda storms off with the car, leaving poor Bob stranded. You've got your gear together and a list of sounds to record, and there's a perfect place just outside of town. Scout the location with your ears, listening for good and bad sounds. Is there traffic in the background? Depending on the area, aircraft is a possibility too. This location is clean, so we'll set up our equipment. Since this is ambience for our video, stereo recording is the way to go. There's plenty of wildlife and water sound, so we'll use the built-in stereo mic on the camera. For a completely natural feel, position the camera just as you would to shoot video. Slate the recording with a short description of the setting or scene number and let the tape roll for a few minutes.

Next on the list is a car door slam and tires throwing gravel as the car speeds away. For this setup, we'll use a handheld or shotgun microphone to isolate the sounds. We'll also record each element separately so we can get the timing just right in post. The door slam is easy—just point the mic at the door and slam it a few times, we can pick the best one later. Don't forget to record the opening sound too. For the drive-off, we'll set the microphone near the car, pointed in the direction it will drive. With safety in mind, we should locate the camera and people to the side of any flying gravel. A long mic cable and some safety glasses wouldn't hurt either. We'll record several takes of this one too, for more flexibility later.

Finally, we need to record a sound that can substitute for feet crunching through the leaves in the woods. Let's set up with

Figure 55-2 *Recording sound effects during the shoot is often easier than trying to find them in a library and they'll always match your scene better.*

the handheld or shotgun this time too. Lay a large towel on the floor and dump a bag of potato chips or corn flakes in the middle. Feel free to crunch with your hands or feet—whichever makes the most convincing sound. Don't worry about matching the pace of the video; we'll record a variety of left and right footfalls to drop on the timeline. I guess we'll have to clean up the mess at some point.

Post It

Once you've recorded your sound effects and dumped them into the computer,

you need to mold them on your timeline. First, we find the perfect version of each sound. Next, let's drop the stereo ambience on the timeline to establish the feel of the scene. The recording of the woods should enhance the feel without overpowering the dialog. Adjust the volume with track sliders or rubber bands to create the right balance. Now we'll add the car noises. Scrub the timeline to the point where Rhonda opens the car door. Add that sound effect on its own track and then do the same for the car door slam, nudging each sound until it matches the action perfectly. For the drive off, we'll do the same thing, but add a keyframed

Figure 55-3 *Using a clapboard will help the editing process later. Recording the perfect sounds separately from your dialog tracks gives you many choices.*

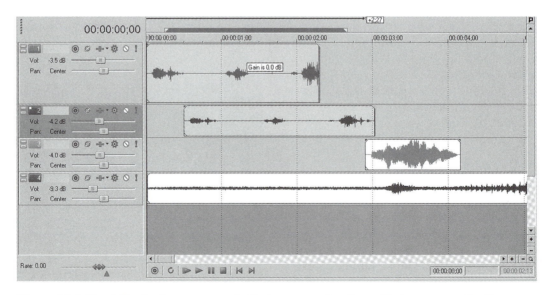

Figure 55-4 *Carefully placing your sound effects on your timeline will give your production a professional sound.*

pan to the mix. The car drives from right to left, so set a keyframe at the beginning of the clip and adjust the pan 50 percent right. Now, go to the end of the clip, set another keyframe and adjust the pan for 50 percent left. Tweak for maximum effect.

We've saved the footsteps for last since they're the most difficult. Play the scene and count how many footsteps you'll need. If the feet aren't in the shot, watch for body movement to determine their locations. Drop a variety of left footfall sound effects on one audio track and then add the right footfalls on another. Slide the sound effects around until you've created a convincing walking sound. If necessary, mute the other audio tracks to improve clarity as you're editing.

To help with timing, it may be possible to reference the dialog track for actual footfalls. Once you're happy with the edit, play it a few times, listening for balance and realism. The sound effects should enhance the scene rather than call attention to themselves.

Lock That Mix

Now, it's up to you to experiment with these techniques on your own projects. Adding your own sound effects to a video is a creatively rewarding process. It's extra work, but you'll gain valuable experience and a newfound respect for the SFX wizards who share their creativity on the big screen.

Grab It Today

I recently worked on an independent movie called *Breaking Ten*. As the sole tech guy, I was responsible for shooting, lighting and audio. Working on tight schedules barely got some scenes shot, so I had to return later to record sound effects. Unfortunately, it was many months later and now the restaurant was out of business, the field with all the crickets had been mowed, and the creek was much lower than the day of the shoot. I know better. Lesson learned: save yourself time, gas and stress by recording sound effects while on location.

56
Sync Sound

Hal Robertson

Figure 56-1

What do you do if your camera doesn't record good audio? With the increased use of DSLRs and cell phone for video shooting, audio syncing skills are a necessity.

We've always advocated the use of external microphones, but not every camera has a mic jack, even those that do often have noisy inputs and limited audio quality. Today, it's very easy to gather location audio the way the big boys do—with a separate recorder—and sync the sound in post. The movie and television industries have done it this way forever. In fact, the reason we expect our cameras to record audio comes from the news world, where everything is included in one package. Maybe the way to move your production quality forward is to take a step back.

Figure 56-2 *Attaching a boom mic to a portable audio recorder is a great way to get the mic as close as possible to the sound source without having to tether the mic to the camera. Record the "clap" from a clapper with your camera mic and the boom mic.*

Get the Gear

There is an incredible range of cameras that record video today. DSLRs, point-n-shoots, pocket cameras and even our cell phones all shoot pretty nice HD video. But they all share one problem: the sound stinks. It's the same problem we've had in the video world for years; a cheap, built-in microphone simply can't record professional audio. This is no longer a problem. By recording the sound separately— sometimes called Dual System Sound— you can build an audio package that meets your specific needs, whether in the studio or on location.

The simplest way to get started is with one of the new pocket audio recorders. Several big manufacturers make these little recorders and there are many models and features to choose from. They all share two common traits: they run on batteries and they record to flash cards. From there, choose a recorder based on your production style and existing equipment. Most have built-in stereo microphones, an 1/8" input and a headphone jack. Others add inputs for line level and a few even have professional, balanced XLR inputs with phantom power. The good news is that even the least expensive models record excellent quality audio with plenty of control, features and battery life.

Another way to record is using a laptop or netbook and a simple USB audio interface. There are several USB-powered audio interfaces available for under $100. Most include balanced XLR inputs, headphone outputs and even phantom power for your condenser microphones. Attach one of these to your laptop or netbook, load your favorite audio software, and hit the record button. This is a simple, portable system that can easily produce professional recordings. Plus, you can use the same interface back in the edit suite for voice overs and sound effects recording.

The Setup

Shooting with sync sound isn't much different from a normal shoot, but there are

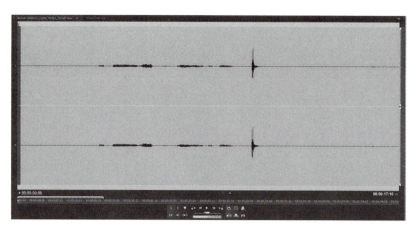

Figure 56-3 *Place the camcorder and portable recorder audio on separate tracks in your timeline. Then enlarge the clapboard spike so you can line up the tracks.*

some changes. Obviously, setting up the video is the same however you shoot, but there are some extra steps in the audio setup. First, you'll have to make sure your audio recording device or software is set to the proper recording mode. A good place to start is the file format. Although most video editing software will accept compressed audio formats like MP3, resist the temptation and record in an uncompressed format—usually WAV files. Set the sampling rate to 48 kHz and the bit depth to 16 bits. This setup replicates the audio system for DV recording, is already DVD friendly, better than CD quality and should give you an excellent recording. Many recorders and interfaces can use higher sampling rates and bit depths, but your file size increases dramatically and it's unlikely you'll hear a significant improvement. While you're in the menu, synchronize the date and time with your camera if possible. It will save you headaches later.

Separating audio from video adds some challenges, but also creates some opportunities. For instance, if you use one of the smaller pocket recorders with a lapel mic, it can function as a virtual wireless microphone without any noise or range problems. An audio person booming a shotgun mic on a pole can monitor with their own headphones untethered from the camera and free to move around as needed.

After you hit the record button on both the camera and the audio recorder, it's important to slate each take. The easy way to do this is with a clap board. With the clapper in clear view of the camera or cameras, state the information about the take and smack the clapper bars together. This provides a simple visual and audible cue that makes sync easy in the edit suite.

iPhone and iPad users have a digital alternative. Search for "DSLR Slate" in the app store. For just a few bucks, you can have a thoroughly professional slate that fits in your pocket or backpack. Of course, you can do something similar by simply clapping your hands. How ever you do it, slating every take is very important when you're recording audio and video separately. You'll learn to appreciate this extra step once you start editing.

Post-it Notes

Following the shoot, it's time to recombine your audio and video elements. After you dump all the files into a folder and load them into your editing program, the fun begins. If you did your homework and followed a consistent workflow during the shoot, you should have one audio clip for every video clip you shot.

If you did, congratulations! Your edit will be easy. For the rest of us, we may have to do some digging. This is where the date, time and slate information comes into play. Essentially, you're comparing each video clip to its corresponding audio clip or slate information. And you may have to split some audio clips into smaller chunks if you recorded continuously during the shoot. This can take some time, but after you've done a few, it gets easier.

Once you've identified matching audio and video clips, drop them on the timeline, zoom in on the audio track and look for the clapper spike. Simply slide the audio spike to match the clapper in the video and link the two files together. Make sure to delete or at least mute the sound from the video clip and your sync sound will become the primary audio. You might have to play with this frame-by-frame from here, until you get a perfect match. Now, just edit as usual. Of course, you have to do this for every set of clips, so this might take a while.

Oh, Oh—The Sound doesn't Match

But what do you do when your sync sound doesn't sync? You can sync up the beginning but, by the end of the clip, it's out of sync. Long-form projects are the most vulnerable here and there are several possible causes. Video frame rates vs. project frame rates, audio sampling rates and even hardware issues could be the culprit. One repair technique is cutting up the audio and re-syncing every few minutes. This is a serious pain, especially on a long project, but it may be the only way. Alternatively, try adjusting the speed of the audio clip, adding or subtracting small percentages as needed—a little goes a long way here. To assist with this, add a clapper to the end of each clip, just before you stop recording. This provides an additional sync reference point for audio stretching. To find out more about some syncing issues a number of our readers have been discussing check out this forums link: http://www.videomaker.com/community/forums/topic/audio-sync-1.

Sound All Around

We tried to keep this chapter non brand-specific, simply because there are so many options for recorders, audio interfaces and software. Each has its merits and any given item might or might not be the perfect fit. However, there is one unique recorder worth mentioning by name: the Zoom H2. This little pocket recorder has one feature not included on any other model we know of—it records in surround sound. With four built-in microphones, the Zoom H2 records two stereo pairs—one facing forward, one facing back. Add a separate dialogue track and you have a nearly perfect surround recording solution. As for another recording device, the Tascam DR-05 has similar features to the Zoom H1 and costs the same. It looks like a solid piece and the Tascam pedigree doesn't hurt.

57
Simple Compositing

Morgan Paar

Figure 57-1

Everyone loves to be awed by movie magic, and you can bedazzle your audience using our simple compositing tips that reveal the secret of see-through layers.

Compositing is omnipresent. It would be nearly impossible to watch a Hollywood film or an hour of television and not see some sort of compositing. Some films, such as Zack Snyder's *Spartan Epic, 300* (2006), is nearly all compositing. But what is this technique, and how do we who have less than a Hollywood budget use it?

Compositing is the combination of two or more images to form a single final image. The six o'clock news meteorologist standing in front of a weather map is a good example. The map is not really behind this person, nor is it projected.

The composite is made in the "booth," where a video engineer combines the feed of the live meteorologist with the image of the map and the icons of clouds, the sun, names of counties or towns, etc.

Another great example of common composites is lower thirds. These can be static graphic or flashy motion visuals which usually identify a person and his profession. You find them often in news programs, documentaries and sporting events such as football and baseball games. Similarly, titles in films, commercials and music videos use this graphic type of compositing.

Now, I know what you are thinking: "Ah, I get it, computer-generated effects." But not all compositing is the product of microchips. George Melies, a stage magician working in France over 100 ago, often gets credit for being the first compositor for moving pictures. Melies admired the works of film pioneers, the Lumière brothers, in 1895 and was inspired to combine some of his sleight-of-hand with film. His famous 16-minute, black-and-white film, *A Trip to the Moon* (*Le voyage dans la Lune*, 1902) can still be found pleasing audiences over a century later.

The Basics

The basic idea behind compositing is transparency. A great analogy is t-shirt silk screening. You stretch fine-mesh cloth or screen over a wooden frame. You can press ink through this screen onto a shirt. Next you adhere a "negative" of the image you want onto the screen. It's a bit like a stencil: the negative image attached to the screen will not let ink through.

When we composite, our "frame" is the pixel dimension of our video, 720 × 480, 1280 × 720, 1440 × 1080, etc. The screen is usually what's called an alpha channel. Instead of using a negative, you place

Figure 57-2 *The checkerboard pattern seen here in the background represents the alpha channel.*

your still or moving image right on your "screen." The "screen," "frame" or alpha channel usually disappears completely, leaving behind your image. That image can also be something more abstract, such as fog—a tint of color which will alter our image.

The alpha channel is important, because it keeps our visible image on the correct x- and y-axis. If we have a lower third which we want to use in a documentary about school teachers, we can make a template of our lower third and switch out the names and occupations of all the teachers, administrators and students in the video. The alpha channel makes sure that this "floating" lower third is always in the same position on the screen relative to height and width. Does this make sense? Without this layer locking in our graphic to its correct x- and y-axis, it could float around our "frame" and be inconsistent.

There are times we need to be very conscious of this alpha channel and make sure we keep it intact. For example, when we export an image from Photoshop and import it into our editing software, we need to make sure the alpha channel is not compromised. If we create graphics, lower thirds, watermarks or any other "layer" for a composite within our editing software, we may not even be conscious of this alpha layer.

To oversimplify what we are talking about, an alpha channel is 100 percent transparent. Your image can be fully opaque or partially transparent, have feathered or gradient transparencies and/ or many other variations, adding to the complexity of your composite. Any of this making sense? Perhaps some examples will make it clearer.

Lower Thirds and Bugs

We call graphics living in the lower area of the screen—usually identifying an on-camera speaker—a lower third. If you're over 40, you may know them as Chyrons, Vidifonts or superbars (or Astons or name straps, if you speak with a British accent).

Figure 57-3 *A sample of a bug generally (but not always) found in the lower right-hand corner of the screen. Most bugs have some transparency, but others use solid colors instead.*

Today's lower thirds, at least in broadcast news and sporting events, are usually fancy, quickly-moving motion graphics, often accompanied by sound effects. Most editing software programs have nice-looking lower-third templates or ways to make custom lower thirds, built right in their titlers. Adobe's Premiere Pro has a robust titler with many lower-third options. Some quite robust third-party titlers that make industry-quality lower thirds include Boris FX, Ulead COOL 3D and Apple's Motion. Adobe's Photoshop and After Effects are 2D and 3D still and motion graphic favorites.

A bug or watermark is usually a semi-transparent graphic icon or logo that you use to tag a video. The broadcast networks, such as NBC and ABC, first used them, but now you find them on most cable channels as well. If you watch YouTube videos embedded in a non-YouTube website or blog, you'll see a YouTube bug in the lower right corner of the video.

Green/Blue screen and Special Effects

Thanks to the behind-the-scenes, extra footage found on many blockbuster Hollywood DVDs, we know the wonders of green- and blue-screen work on movies such as *The Lord of the Rings*

trilogy, *300*, *Sky Captain* and the *World of Tomorrow*, the *Star Wars* prequel trilogy, etc. Many of the scenes in these movies have layer upon layer of composites, such as painted backgrounds, live action footage and many layers of special effects—laser beams, explosions, robots, etc. But this is not only the domain of Hollywood studios with billion-dollar bank accounts. Robert Rodriguez is proud of the fact that he made many of the special effects in the *Spy Kids* series in his garage.

Wipes and Split Screen

You know that typical split-screen/wipe when a character on screen calls another person? Viewers see the footage of a person answering their phone slide into the footage of the caller, usually from the right. This is compositing. Most such wipes are. There are many pre-made wipe transitions in editing programs, but you can also make your own by using your knowledge of compositing.

Special Effects

Remember that holographic SOS message sent by Princess Leia via R2D2 in *Star Wars, Episode IV: A New Hope* (1977)? We can easily do that today with compositing. Want ghosts in your story? No problem. All of these types of special effects can be done easily with compositing. How about an image of yourself talking to yourself? You could now be a triplet even.

But How!?!?

We've arrived at the end of the chapter, and we haven't even talked about how to composite. The concept is fairly simple, but you can get as complex with it as your imagination allows. The main concept involves layers. You will need to work with two or more video layers on your timeline. Put some kind of static or

Figure 57-4 *A studio light for an "eye," a camcorder for a "body" and various other video accessories become our version of R2-D2's holographic feed of our fairy godmother watching over the Videomaker staff.*

moving image on video track 2 with some sort of transparency, and you will be able to see through to video layer 1. That is it, really.

There are all sorts of ways to do this. We have already mentioned alpha channels. Put a bug of your station's name, "Video Wizard Television," in the lower right corner of your frame by placing the logo with invisible alpha channel on video track 2 and this half-transparent gray logo will appear over any video you have on video track 1. Shoot an actor walking toward a camera against a green-screen and "key out" or digitally erase the green background, drop the walking actor on video track 2 over footage of an exploding building on video track 1 and you have a giant Hollywood effect (where you get the footage of the exploding building is your real challenge—be careful). Cropping is also a useful tool, especially for the two-people-talking-on-the-phone example above. All the big editing programs allow you to crop a moving image.

See-Through Layers

This really is not as difficult as it seems. Figure out how your particular editing program handles alpha channels, key effects and cropping, and start making your own Hollywood effects or network television graphics.

58
Be a Good Scout, Have a Backup Plan

Michael Reff

Figure 58-1

Backing up your video files sounds like a wise decision, but it's sometimes kind of scary. How will you know those files will be there next time you need them?

So you've finally made the transition from videotape to digital media management. You've been shooting so long that you feel you've earned all the merit badges needed to move up to the next level. Like a true scout, whose motto has always been, "Be prepared" you think you're ready. But are you? When I was a scout, be prepared meant: have a backup plan. My backup plan was to have two backup plans. Now that you're managing data and erasing your video after every shoot, you have to make sure you have it

right. Because when it comes to backing up your video data, you had better be a freakin' Eagle video scout.

Backing up your data is one of the most terrifying things you will ever do as a shooter. I've been in the business more than 25 years and I still get nervous when I hit the delete button. Whether it's swapping cards in the camera or moving the footage to external hard drives, be sure to always have a plan, and always stick to it. It can't be said enough. Always have a plan, always stick to it!

Tenderfoot Badge

In order to earn your novice video scout badge, one of the first things you should make a habit is marking what is shot and what is not. Whether it's flipping a tab on the card or putting bright colored tape on the card or box, mark it clear and loud. Try taping the ends of the card with hot pink tape to prevent it from making contact to the camera or try taping the box to prevent it from opening. You should also mark your cards so you can tell them apart. Use a permanent marker and put a number or letter on each card. If you have more than one camera, try calling all the cards from one camera "A" and the other one "B" followed by the number. For example 1A, 2A, 3A, then 1B, 2B, 3B. Keeping them clearly different helps to avoid mixing them up in the heat of the battle, especially if you're not doing a lot of daily camera work and there are long gaps of time between shoots.

Another basic media management practice that is essential to start from the very beginning is to build a clear file structure on your computer or hard drive. It needs to be easy to understand and easy to check. In other words, don't copy your video into one folder titled "Video" and let the clip numbers land where they may. Carefully think about how you would search for something. One suggestion would be to build a series of folders that use a combination of date and location and card number.

Professionally we use a main folder with the client name. Inside that folder we break it out into shoot names. Inside that folder we break it out into multiple days if the shoot happens that way, and finally we break it out into card numbers. The more overly precise you are the better. This will help you quickly and clearly check to see if you have copied the entire contents of the card before you go to erase it. Once you have copied the card, check

Figure 58-2 Managing your media can be quite a task, so if you know organization is not one of your strengths, consider helpful software like ShotPut Pro.

to see that all of the clips are there, play a few of them back to be sure they are working. Now you're done. Right? Wrong.

What happens if that drive goes bad? What if your child puts his glass of soda on top of your drive while playing video games on your computer and then loses at the last level after three days of non-stop playing? What happens if you delete it, because you have a copy of it in edit and then forget to save that version of the edit? There goes your parents' fiftieth anniversary video. If you haven't copied your video in at least two places, then you don't have a backup plan, and you definitely don't have a backup to the backup plan. Besides, hard drives are cheap these days and there is even media management software that helps check it for you, like ShotPut Pro. You can even have your backup copy online, if you're in a real pinch. Websites like Vimeo Pro and YouTube may not be the best or safest place to hold your video, but if the choice is between having a second backup and not having a second backup, I would at least know it was somewhere should all your drives crash or be destroyed in some terrible catastrophic event. And trust me, if you don't have a backup, something will happen to it.

Star Video Scout Badge

Once you've started making money with your shooting, you've become a true video scout. It will become more important to back up your data in the field while shooting. Many new videographers don't have a lot of money and can't afford several large memory cards to allow them to keep shooting non-stop throughout the day. If you're one of those shooters and are limited to one or two cards, then you will have to off-load as you go. This is where choosing the right equipment is essential. You will not only need robust drives but they should be bus powered (powered from the computer battery through the connecting data wire) in case you are somewhere that doesn't have access to electricity. The drives should also be very fast, preferably FireWire 800 or USB 2.0 or better. Speed is not only limited to the drives, however; carefully look at your whole system.

Laptops that allow your card to be directly inserted into them are much faster than external readers. If yours doesn't have one that fits your type of card, try running the transfer from the camera. Typically it's faster than an external reader. Of course, this can only be done if you're not shooting with it at the time. Finding the right moment to start off-loading the data is a talent in and of itself. Be sure you have enough unused memory left in the camera so as not to run out of data before the transfer is complete. There is nothing worse than having to stop shooting to wait on a download. And remember we're doing two backups. Just because you're shooting on location doesn't mean you don't make a safety copy, so plan ahead.

Figure 58-3 *Offloading your card directly onto your computer is faster than using a reader, and it eliminates one or more wires for your data to pass through.*

Buying hard drives for every shoot may also not be a reality for you. Professionally we like the client to bring their own portable hard drives when we're not editing for them. This saves you money and allows the client to walk away and keep the footage in their possession. It also passes the responsibility onto the client, to keep track of the footage, should they need it at a later date. If you're a true video scout, you may even wish to bring your own portable hard drive just in case you want a copy of your work or they bring something that won't work with your computer. Just remember if you're not backing up their stuff in two places or more, someone had better do it.

Eagle Video Scout Badge

By the time you have become a professional camera operator you will have advanced in the ways of digital media management. You'll also come to realize that the best way to do media management takes lots of money. Ideally, you should strive to have as many large data cards as possible. Eight hours of record time will probably hold you all day long in most insistences. This allows you to keep shooting continuously until you get to a point where you have the time to safely off-load your data without rushing and making mistakes. If however you are

Figure 58-4 *Create an archive for long-term storage on a RAID. The redundant drives will add lots of security.*

shooting non-stop—like in a live event—or you lack the amount of cards you need to make it through the day, then the other professional way is to hire a media management operator. This person's dedicated job is to do nothing but focus on making sure everything is there, backed up, and working properly. I should stress, however, that this operator must be competent. I once heard a story of a company using a production assistant to do the media management. He did a good job except for one day where he copied over the previous day's work, costing the production thousands of dollars in re-shoot fees. It would have been a whole lot cheaper to have paid a few hundred dollars more and got an expert. Don't fool around with this position. This is not only your work, but your reputation too.

You've Earned your Safety Badge

So it's a wrap and the day has ended. The client has two drives with all the footage and you have your copy, too. But wait a minute—you don't have a drive. How is that possible? Well if you have enough cards and you haven't needed to erase any, your footage is still located where you left it, on the cards. Whatever you do, don't erase your cards until you absolutely have to! I can't tell you the number of times I have been asked to go back to the original cards days later because a clip was corrupt or missing or deleted. I have had several instances where professional media managers have left off a clip or lost the location of the transfer. I have had producers run over their drives, drop them in water and lose them in the mail. If you're not using those cards let the data stay there. I even sometimes reverse the order I use the cards so as to delay the erasure as long as possible.

The other option, if you have the equipment and the money, is to go to home and make a backup to the card backup. Having a long-term storage-safe copy of your footage is good idea too. Very large servers, RAIDs or arrays, work best for this type of storage, but most people don't have the space or the money for this. There are however many companies that offer off-site data storage for reasonable rates too. Check your local yellow pages for one close to you. You never know when a client might need your help, and if you've saved the data, you can save the day. Trust me. I know what I'm talking about. Scout's honor.

Times Two

An optional way to make a backup of what you shoot, is to simul-roll. Simultaneously rolling on a backup drive is done every day. Devices, like a nanoFlash for instance, can be attached directly to the camera and carried around with you, recording as you shoot. They are light weight, can run off the camera's battery (some cameras may need special adaptors) and use CompactFlash drives or other small memory cards, very much like your camera. They can even automatically roll when you roll, by way of connecting to the timecode or SDI output of your camera, should it have that option. This method of making a backup is excellent for clients who need a copy of their footage immediately after the shoot and can't wait for a transfer to happen. The disadvantage of doing it this way, is that the memory size is very small, usually limited to the memory card size of 32GB per card and is very costly when compared to portable hard drives. But it does accomplish the golden rule of backing up your data.

59
Public Access Television

Randy Hansen

Figure 59-1

How to produce video productions with someone else's gear and get them broadcast—for free!

It's a federal mandate to local cable companies (the Federal Cable and Telecommunications Acts of 1984, 1992 and 1996, to be exact): depending on your city or county's franchise agreement with your local cable company, there may be an entire video production organization at your disposal—everything from video gear, video editing computers, studio space and even a way to broadcast your finished masterpiece at no cost to you. All you have to do is provide the labor and brainpower.

In the Beginning . . .

Back in the 1960s, as television cable service was expanding across the United States, cable companies were using the

Figure 59-2 *Many public access channels have their policies and practices available for viewing online. Check their websites to see how to get involved with your local area public access channel, or call the local cable operator.*

public right of ways such as sidewalks, power poles, alleys and the like to string transmission lines from house to house. Various politicians and community activists were searching for a way to charge these for-profit corporations for using the taxpayer-supported right of ways. Eventually, this "rent" culminated in the public access channels we see daily on our local cable systems, as a sort of exchange for the right to use the rights of way. Also, a small percentage of the franchise fee the cable companies pay goes to funding these channels. There are three kinds of public access channels; they carry the acronym PEG: Public, Educational and Governmental. Let's start with educational and governmental before we get to the good stuff.

Educational channels service the needs of the local elementary, middle and high schools for announcements, broadcasts of graduation ceremonies, televised classes and other activities. Video production classes in local schools can take advantage of the broadcast capabilities of the educational channel to show off their latest video work or student-run broadcast.

Government channels provide a look at how local government operates. City council meetings are a very common sight, as are help wanted ads, water restriction announcements, weather conditions and announcements of local interest to the average taxpayer.

Free? Really?

The final piece of the PEG acronym (but the first letter!) is the public access channel. It is open to the general public, and cable systems must provide the equipment, training, studio space and broadcast channels necessary for local community members to express their voices. All types of programming—gardening shows, discussions of city politics and even cooking shows—have a place on the local public channel. For little to no fee, citizens with no video experience at all may sign up for training on camera operation, video editing and studio practices. They may reserve and use video cameras, mics, tripods, lights and other production gear for free. There may be a small fee to join the volunteer group.

One of the few rules is that those wishing to use the equipment should reside in the service area of the cable company. There is no requirement that the user subscribe to the cable system's commercial programming.

If you're unsure about your ability to produce a full-fledged video program, you'll be happy to learn that most access providers are required to teach fledgling video producers how to operate all of the equipment in their facilities. Classes are held regularly to teach those with no experience the care and use of all the video gear in the facility, to ensure the greatest success possible.

For some valuable experience before taking the plunge into the "deep end" of a video production, volunteer on someone else's project as a photographer, editor or a simple go-fer. Keep your eyes open and ask questions, and you'll gain valuable experience while building a base of knowledge to make your idea into a broadcast a reality. Seek out more challenging opportunities from show to show, and keep pushing for improvement in your skills and abilities. You'll also build valuable contacts and friends from these volunteer opportunities. Eventually, you'll need the service of others, both experienced and not, to volunteer on your production—then you will be the experienced one!

No Gear? No Problem

Just as it provides training, the facility will provide video production gear for use by its members. Quality ranges from decent home equipment to prosumer to high-quality broadcast gear. The good news is that they provide more than

cameras for the ambitious producer. The sort of gear package available consists of a camera, tripod, mic and a simple light kit. Additional accessories for creative producers might include boom pole mics, green screens and wireless audio gear. Some larger operators even offer production trucks with an attending engineer for multi-camera uses. And all of this is available for little to no cost!

While the gear is free, it's still the responsibility of the member to care for the equipment. If it's stolen, broken or otherwise rendered unserviceable, you're on the hook for the repair or replacement of the video equipment. Some of the video packages can run into real money—in many cases, a whole video package may be valued at several thousands of dollars, so it's important to take care and secure the gear as if you own it yourself.

You reserve studio space on a first-come, first-served basis. There may be one or a few generic sets (news-like, living room, etc.), and you can certainly build a custom set for any unique needs—at your expense, of course. Two or three cameras are usually present and are controlled and coordinated through a multi-camera switcher and audio production board kept in another room. You may tape your programs for later broadcast or present them live.

Figure 59-3 *A studio setting might be appropriate for your show. Many public access channels will have a studio you can work in, but you can also make your living room your own production studio.*

Programming Choices and the First Amendment

The topic of your show is entirely up to you. The United States Supreme Court has determined that the cable access provider may not interfere or change your message. However, be aware that limited power exists for the provider to deny broadcast of your programming if it's determined to contain pornography or slander.

You can produce a program on local politics, cooking, log cabins or any subject that strikes your fancy. More mainstream shows will attract a larger audience, while shows that tend to be more "out there" will appeal to a more, shall we say, selective audience. Length is usually in the 30- to 60-minute range, although some providers might have different requirements. The scheduled broadcast date is up to the public access provider. Although you may certainly request a certain date and time, the rules of the organization might determine a different time for your debut.

Once in the edit bay, it's time to turn that stack of videotapes into a full-length production. Editing will be most exclusively computer-based, and you may have limited time to edit your masterpiece for broadcast, as others will most certainly be waiting in the hallway for their turn to edit their productions. Plan ahead and jot down notes before the edit session to ensure maximum efficiency and the highest-quality product possible.

Public access video channels serve an important purpose, because they provide an electronic soapbox for local folks to broadcast their unique points of view about the world, the nation and city around them. For those willing to do a little work and sacrifice a little time, the high price of video democracy is free, and it's just around the corner. After all, it's a federal mandate.

Figure 59-4 *Your public access show doesn't have to be a ground-breaking show. Pick a topic where you have expertise and plenty of content.*

Public Access Is More than Just TV

Public access was initially begun as a way for local communities to have their voices heard through the medium of television, but public access providers have begun to seek out new avenues of communication to fulfill their commitments to allow minority voices of opinion and creativity to be heard.

Many operators now offer high-technology solutions beyond television. The internet provides worldwide access via web pages, blogs, vlogs, podcasts and cell-phone distribution to achieve and serve the idea of access for all. Some providers are updating their services to include these technologies.

As new technology emerges, innovative ways of communicating will allow the mainstream, the right and left and the fringes of opinion a more level playing field, when the access to these distribution channels is provided for all. Check with your local provider to see if it has some or all of these technologies available for use. If not, ask it to look into offering these services to its members in addition to television production.

60
As Seen on TV: Citizen Journalism Worthy of Your Local News

Dave Sniadak

Figure 60-1

When news happens are you ready to record it? Used to be just traditional professional news jockeys got the story on the air. Now anyone with a camcorder can cover news as it happens ...

Your local newsman implores you to do it; the morning anchor asks you to share your special moments with her on Facebook; the weatherman isn't just calling for severe weather, but wants to see your best tornado footage. The local media have become increasingly reliant upon their viewing audience to help tell the stories of the day. The only question is: will you be ready to roll when news breaks?

The news cycle has evolved into an around-the-clock intake process for media outlets. With the prevalence of affordable camcorders, smartphones equipped with HD video capabilities and mobile access from coast to coast and across the globe, regular citizens can share their stories—in real-time—with a content-hungry online audience.

But just because nearly everyone has access to video technology, does that mean they should be considered potential citizen journalists? What exactly is citizen journalism? What are ways the average Joe can shoot like a pro? And what exactly is considered "film at 11" material? *Videomaker* talked with some seasoned shooters to find out how anyone can improve their chances of getting their footage seen by the masses.

The Glory Days of Storytellers

Storytellers come in all shapes, sizes and ages. From grandpa retelling the battles of his times served overseas, to the toddler telling the tale of adventures at preschool, how we craft and deliver a message is limited only by our own imaginations. Citizen journalism could be interpreted the same way.

For decades, a credentialed TV film crew was held in very high esteem. Their skill set was unique, requiring the finest education and experience. While anchors and reporters were the faces of newscasts from sea to shining sea, there was an elite force of behind-the-scenes laborers who made the talent look their best. Television production professionals rarely got the credit they were due, but true skill shone through every night with featured stories, scheduled events and during the most important times of the year for broadcast outlets—sweeps. It was the amazing visuals, captured by the best of the best photojournalists, punctuated with the emotional elements edited with just the right copy writing that usually elevated media outlets to the top of the ratings food chain, feasting on the viewers' insatiable desire for good stories.

But the glory days of broadcast news have been forced to give way to less glitz, slashed staffs and an approach where quality has conceded to quickness and quantity, where story count is more important than story content.

The Times, They are a-Changin'

Twenty years ago, Kevin Kjergaard was a wide-eyed novice news photographer. He started working at KELO-TV in Sioux Falls, SD, as a way to get his hands on the latest video equipment. He covered all sorts of stories, and met people from all walks of life. When news broke in South Dakota, there was a lot of real estate that needed covering. From his perspective, covering everything with one camera was great—but there was always the need for more.

"I remember when major events would happen and we'd think how cool it would be to have had a camera there," said Kjergaard, now Chief Photographer at the CBS affiliate. "Now, we do. Technology has made gathering news and images so quick."

Keith Yaskin, owner of The Flip Side, a media and video production company, once roamed the deserts of Phoenix covering news as a reporter and videographer. With more than 17 years of professional experience under his belt, he has seen just about every kind of story you can imagine. With the changing landscape of broadcast news, he's seen a shift in attitudes in the way that news stories are covered.

"It seems like much of broadcast TV is just tossing darts and seeing what stuck," Yaskin noted. "With the audience craving social media content, viewers would rather watch their favorite shows on their DVRs than watch the 5 pm news with stories that aren't interesting."

"Some of broadcast TV is adapting to viewers' habits, finding their niche in this new landscape, while other station managers are like the guy about a century ago trying to sell a horse to someone who just bought a car."

What is a Citizen Journalist

With the expansion of social media being an acceptable form of news gathering, media outlets have leaned more heavily on user-generated content to deliver not only timely updates from breaking news events, but to offer first-person perspectives of topical moments in our lives. Anyone armed with a camcorder—or cell phone for that matter—can deliver real-time content to anyone willing to watch.

CNN is a global news outlet that routinely incorporates footage submitted by viewers. Whether it's cell phone footage, or pocket cam video, if it captures news happening and the chaos or reaction that follows, they want it. The global news network started its iReport program back in 2006 and has seen contributions grow substantially since launch.

Many major network news outlets have followed CNN's suit. FOX News has its uReport; MSNBC encourages viewers to submit photos and videos via email and social media, while ABC News has its i-CAUGHT franchise. Contributors typically grant the networks the authority to use their content, and the fine print eliminates the chance for monetary remuneration. For most, however, simply sharing their perspectives to historical moments is compelling enough reason to submit their footage.

News doesn't dictate when or if it's going to break. How it's captured depends on who's around to capture it. Armed with few of these simple suggestions, you can be prepared to stand in as "TV Crew On the Spot" and get your proverbial 15 minutes of fame, thanks to content that rocks.

Red Light Realities

We live in a "looky loo" society: when there's a car crash, we slow down and take in the scene; if there's a house on fire, we'll stop and watch; if a storm is approaching, our instincts have become such that we stand and ingest instead of seeking shelter. Blame the media, blame an egocentric "Nothing bad will happen to me" psychology of society, blame the president . . . whatever the ridiculous reason, a majority of the global population tends to absorb the realities of the moment, instead of turning away from them.

Either we've become so immune to tragedy and destruction that we've been rewired into thinking it's OK to look, or we just have become so desensitized to it that we aren't affected by it. Whatever the reason, there's a good chance that at some point in your life, you will be witness to some form of breaking news. Be it a hit-and-run, or impromptu tight-rope act, you'll need to be ready. With these tips, you will be.

- Stay energized—much like the persistent pink bunny pounding on its drum, it's important that your camera—be it a cell phone or high-end professional camcorder—has enough juice to capture the scene. Never leave home without a fully charged battery, or make sure you have a car charger or backup power source. Spare batteries are generally

Figure 60-2 *Sometimes the difference between legal video and illegal video is a few paces. Respecting private property and sensitive areas can ensure you won't be bothered.*

easy to find, and really make your life easier when you can also acquire a standalone charger.

- Respect the scene—in the moments following an accident or serious news event, the crush of activity and panic will reach extreme levels. If emergency responders aren't on scene, assess the situation and respond accordingly. No one needs to rescue you trying to play hero, nor should you get in the way of those who are, so use common sense. A medical emergency may require your first aid knowledge or director experience to ensure that help is one the way.

- Safely get as close as possible—"Video does not 'zoom' well after it's been shot," said Sean D. Elliot, president of the National Press Photographers Association. "If you can safely and legally get closer to what you are documenting, do so. The less zooming you do with the camera, the easier it will be to steady your shot." However, if an official tells you to back away from a scene, respect their commands—or you could make news of your own.

- Stabilize your shot—"Keep your camera steady," Yaskin said. "If you have a tripod, great; if not, lean or prop your camera against something. Don't wave your arm back and forth like a windshield wiper. This way, if there are several people shooting the same event, your video has the highest chance of getting picked up."

- Composure while composing—if the scene you're shooting involves lots of action—fire, gunshots, severe weather, fast moving action—the temptation to get 'everything' will make your heart race. By maintaining the basic fundamentals of composition: steady shot, good framing, clear images, sequential shooting, variety of shots—you'll be sure to capture everything the viewers at home will need to follow the story.

- Talk to witnesses—"TV film crews are desperate for eyewitnesses," said Yaskin, who worked on both sides of the camera. "Walk up to people at the scene and ask them questions. People tend to talk first, without asking who you are." You'll have your answers that way, then get their permission for inclusion in your completed video. Follow good TV interview techniques and keep the number of questions to a minimum. Often times, the more witnesses you find, the closer you are to reporting a more factual story.

- News desks on speed dial—having contacts whom you can rely on to take your footage will go a long way toward getting your footage aired. "Instead of just saying, 'Here's your news for the day,' we work with our viewers," said Kjergaard, who says KELO-TV viewers engage with the outlet because the TV video production staff embraces citizen journalism. "We let them become part of the team, they feel it. They want to be a part of something that so many people take to heart."

- Release it to the masses—if your content is compelling enough, a broadcast outlet can give it international television distribution. With affiliates and wire services, like the Associated Press, Reuters and CNN's Pathfire feed, video can be sent across oceans and borders instantly, where TV film crew decision makers will ultimately pick it up and run it during a newscast.

Videomaker's managing editor, Jennifer O'Rourke was a news shooter during the glory days of broadcast TV. Working at several California stations for two decades, she says she had an uncanny sixth sense about being at the right place at the right time when events unfolded—in fact, many of you may have seen some of her footage at one time or another.

"I covered many actions that no other news crew caught which elevated my footage right away to national and international broadcast," she says. "The key is keeping your wits about you, staying emotionally focused on the tasks of good framing, proper coverage and illustrating the event

Figure 60-3 Videomaker's *managing editor, Jennifer O'Rourke, has had her footage seen worldwide as a news shooter. It used to be an elite job using massive gear. Now anyone can do it!*

correctly; and being very alert and aware of what is going on all around you, not just where your camera is focused." O'Rourke adds that if consumer cameras captured those same events back then, the footage would have had to be extremely unique, because the camcorder quality was so poor. "But now, anyone with a small digital camcorder who captures clean, focused and stable footage can get their work seen on TV," she says, "It's a wonderful way of democratizing a once elitists-only world."

Content Comes Before Quality

As a citizen journalist, it's hard to travel with television production gear, let alone afford shooting with it. Your handheld camcorder or smartphone—whether it shoots SD, HD or 3D—will generally be accepted if it captures the moment. Producers and editors will want visuals that are compelling, captivating and emotive. Don't worry about not having the best equipment, just focus on how to use a camcorder in a way that will help paint a picture of what you've just witnessed.

According to both the Federal Communications Commission (FCC) and the American Civil Liberties Union (ACLU), which outlines citizen journalist rights, videographers are legally allowed to shoot photos and videos at crime and accident scenes, as long as it doesn't interfere with the work of law enforcement officials.

Figure 60-4 *To increase the chance that you'll record usable and desirable footage, go for stabilized shots. Even your camera bag can be a source of stability.*

FCC rules state that citizen journalists and TV film crew alike cannot break any other laws while shooting video—if you are standing on private property, and the landowner asks you to leave, you need to leave. You can (and just might) be arrested for trespassing. Business owners may also interact with you in this territory since their image is like that of a public figure, and they won't want to be misconstrued. However, at no time can law enforcement officials take your camera, unless they have a warrant, or you've broken—or are in the act of breaking—a law.

Additionally, the ACLU points out that producers will want to check their state wiretapping laws if they plan to use the audio portion of their video. These laws vary from state to state, so educate

Figure 60-5 and 60-6 *Be aware that there are some rules and regulations that could impact how to shoot videos in public.*

yourself before pressing record. It is not an easy read by any means, but it does refer to eavesdropping and may come into play for your footage.

"Know when to back down, regardless of your legal rights," added Elliot. "Your video won't do you any good if the camera is in the impound and you're in the lockup. Don't get yourself arrested if you can avoid it."

Film at 11, Notoriety for You

What makes good "made for TV" video? There's an industry saying: "If it bleeds, it leads." However, as Kjergaard noted from his two decades of telling stories across South Dakota, it's not always the flashing lights that capture the viewers' attention.

"Good content is the unexpected. What happens right before, what happens immediately after, how people respond, expressions, body language," Kjergaard said. "I think that tragedy is always the best content. Good things happen everyday that people just take for granted. Challenge yourself to share those moments as well."

And while chasing ambulances may get your story on the news, sometimes it's the reaction to the story that generates the most interest.

"Build a relationship" with local television production staff, Yaskin added. "Communicate with them about life's everyday things. Don't be a salesperson (with your video). Be a person. Prove that you understand the difference between what's newsworthy and what's nonsense."

PART V
Distribution

Broadcasting your programs through cable, over-the-air TV and on the internet.

61

Options for Marketing Your Video

Earl Chessher

Figure 61-1

The market for video producers looking to sell video is huge! Video sales can happen if you're willing to invest time and effort into the right marketing plan.

You've got cable channels seeking content—travel, food, investing, shopping. The list is infinite. There's indie productions at Blockbusters, Netflix and other video outlets. Don't forget Blip.tv, CreateSpace, even Vimeo.

Independent producers are setting up websites and marketing their own videos using direct sales, even eBay. Enterprising producers seek sponsors and gain counter space at garden supply centers, hobby stores and do-it-yourself shops. If your production focuses on something of interest to their customer base you might have a niche market video sales opportunity on your hands. Unfortunately the competition is also huge. How can you get the word out, gain eyeballs and attract the consumer, agent or distributor how to get somebody to pay for your video or concept? Can you market your video, not only sell but make money from it? Absolutely!

Sales, success and profits only come if you're willing to work diligently and have patience. There's no guaranteed success method, however enough options and

Figures 61-2 *There is a ton of niche markets for video production that include wedding, funeral, tourism and legal video, just to name a few. Each market has a different opportunity to capitalize on sales from Bridal Fairs to hobby stores.*

opportunities exist that if you actually try you'll get somewhere. It takes more than believing though. You'll have to dedicate yourself to making it happen. Producing and marketing video isn't a one-time effort. You learn as you go. Success will come to those who are in it for the long haul. Be confident but not foolish with your investment of time, money and effort. Know when to cut your losses or when to persevere and develop marketing strategies

The Easiest Quick Way?

Do it yourself is the easiest way to quickly start selling your video products. It has the potential for being the simplest solution with highest returns. You cut out the middleman, aiming straight for the consumer. You control the bottom line because you control the process. There's time enough to

consider a distributor, mass production or expanded market when you've sold or produced a few. Your video could get "picked up" by one of the big operations. Simple, right? It can be but you're going to have to maintain confidence and determination in order to make it happen. You have to be more than a video producer. You have to develop some marketing savvy as well. That might not be so simple.

Your success is measured by your expectations. Are you seeking a million-seller or a hundred-seller; a consistent seller or a pinch-hitter; selective theatrical release or major distribution? You might not hit your first one out of the park but there's a good chance of making it to first base. Having a product to offer is first. Production first isn't for everybody but I suspect that most independent producers rarely test for marketability first. Instead they want to cut to the chase, put a production together then worry about selling it to somebody later. That's the approach producer Bill Mecca, takes.

"I produce these (videos) because the topics interest me and I'm a video guy."

Producer J. Michael Long, takes a similar approach. Grinner Hester, produces video he likes but knows his market and promotes his videos where he wants them to show, sell or share.

Be prepared to deliver on demand, burning, printing, packaging and mailing your video as orders come in. Establish a website dedicated to video sales. Utilize social sites—Facebook and Twitter, along with LinkedIn and a host of others. Make people aware of your video, where and how to find it.

Post a teaser on YouTube, write that blog, comment on other blogs, submit articles to online news feeds, start a podcast, participate on forums and email your friends, ask them to share with others. Ask them to view your video, snippet or teaser and post or write a review. Over time, your video will gain visibility and linkage. You will get some sales.

Who's the Client?

Pick your preference. Weddings? Events? How-to or special interest? Web video for small businesses? Marketing, sales and distribution of special interest videos, either doing it all for yourself or doing it for the other person?

How do you get work? How do you find the clients? Easy answer is you go where the people you want to reach go. A bit of research will disclose where hobbyists, brides-to-be, sports enthusiasts or others go to find out information about what interests them. You need a presence there. Visit the local handicrafts, hobby or bridal shops they visit. This might seem obvious and there's more, but this is where to start.

- Website and email address
- Business address and phone number
- Business cards and demo reels
- Sample clips on your website

Participation in and on social networks, interaction with interest-specific forums and even postings on the Knot, Craigslist, etc., will get the word out, as do blogs and word-of-mouth referrals. A direct-mail campaign that identifies your video products or services, who you are, where you operate and your availability is good. Use testimonials from satisfied clients, ask for and seek referrals and recommendations.

Independent video services providers often must wear multiple hats in addition to being a shooter or editor. You have a virtual hat tree where you hang your graphics artist, marketing specialist, researcher, CPA, boss and administrator hats. Wear them all as well as you can but know when you need to outsource elements.

The single most important thing you can do to take your video products and services business to the top is to use every possible means for getting the word out. While advertising can be an important and expensive contributor to your business success, it's marketing that makes things happen.

Agents and Distributors

Major competition lives here. With all those productions to pick from, agents, creative property buyers and distributors are quite selective in what and whom they decide to promote or invest in. You'll need to research and identify these companies and resources, determine their subjects of interest, restrictions and methods for submission, then submit a promo for your video. If they check it out, judge it worthy and if your production is really good with broad consumer appeal and production value, you could hear from them. It happens.

Mostly these distributors discover or pick up documentary and entertainment productions from the many film/video festivals held each year. Perhaps you've heard of Sundance but have you ever heard of *The Dove Foundation*, a Michigan-based film festival that claims 96,000 in attendance? Research will show a bounty of video and film festivals where your video

Figure 61-3 *VideoUniversity.com, WedVidPro.com, and DVProfessionals.com are all great sites to let other professionals in the field critique your work.*

might attract the attention of a major distributor as well as writers, reviewers and indie video enthusiasts.

Premiere Showings, Festivals and Reviews

This route is similar to the do-it-yourself but kicks things up a notch. You have to do more because there's more to do to make it happen. You can't simply show up at a film festival and expect your production to be accepted. There's a process.

Length, content and production style matter. Documentary and entertainment content have the highest interest quotient at festivals or independent premiere showings at venues ranging from individually-owned movie houses, large meeting rooms or even the local pub.

Figure 61-4 and 61-5 You can either copy multiple DVDs by using a duplicator from a company like Primera, or by using an online service like WTSmedia.com. Choices should depend on the costs, including ink, disks, cases and labeling.

Showing your special interest, how-to or instructional videos at a special interest group meeting or commercial location might also work with a premiere showing. If you produced a how-to video featuring goods from a local hardware store, the business might sponsor you to show your video.

A broad range of video forums exist where you can share your production and get input. In addition to *Videomaker* forums there's Video University, WedVidPro, and DVProfessionals all with video galleries where you can show your work and get the word out. Keep in mind that critiques from your peers often require thick skin and an open mind—the same with other social forums that offer opportunity to garner comments, even recommendations from internet friends and viewers. The purpose is to expose your video to as many people in as many ways as possible. Get recognition. But be careful how much of your production you give away.

"I tried to post articles and videos on related topics," says Mecca. "But then realized I was violating the old adage about giving away the cow, so no one would buy the milk."

Make it and Market it but Outsource Order Fulfillment

Mecca and Long keep their video production plates full, spreading their time thin between video production and a host of other activities intended to keep their name recognition, visibility and linkage active. Having a full video production

lifestyle, maintaining a personal life and more than one area of interest can kick you in the head if you add order fulfillment to the equation—mega sales or not. Mecca and Long have used Kunaki.com for print on demand. "It's worked out really well. I have links on my sales page to the Kunaki sales page for my video and they handle it all and take a very small cut."

CreateSpace, an Amazon Group, offers similar solutions for video entrepreneurs who want to self-publish and sell CDs and DVDs. Mecca says he's tried eBay but instead of sales there, he notes an uptick of sales from his website the next day or two.

Marketing an Idea or Concept

This article assumes you have a video or plan to produce one independently. If you have an idea or concept and want to "pitch" it somewhere many of the same principles apply. Your options are also the same for marketing your video production services.

To sell an idea or concept you need to further identify your market and product focus, pin down specifics of interest to the group you want to approach—market saturation from similar productions, commercial viability, cost of production, level of production quality, budget requirements and time required to deliver. Much more planning and support materials, information and resources are needed up front making it obvious why so many independent producers take the "make it and see if I can sell any" approach instead.

Making the Product

If you're not well established and don't have highly skilled professionals or resources to develop them, save the complex productions for somebody else or for down the road. Avoid the downer of a self-inflicted sense of failure or the disappointment of a mid-production derailment by pursuing and taking on projects you cannot objectively have a reasonable expectation of completing.

There are things you need to deal with that are complex enough without stacking the deck against your success. Things like getting a diversity of shots, point-of-views (POV) are often important when doing product demonstrations and how to videos. Decide on the blend you or your client wants between necessary talking head and preferable narrative with cutaways, B-roll and graphic elements to mitigate the "boring" factor that a droning, lethargic talking head can induce.

Push yourself a bit but know your strengths, skills, abilities and your limitations. Keeping that in mind, development of simple, well-produced, affordable video product is the secret to immediate success or at least a sense of positive accomplishment. One-to-two year production commitments can grind you down.

As long as you use your tools well, just about any camera capable of recording good quality visuals, with mic inputs and microphones that can capture clean and clear audio, backed by a sturdy support system and enhanced with an adequate set of lights, using a decent pair of headphones to monitor, will deliver what you need and get you ready to do business. There's more but that's the short answer. Pay attention to blocking, framing and other basic essential elements for development of pleasing video. Shoot more than you think you need and plan for the production beforehand, not on the fly. Work toward an accurate estimate of the time you need to do the job.

Set your rates so that you're within the range of your market, video production type and in line with the competition that falls just above your perceived level of ability. Work by the hour, starting at $50 an hour and always deliver when you say you will. Don't cave in when the client wants it yesterday and you know that can't happen—not if you want to deliver the quality product the client is expecting. Be up-front, honest and confident. That will often win the day.

Shorter is better. Half-hour productions often work when you're telling somebody how to do something rather than teaching them a skill—no more than an hour. Teasers should be under five minutes, one-to-three minutes actually. Product demos should be long enough to provide the important information, say just enough and end with a call to action. The same can be said for promotional videos about services. Less in video is usually always more, so deviate toward brevity with a tight, informative production. Final word to length: if you cannot compel yourself to view, review, tighten and hone your production until it "feels right" and if you fight to keep from nodding off while doing this, your video is either not interesting or entertaining enough, too long and too slow or both. Like a comma, when in doubt, take it out.

62
Taking it to the Screen

Peter Biesterfeld

Figure 62-1

Getting your hard work shown on a big screen is a dream of many video producers, but it really can be done. The name of the technique in question: four-walling.

The other day I got an e-mail from a long-ago film student of mine. It was an invitation to the premiere screening of *Holy Cow*—the sequel to his comedy short about two inept security guards. The viral blurb went like this: "Outfitted with a two-man cow costume and more enthusiasm than brains, the perilous pair stake out a farmer's field to apprehend a group of elusive cattle-thieves." A colorful poster attachment announced three consecutive screenings at a local pub. Admission was free, but the beer was not.

Although this was a contemporary and snappy DIY movie marketing campaign, I was struck by the throwback of this invitation to the pioneer days of motion pictures, before there were theatres to show them. The road-show era of film exhibition was a time when itinerant showmen bought the films outright, took them on tour and screened them wherever they could mount a projector and a white sheet—in fairground tents, department stores, opera houses, museums, churches—and yes, even in saloons.

More than a century later, finding an audience continues to be the engine that drives moviemaking in all its forms.

Blockbuster marketing machinery aimed at bringing audiences to the big screen is the distribution turf where the big boys play. But there are more and more examples of DIY filmmakers finding captive audiences and the requisite four walls it takes to mount and show their films.

Four-Walling: the Time Capsule

Four-walling simply means you find a theatre, rent it and show your movie. Depending on the deal, you will likely pocket the receipts and the theatre will keep the concessions.

A filmmaker might resort to four-walling because the film needs to score some reviews in order to qualify for the Academy Awards or because a movie deal with a broadcaster is contingent on the film's prior theatrical release.

Or, it could be that exhibitors find the film a risky investment because they're afraid nobody will come to see it, and the filmmaker turns to releasing it himself. This is exactly what Tom Laughlin did with *Billy Jack*, the 1971 box-office phenomenon. Laughlin wrote, directed, produced and starred in the cult classic about a soft-spoken loner who explodes

Figure 62-2 *Locally-owned and operated art theatres are frequently the best places to start in your search for good locations to four-wall your production.*

into a one-man fighting machine when he sees injustices perpetrated on the helpless and downtrodden. Laughlin was unhappy with the way Warner Brothers handled the release of his anti-war opus, so he promoted it himself and rented theatres all across the country. The $32.5 million it earned put *Billy Jack* in the top 100-grossing pictures of all time. Before *Billy Jack* and its 1974 self-released sequel, *The Trial of Billy Jack*, the tried and true approach to finding an audience for a new release was to hold test screenings in select theatres, usually in a single region or market. After Laughlin turned Hollywood's marketing and distribution model inside out, the studios followed suit by releasing new movies in thousands of theatres on the same day in markets all across the country.

DIY Distributors are Like Indie Rockers

Laughlin is remembered as a self-distribution pioneer and risk-taker who was ahead of his time when he thumbed his nose at the powerful studios. The four-walling success story of *Billy Jack* is now ancient movie history, but, more than 30 years later, do-it-yourselfers are no longer debating whether it's a good idea to find your own screens for your movie.

Contemporary DIY movie maker and "cinematic provocateur" Caveh Zahedi

Figure 62-3 *A usual arrangement with local theatres is that you keep ticket revenue and they keep concession revenue.*

put it this way in a 2006 *Filmmaker* interview: "Why should a distributor take half the revenue just because they made a few phone calls that I could have made, designed a poster that I could have designed, cut a trailer that I could have cut, and sent out screeners that I could have sent out myself?"

It's no secret: the DIY filmmaking crowd is adopting the same kind of thinking that goes on in the world of indie rock, where artists have realized that, by controlling all aspects of their work, they no longer need to rely on a major-label recording deal to make a living from their music. Using a web presence, they are taking charge of their own concert promotions, taking their music on the road and selling their CDs, not only in the lobby, but also online.

And that's what one do-it-yourself film-maker did with her labor of love—find an audience by taking it on the road.

BRATS: The DIY Distro Show

The banner headline on the film's web-site reads: "*BRATS: Our Journey Home*, a Donna Musil film featuring narration and music by Kris Kristofferson." For writer/director Musil, the journey was a seven-year filmmaking odyssey fueled by relentless passion. Being passionate about the subject matter is what kick-started

this feature-length documentary about "growing up military," and being relent-less is what ultimately got the film made, financed and delivered to an audience.

After film-funding agencies and broad-casters had raved about the project and made promises when Musil first pitched it to them, they failed to come through with funding. Undeterred, Musil dug deep into her own pockets and began shooting. An army brat herself, she set up a website for the project and connected with her sub-jects by emailing brat groups everywhere. Response was overwhelming, and Musil spent two years collecting interview mate-rial, including talking heads of celebrity brats like Norman Schwarzkopf, Robert Duval and Kris Kristofferson.

Worried about money going out and not coming in, Musil set up an educa-tional non-profit corporation, Brats with-out Borders. Donations ranging from $1 to $1,000 poured in from the military com-munity. Offers of B-roll included brats' 8 mm home movies and stock footage from military archives, broadcasters and even Disney.

BRATS collaborators, advisors and crew came on board as well, either working for a fraction of their day rates or waiving their fees altogether (as did Kristofferson). Military brat and Hollywood veteran Timothy Wurtz offered his services as co-producer. He says it was the "concept-testing" mentality and limited vision of potential funding partners that ultimately propelled Musil and company towards taking *BRATS* on a four-walling road trip.

"They told us appeal for the movie was going to be limited. But they weren't thinking about its built-in market—the 15 million American military brats all over the world," said Wurtz.

The documentary managed to gain entry into small festivals, but it wasn't reaching that built-in audience. Tired of Thursday afternoon festival screenings in venues where few people showed and nobody cared, Musil and her band of collaborators took *BRATS* on the road. First they built an email database to book venues on mili-tary bases and organized their first tour

Figure 62-4 *As with any production a good website is crucial for getting the word out as well as selling copies to your audience and listing upcoming show times and locales.*

to the 26 communities where the largest contingent of military brats lived. They hired a publicist to generate a buzz about the *BRATS* road show in the national press, while Wurtz himself contacted the regional media, often creating local headlines announcing that *BRATS: Our Journey Home* was "coming to a theatre very near you."

At every stop, *BRATS* played to packed halls, churches and theatres. Sometimes as many as four hundred exhilarated military personnel and their families turned out to watch their own stories unfold on the screen.

BRATS sales aren't of *Billy Jack* proportions, but they are impressive. The screenings are usually free or sometimes $5 to help pay for the venue rental, but after every show 10 to 50 percent of the audience buys the DVD at $24.95 each.

At last count *BRATS'* marketing numbers look something like this:

- Website hits: 3.4 million

- Magazine articles: 55

- Radio and TV stories: 11

- Screenings: 100 (and counting)

- Revenues: mid six-figures in the black

While Wurtz is selling *BRATS* DVDs in the lobby, Musil is usually up on stage handling what often turns out to be an emotional Q&A session for both filmmaker and audience. The fledgling documentary maker admits the journey has been life-changing, and that the making and subsequent four-walling of *BRATS* has indeed brought her home. In a telephone interview from Denver, she reflected on the

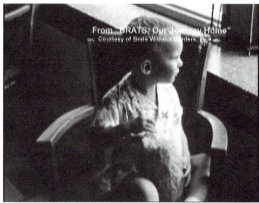

Figure 62-5 *Marketing your video successfully requires engaging your audience on an emotional level. By showing BRATS on or near military bases, the producers guaranteed that archival footage of children and their military parents would trigger an emotional response from an audience that shares a common interest.*

experience: "I will no longer say I'm going to make a film because I think it will do well. I want to make films that tell stories about which I am passionate."

Just like the itinerant movie showmen of yesteryear, Musil and Wurtz keep on rolling, bringing their road show to audiences in venues from Helen, GA, to San Diego, CA, and beyond. Through their non-profit corporation, they are planning to produce educational sequels and DVD companions.

Before the Curtain Goes Up

Ryan Bruce Levey is president of international distributor, Vagrant Films Releasing, in Toronto. When asked in a telephone interview about do-it-yourselfers finding screens for their films, Levey waxed nostalgically but respectfully about movie shlockmeister William Castle. The renegade producer from the 1950s used promotional gimmicks such

as "fright insurance" policies and flying inflatable skeletons to pull audiences into his B-movie horror flicks. Hokey? Yes. But Castle knew his audience.

Levey claims he knows within about 30 minutes into a film who the audience is, "and if there's an angle, I can usually see a marketing plan unfolding."

What makes a film worthy of a sales campaign? "A worthy film challenges you; it makes you think," says Levey. "So, make the film you want, but sell it."

His advice to DIY filmmakers goes something like this: Don't make a theatrical release the only prong of your sales strategy, but rather integrate finding a screen for your movie into other marketing activities. For starters, make sure you get your film reviewed and start a viral campaign.

"It's all one big sales thing," says Levey. "Be prepared for unreturned phone calls and chasing down reviewers and bookers who tell you 'I lost the DVD.'" But, when you score your four walls, he urges, "You've got to make it an event."

63
It Could Happen: Festivals

Peter Biesterfeld

Figure 63-1

Showtime—your epic is finally done. The color corrections you meticulously crafted are perfect, and the audio tracks in the edit timeline are speckled with fades and dissolves—evidence of a carefully-blended soundtrack. You click on Save As and rip the project to DVD. It's showtime.

Rambunctious friends and relatives, even the family dog, gather in front of the digital hearth for your premiere. As they're hooting and hollering and throwing popcorn, you dare to wonder if there might be larger audiences in grander places who might appreciate your opus.

Try to imagine a packed nineteenth-century theatre where Mark Twain once gave a speech, and it's your movie flickering up there on the digital silver screen. When the credits go up, there's applause and questions about your film. During the schmooze-fest afterwards, a sales agent comes up to you and says she might be able to find a buyer for your movie. It could happen. But you have to work for it.

Filmfests: Why Not?

Without an audience, your movie is like the proverbial hand clapping in the forest. How does anybody know it exists? If you're genuinely serious about finding an audience for your film, you have to stop thinking that finishing the movie is the end of your labors.

One of the best things you can do for your film and for your own development as a filmmaker is to have your movie screened at one of the several hundred festivals that dot the North American landscape.

Festivals can do three things for you: deliver audiences for your film, connect you to the industry marketplace and provide learning opportunities for improving your craft. Before launching into the do's and don'ts of getting your film past programmers and screeners and in front of festival audiences, we should first pan across the terrain to explore what kinds of festival experiences are out there.

Festival Landscapes

Filmfest.com reports that, in the last ten years, the number of US festivals jumped from 450 to 650. One of the reasons for the jump is the new kids on the festival block. Boutique fests, student fests and online fests are not only boosting the numbers, but they're also making distribution of original screen stories achievable for non-professional filmmakers. Some of the younger fests are grabbing a foothold by attracting a mix of pros, semi-pros and first-timers. The six-year-old Big Mini-DV Festival out of Long Island University, for example, encourages "filmmakers of all genres and technical levels" to submit their videos.

At the other end of the festival rainbow sit festivals with long traditions, such as the stately but vibrant WorldFest Houston Film Festival. Founded in 1961, WorldFest boasts that it gave Stephen Spielberg, George Lucas, Spike Lee, David Lynch and the Coen Brothers (among others) their first awards.

Festivals can also be niche fests programmed around issues, themes or regions. Take the Midwest Independent Film Festival, which will consider films of all lengths and genres, but prefers submissions from "the eight-state region of Illinois, Indiana, Iowa, Michigan, Minnesota, Missouri, Ohio and Wisconsin."

The goal of your submission is to have it selected from a competing crop and win an award in one of the categories. Although most festivals are competitions, there are non-competitive events, such as the Tulsa Overground. This combination film and music event bills itself as "a festival for the people, by the people. A cinematic grab bag of first-time filmmakers, student directors, professional lensers and big name auteurs." "Anything goes" programmers at the Overground accept only shorts and caution that only two hours of films are screened each night, so the shorter your film, the better its chances for selection.

Once your film is accepted, most festivals will give you an industry pass. This gets you into the formal and informal sessions where filmmakers of all stripes get to mix with industry pros, distributors and sales agents. Whether it's a Q-and-A session with a seasoned filmmaker after a screening, an industry panel on current trends or a boot camp on distribution and marketing, you'll find these sessions indispensable to your career trajectory.

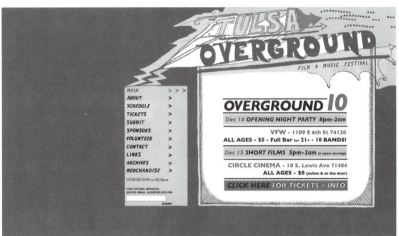

Figure 63-2, 63-3 and 63-4 *There's a festival for everyone nowadays, but make sure you read all the rules. For instance, if you're submitting for teen viewers, you might get rejected if your subjects are smoking, no matter how good your video is. Know your target; they set the rules, not you.*

Festival 101

Festival pros suggest you should know what you want your submission to achieve before you submit it: Is it to get you an agent or a publicist? Or is it to make enough of a splash to get you invited to other festivals? Perhaps you want a distributor or broadcaster to notice your film, because you want to tap them for participation in your next film.

Those who unpack and screen your epic say that wrapping your submission copy in a glossy marketing package is not the way to get their attention. Filmfest mythology has it that the fancier the package, the more the buzz. Don't believe it. Put your heart and attention into your film, not into the wrapper. What interests festival screeners and selection committees is the quality of your storytelling. But if they like your film and select it for competition, you will want to be ready with a high-quality screening copy and a press kit.

If you're too busy making your movie and haven't got the time to market it, get somebody on your team to do it. Right from the outset somebody has to be on festival alert, sniffing out the details of submission criteria and deadlines and preparing an information kit about your film. Start shooting production photos early—you never know.

Many festivals don't accept direct submissions anymore and prefer you go through an online festival submission service. Withoutabox.com is the biggest of the one-stop online festival submission supermarkets. Its signature product, the International Film Submission System, gives beginning filmmakers and Academy Award winners alike access to over 1,200 international festival markets. "We help filmmakers navigate the film festival submission process and make informed and well-researched decisions about their film festival entry choices," says the website.

Festival veteran and Withoutabox junkie, Murphy Gilson, has had his short film *Partially True Tales of High Adventure!* accepted by over 20 festivals around the world, including Cannes'

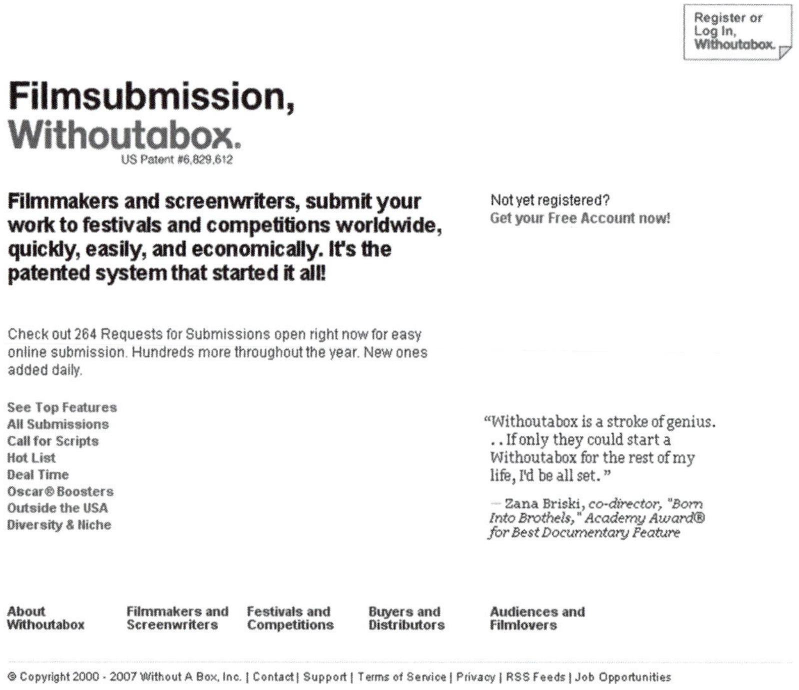

Figure 63-5 Withoutabox is a very powerful ally for the budding film festival producer. Everything you need to get started, without the confines of a distribution agency.

Short Film Corner. The Culver City-based director and writer has these words of wisdom for festival newbies:

"Your DVD is how people think of you as a filmmaker. Are you going to submit a professionally-made disc or some sloppy Sharpie-scribbled thing they lose in their car? A successful festival visit is not only about your screening".

Murphy tells us these points to consider when trying to break into the festival world:

- Go to other screenings and stay for the Q&As and meet other filmmakers.

- Go to the panels and the forums.

- Try to meet distributors, agents and producers.

- Follow up. Go through all the business cards, and send a "nice to meet you" email.

- Promote your film, but don't make an *** of yourself. Seinfeld in a bee suit is funny. A nobody in a bee suit is creepy.

As a final point, Murphy adds, "Don't get too attached to rejection. There are probably a dozen valid reasons why your film was rejected that have nothing to do with the quality of your film."

Submissions: The Final Word

Local programmers pride themselves on bringing something new and fresh to their audiences, and they like to write "premiere" next to an entry's title in the program. But, if your piece has been widely available through the World Wide Web, festival directors can't do that. However, many festivals are more lenient when it comes to short subject films, and there are many who won't insist on the first-time rule. As well, there are plenty of exclusively short film fests out there looking for your "previously enjoyed" masterpiece. Read the rules to see where you fit.

Credit Roll

Excellence is what will get your submission past festival gatekeepers and into the hearts of audiences and jurors. An informal email survey of festival pros all concurred that what programmers and screeners are generally looking for is "quality storytelling, quality performances and intriguing and slightly unconventional docs."

If you want to get plugged into the film festival scene and plan for your first submission, visit online festival forums and discussion groups. You should also check out the festival "idiot guides" and other how-to books available on bookstore and library shelves.

Happy browsing. May all your submissions be worthy. May all your audiences be delighted. And may you hoist a statuette or two.

Press Kit

As soon as a festival announces its selections, the media will want details about the films on the schedule. If yours is one of the lucky ones, you will want to leave a stack of press kits for festival staffers to hand out. To create a pre-screening buzz with your press kit, here's what you might put inside the package:

- Quality 8 × 10 production stills

- Camera-ready word marks and promotional graphics

- Writer and director bios

- Separate actors' bios for all the principals (with photos)

- Crew credits

- Movie synopsis and logline (one-pager)

- Contact information and links to website

- Samples of early reviews

- Quotations from the script

- Posters

- Postcards

- Music soundtracks

- DVD trailer

- Post-production blurbs ("What a wonderful picture it was to work on . . .")

- Peer quotes (Michael Moore: "This has to be the most important doc of the year.")

- CD of all of the above—Electronic Press Kit (EPK) can be made available online

- Clever pocketable trinket (helps with title recognition)

Tip: consider a tasteful mix of the above. Postcard-sized items work best.

64
Video on the Web

Andrew Burke

Figure 64-1

With new mediums come new opportunities—this should be the mantra of the video producer of today. Following are tips to formatting your story for the web.

We have in front of us our newest medium with which to utilize, and it is called web video. Certainly, we have had our share of video media: broadcast TV, VHS home video and DVD. Well, you might say, "Web video is not that new." And you'd be right. But it is a changing medium. It is different and better than ever, and has evolved significantly in the last five years. YouTube's viewership rises by the double-digits each year. Can this be said for the others listed above? Frankly, no. Even though our newest stories are being told on video specifically for the web, our archive of fantastic stories from other

sources can not be left out in the cold! Our past stories can be adapted for this online medium. Using video editing technique, social media optimization and an understanding of story, our videos can thrive like never before.

Adapting Your Shelf

If you've been involved in making video even a short length of time, chances are that you've experimented with making a DVD, or you've even been asked to create one. While DVDs serve a wide audience

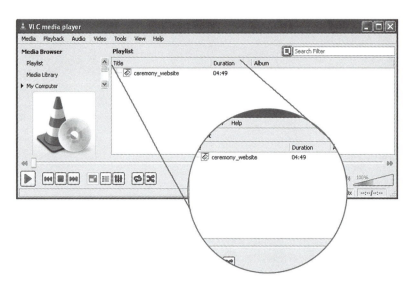

Figure 64-2 *Often, time-restrictions will not allow the entire video to be uploaded. Segmenting the video into shorter chapters can help as well as improve the viewer's experience.*

(most laptops include players, and stand-alone units can be had for under 20 bucks), videos on DVD can also be thoughtfully ported to online video. So, let's do something new with our shelf of DVDs. Whether you have an instructional video or even a feature-length movie, here are a few ways to make them fit in online:

1. *First, a full DVD is too long for most viewers to watch online.* Since online video's sweet spot is typically under five minutes (and sometimes less than two), time spent pondering good edit points is very valuable to you, the video producer. Consider uploading each chapter as a separate video. Chapter breaks found on DVDs serve as natural cutting points, though they may run longer than five minutes. Shorter video segments also allow the viewer to download less material— freeing up internet bandwidth for other family members or coworkers to enjoy the Web.

2. *While the segmented approach mentioned above is best for heavily segmented DVDs such as Instructional DVDs, a different approach can be helpful for narrative films.* Keeping the narrative story together is key. Consider uploading your story in three parts; one for each of the three-story acts. Editing may again be required, but longer video segments of up to 10 minutes are generally accepted. You can also track which acts or scenes are the most popular with viewers using tools like YouTube's video stats.

3. *Uploading episodic stories, or serials, is ideal using video-sharing communities such as YouTube and Vimeo.*

These sites allow other people to follow your story and add comments that could, in turn, help refine your video. Utilizing good feedback is way to engage with your audience, and inspire more viewers to contribute to your success. Some non-video communities like Twitter are also ideal for distributing serials. While you can't embed a video in Twitter, you can link to your video in a tweet. Sharing tweets at regular intervals, each with a video link, creates the serial story.

Consider advertising an "announcement" using tweets that you've uploaded your video. Include a Twitter contact and a keyword (on Twitter, a keyword is called

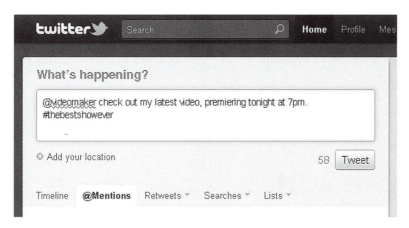

Figure 64-3 *Using Twitter to advertise your freshly uploaded videos can help increase the number of people who view them. A hashtag will improve the visibility of your video series when it is searched.*

a hashtag) that relates to your project. An example tweet may look something like this,

> "@arlohemphill Drop everything and make sure to check out the latest episode—4PM Thursday! #theottermovieproject".

In this case, "@arlohemphill" is the account of a Twitter contact who I think will enjoy and share the show. Our hashtag is "#theottermovieproject", and when it's applied to many tweets, it will improve the visibility of our video series when prospective viewers are looking for it. When you "@" someone, they are alerted to the mention, though all twitter contacts would see the tweet. The hashtag "#" is mostly used for Places, Things or Events. And sometimes fun tongue-in-cheek stuff. Example tweet: Watching news with @GabriellaDago Anchors seem sleepy! #ABCpleasecaffeinateyourstaff

Adapting Television

We're all familiar with TV and its two closely-knit parts: television shows and those pesky advertisements that seem to show up just before the car goes off the cliff on-screen. A television show's length is approximately 20 minutes of story,

which allows a TV station to insert breaks in the action for said advertisements. If you've made a documentary or narrative show for TV, you've already made some changes to your original story to accommodate the television medium. When adapting your story for the Web, you'll also have to make some story adjustments. Some scenes may be cut short, and others may even be removed to fit the broadcaster's guidelines. The guidelines for formatting your story for the Web are less regimented—but no less important. At its most basic, a Web version of your story may be a "cut down" of your original, full-length video. In this instance, your new video would aim to keep all of the elements that made your original story engaging—be it a powerful narration, smooth pacing or punchy graphics—just shorter in length by a factor of two or three minutes. Complex stories may require more complicated editing techniques, such as re-arranging scenes or adding parallel storylines. An abbreviated intro sequence is a must. This may mean re-working graphics and titles. Keep in mind, the Web audience is interested in short, pointed stories that can keep their attention right away.

TV advertisements have found a home online as well. While any small business can upload their 30 or 60 second TV spots, success is often found by sandwiching them with unique content. Popular videos

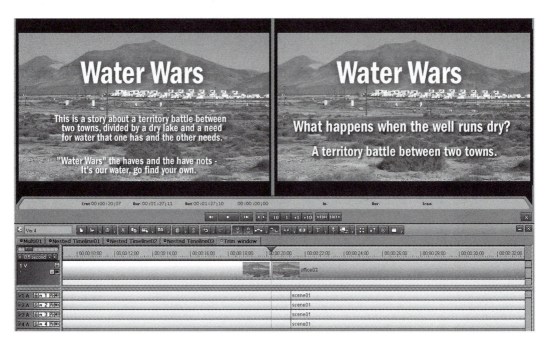

Figure 64-4 *Keep it short; keep it sweet. Making adjustments to your video to better fit a web audience may be needed. This can include cutting down your story, shortening your titles, eliminating graphics, or a combination of all of the above.*

to include alongside your ads are documentary or cinema verité style short videos. These can describe a business in greater detail or show "real" employees having fun at their job. The idea here serves to contrast the polished TV ad, while continuing the story of the business or product. At the top of the top lies Old Spice and their most recent web campaign featuring Isaiah Mustafa. Pairing with creative giant Wieden + Kennedy, Old Spice uploaded its original TV ad to YouTube, and found gold in viewers' responses. The ad gathered hundreds of responses, and Old Spice responded by uploading new videos with Mustafa addressing individual viewers directly—in near real time. Word spread fast online, which fueled millions of views for the ad.

Looking Ahead

Back in the early days, you know, around 2005, a very interesting phenomenon started occurring: some stories were being shared expressly for the Web, while others were being copied-and-pasted from traditional media. This was before YouTube's rise to online video stardom, and when video podcasts numbered in the low hundreds. The result of transplanting broadcast shows to the web amounted to putting 'TV on the radio'. Something was definitely missing! Since television consists of two distinct parts: picture and sound, both are needed to make the experience a good one. Just think of listening to an episode of "*Seinfeld*"—on the radio. The story no longer fits the medium, and borders on something of experimental art. You'd probably be able to follow certain parts of the *Seinfeld* story, but you'd miss Cramer's funny facial expressions and the textured big-city backdrops that are key to the show. So it goes for video, television and movies that are simply copied-and-pasted to the Web, without any thought of how the Web can work in our favor. The Web is changing storytelling; it allows us access to large audiences and to connect with them. It allows us to share experiences in ever-meaningful ways. And with your help, these changes will be for the better.

65
Compression Software for Web Video

Andrew Burke

Figure 65-1

Web video is everywhere, playing on laptops, through video game consoles, in digital magazines on tablet computers, and even on TVs and mobile phones.

There are many Web enabled devices (electronics which connect to the internet) that produce video and have made quite an impact on our everyday lives. All this Web video comes from somewhere, but most camcorders typically don't record video fit for immediate viewing on the Web. Herein lies the challenge: how to get our video playing on the Web, and to make sure it looks its best! Some tweaking to the video is needed; our video must be compressed for the Web.

Video compression is needed to change our large video files into smaller video files so that they can be shared more easily and viewed online. Luckily for us, there's a whole world of video compression software to get our video ready for the Web. Basic video editing software like Windows Live Movie Maker, usually includes an AVI compressor option for the Web. Professional video editing software like Adobe Premiere Pro CS5, gives us more advanced, detailed compression options. There are even stand-alone compression software tools like Sorenson's Squeeze, Apple's Compressor 4 and MPEG Streamclip that handle video compression without the need for any other software. So whether you want your video looking its best on YouTube, or playing loud and proud on an iPad, video compression software makes it happen.

What is the Best Compression Format for you?

It's hard to write a video compression comparison because everyone's needs will differ. However, whether it's the best video compression software you're looking for or the best video format for YouTube, we can get started compressing right away. Most desktop and laptop computers actually ship with video compression software built-in. On the Mac side, this means Apple iMovie, which comes

standard on every new computer (or as a $15 download from the App Store). On the PC side, it's Movie Maker, which you have to download, but it's free. Both of these offer preset options that produce good-looking Web video. iMovie is technically a video editing application, so it does much more than compress video for the Web. The software includes many basic compression features under its share menu, which gives you options to compress and upload to several online social networks like YouTube, Vimeo and Facebook. Since iMovie accepts video from most types of camcorders and point-and-shoot cameras, we think it's a no-brainer for your first Web video.

On the PC side, you can download Movie Maker free on most computers. Like iMovie, Movie Maker is a basic video editor that includes a handful of compression features for the Web. Movie Maker accepts video from a variety of camcorders and users can make online

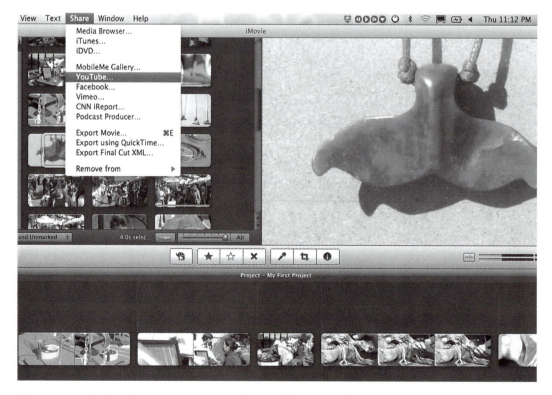

Figure 65-2 *Rather than compress your video and burn it to DVD, iMovie makes it easy to share to various social networks by using preset formats for each type of network.*

video compression for many outlets including email, YouTube, Facebook and to Windows Live SkyDrive (Microsoft's online storage service).

A third basic tool to use for compression is QuickTime player. This small application for both the PC and Mac offers video compression features in a simple package. Compression options for the Web include presets for YouTube, Vimeo, Flickr and Facebook. Custom compression options are available, too. Both Movie Maker and iMovie use presets to compress for the Web. If we want more control (and even better looking video), we'll want to look past these presets, to some professional tools and video compression techniques.

The Big Time: Specialized Compression Software

If we want to make the very best Web video, and attract the largest viewing audience, we'll have to use some more advanced tools. These tools allow us to compress HD video for more than just social networks—think Web video streaming from your website or onto a tablet computer.

Custom settings like bit rate, resolution, format and adaptive streaming are features to look for. These settings allow for fine control of video quality, but it takes time to master. With Web video now playing in glorious 1080p HD resolution, the need for exceptional video compression is greater than ever. HD video has a lot more pixels to compress than standard video. So the demands on our video compression software are higher. You may also want to compress many video clips all at once. And what about all the Web enabled devices? They each require video with slightly different compression. It's easy getting so many pixels to look good online. We just need the right tools.

Adobe Premiere Pro and Media Encoder

Adobe Premiere Pro CS5.5 is a full-featured video editor with many customizable

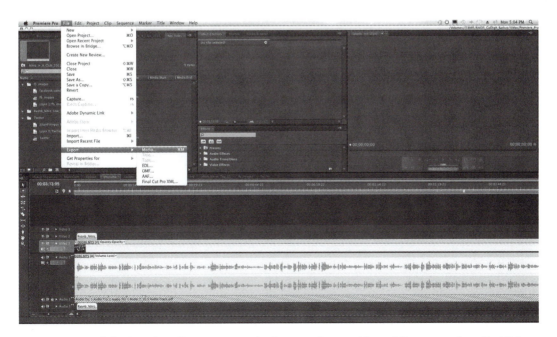

Figure 65-3 *Adobe Premiere Pro preserves the format of your video while you work so that it is faster when it comes to compressing.*

compression options, and is available for both Mac and PC. Since Premiere Pro CS5.5 ($800) allows video to be edited natively, or in an original format, compression times are shortened. Pair that with special CUDA hardware acceleration (certain video graphics cards which speed up compression), and you have a very fast tool. Premiere Pro CS5.5 works seamlessly with its included partner app, Adobe Media Encoder. This partner app allows for even greater control over compression settings, and offers adjustable setting for compressing Web video for mobile devices. And since these applications run at 64-bit (basic compression software usually runs at only 32-bit), adding more RAM to our computer helps speed up each compression task.

"Once I'm done with my edit in Premiere", says Ryan Brown owner of Downtown Brown Entertainment, "I click File -> Export Media, and Adobe Media Encoder launches." Ryan modifies Adobe's YouTube settings to 1920 × 1080 resolution and 23.976 frames-per-second, for an even better video. Taking full advantage of Premiere Pro CS5.5, Ryan compresses video for the Web using an Apple MacPro 8-core with 32GB of RAM, and an NVIDIA Quadro FX 4800 CUDA-supported graphics card.

Apple Final Cut Pro and Compressor

Final Cut Pro X is another top-quality video editor that includes a host of options to compress for the Web, but is only available on the Mac. Final Cut Pro X ($300 download from the Apple Store) offers similar publishing features to iMovie, such as a direct-to-YouTube setting, though Final Cut Pro compresses much faster using its 64-bit capabilities (iMovie is 32-bit). Other features include optimized compression for all of Apple's Web enabled devices: iPhone, iPod touch, Apple TV and the iPad.

Another standout feature is compressing for HTTP live streaming. This gives us the ability to compress multiple versions of the same video at once, for playback that matches the viewer's internet speed. For finer control, Final Cut Pro X pairs with its partner app, Compressor 4 ($50 download from the Apple Store). We can also keep editing our video in Final Cut Pro while our Compressor 4 is compressing Web video, since Compressor is a separate, stand-alone application.

Sorenson Squeeze

If we want a bundle of the top compression features without being affiliated with

Figure 65-4 *Premiere Pro CS5.5 is well set to work in conjunction with Media Encoder.*

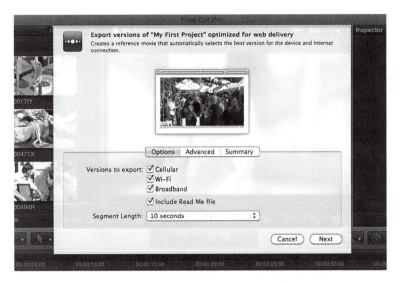

Figure 65-5 *HTTP live streaming beats the queue by compressing multiple videos at once.*

a particular video editing app, Sorenson's Squeeze 8 ($600) fits the bill. Squeeze 8 is a full-featured stand-alone application for making Web video, featuring adaptive bit rate compression for mobile devices, batch processing (an easy way to make many different compressions), and support for the latest Web video formats such as WebM. The Sorenson community also highlights custom settings, like this one for compressing to the Web enabled Xbox 360 gaming console: Xbox 360 1080p Â Codec = H.264, Data Rate = 3000 kbps, Frame Size = 1280 × 720, Method = 2-Pass VBR. That's quite a mouthful! But to make the best Web video, we'll know these settings eventually.

Close

It's more important than ever to have great looking video on the Web. This is made possible by using the right video compression software and practicing sound techniques. If your needs are basic, chances are you already have the tools to compress a video for the Web. If you're a stickler for details, prepare your wallet and your calendar (to learn top-notch software, naturally). There are still many types of video to navigate, with many devices like the Android video format playing Web video (and growing). The importance of compressing video for the Web has never been greater!

Open and Free

Open source free video compression software is still an elusive tool. These apps, while free, are basic and can complete small tasks. One such product is HandBrake (Mac/PC/Linux), a free and open source application. HandBrake compresses video into a few of the regular formats including MPEG-4 and H.264, along with open source Theora and Ogg Vorbis (for audio). MPEG Streamclip is a free application that is quite powerful; it includes many of the popular Web video formats and allows for resizing, retiming and cropping of video for the Web.

66
Streaming Video, No Longer an Upstream Row

Peter Zunitch

Figure 66-1

Streaming video has evolved tremendously over the years. It's as stark a contrast as Dorothy's barren black and white farm was to the glory of the Emerald City.

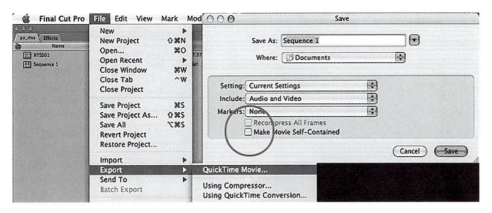

Figure 66-2 *To make a Reference Movie in Final Cut Pro, un-check the*
"Self-Contained" option.

My dear friends, we've reached the Promised Land, the ability to stream high definition video from one computer to many with a quality everyone predicted, but no one believed we'd actually achieve.

More accurately termed a progressive download, the streaming video we're talking about here refers to watching a video as the data arrives on the viewer's machine, without having to download first. Besides being slightly more secure, streaming brings a viewer much closer to instant gratification, a big plus in an era where our attention span has become too short to even watch an entire music video. Plus, given the advances in compression, computer speed and bandwidth, the additional resources streaming requires become largely mitigated.

So how's it done? More importantly, how is it done correctly? We'll take you from edit to distribution in no time. The steps are generally the same no matter which encoder you choose and the information here can easily be adapted to run with your particular setup.

Out with the Edit

Many video edit systems provide built-in support for creating a stand-alone video file. However most have limited options, are slow, and/or provide inferior quality. It is for this reason I highly recommend using an external transcoding program whenever possible.

When your edit is complete, look for the "Export" function in your editor. The specific steps will vary by edit system, and possibly by the user preferences you've set up, but typically you'll have to select the sequence you want, mark in and out points, and select the tracks to include (Check your product manual for more specific information.) You'll also need to choose an output format. Select a format compatible with both your editor and compressor. Choose "QuickTime Reference" if it's available. If it isn't, choose the native format of your edit sequence. Likewise, select.wav for audio when possible. The idea is you don't want to compress your movie at this point. You simply want a file of your edit that you can work with elsewhere.

A Short Cut

If you're going to a video-sharing site like YouTube or Veoh, then you might be in luck here if you forgo the reference file and export an actual movie. Most of these sites support a massive amount of file types for upload, and will likely take your video as it stands. Know however that doing so basically means leaving the transcoding up to them, and you'll probably be sacrificing some quality. Being the consummate professionals we are though, we're going to do it ourselves, right?

Figure 66-3 *Sorenson Squeeze offers many options for loading video.*

Taking Control

Now open up the transcoding program of your choice. Which one you choose should depend primarily on if it can import your source footage without re-encoding it, and if it can output all of the file formats you need in a fast, efficient and reliable manner. You'll then want to add or import the file to be compressed (most of the time you can simply drag the file to the source window).

For video, our most important issues are quality followed by size. So choose your codec and settings based on site and Webmaster recommendations whenever possible. Once you've decided, double click it, or drag and drop it on top of your video to apply the presets. Depending on what codec you use, you'll be presented with different options. The major settings to be concerned with are in the chart provided. It's OK to leave everything else alone in most cases.

If you're entirely confused as to where to begin, and have no input from those in the know, then consider optimizing your sequence for 300 kbps. This will allow most broadband users to play the file with

no problem. Many transcoding programs provide presets for streaming. It can be helpful to start with these and tweak for your needs, but in a pinch you can rely on them to do a decent job.

Your frame size should be set to accommodate your web page, but consider that a good percentage of users still have a 1024 × 768 monitor. Your web page should fit inside that, and your video should be comfortable within the page. Leaving the video around the 640 or 720 range will work nicely and also avoids up-scaling. The video codec you need must obviously be compatible with your streaming platform.

Which audio codec you choose will largely depend on which media container and video codec you choose, but Mp3 (if supported) is always a safe starting point. Generally 112 kbps or more will be acceptable for dialogue with music, and unless you have a specific reason, don't bother with anything other than mono or stereo. Most people only have two speakers on their computer setups.

As your last step, add any metadata you feel is necessary, set your destination and hit "go." When rendering is done, verify that the video is within file size limits and that it plays back satisfactorily. You may have to tweak settings a bit to find optimal balance.

The Great Reveal

Now it's time to publish. Log in to your destination site and upload your file. There are many options. YouTube is an obvious choice, as are sites like Veoh, Metacafe, Yahoo, etc. They all differ in what options, file formats/size allowed, acceptable content and promotion choices you get at what price point. You'll need to explore the options of each.

Choose a category for your video and a catchy, yet relevant title. Be sure to fill in the tags with relevant keywords. Careful choices here will help promote your video both within the site and with search engines. Most likely there's also boxes for linking your video to a website at the bottom. You'll also want to select if your file is to be viewed by the world at large, or by private invite only.

If you're creating your own site and you're using Flash or Silverlight, you'll also need a player front-end. Advanced users can build their own interface, but options like flowplayer.org and slvideo-player.codeplex.com respectively are good free alternatives. Make sure you find a web hosting service that supports streaming video.

Now that you've tested your video (you remembered to do that, right?) you're ready to announce it to the world. Most of the video hosting sites have options for linking to your site through Facebook, Myspace, etc. Consider also what special interest groups might be interested in your video and put a post on any forums you can find. Remember, too, that there's nothing keeping you from uploading to more than one site. And of course don't forget to email a link to everyone in your address book. Yours could be the next viral video hit!

Streaming Platforms

There are two major contenders for streaming video right now. Over the past few years Flash has all but dominated this area. Recently however it has fallen under criticism, mainly for security issues. Microsoft's Silverlight, which first launched officially in 2007 is quickly gaining popularity. Touted as an interactive development platform, it offers some flexibility not previously offered, and appears less vulnerable at the present time. Other streaming possibilities, like Divx, have their shortcomings, if for no other reason than not everyone has the playback codec already installed in their system. Others may lack hardware acceleration support. All of these are still great options and which you choose may be predetermined based on your destination. The good news is that many of the prominent video formats these days can be streamed in one way or another.

Setting up a Flash Stream on Your Own Site

A Flash player is customizable and skinable. However you must provide this information at the source. Flash then reads the information when it plays the video through the client browser. Let's use the free Flowplayer front-end to stream our video.

Render your video with the.flv extension. We're going to call it "video1.flv" here.

First, head over to Flowplayer.

Upload your video to your server, as well as the "flowplayer-3.1.1.min.js", "flowplayer-3.1.1.swf", and the "flowplayer.controls-3.1.1.swf" files.

In the head of your web page, type:

<script src="flowplayer-3.1.4.min.js"></script>

In the body, type: <a href="video1.flv" style="display:block;width:480px;height:360px" id="player">

Save and upload your Web page. Check out the Flowplayer website for help and information on customization. You will have to work with a Web hosting service that provides support for streaming. 110mb.com is a free service I've found with streaming support and no ads, though as its name implies, there's a severe limit on web space size.

67
Tips to Promote Your Video Online

Teresa Echazabal

Figure 67-1

There has never been a better time for video producers to promote and distribute their own work. You don't have to hire someone to do it nor spend a lot of cash getting it done.

If you are a little digital-savvy, or if you already have a blog or website of your own, you can market your own video and services just as effectively as any professional marketing agency.

You have put your heart and soul into your video production—now you want the whole world to see it, but you are not sure what to do about it. The good news is that these days you have many options from which to choose. Web-savvy videographers have been inventing new markets and opening up distribution opportunities with minimal resources. You have the potential to reach millions every day using such tools as blogs, social networks, even your own website. They are your opportunity to let your work be seen by the right people and they are all as effective, if not more, than if you hired an advertising agency to do it for you.

Figure 67-2 *There are lots of opportunities for videographers to distribute content to millions of viewers through a myriad of websites.*

Podcasts

Often overlooked by videographers, Podcasts are a great way to distribute your work. Podcasts are audio or video clips that are downloadable at no cost. Because a podcast is subscription-based, it uses "teaser videos" like the behind-the-scenes of your video or interviews with cast members to get people to subscribe. Once you have a significant number of subscribers, you will be ready to debut your video or film.

Video Portals and Social Networks

Video portals and social networks can establish the value of your video with like-minded people sharing common interests. Getting their attention can be as effective as meeting in person. Your profile page can serve as your website, and using their tools, you can embed video clips, launch podcasts, and even link back to a blog or a website.

YouTube is the most popular video portal in the world. Create your own channel on YouTube, upload your video and send out invitations to people interested in watching it. Asking for comments and feedback is a great way to establish relationships. Publishing videos on *YouTube* has propelled some videographers to celebrity status. Amanda Baggs' video about autism caught the attention of CNN executives. Amy Walker's video *21 Accents* has received 4 million hits and an invitation to appear on *The Tonight Show*.

VodPod is another social networking video sharing site. As with *YouTube*, you can get your very own video channel up and running in minutes. Use your video channel to power your own video site and connect your channel to your blog, *Facebook*, even *Twitter*. Take advantage of their stock templates or customize your video site from scratch.

Facebook is by far the most popular social network in the world. If you have a *Facebook* account, you can upload your video to your profile page and let the comments pour in. For a more professional presence, create a *Facebook Business Page*, just for your video distribution.

Although *MySpace* has lost some of its popularity in recent years, it is still a favorite among musicians. *MySpace* boosted Tila Tequila to celebrity status, a singer who became an overnight sensation through her *MySpace* appearances and singing.

Flickr is yet another social network where you can show your video to millions. Upload your video as you would a photo and make it "public."

Do you have a Blog or Website?

If you have your own blog or website, you are already ahead of the game. Use them to distribute your video. However, before you upload it to your blog or site, you need to attend to a few technical details that are necessary to ensure optimal video quality. You will need to convert your video to a Web-optimized format. The most widely used video format on

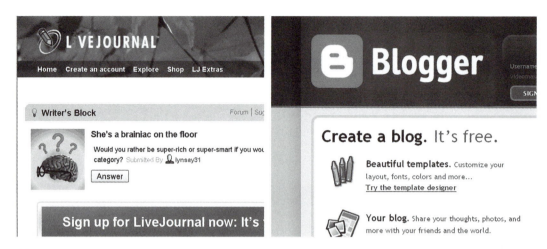

Figure 67-3 *Blogger.com and LiveJournal.com are both great websites for promoting and showcasing your work.*

the Web today is Flash. Any video conversion program can help you with this. You might already have a built-in video conversion plug-in inside your video editing application. Some of the more popular video converters are Handbrake, Sorenson Squeeze, and QuickTime Pro.

You will want to add search-engine friendly (SEF) metadata keywords along with your video as well as to your video page so that search engines can find it and list it. Use Google's Webmaster Tools to submit your video information so they can list it on their video index.

After you have converted and optimized your video for search engines, you can then upload it to your blog or site. Every video portal and social network site has its own uploading requirements. However, they are all very similar and not hard to figure out. If you are uploading to your own website, you can use an FTP client like FileZilla to upload your video.

But what if you don't have a blog or a website, and you don't know squat about how create either one? Lucky for you there are thousands of free tools available that you can use to create a blog or website. Here are just a few of the more popular ones:

Blogger is one of the most used blogging tools in the world, no doubt in part because it is so easy to manage and because it is free. Using *Blogger*, you can have your

own blog in minutes. Moreover, because it is a Google product, you can easily link all of your other Google applications, like Google docs, spreadsheets and gmail to your blog. These are useful tools to have for communicating with clients, buyers, and other distributors.

LiveJournal describes itself as "a community publishing platform, willfully blurring the lines between blogging and social networking." It's a virtual global community where users can interact on common interests. Using *LiveJournal*, you have a combination of blogging and social networking tools, giving you the opportunity to double the distribution of your video without doubling the effort.

Hire a Professional

OK, all these services are great, you say, but you want something a little bit more customized, more professional, something that will say you are a serious video producer and you will spare nothing to get the attention your clients deserve. With so many videos on the Web these days and so many "free" blogs and websites to post them in, it's easy to get lost in the shuffle. You want to make sure you stand out above the crowd.

If you are in this position, then either you can build your own custom website

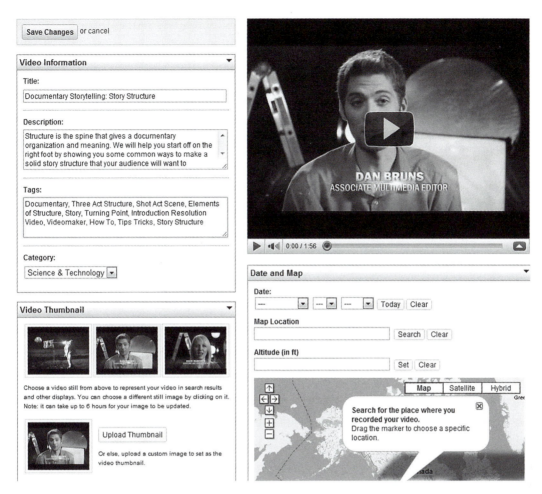

Figure 67-4 *Be sure to include description tags that are appropriate to the focus of your video topic. This will improve your search engine result ranking.*

or you can pay someone else to do it for you. Some domain and hosting companies provide free Web design services when you sign up with them. However, these services are simple, and you will end up with a website that looks "cookie-cutter" made.

The next option is to have professional do it for you. There are countless Web design companies, as well as freelance Web designers, that you can commission to build your custom website. Shop around for good Web designers. Ask friends or colleagues whom they might recommend. Make sure you commission a Web designer who will understand what you want and what you need. Tell him or her what your goals are and what

you would like your website to accomplish for you.

Full-Serve Online Video Platforms

An online video platform is a software-on-demand-based solution that offers services for the management and publication of video. The services include asset management, encoding, video players, video editing, syndication, analytics, hosting, and distribution, to name a few. While they mostly cater to businesses and corporations, the entrepreneurial video producer can also use them. *Brightcove* is one company that produces an online video platform. When you sign up with them, you upload your video to their servers and then take advantage of their services to create your custom video website. *Brightcove* has various service plans, starting at $99 a month.

Another company that will do it all for you is *CreateSpace*. On *CreateSpace*, you can sell your videos for a fraction of the cost of traditional manufacturing, while maintaining more control over your product. Your audience can choose "Download to Own and Download to Rent" your video through Amazon Video On Demand or they can purchase a professional DVD of your video on Amazon.com, your own website or other retailers without setup fees or inventory.

So Which One Do You Choose?

No one can say that there is a shortage of opportunities for today's video producers to show their work to millions. Thanks to the Web, this is now very easy and relatively inexpensive. This is probably the best time in history to be a video producer or filmmaker. With so many choices and opportunities to get your work noticed, the only thing keeping you from fame and fortune is your own talent, or lack thereof.

68

How to Make a Documentary: Distribution

Morgan Paar

Figure 68-1

You found a compelling story that the world needs to know about; you gathered up enough money to get the documentary through pre-production, shooting and post-production and your family and friends loved it. Now put your finished doc in your closet and go watch TV. NO! You're not done yet.

Distribution is something that you should have been thinking about since pre-production; not only thinking about but also including in your planning and budgeting. Every filmmaker should know from the beginning what is most important to them in regards to their product. Are you hoping to be the next Francois Truffaut who is mobbed at Sundance and Cannes by reporters and fans or are you more interested in selling your film? Both are admirable goals but their paths may vary.

Film Festivals

For many, the festival circuit is the first and maybe only step they will take.

Figure 68-2 *Withoutabox.com is a platform that allows the user to search more than 3,000 film festivals. A great resource for independent video producers who want to distribute their documentary.*

Research five to 20 festivals that your documentary will have a good chance to compete or screen in. Find some safe ones and some ambitious ones. Does your hometown sponsor a local festival where your doc will have local relevance? Be sure to send your work to one or more of the majors: Cannes, Sundance, The Academy Awards, etc. Why not? Aim high. During pre-production you took note of the festival's requirements, so you have everything you need: release forms, production stills, multiple DVDs of your video, subtitles if necessary, entry fee, etc. Mail them in before the deadline and prepare your acceptance speech for the big win.

The website Withoutabox seems to be the most comprehensive hub for festivals these days (withoutabox.com). In fact, many festivals insist you use this service. Set-up a profile and let it work for you. You can also search the Web for festivals that are appropriate for your documentary. Most have a $30–$50 entrance fee. With all the other supporting material (e.g. production stills, multiple DVD copies, shipping costs, etc.), a single entry could cost

close to $100 so pick your festivals carefully. And you may want to budget airfare and accommodation to a festival or two in order to accept the statuette in person.

Film Markets

Film markets are the place to sell your documentary. Generally speaking, this is the route towards fortune as opposed to the dream of fame at a festival. Film markets are usually large, chaotic "swap meets" where distribution companies or sales agents meet face to face with filmmakers to make deals for television, theatrical or DVD sales. To add a layer of complication, many agents will represent specific foreign markets so you might be negotiating with one agent to have your documentary play in theatres in India and another company to air on Argentine TV.

Many markets are associated with big film festivals such as the European Film Market at the Berlin Film Festival (EFM), TIFFCOM at the Tokyo International Film Festival and Cannes Film Market at the

Cannes Festival. Others are not attached to festivals such as the American Film Market in Santa Monica, California. Find out as much as you can about a distributor's desires and needs so that you are prepared to successfully sell your documentary.

Distributors

Finally, if schmoozing and negotiating at film markets is not for you, you can approach distributors directly. The internet is your friend here as there are all sorts of niche companies offering just about any kind of distribution deal you can think of. For example, if your documentary has educational relevance, there are a number of organizations that specialize in distributing to schools. Some of these distribution companies are very niche, so do your research and don't hesitate to contact them with questions (preferably in pre-production). Remember, they are making money from your hard work so they should be happy to answer your questions. Wikipedia.com and Filmforum.org are two websites that list film distributors around the world.

There are new websites popping up (and disappearing) every day that "distribute" documentaries. Some will pay you and some won't. Some will attach an advertisement to your work and share the ad revenue with you. Even if you don't get paid, it might pay off in the end if someone from a production company sees your documentary, contacts you and wants you to shoot their next documentary.

Website

Whichever path you take, it's a wise idea to have a website solely for your documentary. It doesn't have to be fancy, in fact, many times simple is better. A relevant URL name helps. If my documentary is called *The Cute Kittens of Kansas City*, www. CuteKittens.com would be great. It's probably taken, so www.CuteKittensTheDoc. com could work. Have a trailer and contact information at a minimum. Production stills, crew bios, subject bios, names of festivals where the documentary played or won awards, etc., are all relevant.

Figure 68-3 *A simple website with a trailer and contact information as well as production stills, crew bios, and awards is a great idea for showcasing your documentary. Be sure to use a URL that is relevant to the documentary and is SEO (Search Engine Optimizing) friendly.*

Television

Public Television, cable television and syndication are all avenues worth looking into. This route has become a less traveled road with the rise in popularity of the internet but if you had aired your documentary on the Discovery Channel or the National Geographic Channel, you'd have bragging rights for sure. Make some official looking letterhead, find out who makes the programming decisions and snail-mail them a skillfully written one page letter describing why their station needs to air your documentary. Chances are they will not call you back. After about two weeks, contact them again. Persistence is the name of this game.

You will need to know exactly what the station wants and needs before you roll tape. PBS has their Proposal Guidelines and Red Book (technical and legal guidelines) online as a downloadable PDF file. If you can't find a station's guidelines online, call the station directly and ask to speak with the program or editorial management.

Public-access television used to be the way us "little folk" got our videos seen. These stations, and sometimes full production and post-production studios still exist, but have taken a back seat to cable television and the internet. Wikipedia has a list of public access TV stations in the United States.

RSS and Web Syndication

We've heard some success stories of ambitious filmmakers getting their docs out via RSS feeds (Really Simple Syndication). You'll need to create some buzz (see below) in order to get the word out that

Figure 68-4 *Romeo-Theater.com is a place for independent video producers to submit their work and be featured on the site.*

your documentary is available for download via an aggregator site. John Romeo, a Richmond, Virginia filmmaker, started a sight that shares short videos through the Web or by RSS from iTunes. You can submit your doc to his site: Romeo-Theater. com. He also has some interviews with the directors of some of the movies you'll find there—good insight.

Do-It-Yourself

"Four-Walling" is a technique that has been used by indie filmmakers over the years. Typically, one rents a movie theatre and its staff for a flat fee. The filmmaker is responsible for filling the seats (read: advertising) and decides if admission will be charged. Four-Walling is a bit more challenging with the near disappearance of small, "mom and pop" type, art theatres.

The worker-owned and operated Red Vic in San Francisco is a good example of a theatre that rents its 145-seat theatre to independent filmmakers. They even have a marquee! Colleges or even high school theatres are a viable though less glitzy option to project your doc in a typical theatre atmosphere.

Create that Buzz

And finally, no matter which of these directions you take to get your documentary out to the masses, you'll want to think about creating a bit of "buzz" for your project. Put together a press kit (synopsis, cast and crew bios, technical information, director's statement, production stills, reviews and contact information), your website, as mentioned above and possibly postcards if you are headed to festivals (these are cheap to print these days, have an experienced designer lay the design out digitally for printing). If you fancy yourself to be a creative entrepreneur, you may be able to figure out a way to make your doc, trailer or project concept "go viral" before you even approach a festival or market, similar to the way *The Blair Witch Project* was being talked about before it reached theatre. Create that buzz.

You are Now a Documentary Filmmaker

Almost every one of these paragraphs, sentences even, can be an article in itself.

Figure 68-5 *Four Walling is used by many independent video producers to showcase their film to audiences. Many locales have independent theatres they can rent for the occasion.*

This was a sprint through the entire process, from initial idea to final distribution. There are many excellent books that further detail each of these steps in producing and distributing a documentary.

I hope this article inspires you to research each of these steps further and, ultimately, I hope it inspires you to take the first step in producing your story.

See you at the awards ceremony.

69
What's Legal

Mark Levy

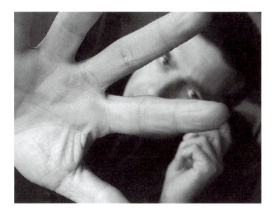

Figure 69-1

As video producers, we're often gifted with an intimate look at people, places and events in the world around us ... but we're surrounded by legal time-bombs waiting to blow our video apart.

Your life as a producer is not always easy. In addition to dealing with myriad creative and technical issues, you have to try not to be sued and not be arrested just trying to perform your job.

Creating videos under the law is all about trade-offs and compromises. As a lawyer, I am often called upon to weigh the rights of creators, such as movie makers and news reporters, against the rights of private individuals. Although you live in a free country and have the right to say almost anything about any subject, you still have limitations on those free speech rights. The public's right to know must be balanced against private citizens' right of privacy. You cannot infringe on the copyright and privacy rights of others.

The Copyright Act

When it comes to making videos, perhaps the simplest law to be aware of is the Copyright Act (Title 17 of the United States Code, www.copyright.gov), which is a federal statute, applying to people in all states. In fact, some of the Act

Figure 69-2 *If a Cease and Desist letter arrives in your mailbox, take the issue seriously. At best, it's just a warning. At worst, it's the first step to a lawsuit. At this point, you may want to consider professional legal help.*

applies to people in other countries, as well. Our copyright laws are based on the US Constitution (Art. 1, Section 8, Clause 8), written long before camcorders were invented. As a matter of fact, the Constitution became effective in 1789, before photocopiers, computers, cell phone cameras, videotape and DVDs. But copyright laws are updated from time to time and now cover all of the technology you are likely to use.

Simply stated and without an agreement to the contrary, a person who creates an original work is automatically given the exclusive right to:

- Reproduce the copyrighted work in copies or phonorecords. (Some of this terminology was last updated in 1905 . . . that's right; this update was more than 100 years ago.)

- Prepare derivative works (i.e., works that modify and are based upon the copyrighted work).

- Distribute copies of the copyrighted work to the public by sale or rental.

- Perform the copyrighted work publicly.

- Display the copyrighted work publicly, in the case of individual images of a motion picture.

- Perform the copyrighted work publicly by means of a digital audio transmission, in the case of sound recordings.

As used in the Copyright Act, what does "exclusive" mean? In this context, it means the creator of the work has a negative right: the right to exclude others from performing these activities.

If you decide to use someone else's music or sound effects or still images or film or video moving images without permission, you can be subject to a lawsuit or, when the infringement is willful, even criminal charges.

What to Do?

The absolute best solution to the copyright quandary is to create everything yourself—shoot original video, add original sound effects, and compose and perform your own music. Unfortunately,

Figure 69-3 *You can find a large array of forms from talent releases and rental agreements to shot logs in* Videomaker's Book of Forms: *www.videomaker.com/store. You can also download legal forms at www.copyright.gov.*

for most of us, this is easier said than done. Alternatively, you may hire someone to do at least some of this work. In that case, if the creator is an employee, the work would be a "work made for hire," as defined in the copyright statute: a work prepared by an employee within the scope of his or her employment, or a work specially ordered or commissioned for use as a part of a motion picture or other audiovisual work. Be sure you have the creator or performer give you a written, signed statement that assigns the copyright to you or, at the least, licenses you to use the work in your production.

In the case of music, as an example, if you want to use someone else's work, you may have to obtain permission from the copyright holders: the composer, the publisher, the arranger, and the performer. Knowing whom to approach for

permission and how to do it is often bewildering. Unfortunately, there is no simple solution to the problem. Requesting permission to use commercial sound recordings can be time-consuming, expensive and frustrating. Hollywood producers, for example, can easily pay thousands of dollars to obtain the rights to a released song. Nevertheless, if you are intent on using another person's material, get permission in writing to do that. That way, you may never have to see the inside of a courtroom.

Another popular alternative is to use royalty-free music that is available from a number of suppliers and conveniently categorized with headings, such as Contemporary, Classical, Corporate or Industrial, Rock, Popular, etc. Once you obtain a license to use the library of music, you can reuse it as many times as you like for almost any purpose.

What Material is Available?

A number of other approaches, besides creating your own, original work or employing someone to create or perform material, can be used to solve your problem. For example, any intellectual property created before 1922 is out of copyright. Certain works created after 1922 are also out of copyright, but it can be difficult to know for sure without a search of Copyright Office records. In any event, you are free to video a Rembrandt painting, say, as long as the book that contains it was published before 1922. You can also perform a Beethoven sonata, as long as the recording or sheet music that you use was published before 1922.

The Copyright Act also includes a provision for "fair use." Under this exception to copyright principles, you can use at least some of another person's copyrighted material without permission if your purpose is for criticism, comment, news reporting, teaching, scholarship, or research. Tests for fair use include how much of the work is copied and whether the copyright holder will be harmed by your use of his material. A certain case involved a circus performer, whose 10-second performance of being shot out of a cannon and into a net was captured by TV news people and broadcast on the evening news. Yes, the purpose for broadcasting the act came under the heading "fair use – news reporting," but once TV viewers saw the entire performance on the TV news, attendance at the circus was drastically reduced. Even a 10-second portion of a work can be considered too much under the fair use provision. Ask yourself whether your use of part of a song such as Dean Martin's *That's Amore*, in a documentary about penguins, will actually dissuade viewers from buying the original song. Unlikely. In fact, you can make an argument that more people will buy the record after seeing your movie.

Right of Privacy

Now that you understand what you can and cannot do regarding the works of others, it is time to discuss limitations on your own, original work. You have the right to videotape any subject—animal, mineral or vegetable—as long as the subject does not object, and as long as videotaping the subject matter does not subject you to criminal sanctions, such as child pornography or espionage laws. Remember, though, that a private citizen has the right to be left alone. If you sneak into a person's backyard and videotape the occupants of the house through a window, you are likely to be sued by the person or persons you videotaped. You may even be arrested. People who are in their own home, in a motel room, or in a bathroom have a great expectation of privacy.

On the other hand, if a person is well known as a politician, say, or a sports figure, a rock star, a movie actor, or a hero of any other description, he is entitled to a lesser degree of privacy than a non-celebrity, private citizen has. The more famous the person, the less right of privacy he has. Famous celebrities will be the first to admit that they have almost no right of privacy.

Similarly, if a private citizen shows up at a parade or a football game or a protest march, he has put himself in a public place and should not expect the same degree of privacy that he has in his home. Sometimes, a person happens to be at a location in which a newsworthy event, like a fire, a hurricane, a bridge collapse or a police shoot-out occurs. In those cases, even though the person did not intentionally seek publicity, he still may have forfeited his right of privacy, due to circumstances beyond his control.

If a small group of people happens to be at your daughter's dance recital or confirmation at your church, they may not expect to be videotaped. Do not let your camera linger on those bystanders for more than a few seconds. Do not single them out, especially if they are doing something impolite or inappropriate that would subject them to ridicule.

If you do not know whether the person's appearance qualifies as a public one, it is

Figure 69-4 *Different locations have different privacy expectations. In between these places lie gray areas. The only way to protect yourself for sure is to have talent and location releases.*

best to obtain a photo or talent release from that person. Always carry a few of them in your camera bag. Sadly, many wonderful, hilarious performances that would otherwise appear on *America's Funniest Home Videos* or on *Candid Camera* cannot be aired on TV because the subjects did not sign a talent release giving permission to the producer to show their image.

Conclusion

Many legal pitfalls await a videographer, but if you keep in mind the balance between the copyright and privacy rights of others and your constitutional right of free speech (or free videotaping), you will sense, if nothing else, when to call a lawyer.

In consideration of the sum of $1.00 and other good and valuable consideration, receipt of which is hereby acknowledged, I, being of legal age, hereby give _____ (hereinafter MOVIE MAKER), and all licensees, successors, legal representatives and assigns of MOVIE MAKER, the absolute and irrevocable right and permission to use my name and to use, reproduce, edit, exhibit, project, display, copyright, publish and/or resell photographic pictures and/or moving pictures and/or videotaped images of me with or without my voice, or in which I may be included in whole or in part, and any of my possessions, including real and personal property, which pictures, images and possessions are photographed, taped, videotaped, and/or recorded on [date] _____, 20__ and thereafter, and to circulate the same in all forms and media for art, advertising, trade, competition of every description and/or for any other lawful purpose whatsoever. I also consent to the use of any printed matter in conjunction therewith.

I hereby waive any right that I may have to inspect and/or approve the finished product or products or the editorial, advertising or printed copy or soundtrack that may be used in connection therewith and any right that I may have to control the use to which said product, products, copy and/or soundtrack may be applied.

I hereby release, discharge and agree to save harmless MOVIE MAKER, his/her licensees, successors, legal representatives and assigns from any liability by virtue of any blurring, distortion, alteration, optical illusion or use in composite form whether intentional or otherwise, that may occur or be produced in the making, processing, duplication, projecting or displaying of said pictures or images, and from liability for violation of any personal or proprietary right that I may have in connection with said pictures or images and with the use thereof.

    Individual:_____

    Print:_____

    Witness:_____

    Date:_____

70
Jacks of All Trades

Charles Fulton

Figure 70-1

Way back in 1999, CD-burning drives were just beginning to cross into practical price ranges. A video-editing computer was still an expensive and tricky beast to configure and no one thought DVD burners would be inexpensive and widely available anytime soon.

The typical software bundled with a typical circa 1999 CD-R drive was barely enough to burn a data CD or audio CD. Even today, the software packages that come in the box with most CD and DVD burners are not the same as the full-featured premium suites a number of companies offer. The core of this software is still burning discs and the software is usually very good at this. As these packages have gone from simple data burning to also include audio CDs, MP3 ripping and video DVDs, most companies have built more comprehensive packages of applications, or suites. These suites handle all of your needs as far as basic disc authoring is concerned. Let's investigate some of the features found in a typical disc-authoring suite.

Video Editing

Frequently, the video editing features found in a suite tend to be rather basic, but functional. They're great if you need to throw a simple, quick project together. They're no replacement for your beloved copy of Avid, Premiere Pro or Vegas if you're embarking on a more involved project, but if you're just cutting up a single-track project and audio needs are simple, you'll find what you need.

Disc Authoring

Most disc authoring suites support a wide array of disc formats. Most packages burn DVD-video projects and audio CDs to a broad variety of discs, which can include CD-R and DVD-R data discs and burning MP3 discs for use in mobile digital audio players.

When it comes to burning DVD-Video projects, most of the packages include templates for menus, which will help you create your project quickly. Interestingly, Dolby Digital audio encoding has found its way into a large number of these packages, which we applaud. Dolby Digital audio is widely considered to be the ideal format for audio on DVD, since it's defined as one of the mandatory formats in the DVD standard, yet it doesn't take excessive amounts of data to encode.

Audio Management

Music management has become an increasingly common feature in disc authoring suites. Most suites now handle a staggering array of formats. MP3 is by far the most common audio format, but a number of other formats have become popular with internet audio fans. These include the open-source Ogg Vorbis format, Microsoft's WMA, as well as AAC, which was co-developed with Dolby Laboratories and popularized by Apple.

Almost all of the packages can also rip (extract) CD audio tracks from discs that conform to the CD Digital Audio standard. This allows you to copy the tracks to the format of your choice for your own personal use, such as cataloguing music on your hard drive for use with jukebox applications or using your music with portable personal audio players.

Other Features

A number of suites offer data backup and restore features. Like many functions performed by suites, data backup capabilities tend to be on the light side when compared to other dedicated backup utilities. You can create and print basic labels and inserts using the included layout software, but, again, the features are limited compared with a dedicated labeling application.

A disc authoring suite is a software upgrade that is always worth considering. They're inexpensive, very useful and often surprisingly powerful. If you're ready to proceed deeper into the world of media creation than that which your basic burning software can handle, it's time to give a disc authoring suite a careful look.

71
To DVD or not to DVD?

Bill Davis

Figure 71-1

There is no question—we're now officially smack dab in the middle of the era of the "homemade" DVD.

DVD burners are included with most modern computers and the ubiquitous shiny discs are rapidly pushing aside VHS tape as the "home recording" format of choice. So if you haven't made the switch to your own home DVD authoring environment, now's the time.

I use the term "environment" rather than "program" because quite a few people who

want to create their own DVDs are turning to stand-alone DVD burners, rather than authoring their DVDs in a software application on a computer. Both approaches yield similar results—take your pick. This chapter focuses on computer-based DVD burning, but if you're considering a standalone DVD recorder, see the sidebar "Standing Alone."

Figure 71-2 *Many DVD authoring programs will allow the user to alter or replace buttons, backgrounds and other design elements in the included menu templates.*

Getting Started

All DVD authoring requires at least some basic menu creation. This is the process of building a navigation "front end" so that the end-user can locate and play the content that is burned onto the disc.

Most DVD authoring software typically comes with pre-packaged menu templates, so if you just want to get the job done fast and easy, look for these templates to give you a head start or inspiration, or cues for how to proceed in making your own templates down the road. More robust software provides customization options, including control over the "look and feel" of your interface. The best software programs allow you to start with a professionally built template but essentially "deconstruct" them in order to customize them for your particular use.

For example, if the original template designer specified four animated picons (picture icons, or thumbnails) for scene selection, but you have five scenes that you want to fit onto your menu page, you can almost always copy and paste another picon link and, with a few clicks and some simple drag-and-drop screen re-arrangement, be ready to go.

Going Outside to Play

Power users will typically do a substantial amount of their menu design outside the DVD creation process, using tools like Adobe Photoshop or similar high-end image editing (or other design) software to precisely specify every background, button, nuance and shading of the interface that they are creating. After you have your menu design developed, you need to link it to the actual actions the buttons or hot zones should invoke. (A Hot Zone is basically a place on a DVD menu where a change occurs in the look of the area when the cursor reaches it—often used for highlighting buttons or other interface elements.) DVD programs have various ways of accomplishing this linking process.

Some use a table-like interface, where you link actions on one side to button titles on the other. Other programs provide robust graphical linking environments, where you drag connecting lines between the button itself and the action you want that button to invoke. Each software implementation might be different, but there *must* be a way—either automated or manual—to link buttons to actions, or your DVD won't be able to do anything.

Figure 71-3 *Imaging software can be used to make assets for your menus such as backgrounds and interactive buttons.*

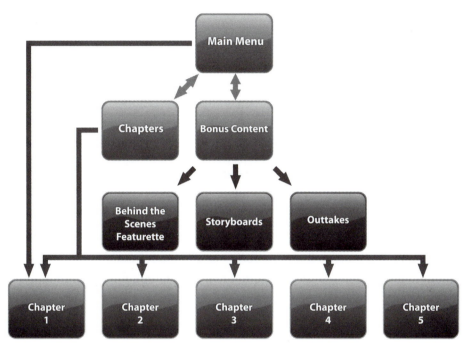

Figure 71-4 *The arrowheads in this schematic represent buttons which the user will need to navigate to and from areas that do not automatically return to the previous menu.*

Simplicity—Its Own Reward

The challenge with linking is that, if you have a lot of menu actions, the navigation can get complex. And there are lots of stories of beginners forgetting, for example, to link the END of a block of content to a "return to menu" function. So essentially someone will play a part of your DVD and get stuck in a blind alley, unable to do anything but eject and re-install the disc. Bummer.

Clear navigation that makes sense to the user and always provides clues to "what to do next" is an art. Studying the templates in good software can give you clues such as placing "home" buttons on all screens and making sure your user choices are clear.

DVD is *not* Videotape!

Finally, all of us trained to make videos are conditioned to thinking in a beginning-middle-end linear process. The magic of the DVD is that it's non-linear in nature. As a DVD designer, you need to think differently. Are there parts of your project that your audience would enjoy being able to skip directly to? What about "special content" like outtakes and bloopers? The very non-linear nature of DVD makes it a perfect vehicle for providing your viewers with extras like these.

The flexibility of the DVD format makes it a much more robust way to store and play back video, but that same flexibility makes it a bit more complicated to burn even a simple DVD than it was, for example, to record to VHS tape. As with any complex endeavor, the key is to dive in, experiment and learn. Your first discs probably won't be perfect, but before too long, you'll be burning DVDs like a pro. And taking comfort in the fact that your creations should look better and be much more durable than the tapes of yesterday.

Happy Authoring!

Standing Alone

For a lot of occasional users, complex computer-based DVD authoring is just too much trouble. So consider the "stand-alone" DVD burner's "all in one" approach.

Figure 71-5

Gone is the computer. In its place is a dedicated box that contains the burner, the MPEG-2 encoder needed to make DVD player-compliant files and in many cases a hard drive that stores the video footage during the encoding and burning process. These units make DVD creation about as easy as it can be. But not as easy as the "one button" VHS recording you're likely accustomed to.

Figure 71-6

That's because at least some basic titling, chapter marking and navigation are required for any DVD. In the stand-alone recorder, the typical process is a guided series of menus where you enter your text for titles and mark your chapter breaks by pushing control buttons on a handheld remote control. It's a little like text messaging on a cell phone. Still, the resulting DVDs work just like those authored on computer based systems. And while the menus might not be as fancy, at least your computer is free for other work while your standalone DVD recorder is burning your latest video project to disc.

PART VI
Authoring DVDs and CDs

Burning video onto discs that will play in DVD players and computers.

72
DVD Authoring Buyer's Guide

Peter Zunitch

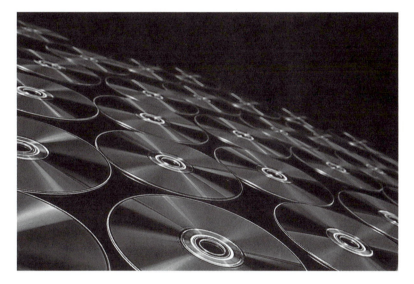

Figure 72-1

What to Buy, What to Know

I had a simple goal: authoring a DVD. It's something I've done hundreds of times over the past eight years; not a big deal. Typically there are at least three programs capable of making a DVD on my system at any given time. The trouble is none of them were capable of making the DVD exactly the way it needed to be done. Each of them was missing some functionality that prohibited continuing. It seemed like I was stuck.

Then it occurred to me that my most recent program hadn't seen any updates in over four years. It had come bundled with my editing software (which in itself usually means reduced functionality than the full retail version). There must be a more recent, more functional version out there. Surely others are looking for the perfect solution as well? The market landscape has changed a lot in the past few years. Companies have folded, merged with others, or canceled product lines. It's a whole new authoring world. So the quest for an answer had begun. In this stage of DVD's reign, is there one piece of authoring software that can satisfy all of our authoring needs?

Let's first define those needs. The options considered essential are noted in the accompanying grid, along with a few other items that aren't needed per se, but go a long way towards a professional product and pleasant operating experience. Most features are self-explanatory, but let's talk about why some of the more questionable inclusions are necessary.

Menu Customization

Templates are a nice starting point, and good if you're making a disc for your niece's eighth birthday, but after that they become boring. Creativity comes out in the menu, so it's essential to be able to tailor every aspect of it to your needs. A proper authoring program should let you internally and/or externally design every item that makes up your menu navigation.

Blu-ray: I don't actually know anyone who has ever been asked by a client to make a Blu-ray disc, however, the ability to make one is important for future-proofing as well as learning.

Dolby Digital (AC-3): smaller audio files means more room for video, which in turn leads to less compression, and thus better picture quality. Dolby's compression scheme provides equivalent quality at file sizes far smaller than PCM.

Multiple audio and subtitle tracks: commentaries, alternative music, karaoke mode, other languages, aid for the impaired; 20 different ways to use multiple audio and text tracks spring to mind. The ability to process at least one alternative track of each type is essential.

Copy protection: any copy protection scheme on DVDs and Blu-ray can be defeated. However, there are instances when something, anything, even if imperfect, would be "good enough." Most people out there know they can break Digital Rights Management (DRM), but either don't bother, don't know how, or don't have the tools on-hand to do it. So, yes, it can be useful.

Multi-core support/Advanced encoding: sharing encoding time among multiple cores (or even computers) can significantly speed up disc creation. The question is, what programs support it? Also helpful are features like smart rendering (encoding only those parts that have changed), batch processing, encode scheduling, and post-encode functions (auto-shutdown, email notification, etc). All these things make authoring a lot less agonizing.

The ultimate solution for DVD authoring is obviously a hardware/software system like Sonic Scenarist, but let's be realistic. Few of us would ever be able to justify giving away four digits to the left of the decimal point and more for an authoring system. So just how much does one have to spend to get a similar level of ability?

The $100 Mark

Software under $100 is dominated by consumer-level authoring programs. These programs are good if you just want to put together a DVD. Nero Multimedia Suite 10 is the first program that stands out above the rest. It does all that the others in this range do, and offers a whole suite of programs for editing, mixing, viewing, etc., to boot. The sacrifice you'll make here is in menu customization. Users with this program work from pre-made graphics.

Nero's new system allows you to swap out buttons and thumbnails for designs more to your liking, but you can only choose from what they provide.

Roxio Creator 2011 Pro offers full 3D support, if that's your cup of tea (a trick that can only be done in most other programs with AviSynth scripts). You can import and edit, and also export 3D video for display on 3D TVs and 3D computer displays, and sharing on YouTube.

CyberLink's PowerProducer 5.5 has an extremely enjoyable interface that is very easy to understand, even if you've never touched authoring software before. It might be the ideal program for someone just starting out, or who makes more slideshows than videos, but users may quickly

 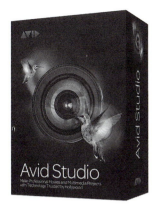 

Figure 72-2 *The DVD authoring software programs used by most consumers runs in the $100 or less range.*

become frustrated at its inability to recognize popular file formats.

Corel's DVD MovieFactory was just the opposite. It lacked features, but accepted virtually every codec thrown at it.

Sony's DVD Architect Studio edition has navigation features not available in any other program in this price range. Its ability to handle external graphics, customize remote control buttons, and produce playlists makes for some nice menu building.

If you want a serious DVD authoring program with professional options in this price range, TMPGEnc offers a phenomenal amount of tools, many of which are only found in programs that cost twice as much. There is a moderate learning curve here, though.

Figure 72-3 *Higher priced programs usually offer more manual features.*

$200–$400

If you're willing to step up to the next price range, Roxio DVDit 6 Pro is the way to go. The interface is one of the most pleasant to work with, offering a logical workflow even for the most advanced of options. It is a bit of a shame that Roxio does not offer trial versions of any of its current DVD software though, and we find it interesting that they charge more than double the cost of the program for the Blu-ray version. The Pro and HD versions both support AC-3.

Another program worthy of note in this price range is DVD-lab PRO2. It's kind of

hard to put this program in the same class as the others. DVD-lab PRO2 sacrifices any semblance of a kind of simple interface and replaces it with the power to author truly intricate and complex DVDs. If you wanted to make a DVD game, or a DVD that changes based on user input, this would be the ideal program. It does, however, lack amenities like drag and drop support, and does not accept many common codecs.

$400 and Up

All of the other high-end authoring tools would probably fall into the same price range as DVDit 6 Pro . . . that is if they were offered as stand-alone products. Unfortunately, they only come as parts of

Figure 72-4 *Working in a suite like those offered by Adobe or Apple cost more, but include other programs along with the DVD authoring. These authoring programs have all the whistles and bells you'd use for your DVD publishing form custom menus to copyright protection management.*

larger, and much more expensive packages. If you work in Final Cut Pro for example, then you know how good DVD Studio Pro 2 is. It offers virtually identical abilities as DVDit 6 Pro.

The same can be said for Adobe's Encore. It's a cornucopia of professional authoring options if you're willing to shell out for Premiere Pro or the CS5.5 Master Suite. The benefit, however, is the tight integration with all of Adobe's other products. The latest version of Encore is 64-bit only. 32-bit users are just plain out of luck. We understand that 64-bit operating systems are superior, but this still seems a little premature. While other companies should be moving to 64-bit eventually, this makes Encore out of anyone's ability unless they have a newer operating system. (Computers have been shipping for years with 64-bit capable processors. You can verify your system's capabilities with the Intel Processor Identification Utility.)

However, once you go this route you'll enjoy the speed and stability 64-bit offers.

The Pro version that comes with Sony Vegas is where DVD Architect really shines. Blu-ray support, copy protection, multiple tracks of all types and more all round out an already feature rich product. The interface retains the same lackluster style though.

Free With a Price

So how did the no-cost offerings hold up? Well, to be honest, mostly as expected. DVD Flick is an enjoyable program with an easy to understand interface. Unfortunately, menu customization is almost non-existent. GUI for DVDauthor had a less friendly interface. It did, however, offer some interesting options not seen in many other programs, like auto-shutdown upon completion. Its biggest drawback is that it only accepts MPEG-2 video, forcing the user to use external transcoders.

These programs aren't really comparable to the polished offerings of the popular consumer products, but many of these projects build upon each other as well, so it's conceivable that you could put together a feature rich package eventually, but it's not recommended.

The Quest Continues

It's quite surprising, but there's still no authoring system out there that will ever satisfy all the features you need, unfortunately, when it comes to DVD authoring, "one size does NOT fit all!" We're all shooting to different formats, and our DVD needs differ greatly, too.

If you want something simple, there's plenty of choices all with a variety of options. If you've obtained Encore, DVD Studio Pro, DVD Architect or DVDit as part of a package, there's no reason you shouldn't stick with those, as they're all about equal (though, if you have the Avid-bundled standard DVDit, we do recommend upgrading to Pro). In the end, each one has its shortcomings, however small they may be. There are many more we didn't have room for, so let this be your starting point, and go for the features you need most. If you weigh the options, you can walk away satisfied.

Format Rant

Today, support for the insane amount of different file types in circulation remains an issue in many DVD authoring programs. As users, we want the program to simply accept any format thrown at it and have it work. Sadly, this is not the case. While there are some shining standouts, most authoring programs still lack support for a wise range of file types. What's interesting is that this is one problem that does not go away simply by throwing money at it. In other words, you'll find just as many high cost programs fail to support codecs as you'll find low cost ones that do.

Even more perplexing is what codecs certain programs kicked back. It wasn't just the obscure file types that went unsupported. Almost half of the programs tested wouldn't accept mov files. Others rejected avi containers, mp3, or even wav! At this point, there's just no excuse for such lack of support. Users shouldn't have to rely on external transcoders, especially since one of the free offerings we looked at accepted almost anything under the sun.

The bottom line here is that you should take stock of the file types you use most often before deciding on one of these programs, and make sure they are natively supported. You should also make sure you have a decent transcoding program for all the rest. Nothing's worse than getting stuck up the authoring tree without a codec.

Video's Neglected Sibling

If the program you're using to compile your final product has no option for regulating audio, then balancing levels across titles can become tedious and frustrating. You might even find yourself going back to your edits and remixing, only to have to export and re-insert into the compilation again. It's baffling why more DVD authoring programs don't include level monitors and volume adjustments, or a simple normalize function at least. One could make the argument that all your sources should be finalized before the DVD stage, but having an authoring program that includes some kind of audio tweaking or filters can save you a lot of time, and a very large headache.

73

DVD Authoring Freeware: A Guide to Free Tools

Mark Montgomery

Figure 73-1

You don't have to look too far to find a bunch of DVD authoring freeware options on the internet. However, not all free DVD authoring software is created equal. What's safe? What works best? What should you avoid?

It can be tricky sorting out the good DVD authoring software from the ones that will crash frequently or leave you high and dry with technical issues. Let's take a closer look at how to choose the best free DVD authoring software for your needs.

What is DVD Authoring Freeware?

DVD authoring freeware is exactly what it sounds like: free software. Yes, free DVD authoring software does exist and there are quite a few options. But the

Features

- create and burn DVD video with interactive menus
- design your own DVD menu or select one from the list of ready to use menu templates `v1.8.0`
- create photo slideshow
- add multiple subtitle and audio tracks
- support of AVI, MOV, MP4, MPEG, OGG, WMV and other file formats
- support of MPEG-2, MPEG-4, DivX, Xvid, MP2, MP3, AC-3 and other audio and video formats
- support of multi-core processor
- use MPEG and VOB files without reencoding, see FAQ
- put files with different audio/video format on one DVD (support of titleset)
- user-friendly interface with support of drag & drop
- flexible menu creation on the basis of scalable vector graphic
- import of image file for background
- place buttons, text, images and other graphic objects anywhere on the menu screen
- change the font/color and other parameters of buttons and graphic objects
- scale any button or graphic object
- copy any menu object or whole menu
- customize navigation using DVD scripting

See Documents for more information.

__Figure 73-2__ Softpedia provides a seal of approval and is revocable. There is also a 100-percent clean certification that is good for personal use—not commercial.

truth of the matter is that many of the options are free for a reason. They're generally not as feature-rich as their commercial counterparts and they may not be as stable, too. As long as all you need is some simple DVD authoring tools, they're definitely worth a closer look. After all, free is hard to beat.

What to Watch Out For

Freeware has gotten a bad rap with a host of problems related to the free software market, and DVD authoring freeware is no stranger. There are a few bad apples out there that have spoiled the mood over free DVD authoring software.

Spyware: They're Watching You

You may have heard of the term spyware. It's a version of software called malware and it's no good. Spyware is usually installed inconspicuously onto the user's computer and it secretly collects data about the user, such as private information and Web viewing history. This data

can then be sent to another party via the internet. Spyware can also install other software and/or mess with your computer's settings and ultimately create quite a nightmare for you. So, naturally, you'll want to avoid this when you go looking for DVD authoring freeware.

Our most important tip for free DVD authoring software is to fully research the software developer. One nice assurance often found on the best options is "100% Free" Softpedia.com certification. The certification process is done by Softpedia and guarantees that the software does not contain any malware, including spyware, viruses and other nasty stuff that would put your personal and private data at risk. We highly recommend you steer clear of any options that aren't certified. It's not worth it.

Stability Issues

As you might imagine, some free DVD authoring software options just aren't as stable as the more professional (and expensive) options. Some of the software developers in this category are

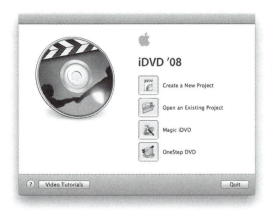 

Figure 73-3 *Included with many computer software packages are iDVD and Windows DVD Maker. Both are adequate and tailored for simplicity.*

one-man-bands. They are indeed talented developers, but even for them, keeping software bug-free can be a real challenge. Always check the forums and FAQs for a glimpse into some of the technical issues that might arise. Check if the DVD authoring freeware provider has a tech support area on its site or a way to contact the creator. Also, check to see when the last release was for the current version of the DVD authoring software. If it's several years old, then it's probably a personal project of someone that has gone by the wayside.

We've come to expect a few bugs here and there. You get what you pay for. This is especially true if you're pushing these applications to their limits. The good news is that the best providers do try their best to correct any bugs and even the big software companies out there have bugs too. At the end of the day, though, if you absolutely need to have a disc burned and ready to go to a client, free DVD authoring software is probably not a good fit for you.

Solutions for all Operating Systems

By far, Windows has the greatest selection of the best DVD authoring software. Linux also has a few good options, and the Mac is just ho-hum. But all three of these operating systems (OS) do have DVD authoring freeware options, so

whatever OS you're running it will not be a factor. There are two interesting points, however. First, Windows has bundled Windows DVD Maker with Windows 7 or Vista packages. This means that it integrates nicely with the free Windows Live Movie Maker software. These two freeware options team up nicely (we'll cover this option in greater detail later). Second, while Windows has its DVD Maker software available as a free download, Mac has its iDVD software bundled with its OS. Both options seem like freeware even though the cost of admission is owning those respective operating systems.

DVD Authoring in the Web World

We're keeping an eye out on this field of DVD authoring freeware for one good reason: we can't help but wonder if many of these solutions can sustain development and technical support in a world with YouTube being so prevalent today. We know that home video enthusiasts still want to watch their videos on their big screen TVs, and DVD is just the tool for the job. But we wouldn't be surprised to see a few of these options lose steam and wither away. For this reason, we also highly recommend DVD authoring software that is open source. This means that they are not only free to use for the end user, but free for other developers to use

Figure 73-4 *After being malware free, or having few stability issues, open source freeware—with many supporting developers, is the next fallback for choosing DVD authoring software.*

and contribute to the source code of the project. Open source DVD authoring software generally has more support from a community of developers and therefore is more likely to survive difficult market conditions. We can't predict the future, but we feel more confident about the open source solutions outlasting any others (except maybe Microsoft).

DVD Authoring Software Review

Let's quickly review our main tips about selecting DVD authoring freeware. First, choose solution providers that are "100% Free" Softpedia certified and avoid installing malware on your computer. Second, thoroughly research what stability issues might exist and what options you'll have for tech support. You don't

want to be left with a bug and no support. Third, when in doubt choose open source DVD authoring software as it is typically more likely to have development support and a longer future. Now let's get into some of our choices for the best DVD authoring software for free.

Windows DVD Maker

If you're using a Windows computer, I can't think of a better option for you. This one is free, works nicely with Windows Live Movie Maker (the free video editing software) and is designed by one of the best software development companies in the world. Hands down, this is probably your best bet. It's got a nice user interface with a relatively low learning curve. There's no malware. It has stability and thorough technical documentation. Although it's not open source, this application is such a nice complement to the operating system that I don't see how or why it would be discontinued in the near future. However, if you are working with Windows Vista, DirectX 9 must be supported by your video card. Earlier versions are not supported.

If you have an earlier version of Windows, there is another DVD authoring software solution for you. DVDStyler is one of our favorites.

DVDStyler Version 1.8.4.2

DVDStyler is an easy to use DVD authoring software solution. It's an open source project and has the support of a team of developers working on the project. They're frequently posting fixes to the software and making improvements and taking feature requests. It's also proudly "100% Free" Softpedia.com certified. But most of all, we like that it's available for

Windows (XP, Vista, 7, and 2000), Mac OS X, and Linux, too. So, it's cross-platform compatible, which makes it great for schools or classrooms that have different computers with different operating systems. DVDStyler is compatible with a long list of different video and audio codecs, including the most common types, like H.264, AVI, DV, WMV, MPEG-4, QuickTime, AC-3, WAV and many more.

These are our top choices for DVD authoring freeware. Both combine an easy-to-use interface that should please the home video hobbyist. If you're using a Windows 7 computer, your best bet is Windows DVD Maker, Mac users can rely on the bundled iDVD application, and earlier Windows versions and computers running Linux can take advantage of DVDStyler.

There's certainly nothing wrong with freeware, however, be wise about your selection process and follow our tips to keep yourself out of trouble. The last thing you need is a nightmare virus keeping you from enjoying your vacation video and a bag of popcorn.

74
Authoring Blu-ray Discs

John Joyner

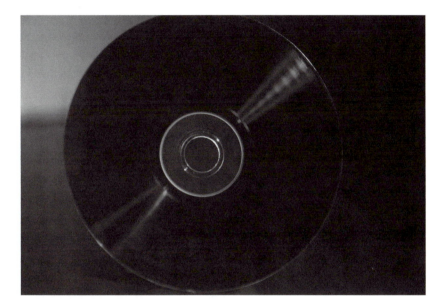

Figure 74-1

We are living in a revolutionary time. Blu-ray Disc technology has taken its place as the vessel for viewing High Definition (HD) media. More excitingly, Blu-ray Disc creation is available to anyone who wishes to use it, whether you're creating an experience for major distribution or for viewing on your family room's new digital wide screen.

If you don't know what you're doing, HD output can prove a frustrating task. To give some perspective, a minute of uncompressed HD video equals a gigabyte of memory! The answer to this problem is compression. The time has come to empower yourself! By understanding HD compression you will minimize your problems when outputting to Blu-ray. This will save on time and aspirin. In this chapter, we'll walk you through the process of compressing video for Blu-ray distribution.

The following examples will draw from Adobe Premiere and Adobe Encore, as these are the systems the author has worked most extensively with.

Getting Started

Compressing for Blu-ray is a two-step process.

1. Creating the HD media file (encoding and formatting)
2. Putting it on a Blu-ray disc (building and burning)

The first step can be approached in two ways. You can use your editing platform, Adobe Premiere in this case, or you can use your disc authoring system, Adobe Encore.

For step number one, I recommend using your editing platform (Adobe Premiere in this case) to compress your masterpiece. There are a couple of reasons for this. The editing platform gives more options for output, while encoding within it allows the system to focus all its energy on creating a crisp media file for you. I find the overall quality tends to be better.

If you choose to export your video via the DVD authoring system (Encore), it will be pulling double duty as an encoder and a Blu-ray burner. Remember, you're dealing with HD here. While the encode step happens before the burning takes place, the entire operation puts tremendous pressure on the authoring system. As such the entire process takes a long time (at most a few days,) and that's if the congestion of data doesn't crash the platform. We recommend saving often, and we've experienced greater overall stability when we manually transcode clips before beginning the build process.

Step 1: Codecs

In Adobe Premiere click File and then Export, where the drag down will display a series of options. Choose Adobe Media Encoder, as shown (Figure 74-2)

This will open the Encoder's export settings sub-screen (Figure 74-3).

This is where the encoding process will take place.

Adobe Media Encoder is very straightforward and the options are all very accessible.

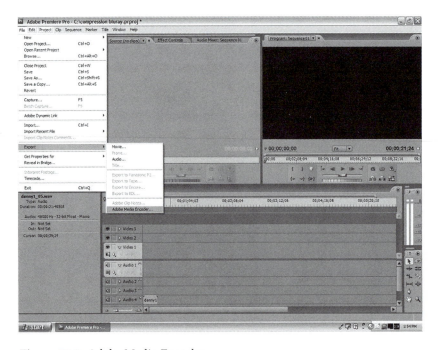

Figure 74-2 Adobe Media Encoder.

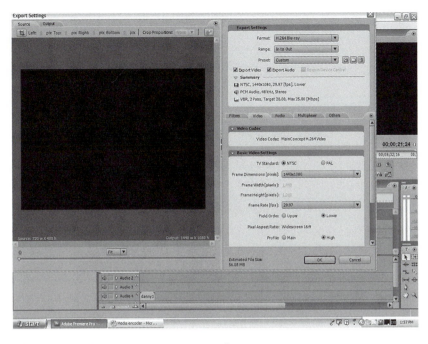

Figure 74-3 *Encoder's export setting subscreen.*

First you want to choose a codec. The primary video codecs that support Blu-ray are as follows: (Figure 74-4)

- MPEG-2 (Blu-ray)

- H.264 Blu-ray (MPEG-4 AVC)

- SMPTE VC-1

MPEG-2 (Blu-ray) is the first-generation HD codec and is more akin to the limited 4.7GB DVD format. As such, the quality is compromised.

H.264 Blu-ray or MPEG-4 is newer and much stronger in both quality and efficiency in use of the available bits on the Blu-ray Disc.

SMPTE VC-1 is Microsoft's answer to H.264 (MPEG-4). Due to its reliance on the Windows Media architecture, this codec is only available on Windows-based outputting platforms.

As part of the spec, all Blu-ray players will support any one of these codecs, but for the sake of this example, we will choose H.264 Blu-ray (MPEG-4).

Below the format options you will see the range options (shown in Figure 74-3).

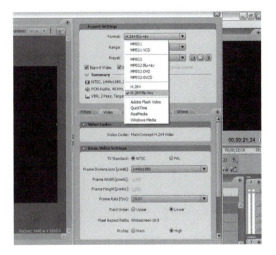

Figure 74-4 *Video codecs that support Blu-ray.*

This refers to the exporting of your entire video or just a part, as marked on the Premiere timeline by in and out points.

Step 2: Resolution

As seen in the example (Figure 74-5).

There are many choices for pixel resolution. Most of your choices are similar.

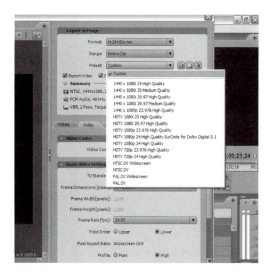

Figure 74-5 Pixel resolution choices.

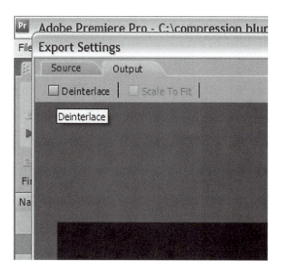

Figure 74-7 Deinterlace.

You'll notice the 29.97 next to the 1080i. 29.97 is the rate of frames per second of playback, or simply frame rate. The frame rate affects how the motion of your video is perceived.

When video is shot, the presets of a camera will provide you with frame rate options. The vast majority of video in North America is shot at 29.97 frames/sec. Film is usually shot at 24 frames/sec. It's important to know what frame rate your project requires, because if it is heavily altered from its original settings the quality of the finished product may suffer.

Figure 74-6 1440 × 1080i.

If you're exporting for a movie or home video, 1440 × 1080 is usually the way to go. You'll notice a small i or p next to the 1080.

The standard HD video mode is 1080i. The 1080 is the vertical resolution of the image, while the i means interlaced scan. Up till recently, most digital video was shown interlaced. The newer format is 1080p. The p stands for progressive scan.

In this case we'll choose 1440 ×1080i (Figure 74-6).

Here I chose 1080i because the video was originally shot interlaced.

Note: Progressive vs. Interlaced

Progressive is newer and cleaner, but it can only be viewed in all its glory on a progressive scan monitor. Digital TV broadcasting has already made the shift to progressive, though most affordable TVs have not yet. The smaller 720p has a number of monitors available to it. 1080p still commands a premium price, but the equipment is getting more reasonably-priced all the time.

If it is your wish to go progressive (maybe you are in broadcasting) you will want to choose a progressive format that suits your needs. You will then need to make your interlaced video compatible with it. So you must deinterlace! To deinterlace, go to the left-hand corner of the export settings subscreen. That option waits above the viewer, under the Output tab (Figure 74-7).

If you shot in 1080i and choose to deinterlace it to go progressive, that shuffling of image data may affect quality. This is not necessarily true on every system, though.

When you are ready to export, make sure you have enough room on your hard drive. Avoid exporting to external USB or FireWire drives (though eSATA is OK). That simple degree of separation will usually crash the program and maybe the whole computer. When exporting HD, close all other programs and take a break. It's a process that could take several hours.

Step 3: Building and Burning

Once the video is compressed in Premiere all you have to do is transfer it into the Adobe Encore disc authoring system. Open up Adobe Encore and make certain its settings match the ones you chose when compressing in the Media Encoder. Be sure to specify the project is Blu-ray Format in the authoring mode (Figure 74-8).

Authoring the disc is a process unto itself, but for the purposes of this chapter we will focus on the compression. Go to File and import your video and audio as assets and drop into the Encore timeline at the bottom. Author the Blu-ray as you see fit. This includes menus, chapters, and extras, etc. Photoshop is a strong companion with Encore. Just be aware of how much space you are using (Figure 74-9).

Note: Burning—many computers do not yet have Blu-ray burners. As this is the case, you may need to purchase an external burner to finish the job (Figure 74-10).

When you are ready to finish you will go to the build tab. Here are the pitfalls to look out for (see Figure 74-9).

Make certain you set your format and output to Blu-ray.

Make sure your disc info does not exceed the allotted amount of memory. There are two types of Blu-ray Discs, 25GB (single-layer) and 50GB (dual-layer). Some burners (and some software) only support 25GB discs for burning.

Fix any authoring issues that may arise in Encore. The computer will prompt you if you need to correct something that has been neglected.

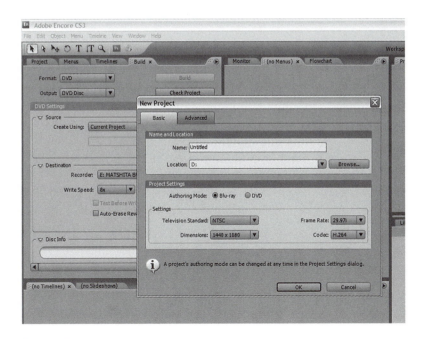

Figure 74-8 *Blu-ray Format.*

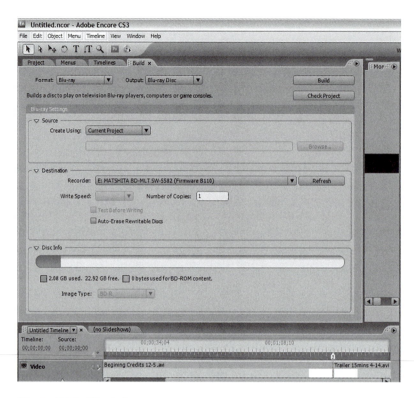

Figure 74-9 *Disc info.*

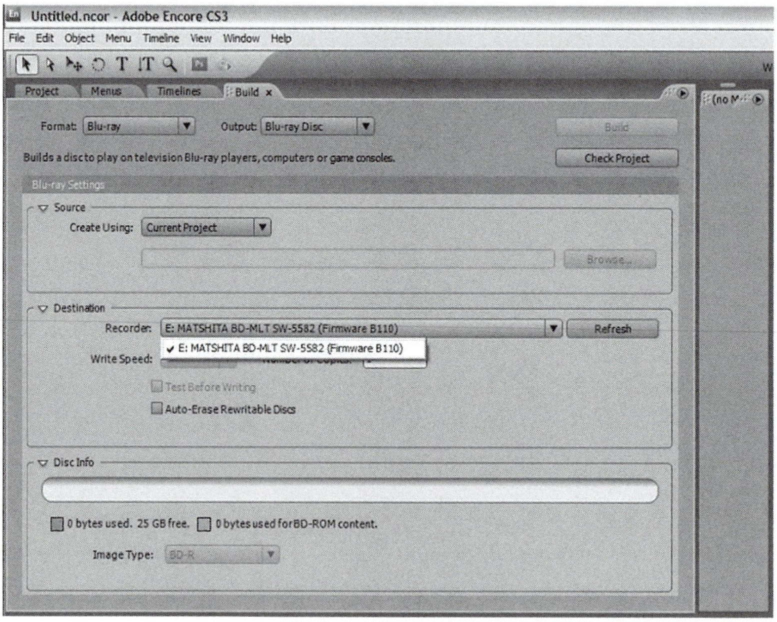

Figure 74-10 *Recorder.*

Press *build*. Depending on the complexity of your project, e.g. whether there's a lot of recompression involved, it could take as long as a day for your disc to be ready; but it might only take a few minutes.

Note: Duplicating

While Blu-ray Disc burners have already gotten reasonably fast in their short history, sometimes you need to make more than a few discs. If you want to make many copies, I recommend purchasing a Blu-ray duplicator to free up your computer. They're easy to find on the internet (generally not in stores) and fairly reasonably priced, considering the time they'll save you.

A Final Thought

The most up-to-date editing platforms, (AVID, Adobe Premiere, etc.) and their DVD authoring counterparts, (Adobe Encore, etc.) all provide functions for creating Blu-ray Discs. As separate systems they each have merits and flaws in how they approach HD output. What makes them all accessible is that each platform follows a similar set of rules. Bottom line: choose a platform you like and learn to navigate it. It's all about troubleshooting, my friends. Good luck!

75
DVD/Blu-ray Duplication Services versus Home-Use Duplicators

Stephen Smith

Figure 75-1

A guide to which DVD mass-production option works best for you.

You've burned a master disc of your *pièce de résistance* and are ready to ship it all over. Just one problem: you have only one disc, and burning hundreds by yourself isn't feasible. Or is it?

Both duplication services and home-use duplicators create the same outcome, so which one should you go with? This article will arm you with the information you need to choose the option that works best for you, so you can tackle your next big project with ease.

Duplication

The duplicator works just like a photocopier, except this process uses a laser to burn pits into the dye of the recordable area of the disc. You'll end up creating a carbon copy of your original. And unlike photocopies, which can be hard to read if ink is low, your discs will end up identical every time. If there is a problem with any disc, the duplicator will reject it.

Now that we have a better understanding of what duplication is, let's delve a little deeper into the subject matter and explore the difference between duplication services and home-use duplicators.

DVD/Blu-ray Duplication Services

If you have occasional orders for more discs than you can reasonably burn yourself, you'll find that a duplication service company can be very helpful. You don't have to have a job with hundreds of discs; the duplication service can provide you with varying numbers of duplicates.

Duplication services can be convenient when you don't have time to fuss with doing it yourself. All you have to do is supply them with your master disc. They save you time and the hassle of doing it yourself.

Regardless of the number of discs you choose to duplicate, your order can take a few business days, depending on the duplication company. If you have a limited amount of money, are short on time

and don't need to duplicate discs that often, then using a duplication company to fill your order is ideal.

In-House Duplication

Burning discs one at a time on your computer is a daunting task when you need large numbers. If you're duplicating large orders of discs more often than not, you should look into getting a duplicator. There are many options available that are easy to use and affordable. The greatest thing about most of these duplicators is that they require no software, and they can be standalone units, which makes them very easy to set up. We'll look at manual and automated duplicators.

Manual Duplicators

Manual duplicators look like a rack of DVD burners stacked on each other, with a simple menu system. One drive acts as the reading drive, while the rest burn a duplicate of what's in the reading drive. Their design is simple, and they usually have only a few buttons. Many of them require you to just turn on the tower, load all the trays and let the duplicator do the rest.

The number of discs a tower can burn depends on how many drives it has. It can range from one duplicate at a time to how ever many you're willing to buy. Higher-end models can come with a built-in hard drive for storing DVD images. This can free up the tray that would have held the master disc and is great for quickly returning to a past project.

Manual duplicators are the most cost-effective option for burning multiple discs yourself. This option is ideal for lots of little jobs, but you can also use it for bigger ones, if you have the time to reload the trays.

Automated Duplicators

Automated duplicators are a lot like manual duplicators, except they'll save you

Figure 75-2 *A robotic arm, as found on automatic duplicators, will allow the duplicator to finish a job without your having to babysit and feed your duplicator fresh discs.*

Figure 75-3 *DVD/Blu-ray inkjet printers can print on inkjet-surfaced media to give your discs a full-color label.*

even more time and effort. This will come in handy when you're routinely duplicating large numbers of discs. With the automated duplicator, you place a stack of discs on a spindle, and the duplicator's robotic arm will retrieve the discs when it's ready to start burning them. This is why some people call them autoloader duplicators.

Because of the autoloader feature, the duplicator can usually complete a duplication job from start to finish without you, once the discs are loaded. That way you can give your full attention to other things and even let it operate overnight. This allows you to get your duplication project done and have a life. Some of the higher-end models can print labels and burn discs in bulk as well. They are often referred to as publishers.

Automated duplicators cost more than manual duplicators, but they take a lot less time to load. If you're burning large numbers of discs and have limited time to babysit your duplicator, then an automated duplicator is the product for you.

What About the Labels?

If you're going to take the time to burn all of your discs, you should make sure they have a high-end look. Could you imagine going into your local video store and

seeing the latest Hollywood title with a handwritten label? *Videomaker* always recommends that you print labels directly on the disc instead of using paper labels. Fortunately, you have a lot of options for creating your own professional-grade labels. Duplication service companies can help you out, or you can do it yourself.

Print Services

Duplication service providers can print the label on the discs when they burn your order. You can also order blank media with labels printed on them, so you can burn the discs yourself and not have to worry about the print job. Most duplication houses offer inkjet or thermal printing, which adds a professional feel to your discs. For even higher-quality labels, companies like Disc Makers offer silkscreen printing on duplication projects. Because these options look and feel different, don't hesitate to request a print sample or drop by their facility to see which look works best for you.

Print Yourself

If you know you're going to print a lot of labels or simply want the convenience of at-home production, you can do it yourself with a DVD/Blu-ray printer. These printers can print labels directly on your discs. These devices vary in the number of discs they can print at a time, as well as whether they use inkjet or thermal printing. Unlike a lot of duplicators, they require a computer. As with home-based duplicators, you can choose between manual and automated printers.

Manual and Automated Printers

Manual printers work well for small jobs of 25 or fewer. Unfortunately, they can print only one at a time, which can constantly take you away from working on other projects. If you have the time and mostly small jobs, this works great and is the most cost-effective way to print DVD/Blu-ray labels yourself.

Automated printers operate a lot like automated duplicators. The number of discs they can do at a time varies greatly. If you need to print a large number of labels, these printers can save you time and trouble.

The Biggest Bang for Your Buck

With so many options, what should you do? There are a lot of factors to consider when deciding on which option will work best for your needs. In the end, it will boil down mainly to time and money.

A duplication service company can provide high-quality duplication with very little work on your part, giving you time to focus on what you do best. You don't need to worry about the process once the master disc is in their hands. However, it can be quite expensive if used routinely.

Doing it yourself allows you to duplicate your project within your own time frame. If you do enough duplication jobs, this can be a cost-effective investment and another arrow in your quiver. The main drawback is keeping track of your ink supply and maintaining and repairing the duplicator.

Vendors

OK, you've figured out which process will work best for your requirements. So what's next? Obviously, the neighborhood Giganto-Mart doesn't carry duplicators or offer duplication services.

DVD Duplication Solutions

RACK MOUNT

Applied Magic is happy to announce our latest DVD/CD Duplicator series, the Rackmount DVD Duplicator. These duplicators are designed to maximize space and meet your growing duplication demands.

CLICK HERE for more information

NEW BLU-RAY

The Applied Magic Blu-Ray DVD Duplicator is one of the first Blu-Ray duplicators available at a competitive price.

CLICK HERE for more information

The Applied Magic DVD Duplicator System is a perfect way to expand your current production capabilities. The 18X easy-to use system will duplicate a video from any format including DVD +R/RW, -R/RW and CDR. The Duplicator is also capable of double layer recording. Available in 4-Bay or 8-Bay Towers.

Limited Time Offer: FREE hard drive included

CLICK HERE for more information

Bravo II is *The World's Best-Selling Automated CD/DVD Duplicator!* It is Primera's newest and most advanced "all-in-one" disc publishing system. It combines fast, automated robotic CD/DVD duplication along with full-color, 4800 dpi direct-to-disc printing - all in one compact, desktop unit.

CLICK HERE for more information

PRIMERA
TECHNOLOGY, INC.

Contact Us | Search | Home | Primera Europe | Primera Asia Pacific

Healthcare Solutions | Why Bravo? | Bravo Fan Club | Store

| PRODUCTS | MARKETS | SUPPORT | DEVELOPERS | COMPANY |

"Your product ROCKS. It is a huge time saver, easy to use, and really does produce professional results."

– J.K.
Marketing Asst.
Cresswell, OR

CLICK HERE »

BravoPro Disc Publisher

The World's Leading Manufacturer of CD & DVD Duplication and Printing Equipment!

Award-Winning CD and DVD Duplicators

Primera Technology is the world's leading developer and manufacturer of automated DVD, BD and CD duplication and printing systems. Primera is well known for its award-winning Bravo-series Disc Publishers.

Primera's DVD / BD / CD duplication and printing equipment is used by more than 80 percent of Fortune 500 companies as well as companies and organizations in over 85 countries. List of companies.

You'll see you're in very good company when you purchase Primera's best-selling DVD / BD / CD duplicators, CD / BD / DVD printers and CD / BD / DVD copiers! Read what users are saying about Primera's CD / BD / DVD duplicators.

PRIMERA PRODUCTS

▸ **Entry-Level CD / DVD Publisher**
Compact, reliable and affordable the Bravo SE Disc Publisher and Bravo SE AutoPrinter meet limited home and small business needs by recording and printing CDs, Blu-ray Discs and DVDs. Read testimonials.

▸ **Mid-Range CD / DVD Duplicators & More**
Professional disc publishing solutions for all office environments. Includes the world's best-selling Bravo II and BravoPro Disc Publishers to automatically record and print CDs and DVDs as well as the Bravo II and BravoPro AutoPrinters. Read testimonials.

▸ **High-End Disc Duplicators & Printers**
The Bravo XR-Series includes CD, DVD and BD duplicators for mission-critical applications including medical imaging, digital photo processing, banking, insurance, government, mobile video archive and more.

▸ **Label Printers**
The LX-Series Color Label Printers inkjet print short-run, full-color product and box-end labels. Applications include wine, coffee, bottled water, gourmet foods, candy, industrial products, cosmetics, pet food and more. Read testimonials.

PRIMERA NEWS

▸ **PTPublisher NE Software Now Available**
Primera's PTPublisher NE software allows you to share your Bravo II, Bravo XR, BravoPro or Bravo XRP over a network. PTPublisher NE comes with an unlimited number of client licenses. Try it FREE for 30 Days.

▸ **New! Bravo SE Rental for CD Ripping**
Rent a Bravo SE and Revive your Music Collection. Ripping CDs one a time takes a lot of time. But with the Bravo you can upload your personal CD collection into iTunes™ or Windows® Media Player - automatically and hands-free. Rent it now.

▸ **We'll Print Your Labels for You**
Not ready to buy a LX-Series printer? We'll print your labels for you. Professional-quality, full-color labels at an affordable price. Labels are available in many sizes and shapes. Get an Instant Quote.

▸ **Free PTRip Software**
Primera introduces its new PTRip software which gives users of Primera's Bravo-Series Disc Publishers the ability to automatically upload their personal music CDs into iTunes™ or Windows® Media Player using their units' built-in CD/DVD drives and robotics.

There is a large assortment of duplication houses on the internet and pricing depends on the number or dupes as well as cover art, labels and boxes or jewel cases.

Conclusion

Sometimes, using only one of these options is not enough. Consider using multiple duplication options. The company I work for has a manual duplicator we use for all our small jobs. Occasionally, for bigger duplication jobs (200 to 1,000 discs or more), we'll turn to an outside duplication service company to make our product look good. For jobs beyond that, we rely on replication, which is a whole new story. (In replication, the information is put onto the disc as it is manufactured, rather than burned onto an already-created disc.)

The next time you burn multiple discs from your computer's burner, consider the time you can save with duplication. Anyone who needs to burn and print discs will benefit from DVD/Blu-ray duplication services and/or home-use duplicators.

76
Special Features: DVD Extras

Nathan Beaman

Figure 76-1

People love movies, and many people love them enough to want to watch movies about the movies they love.

Special features are any additional audio, visual or interactive media that exist beyond the original version of a film on a DVD. These features may be items such as extended versions, director's cuts of the film, audio commentaries, behind-the-scenes featurettes, documentaries, production stills, cast and crew bios, alternative endings, animatics, interactive games . . . the list goes on and on. So, if you can dream it up as an added feature, someone somewhere is going to appreciate it. Let's take a closer look at a few common special features you can add to your own DVDs.

Audio Commentary

Audio commentary is an alternative audio track that plays over the film and discusses other aspects of the movie. The typical commentary is the director discussing specific scenes, motivations or challenges. Often you may find commentaries from the actors, special effects artists, editors or even a whole group of people. Audio commentaries have become standard on most DVD releases, partly because they are incredibly inexpensive to do and easy to add.

You can include an audio commentary on your own discs by recording yourself talking about the film as you watch it and adding it as an alternative audio track to the disc. This is great when bit-budgeting your DVD for space, as it does not need to duplicate any media. In short, you're adding an additional track of audio rather than introducing a second copy of the whole movie.

Director's Cuts and Extended Versions

Many studio releases feature a director's cut of the film as a special feature. Often in the studio system, the director doesn't maintain 100 percent of the decision-making in the theatrically-released version of the film. This happens for a variety of political and profit-based reasons that we won't get into here. Sometimes the director's wishes for the film differ greatly from what the studio releases, and other times it may just be a scene or two—maybe even the ending! DVD is a great place to exhibit this alternative version of the film. Extended versions function in the same way. Often they include footage that editors cut for time purposes or that they deemed unnecessary for the film.

If you're authoring your own DVD, chances are that a director's cut may not be necessary, as no one is probably telling you what you can and can't do. There's always a chance that you might have various cuts of the film that you'd like to share, though, or an extended version. Putting an alternative cut of the entire film on DVD requires another complete copy of your film to play back smoothly. So, if your movie is 90 minutes and the director's cut is 110 minutes, you'll need 200 minutes of disc space. When you are bit-budgeting, something like this is critical, because it essentially doubles the amount of space you need.

Often, a decision like this will force you to make a compromise between compression quality, going from a 4.7GB to an 8.5GB disc or adding an additional disc to your DVD set. It is good to be mindful of these things when your disc is going to duplication or replication, as upgrading disc capacity or the number of discs in your release can be very costly.

Deleted Scenes

Deleted scenes are portions of the film that were shot and edited but removed from the final version of the film for any of a variety of reasons. You'll often find a ton of these in comedy films: jokes that didn't work, were just too risqué or would push a PG-13 movie to an R.

One of the easiest and most fun additions to your DVD masterpiece might be the deleted scenes feature. You can treat each individual scene as its own piece or cut them together as one seamless group of outtakes. Deleted scenes add to the amount of bittage on the disc, so it's good to keep an eye on just how many you may add. However, the added data is nowhere near the amount required for adding multiple versions of the film, so it is less of a concern.

Alternative Endings

Alternative endings are a great and exciting draw to our favorite films. This is

Figures 76-2, 76-3, and 76-4 *Behind-the-scenes segments showing how the production went down and how some of the FX were made are some of the extras found on many DVDs and Blu-ray discs.*

especially true when a film has a lot of mystery and open-ended possibilities. Some thrillers may have alternative endings with different characters ending up as the killer, or a drama may end with a key player dying, changing the whole feel of the film. For the most part, alternative endings provide a much less dramatic difference from the theatrical ending of the film, but they are an intriguing addition to the DVD nonetheless.

Adding alternate endings to your own DVDs is very much like adding deleted scenes. You're essentially adding another movie track that a viewer can choose to play. You can take it a step further by having the entire film watchable with the alternate ending rather than the theatrical ending. Doing it this way requires either duplicating the files or creating a playlist that tells the main film to stop playing at some point and jump to the video of the alternative ending.

Behind the Scenes

Behind-the-scenes featurettes are short videos that focus on events that happen behind the camera lens. They may show how the crew accomplished specific shots or effects or how various aspects of the film came to be. They may feature the actors discussing the film out of character. *The Lord of the Rings* has countless hours of amazing BTS footage on just about every aspect, from hand-making each costume to the final digital effects shots. *Pirates of the Caribbean* illustrates how the film merged CG with practical acting to bring life to the tentacles on Davy Jones' face. *Superman Returns* shows how the editor digitally manipulated existing footage of Marlon Brando long after his death to incorporate him into the film. Things like this provide an amazing and in-depth look at the filmmaking process.

Of all the features we've looked at so far, a behind-the-scenes feature is the only one that requires additional filming to make it happen. All the others mentioned, with the exception of audio commentaries, use materials gathered for the film to make the features. A typical behind-the-scenes featurette uses footage as it happened on set and often features additional footage of people discussing its importance after the fact. You can film your own behind-the-scenes footage while you shoot the main movie, by shooting interviews or supporting materials specifically for the creation of a behind-the-scenes feature. Adding

Figure 76-5 *The packaging for your production is definitely an extra all by itself, but it's usually only good value in large duplication runs.*

Figure 76-6 *There are now entire websites dedicated to finding and sharing DVD Easter eggs with fellow enthusiasts.*

this footage to the DVD is just as easy as adding your original film.

The Easter Egg

The Easter egg is a hidden special-feature link on a DVD menu. These invisible buttons link to outtakes, secret endings or many of the features we've discussed thus far. They are fun to find and exist on many of the DVDs you may own. In the first *Pirates of the Caribbean* DVD, there is an Easter egg linking to an interview with Keith Richards talking about being the motivation for Johnny Depp's character, Captain Jack. On the *Star Wars: Episode I* DVD, you can access bloopers of the film by entering a specific number sequence in the right menu.

You can make Easter eggs as easy as an invisible button on a menu or as complex as a series of invisible buttons that force the user to enter the right key combination to get there. When authoring, you can even program specific numbers on the remote to trigger playback of hidden clips. The key in making your own Easter eggs is making someone want to take the time to find them. There are websites dedicated to finding known and unknown Easter eggs in movies.

Many DVD releases are marketed using the special features as a sales hook. Some films release a DVD with few or no extras and later release special editions with loads of additional material. The presence of special features gives an added value to your DVD product and offers the viewer a more involved viewing experience. Many types of features are incredibly easy to add to your own films from existing footage you acquired as part of making the movie or from materials gathered during the filmmaking process. For other types of features, like interactive games or bonuses that feature materials not acquired during filmmaking, you must meticulously plan in advance.

With DVD extras, if you can make it, someone will probably watch it.

Jargon:
A Glossary of Videography Terms

8 mm: Compact videocassette format, popularized by camcorders, employing 8-millimeter-wide videotape. (see Hi8).

720 p: An ATSC high definition video standard size of 1280 ×720 pixels, progressive scan at various frame rates.

1080 i: An ATSC high definition video standard size of 1920 × 1080 pixels, interlace scan at various frame rates.

1080 p: An ATSC high definition video standard size of 1920 ×1080 pixels, progressive scan at various frame rates.

A/B roll editing: Two video sources played simultaneously, to be mixed or cut between.

A/V (Audio/Video): A common shorthand for multimedia audio and video.

action axis: An imaginary line drawn between two subjects or along a line of motion to maintain continuity of screen direction. Crossing it from one shot to the next creates an error in continuity. It is also referred to as the "180-degree rule," "green rule."

ad-lib: Unrehearsed, spontaneous act of speaking, performing, or otherwise improvising on-camera activity without preparation.

aDSL: (Asymmetric (or Asynchronous) Digital Subscriber Line) A "fat pipe." New technology to carry high-speed data over typical twisted-pair copper telephone lines. ADSL promises be up to 70 times as fast as a 28.8 modem.

AFM: (Audio Frequency Modulation) The analog soundtrack of the 8 mm and Hi8 video format (see PCM).

AGC: (Automatic Gain Control) A circuit on most camcorders that automatically adjusts a microphone's gain (volume) to match environmental sound levels.

ambient sound: (ambience) Natural background audio representative of a given recording environment. On-camera dialogue might be primary sound; traffic noise and refrigerator hum would be ambient.

amplify: To magnify an audio signal for mixing, distribution and transducing purposes.

analog: An electrical signal is referred to as either analog or digital. Analog signals are those signals directly generated from a stimulus such as a light striking a camera picture tube. You can convert an analog signal to a digital signal by using an analog to digital converter.

animation: Visual special effect whereby progressive still images displayed in rapid succession create the illusion of movement.

aperture/exposure: A setting that manipulates the amount of light falling onto the camera's CCD(s). This control adjusts the size of the camcorder's iris.

apps: (application) Software that performs a specific function.

artifacting: The occurrence of unwanted visual distortions that appear in a video image, such as cross-color artifacts, cross-luminance artifacts, jitter, blocking, ghosts, etc. Artifacting is a common side effect of compression, especially at lower bit rates.

artifacts: Unwanted visual distortions that appear in a video image, such as cross-color artifacts, cross-luminance artifacts, jitter, blocking, ghosts, etc.

artificial light: Human-made illumination not limited to "indoor" variety: fluorescent bulbs, jack-o'-lanterns and a car's headlights all qualify. Typically, it has lower color temperature than natural light, and thus more reddish qualities (see color temperature, natural light).

asf: Active Streaming Format

aspect ratio: Proportional width and height of on-screen picture. Current standard for a conventional monitor is 4:3 (four-by-three); 16:9 for HDTV.

assemble edit: Recording video and/or audio clips in sequence immediately following previous material; does not break control track. Consecutive edits form complete program (See edit, insert edit).

ATSC: Advanced Television Systems Committee. A new TV broadcast standard (replacing NTSC) for high definition televison. It is composed of several frame rates and sizes, including standard definition formats, as well 720p and 1080i video.

ATV: (Amateur Television) Specialized domain of ham radio, transmits standard TV signals on UHF radio bands.

audio dub: Result of recording over pre-recorded videotape soundtrack, or a portion thereof, without affecting pre-recorded images.

Audio Frequency Modulation: (AFM) Method of recording hi-fi audio on videotape along with video signals. Used in VHS Hi-Fi Audio, and also the analog soundtrack of the 8 mm and Hi8 video formats.

audio mixer: The piece of equipment used to gather, mix and amplify sounds from multiple microphones and send the signal on to its destination.

automatic exposure: Circuitry that monitors light levels and adjusts camcorder iris accordingly, compensating for changing light conditions.

Automatic Gain Control: (AGC) Circuitry found on most camcorders that adjusts incoming audio levels automatically to match environmental sound levels.

available light: Amount of illumination present in a particular environment: natural light, artificial light or a combination of the two.

AVCHD: Advanced Video Codec High Definition: an MPEG-4 based codec used to record high definition video to camcorders using hard drives, DVD discs, or flash memory cards.

AVI: (Audio Video Interleave) One of the oldest file formats for digital video on PCs.

avi: Short for Audio Video Interleave, the file format for Microsoft's Video for Windows standard.

back light: Lamp providing illumination from behind. Creates sense of depth by separating foreground subject from background area. Applied erroneously, causes severe silhouetting (see fill light, key light, three-point lighting).

balanced line: Audio cables that have three wires: one for positive, one for negative and one for ground.

bandwidth: A measure of the capacity of a user's data line. Video looks its best on a high-bandwidth connection, like DSL, cable modems or satellite modems. Conversely, trying to download or stream video on a low-bandwidth connection like a dial-up modem can be a frustrating experience.

bandwidth compression: Reducing the bandwidth that is required for transmission of a given digital data rate.

barndoors: Accessories for video lights; adjustable folding flaps that control light distribution.

batch capture: The ability of certain computer-based editing systems to automatically capture whole lists or "batches" of clips from source videotapes.

Betamax: More commonly known as "Beta," half-inch videotape format developed by Sony, eclipsed by VHS in home video market popularity (see ED Beta).

bidirectional: Microphone pickup pattern whereby sound is absorbed equally from two sides only (see omnidirectional, unidirectional).

black box: Generic term for wide variety of video image manipulation devices with perceived mysterious or "magical" capabilities, including proc amps, enhancers, SEGs, and TBCs.

bleeding: Video image imperfection characterized by blurring of color borders; colors spill over defined boundaries, "run" into neighboring areas.

Blu-ray: A high definition optical disc format, using a blue laser. It has a capacity of 50 GB for dual layer discs. Hoping to be the successor to the popular DVD format.

BNC: (Bayonet Fitting Connector aka British Naval Connector) A durable "professional" cable connector, attaches to VCRs for transfer of high-frequency composite video in/out signals. Connects with a push and a twist.

boom: Any device for suspending a microphone or camcorder above and in front of a performer. See also Jib.

booming: Camera move above or below subject with aid of a balanced "boom arm," creating sense of floating into or out of a scene. Can combine effects of panning, tilting, and pedestaling in one fluid movement.

C: See chrominance.

cable/community access: Channel(s) of a local cable television system dedicated to community-based programming. Access centers provide free or low-cost training and use of video production equipment and facilities.

cameo lighting: Foreground subjects illuminated by highly directional light, appearing before a completely black background.

Cannon: See XLR.

capacitor: The part of the condenser mic that stores electrical energy and permits the flow of alternating current.

capture card: A piece of computer hardware that captures digital video and audio to a hard drive, typically through a FireWire (IEEE 1394) port.

cardioid: A microphone that picks up sound in a heart-shaped pattern.

CCD: (Charge Coupled Device) Light-sensitive integrated circuit in video cameras that converts images into electrical signals. Sometimes referred to as a "chip."

character generator: A device that electronically builds text which can be combined with a video signal. The text is created with a keyboard and program that has a selection of font and backgrounds.

chroma: Characteristics of color a videotape absorbs with recorded signal, divided into two categories: AM (amplitude modulation) indicates color intensity; PM (phase modulation) indicates color purity.

chromakey: Method of electronically inserting an image from one video source into the image of another through areas designated as its "key color." It is frequently used on news programs to display weather graphics behind talent.

chrominance: Portion of video signal that carries color information (hue and saturation, but not brightness); frequently abbreviated as "C," as in "Y/C" for luminance/chrominance (see luminance).

clapstick: Identification slate with hinged, striped top that smacks together for on-camera scene initiation. Originally used to synchronize movie sound with picture (see lip-sync).

closeup: (CU) A tightly framed camera shot in which the principal subject is viewed at close range, appearing large and dominant on screen. Pulled back slightly is a "medium closeup" while zoomed in very close is an "extreme closeup (ECU or XCU)."

CODEC: (compressor/decompressor) A piece of software that converts a raw stream of uncompressed video to a compressed form. The same piece of software can also play the compressed video on-screen.

color bars: Standard test signal containing samples of primary and secondary colors, used as reference in aligning color video equipment. Generated electronically by a "color bar generator," often viewed on broadcast television in off-air hours (see test pattern)

color corrector: Electronic device that dissects the colors of a video signal, allowing them to be adjusted individually.

color temperature: Relative amount of "white" light's reddish or bluish qualities, measured in degrees Kelvin. Desirable readings for video are 3,200 K indoors, 5,600 K outdoors (see artificial, natural light).

comet tailing: Smear of light resulting from inability of camera's pickup to process bright objects — especially in darker settings. Object or camera in motion creates appearance of flying fireball (see lag).

component video: Signal transmission system, resembling S-video concept, employed with professional videotape formats. Separates one luminance and two chrominance channels to avoid quality loss from NTSC or PAL encoding.

composite video: Single video signal combining luminance and chrominance signals through an encoding process, including RGB (red, green, blue) elements and sync information.

compositing: Superimposing multiple layers of video or images. Each layer may move independently. Titles are a simple and common example of compositing.

composition: Visual make-up of a video picture, including such variables as balance, framing, field of view and texture—all aesthetic considerations. Combined qualities form an image that's pleasing to view.

compression: An encoding process that reduces the digital data in a video frame, typically from nearly one megabyte to 300 kilobytes or less. This is accomplished by throwing away information the eye can't see and/or redundant information in areas of the video frame that do not change. JPEG, Motion-JPEG, MPEG, DV, Indeo, Fractal and Wavelet are all compression schemes.

condenser mic: A high-quality mic whose transducer consists of a diaphragm, backplate, and capacitor.

continuity: (1:visual])Logical succession of recorded or edited events, necessitating consistent placement of props, positioning of characters, and progression of time.

contrast: Difference between a picture's brightest and darkest areas. When high, image contains sharp blacks and whites; when low, image limited to variations in gray tones.

control track: A portion of the videotape containing information to synchronize playback and linear videotape editing operations.

Control-L: A two-way communication system used to coordinate tape transport commands for linear editing. Primarily found in Mini DV, Digital8, Hi8 and 8 mm camcorders and VCRs (see Control-S, synchro edit).

Control-S: A one-way communication system that treats a VCR or camcorder as a slave unit, with edit commands emanating from an external edit controller or compatible deck. Primarily found on 8 mm VCRs and camcorders. (See Control-L, synchro edit).

cookie: See cucalorus.

crawl: Text or graphics, usually special announcements that move across the screen horizontally, typically from right to left across the bottom of the screen.

cross-fade: Simultaneous fade-in of one audio or video source as another fades out so that they overlap temporarily. Also called a dissolve.

cucalorus: (cookie) Lighting accessory consisting of random pattern of cutouts that forms shadows when light passes through it. Used to imitate shadows of natural lighting.

cue: (1) Signal to begin, end, or otherwise influence on-camera activity while recording. (2) Presetting specific starting points of audio or video material so it's available for immediate and precise playback when required.

cut: Instantaneous change from one shot to another.

cutaway: Shot of something other than principal action (but peripherally related), frequently used as transitional footage or to avoid a jump cut.

cuts-only editing: Editing limited to immediate shifts from one scene to another, without smoother image transition capabilities such as dissolving or wiping (see cut, edit).

D1, D2, D3, D5, Digital-S, DVCPRO, DVCAM, Digital Betacam: Entirely digital "professional" videotape recording formats.

decibel: (dB) A unit of measurement of sound that compares the relative intensity of different sound sources.

decompression: The decoding of a compressed video data stream to allow playback.

deinterlace: To convert interlaced video into progressively-scanned video, for use with computers.

depth of field: Range in front of a camera's lens in which objects appear in focus. Varies with subject-to-camera distance, focal length of a camera lens and a camera's aperture setting.

Desktop Video: (DTV) Fusion of personal computers and home video components for elaborate videomaking capabilities rivaling those of broadcast facilities.

diaphragm: The vibrating element in a microphone that responds to the compressed air molecules of sound waves.

diffused light: Indistinctly illuminates relatively large area. Produces soft light quality with soft shadows.

diffuser: Gauzy or translucent material that alters the quality of light passing through it to produce less intense, flatter lighting with softer, less noticeable shadows.

diffusion filter: Mounted at front of camcorder lens, gives videotaped images a foggy, fuzzy, dreamy look (see filter).

digital audio: Sounds that have been converted to digital information.

Digital Video Effects: (DVE) Electronic analog-to-digital picture modification yielding specialty image patterns and maneuvers: tumbling, strobing, page turning, mosaic, posterization, solarization, etc.

digitization: The process of converting a continuous analog video or audio signal to digital data for computer storage and manipulation.

digitizer: Device that imports and converts analog video images into digital information for hard drive-based editing.

directional light: Light that illuminates in a relatively small area with distinct light beam; usually created with spotlight, yields harsh, defined shadows.

dissolve: Image transition effect of one picture gradually disappearing as another appears. Analogous to audio and lighting cross-fade (See cross-fade).

distribution amp: (distribution amplifier) Divides single video or audio signals, while boosting their strength, for delivery to multiple audio/video acceptors. Allows simultaneous recording on multiple VCR's from the same source, especially useful for tape duplication.

DivX ;-): A recent codec for MPEG-4 video, developed on the internet.

dolly: Camera movement toward or away from a subject. The effect may seem to be the same as zooming, but dollying in or out results in a more dramatic change in perspective than using the zoom.

dollying: Camera movement toward or away from a subject. Effect may appear same as zooming, which reduces and magnifies the image, but dollying in or out maintains perspective while changing picture size.

dongle: A device that prevents the unauthorized use of hardware or software. A dongle usually consists of a small cord attached to a device or key that secures the hardware. The term is also used to signify a generic adapter for peripherals.

download and play: A way of viewing Web video that requires a user to download a video before playing it. Download and play files are usually higher quality than streamed video.

dropout: Videotape signal voids, viewed as fleeting white specks or streaks. Usually result of minute "bare spots" on a tape's magnetic particle coating, or tape debris covering particles and blocking signals.

DSLR: (Digital Single-Lens Reflex Camera) When used in reference to video production, this term usually implies the presence of a video option.

DTV: Desktop video. Also, digital television.

dub: (1) Process or result of duplicating a videotape in its entirety. (2) Editing technique whereby new audio or video replaces portion(s) of existing recording.

DV: (Digital Video) With a capital "D" and a capital "V," DV is a specific video format; both a tape format (like Hi8) and a data format specification.

DVE: (Digital Video Effect) Electronic special effects and picture modification yielding specialty image patterns and maneuvers, such as tumbling, strobing, page turning, mosaic, posterization, solarization, etc. (see F/X).

dynamic mic: A rugged microphone whose transducer consists of a diaphragm connected to a moveable coil.

ED: Beta (extended definition Beta) Improved version of the original half-inch Betamax video format, yielding sharper pictures with 500-line resolution (see Betamax).

edit: Process or result of selectively recording video and/or audio on finished videotape. Typically involves reviewing raw footage and transferring desired segments from master tape(s) onto new tape in a predetermined sequence (see assemble edit, in-camera editing).

edit control protocols: Types of signals designed to communicate between editing components, including computers, tape decks and camcorders. Allows components to transmit instructions for various operations such as play, stop, fast forward, rewind, record, pause, etc.

edit controller: Electronic programmer used in conjunction with VCRs/camcorders to facilitate automated linear videotape editing with speed, precision, and convenience.

Edit Decision List: See EDL.

edited master: Original recorded videotape footage; "edited master" implies original copy of tape in its edited form. Duplications constitute generational differences.

editing appliance: An self-contained machine, essentially a small computer, which only edits video. Editing appliances usually contain most features found in standard computer-based editing systems.

EDL: (Edit Decision List) Handwritten or computer-generated compilation of all edits (marked by their time code in points and out points) planned for execution in a video production.

EFP: (Electronic Field Production) Film-style production approach using a single camera to record on location. Typically shot for post-production application, non-live feed.

EIS: (electronic Image Stabilization) A process of limiting shaky camera shots with digital processing within a camcorder (see OIS).

electric condenser: Microphone type incorporating a pre-charged element, eliminating need for bulky power sources (see condenser).

Electronic Image Stabilization: (EIS) A process that limits shaky camera shots with digital processing found within a camcorder (see OIS).

encoder: Device that translates a video signal into a different format — RGB to composite, DV to MPEG,etc.

encoding: The actual process of compressing video for streaming or for downloading.

ENG: (Electronic News Gathering) Use of portable video cameras, lighting and sound equipment to record news events in the field quickly, conveniently, and efficiently.

enhancer: (Image enhancer) Video signal processor that compensates for picture detail losses and distortion occurring in recording and playback. Exaggerates transitions between light and dark areas by enhancing high frequency region of video spectrum.

EP: (Extended Play) Slowest tape speed of a VHS VCR, accommodating six-hour recordings (see LP, SP).

equalization: Emphasizing specific audio or video frequencies and eliminating others as signal control measure, usually to produce particular sonic qualities. Achieved with equalizer.

equalize: To emphasize, lessen or eliminate certain audio frequencies.

essential area: Boundaries within which contents of a television picture are sure to be seen, regardless of masking differences in receiver displays. Also called the "critical area" or "safe action area," it encompasses the inner 80 percent of the screen.

establishing shot: Opening image of a program or scene. Usually, it's a wide and/or distant perspective that orients viewers to the overall setting and surroundings.

extra: Accessory talent not essential to a production, assuming some peripheral on-camera role. In movie work, performers with fewer than five lines are called "under fives."

f-stop: Numbers corresponding to variable size of a camera's iris opening, and thus the amount of light passing through the lens. The higher the number, the smaller the iris diameter, which means less light enters the camcorder.

F/X: Special effects. Visual tricks and illusions—electronic or on camera—employed in film and video to define, distort or defy reality.

fade: Gradual diminishing or heightening of visual and/or audio intensity. "Fade out" or "fade to black," "fade in" or "up from black" are common terms.

feed: Act or result of transmitting a video signal from one point to another.

feedback: (1:video) Infinite loop of visual patterns from signal output being fed back as input; achieved by aiming live camera at receiving monitor. (2:audio) Echo effect at low levels, howl or piercing squeal at extremes, from audio signal being fed back to itself.

field: Half a scanning cycle. Two fields comprise a complete video frame. Composed of either all odd lines or all even lines.

field of view: Extent of a shot that is visible through a particular lens; its vista.

fill light: Supplementary illumination, usually from a soft light positioned to the side of the subject, which lightens shadows created by the key light (see back light, key light, three-point lighting).

film-style: Out-of-sequence shooting approach, to be edited in appropriate order at post-production stage. Advantageous for concentrating on and completing recording at one location at a time, continuity and convenience assured.

filter: Transparent or semi-transparent material, typically glass, mounted at the front of a camcorder's lens to change light passing through. Manipulates colors and image patterns, often for special effect purposes.

filter effect: Digital effect added to colorize or otherwise alter a clip in post-production.

FireWire: (IEEE 1394 or i.LINK) A high-speed bus that was developed by Apple Computer. It is used, among other things, to connect digital camcorders to computers.

fishpole: A small, lightweight arm to which a microphone is attached, hand held by an audio assistant outside the picture frame.

flare: Bright flashes evident in video. Caused by excessive light beaming into a camera's lens and reflecting off its internal glass elements.

flat lighting: Illumination characterized by even, diffused light without shadows, highlights or contrast. May impede viewer's sense of depth, dimension.

floodlight: Radiates a diffused, scattered blanket of light with soft, indistinct shadows. Best used to spread illumination on broad areas, whereas spotlights focus on individual subjects.

fluid head: Tripod mount type containing viscous fluid which lubricates moving parts, dampens friction. Design facilitates smooth camera moves, alleviates jerkiness (see friction head).

flying erase head: Accessory video head mounted on spinning head drum, incorporated in many camcorders and VCRs to eliminate glitches and rainbow noise between scenes recorded or edited. By design, all 8 mm-family and DV-family equipment has flying erase heads.

focal length: Distance from a camcorder's lens to a focused image with the lens focused on infinity. Short focal lengths offer a broad field of view (wide angle); long focal lengths offer a narrow field of view (telephoto). Zoom lenses have a variable focal length.

follow focus: Controlling lens focus so that an image maintains sharpness and clarity despite camcorder and/or subject movement.

foot-candle: A unit of illumination equal to the light emitted by a candle at the distance of one foot. One foot-candle equals 10.764 lux (see lux).

format: Videotape and video equipment design differences—physical and technical—dictating compatibility and quality. In most basic sense, refers to standardized tape widths, videocassette sizes (see Betamax, D1/ D2, 8 mm, three-quarter-inch, VHS)

FPS: (frames Per Second) Measures the rate or speed of video or film. Film is typically shot and played back at 24 fps. Video is recorded and played back at 30 fps.

frame: 1) One complete image. In NTSC video. a frame is composed of two fields. One 30th of a second. 2) The viewable area or composition of an image.

framing: Act of composing a shot in a camcorder's viewfinder for desired content, angle and field of view.

freeze frame: Single frame paused and displayed for an extended period during video playback; suspended motion perceived as still snapshot.

frequency: Number of vibrations produced by a signal or sound, usually expressed as cycles per second, or hertz (Hz).

frequency response: Measure of the range of frequencies a medium can respond to and reproduce. Good video response maintains picture detail; good audio response accommodates the broadest range, most exacting sound.

friction head: Tripod mount type with strong spring that counterbalances camera weight, relying on friction to hold its position. More appropriate for still photography than movement-oriented videomaking (see fluid head).

full-motion video: A standard for video playback on a computer; refers to smooth-flowing, full-color video at 30 frames per second, regardless of the screen resolution.

gaffer: Production crew technician responsible for placement and rigging of all lighting instruments.

gain: Video amplification, signal strength. "Riding gain" means varying controls to achieve desired contrast levels.

GB: (Gigabyte) Giga- is a prefix that means one billion, so a Gigabyte is 1,000,000,000 bytes. Most commonly used to measure hard disk space.

gel: Colored material placed in front of a light source to alter its hue. Useful for special effects and correcting mismatches in lighting, as in scenes lit by both daylight and artificial light.

generation: Relationship between a master video recording and a given copy of that master. A copy of a copy of the original master constitutes a second-generation duplication.

generation loss: Degradation in picture and sound quality resulting from an analog duplication of original master video recording. Copying a copy and all successive duplication compounds generation loss. Digital transfers are free of generation loss.

genlock: (Generator Locking Device) Synchronizes two video sources, allowing part or all of their signals to be displayed together. Necessary for overlaying computer graphics with video, for example.

ghosting: Undesirable faint double screen image caused by signal reflection or improperly balanced video circuitry. "Ringing" appears as repeated image edges.

gif: Graphics Interchange Format—a bit-mapped graphics file format used by the World Wide Web, CompuServe and many BBSs. GIF supports color and various resolutions. It also includes data compression, making it especially effective for scanned photos.

giraffe: A small boom that consists of a counterweighted arm supported by a tripod, usually on casters.

glitch: Momentary picture disturbance.

grain: Blanketed signal noise viewed as fuzziness, unsmooth images—attributable to lumination inadequacies.

grip: Production crew stagehand responsible for handling equipment, props, and scenery before, during, and after production.

group master fader: A volume control on an audio board that handles a subgroup of input channels before they are sent to the master fader.

handheld mic: A microphone that a person holds to speak or sing into.

hard disk: Common digital storage component in a computer.

HDMI: (High Definition Multimedia Interface) A connection type that combines high-definition video and multi-channel audio into a single cable.

HDTV: (High Definition Television) A television system standard affording greater resolution for sharper pictures and wide-screen viewing via specially-designed TV equipment.

HDV: High Definition Video. A videotape format that records 1080i or 720p using MPEG-2 compression video on DV tape.

head: Electromagnetic component within camcorders and VCRs that records, receives and erases video and audio signals on magnetic tape.

headroom: Space between the top of a subject's head and a monitor's upper-screen edge. Too much headroom makes the subject appear to fall out of the frame.

hi-fi: (high fidelity) Generalized term defining audio quality approaching the limits of human hearing, pertinent to high-quality sound reproduction systems.

Hi8: (high-band 8 mm) Improved version of 8 mm videotape format characterized by higher luminance resolution for a sharper picture. Compact "conceptual equivalent" of Super-VHS (see 8 mm).

high impedance: A characteristic of microphones that have a great deal of opposition to the flow of alternating current through them and therefore must have short cables; they are less likely to be used in professional situations than low-impedance microphones.

hiss: Primary background signal interference in audio recording, result of circuit noise from a playback recorder's amplifiers or from a tape's residual magnetism.

horizontal resolution: Specification denoting amount of discernable detail across a screen's width. Measured in pixels— the higher the number, the better the picture quality.

IEEE 1394: (Institute of Electrical and Electronics Engineers) Pronounced "eye-triple-E thirteen-ninety-four" the institute establishes standards and protocols for a wide range of computer and communications technologies, including IEEE 1394, which is a specification FireWire

data transmission widely used in DV. Sony refers to the ports on its products with the proprietary term "i.LINK."

image enhancer: Video signal processor that compensates for picture detail losses and distortion occurring in recording and playback. Exaggerates transitions between light and dark areas by enhancing high frequency region of video spectrum.

image sensor: A video camera's image sensing element, either CCD (charge coupled device) or MOS (metal oxide semiconductor); converts light to electrical energy (see CCD).

impedance: Opposition to the flow of an audio signal in a microphone and its cable.

in-camera editing: Assembling finished program "on the fly" as you videotape simply by activating and pausing camcorder's record function.

incident light: That which emanates directly from a light source. Measured from the object it strikes to the source (see reflected light).

indexing: Ability of some VCRs to electronically mark specific points on videotape for future access, either during the recording process (VISS: VHS index search system) or as scenes are played back (VASS: VHS address search system).

input channel: On an audio board, the control into which a microphone, tape recorder or other source is plugged.

insert edit: Recording video and/or audio on tape over a portion of existing footage without disturbing what precedes and follows. Must replace recording of same length.

interlace: To split a TV picture into two fields of odd and even lines. Under the interlaced method, every other line is scanned during the first pass, then the remaining lines are scanned in the second pass. All analog TV formats (NTSC, PAL and SECAM) use interlaced video.

interlaced video: Process of scanning frames in two passes, each painting every other line on the screen, with scan lines alternately displayed in even and odd fields. NTSC video is interlaced; most computers produce a noninterlaced video signal (see noninterlaced video).

iris: Camcorder's lens opening or aperture, regulates amount of light entering camera. Diameter is measured in f-stops (see f-stop).

jack: Any female socket or receptacle, usually on the backside of video and audio equipment; accepts plug for circuit connection.

jib: A boom of varying lengths that supports a camcorder on one end and counter weights on the other. Primarily used for smoothly moving the camcorder up and down.

jitter: Video image aberration seen as slight, fast vertical or horizontal shifting of a picture or portion of one.

jog/shuttle: Manual control on some VCRs, facilitates viewing and editing precision and convenience. Jog ring moves tape short distances to show a frame at a time; shuttle dial transports tape forward or reverse more rapidly for faster scanning.

jpeg: Joint Photographic Experts Group image format. A popular Internet compression format for color images.

jump cut: Unnatural, abrupt switch between shots identical in subject but slightly different in screen location, so the subject appears to jump from one screen location to another. Can be remedied with a cutaway or shot from a different angle.

Kelvin: Temperature scale used to define the color of a light source; abbreviated as "K" (see color temperature).

key light: Principal illumination source on a subject or scene. Normally positioned slightly off-center and angled to provide shadow detail (see back light, fill light, three-point lighting).

keyframe: A complete image, used as a reference for subsequent images. To keep the data rate low, other frames only have data for the parts of the picture that change.

keystoning: Perspective distortion from a flat object being shot by a camera at other than a perpendicular angle. Nearer portion of object appears larger than farther part.

killer app: An application of such technological importance and wide acceptance that it surpasses (i.e., kills) its competitors.

lag: Camera pickup's retention of an image after the camera has been moved, most common under low light levels. Comet tailing is a form of lag.

lapel mic: A small mic often clipped inside clothing or on a tie or lapel.

lavalier: A small mic that can be worn around the neck on a cord.

LCD: (Liquid Crystal Display) Commonly used in digital watches, camcorder viewscreens and laptop computer screens, LCD panels are light-weight and low-power display devices.

liIon: (lithium Ion) The most common battery type among new camcorders. More expensive, but has a higher capacity and fewer memory rechanging problems.

linear editing: Tape-based VCR-to-VCR editing. Called linear because scenes are recorded in chronological order on the tape.

lip sync: Proper synchronization of video with audio—lip movement with audible speech.

long shot: (LS) Camera view of a subject or scene from a distance, showing a broad perspective.

LP: (Long Play) Middle tape speed of a VHS VCR, accommodating four-hour recordings (see EP, SP).

LTC: (Longitudinal Time Code) Frame identification numbers encoded as audio signals and recorded lengthwise on the edge of a tape, typically on a linear audio track of VHS or S-VHS tape (see time code, VITC).

luminance: Black-and-white portion of video signal, carries brightness information representing picture contrast, light and dark qualities; frequently abbreviated as "Y."

lux: A metric unit of illumination equal to the light of a candle falling on a surface of one square meter. One lux equals 0.0929 foot-candle.

macro: Lens capable of extreme closeup focusing, useful for intimate views of small subjects.

master: Original recorded videotape footage; "edited master" implies original tape in its edited form.

master fader: The audio volume control that is located after all the input channel controls and after the submaster controls.

matched dissolve: Dissolve from one image to another that's similar in appearance or shot size.

media player: A program that plays back audio or video. Examples include Microsoft Windows Media Player, Apple's QuickTime Player, and RealPlayer.

medium shot: (MS) Defines any camera perspective between long shot and closeup, viewing the subjects from a medium distance.

memory effect: Power-loss phenomenon alleged of NiCad — camcorder batteries, attributed to precisely repetitive partial discharge followed by complete recharge, or long-term overcharge. Considered misnomer for "voltage depression" and "cell imbalance."

MIDI: (Musical Instrument Digital Interface) System of communication between digital electronic instruments allowing synchronization and distribution of musical information.

mic: (also "mike") Short for microphone.

mix: (1:audio) Combining sound sources to achieve a desired program balance. Finished output may be mono, stereo or surround. (2:video) Combining video signals from two or more sources.

model release: Agreement to be signed by anyone appearing in a video work, protecting videomaker from right of privacy lawsuit. Specifies event, date, compensation provisions, and rights being waived.

monitor: (1:video) Television set without receiving circuitry, wired to camcorder or VCR for display of live or recorded video signals. Most standard TVs have dual-function capability as monitor and receiver (see receiver). (2:audio) Synonymous with speaker.

monopod: One-legged camera support (see tripod).

montage: A sequence of shots assembled in juxtaposition to each other to communicate a particular idea or mood. Often bridged with cross-fades and set to music.

mosaic: Electronic special effect whereby individual pixels comprising an image are blown up into larger blocks—a kind of checkerboard effect.

mov: File extension used with QuickTime movies.

mov: File extension used with QuickTime, a popular file format for video on a computer developed by Apple.

MPEG: (MPEG-1) A video compression standard set by the Moving Picture Experts Group. It involves changing only those elements of a video image that actually change from frame to frame and leaving everything else in the image the same.

MPEG-2: The highest quality digital video compression currently available. MPEG-2 is less blocky than MPEG-1 and is used in DVDs and DBS satellite TV systems.

MPEG-4: A recent data compression format that can get better quality out of a given amount of bandwidth. MPEG-4 can compress a feature film onto a CD-ROM disc with VHS quality.

natural light: Planetary illumination— from the sun, the moon, stars— whether indoors or out. Has higher color temperature than artificial light, and thus more bluish qualities (see artificial light, color temperature).

neutral-density filter: (ND) Mounted at front of camcorder lens, reduces light intensity without affecting its color qualities (see filter).

NiCad: (nickel cadmium) Abbreviation coined and popularized by SAFT America for lightweight camcorder battery type designed to maintain power longer than traditional lead-acid batteries. Rare among new camcorders, supplanted by Li-Ion and NiMH.

NiMH: (Nickel Metal Hydride) Battery technology similar to NiCad, but more environmentally friendly, with higher capacity and fewer memory recharging problems.

NLE: (Nonlinear Editor/editing) Hard drive-based editing system defined by its ability to randomly access and insert video in any order at any time. This is in contrast to linear, tape-to-tape editing which requires rewinding and fast forwarding to access material.

noise: Unwanted sound or static in an audio signal or unwanted electronic disturbance of snow in the video signal.

noninterlaced video: Process of scanning complete frames in one pass, painting every line on the screen, yielding higher picture quality than that of interlaced video. Most computers produce a noninterlaced video signal; NTSC is interlaced. AKA progressive scan.

nonlinear editing: Digital random access editing that uses a hard drive instead of tape to store video. Random access allows easy arrangement of scenes in any order. It also eliminates the need for rewinding and allows for multiple dubs without generation loss.

nonsynchronous sound: Audio without precisely matching visuals. Usually recorded separately, includes wild sound, sound effects, or music incorporated in post-production (see synchronous sound).

nose room: The distance between the subject and the edge of the frame in the direction the subject is looking. Also called "look room."

NTSC: (National Television Standards Committee) US television broadcasting specifications. NTSC refers to all video systems conforming to this 525-line 59.94-field-per-second signal standard (see PAL, SECAM).

Off-line: Until recently, the low quality of computer video images limits the DTV computer to "off-line" work. That is, making the edit-point decisions (EDL) for use in a later "on-line" session, using the original tapes to assemble the edit master. Today's editing systems are capable of on-line quality output by themsleves, relegating this term to history.

OIS: (optical image stabilization) A process of limiting shaky camera shots with mechanical movement of the optical system within a camcorder (see EIS).

omnidirectional: A microphone that picks up sound from all directions.

outtake: Footage not to be included in final production.

over-the-shoulder shot: View of the primary subject with the back of another person's shoulder and head in the foreground. Often used in interview situations.

PAL: (Phase Alternate Line) 625-line 50-field-per-second television signal standard used in Europe and South America. Incompatible with NTSC (see NTSC, SECAM).

pan: Horizontal camera pivot, right to left or left to right, from a stationary position.

PCM: (Pulse Code Modulation) A popular method of encoding digital audio. (see AFM).

pedestal: A camera move vertically lowering or raising the camcorder, approaching either the floor or ceiling, while keeping the camera level.

phone plug: Sturdy male connector compatible with audio accessories, particularly for insertion of microphone and headphone cables. Frequently referred to by their sizes, usually 1/4-inch and 1/8-inch. Not to be confused with phono plug.

phono plug: (RCA) Shrouded male connector used for audio and video connections. Frequently referred to as RCA plugs, they only come in one size. Not to be confused with phone plugs.

pickup: (1) A video camera's image sensing element, either CCD (charge coupled device) or MOS (metal oxide semiconductor); converts light to electrical energy (see CCD) (2) A microphone's sound reception.

pickup pattern: Defines a microphone's response to sounds arriving from various directions or angles (see omnidirectional, unidirectional).

PiP: (picture in picture, p-in-p, pix in pix) Image from a second video source inset on a screen's main picture, the big and small pictures usually being interchangeable.

playback: Videotaped material viewed and heard as recorded, facilitated by camcorder or VCR.

playback VCR: Playback source of raw video footage (master or workprint) in basic player/recorder editing setup (see recording VCR).

point-of-view shot: (POV) Shot perspective whereby the video camera assumes a subject's view and thus viewers see what the subject sees.

polarizing filter: Mounted at the front of camcorder lens, thwarts undesirable glare and reflections (see filter).

Post-production: (post) Any video production activity following initial recording. Typically involves editing, addition of background music, voiceover, sound effects, titles, and/ or various electronic visual effects. Results in completed production.

posterization: Electronic special effect transforming a normal video image into a collage of flattened single-colored areas, without graduations of color and brightness.

POV: (Point Of View) The apparent position of the observer in a shoot that defines the camera's position.

pre-roll: (1) Slight backing-up function of camcorders and VCRs when preparing for linear tape-to-tape editing; ensures smooth, uninterrupted transitions between scenes.

preamp: An electronic device that magnifies the low signal output of microphones and other transducers before the signal is sent to a mixing board or to other amplifiers.

proc amp: (processing amplifier) Video image processor that boosts video signal's luminance, chroma, and sync components to correct such problems as low light, weak color, or wrong tint.

progressive scan: A method of displaying the horizontal video lines in computer displays and digital TV broadcasts. Each horizontal line is displayed in sequence (1, 2, 3, etc.), until the screen is filled; as opposed to interlaced (e.g. first fields of odd-numbered lines, then fields of even-numbered lines).

props: Short for "properties," objects used either in decorating a set (set props) or by talent (hand props).

PZM: (pressure zone microphone) Small, sensitive condenser mic, usually attached to a metal backing plate. Senses air pressure changes in tiny gap between mic element and plate. Trademark of Crown International. Generically, "boundary microphone" is preferred.

QuickTime: Computer system software that defines a format for video and audio data, so different applications can open and play synchronized sound and movie files.

rack focus: Shifting focus between subjects in the background and foreground so a viewer's attention moves from subject to subject as the focus shifts.

RAID: (Redundant Array of Independent Disks) Hard drives installed in multiples that are accessed as a single volume. RAID 0 systems (stripe sets) are common in higher-end video editing systems, as they allow for faster access to video. Other RAID configurations are used in some servers to keep important data accessible and protected, allowing access to data even after one of the hard drives crash.

RAM: (Random Access Memory) The short-term memory of a computer which temporarily holds information while your computer is on. Distinct from storage, which is more permanent and is held on hard disks or some other media, such as CD-ROM.

raw footage: Pre-edited footage, usually direct from the camcorder.

RCA plug: (Recording Corporation of America) A popular cable connector for home audio as well as video components. The standard connection for direct audio/video inputs and outputs.

RCTC: (Rewritable Consumer Time Code) The time-code format used with 8 mm and Hi8 formats.

reaction shot: A cutaway to someone or something showing their facial response to the primary action or subject.

real time: Occurring immediately, without delay for rendering. If a transition occurs in real time, there is no waiting; the computer creates the effect or transition on the fly, showing it immediately. Real-time previewing is different from real-time rendering.

real-time counter: Tallying device that accounts for videotape playing/ recording by measure of hours, minutes and seconds.

RealNetworks: Developed the leading streaming technology for transmitting live video over the internet using a variety of data compression techniques and works with IP and IP Multicast connections.

RealPlayer: A program developed by RealNetworks to play live and on-demand RealAudio and RealVideo files.

RealVideo: A streaming technology developed by RealNetworks for transmitting live video over the internet. RealVideo uses a variety of data compression algorithms.

recording VCR: Recipient of raw video feed (master or workprint) and recorder of edited videotape in basic player/recorder editing setup (see playback VCR).

reflected light: That which bounces off the illuminated subject. Light redirected by a reflector (see incident light).

reflector: Lighting accessory helpful for bouncing light onto a subject. Often made of lightweight reflective material.

remote: Video shoot performed on location, outside a controlled studio environment.

render: The processing a computer undertakes when creating an applied effect, transition or composite.

render time: The time it takes an editing computer to composite source elements and commands into a single video file so the sequence, including titles and transition effects, can play in full motion.

resolution: Amount of picture detail reproduced by a video system, influenced by a camera's pickup, lens, internal optics, recording medium and playback monitor. The more detail, the sharper and better defined the picture (see horizontal resolution).

Rewritable Consumer: (RC) Time code sent throug Control-L interface permitting extremely accurate edits. Each frame is assigned a unique address expressed in hours:minutes:seconds:frames.

RF: (Radio Frequency) Combination of audio and video signals coded as a channel number, necessary for television broadcasts as well as some closed-circuit distribution.

RF converter: Device that converts audio and video signals into a combined RF signal suitable for reception by a standard TV.

RGB: (Red, Green, Blue) Video signal transmission system that differentiates and processes all color information in separate red, green and blue components—the primary color of light—for optimum image quality. Also defines type of color monitor.

ringing: Undesirable faint double screen image caused by signal reflection or improperly balanced video circuitry. "Ringing" appears as repeated image edges.

RM: (Real Media) A popular file format used for streaming video over the internet.

rm: Most common file extension used with RealMedia files.

roll: Text or graphics, usually credits, that move up or down the screen, typically from bottom to top.

rough cut: Preliminary edit of footage in the approximate sequence, length and content of finished program.

rule of thirds: Composition theory based on dividing the screen into thirds vertically and horizontally and the placement of the main subject along those lines.

S-video: Also known as Y/C video, signal type employed with Hi8 and S-VHS video formats. Transmits luminance (Y) and chrominance (C) portions separately via multiple wires (pins), thereby avoiding the NTSC encoding process and its inevitable picture-quality degradation.

S/N Ratio: Relationship between signal strength and a medium's inherent noise. Video S/N indicates how grainy or snowy a picture will be, plus color accuracy; audio S/N specifies amount of background tape hiss present with low- or no-volume recordings.

safe title area: The recommended area that will produce legible titles on most TV screens; 80 percent of the visible area, measured from the center.

scan converter: Device that changes scan rate of a video signal, possibly converting it from noninterlaced to interlaced mode. Allows computer graphics to be displayed on a standard video screen.

scan line: Result of television's swift scanning process which sweeps out a series of horizontal lines from left to right, then down a bit and left to right again. Complete NTSC picture consists of 525 scan lines per frame.

scan rate: Number of times a screen is "redrawn" per second. Computer displays operate at different scan rates than standard video.

scene: In the language of moving images, a sequence of related shots usually constituting action in one particular location (see shot).

scrim: Lighting accessory made of wire mesh. Lessens intensity of light source without softening it. Half scrims and graduated scrims reduce illumination in more specific areas.

script: Text specifying content of a production or performance, used as a guide. May include character and setting profiles, production directives (audio, lighting, scenery, camera moves), as well as dialogue to be recited by talent (See storyboard).

SECAM: (Sequential Color and Memory) 625-line 25-frame-per-second television signal standard used in France and the Soviet Union. Incompatible with NTSC; PAL and SECAM are partially compatible (see NTSC, PAL).

SEG: (Special Effects Generator) Permits video signal mixing from two or more sources—cameras, time-base correctors and character generators—for dissolves, wipes, and other transition effects.

selective focus: Adjusting focus to emphasize desired subject(s) in a shot. Selected area maintains clarity, image sharpness while remainder of image blurs. Useful for directing viewer's attention.

sepia: Brassy antique color effect characteristic of old photographs.

shooting ratio: Amount of raw footage recorded relative to the amount used in the edited, finished program.

shot: Intentional, isolated camera views, which collectively comprise a scene (see scene).

shotgun: A highly-directional microphone used for picking up sounds from a distance.

signal-to-noise ratio: (S/N) Relationship between signal strength and a medium's inherent noise. Video S/N indicates how grainy or snowy a picture will be, plus its color accuracy; audio S/N specifies amount of background tape hiss present with low- or no-volume recordings. Higher figures represent a cleaner signal. Usually cited in decibels (dB).

skylight: (1 A) or haze (UV) filter Mounted at front of camcorder lens, virtually clear glass absorbs ultraviolet light. Also excellent as constant lens protector (see filter).

slider: A smooth narrow track with a low friction movable plate on which a camera may be mounted to simulate a variety of moving shots.

SMPTE: Time-code standard which addresses every frame on a videotape with a unique number (in hours, minutes, seconds, frames) to aid logging and editing. Format used for film, video and audio. Named for the Society of Motion Picture and Television Engineers, which sanctions standards for recording systems in North America.

snake: A connector box that contains a large number of microphone input receptacles.

snoot: Open-ended cylindrical funnel mounted on a light source to project a narrow, concentrated circle of illumination.

snow: Electronic picture interference; resembles scattered snow on the television screen. Synonymous with chroma and luma noise.

solarization: Electronic special effect distorting a video image's original colors, emphasizing some and de-emphasizing others for a "paint brush" effect (see DVE).

sound bite: Any short recorded audio segment for use in an edited program—usually a highlight taken from an interview.

sound effects: Contrived audio, usually prerecorded, incorporated with a video soundtrack to resemble a real occurrence. Blowing on a microphone, for example, might simulate wind to accompany hurricane images.

soundtrack: The audio portion of a video recording, often multifaceted with natural sound, voiceovers, background music, sound effects, etc.

SP: (Standard Play) Fastest tape speed of a VHS VCR, accommodating two-hour recordings (see EP, LP).

special effects: F/X. Tricks and illusions—electronic or on camera—employed in film and video to define, distort, or defy reality.

special effects generator: (SEG) Video signal processor with vast, but varying, image manipulation capabilities involving patterns and placement as well as color and texture: mixing, multiplying, shrinking, strobing, wiping, dissolving, flipping, colorizing, etc.

spotlight: Radiates a well-defined directional beam of light, casting hard, distinct shadows. Best used to focus illumination on individual subjects, whereas floodlights blanket broader areas.

stabilizer: Video signal processor used primarily for tape dubbing to eliminate picture jump and jitter, maintain stability. Also a mechanical device on which a camcorder can be mounted to physically isolate operator movement.

star: Filter mounted at front of camcorder lens, gives videotaped light sources a starburst effect. Generally available in four-, six-, and eight-point patterns (see filter).

stereo: Sound emanating from two isolated sources, intended to simulate pattern of natural human hearing.

stock shot: Common footage—city traffic, a rainbow—conveniently accessed as needed. Similar to a "photo file" in the photography profession.

storyboard: Series of cartoon-like sketches illustrating key visual stages (shots, scenes) of planned production, accompanied by corresponding audio information (see script).

streaming: Playing sound or video in real time as it is downloaded over the internet as opposed to storing it in a local file first. Avoids download delay.

strobe: Digital variation of fixed-speed slow motion, with image action broken down into a series of still frames updated and replaced with new ones at rapid speed.

Super VHS: (S-VHS, S-VHS-C) Improved version of VHS and VHS-C videotape formats, characterized by separate carriers of chrominance and luminance information, yielding a sharper picture (see VHS, VHS-C).

superimposition: (super) Titles, video or graphics appearing over an existing video picture, partially or completely hiding areas they cover.

sweetening: Post-production process of adding music and sound effects or otherwise enhancing the existing audio with filters and effects.

swish pan: Extremely rapid camera movement from left to right or right to left, appearing as image blur. Two such pans in the same direction—one moving from, the other moving to a stationary shot— edited together can effectively convey passage of time or change of location.

switcher: Simplified SEG, permits video signal mixing from two or more sources—cameras, time base correctors, character generators—for dissolves, wipes, and other clean transition effects.

sync: (synchronization) Horizontal and vertical timing signals or electronic pulses—component of composite signal, supplied separately in RGB systems. Aligns video origination (live camera, videotape) and reproduction (monitor or receiver) sources (see also synchronous sound).

synchronous sound: Audio recorded with images. When the mouth moves, the words come out.

talent: Generic term for the people assuming on-screen roles in a videotaping.

tally light: Automatic indicators (usually red) on a camera's front and within its viewfinder that signal recording in progress—seen by both camera subject(s) and operator.

telecine converter: Imaging device used in conjunction with a movie projector and camcorder to transfer film images to videotape.

telephoto: Camera lens with long focal length and narrow horizontal field of view. Opposite of wide angle, captures magnified, closeup images from considerable distance.

teleprompter: (prompter) Mechanical device that projects and advances text on mirror directly in front of camera's lens, allowing talent to read their lines while appearing to maintain eye contact with viewers.

test pattern: Any of various combinations of converging lines, alignment marks, and gray scales appearing on screen to aid in video equipment adjustment for picture alignment, registration, and contrast. Often viewed on broadcast television in off-air hours (see color bars).

three-point lighting: Basic lighting approach employing key, fill and back lights to illuminate subject with sense of depth and texture. Strategic placement imitates natural outdoor lighting environment, avoids flat lighting (see back light, fill light, key light).

three-quarter-inch: (U-matic) An analog video format utilizing 3/4" tape. Very popular in professional, industrial and broadcast environments in the past, though beginning to be supplanted by digital formats.

three-shot: Camera view including three subjects, generally applicable to interview situations.

three-to-one rule: A microphone placement principle that states if two mics must be side by side, there should be three times the distance between them that there is between the mics and the people using them.

tilt: Vertical camcorder rotation (up and down) from a single axis, as on a tripod.

Time Base Corrector: (TBC) Electronic device that corrects timing inconsistencies in a videotape recorder's playback, stabilizing the image for optimum quality. Also synchronizes video sources, allowing image mixing (see sync).

time code: Synchronization system, like a clock recorded on your videotape, assigning a corresponding hours, minutes, seconds, and frame-number designation to each frame. Expedites indexing convenience and editing precision (See SMPTE).

time-lapse recording: Periodically videotaping a minimal number of frames over long durations of actual time. Upon playback, slow processes such as a flower blooming may be viewed in rapid motion.

timeline editing: A computer-based method of editing, in which bars proportional to the length of the clip represent video and audio clips are represented on a computer screen.

titling: Process or result of incorporating on-screen text as credits, captions or any other alphanumeric communication to video viewers.

tracking: Lateral camcorder movement that travels with a moving subject. The camcorder should maintain a regulated distance from the subject.

transcode: To convert analog video to a digital format, or vice-versa. Also to convert from one digital format to another.

tripod: Three-legged camera mount offering stability and camera placement/movement consistency. Most are lightweight, and used for remote recording (see monopod).

turnkey DVD authoring system: Any computer system designed to author (and usually burn) DVDs right out of the box, needing only trivial changes in its configuration.

turnkey nonlinear editing system: Any computer system designed to edit video right out of the box, needing only trivial changes in its configuration.

turnkey system: Any computer system which is considered ready-to-use right out of the box, needing only trivial changes in its configuration.

two-shot: A camera view including two subjects, generally applicable to interview situations.

U-matic: An analog video format utilizing 3/4" tape. Very popular in professional, industrial and broadcast environments in the past, though beginning to be supplanted by digital formats.

umbrella: Lighting accessory available in various sizes usually made of textured gold or silver fabric. Facilitates soft, shadowless illumination by reflecting light onto a scene.

unbalanced line: Audio cables that have two wires: one for positive and one for both negative and ground.

unidirectional: Highly selective microphone pickup pattern, rejects sound coming from behind while absorbing that from in front (see bidirectional, omnidirectional).

Variable Bit Rate (VBR): A way of coding video to maximize image quality over a connection's available bandwidth, usually provided by more recent codecs.

VCR: (Video Cassette Recorder) Multifunction machine intended primarily for recording and playback of videotape stored in cassettes.

vectorscope: Electronic testing device that measures a video signal's chrominance performance, plotting qualities in a compass-like graphic display.

Vertical Interval Time Code: (VITC) Synchronization signals recorded as an invisible component of the video signal, accessed for editing precision (see time code).

VHS: (Video Home System) Predominant half-inch videotape format developed by Matsushita and licensed by JVC.

VHS-C: (VHS Compact) Scaled-down version of VHS using miniature cassettes compatible with full-size VHS equipment through use of adapter (see Super VHS).

Vidcast: An episodic video production produced primarily for regular distribution on the internet.

video card: The PC card that controls the computer's monitor display. Don't confuse the computer's video (VGA, SVGA, Mac monitor and so on) which is non-interlaced, with NTSC video. PC cards for DTV are also called capture, overlay or compression cards. Most do not generate NTSC video output.

video prompter: A mechanical device that projects and advances text on a mirror directly in front of a camera lens, allowing talent to read lines while appearing to maintain eye contact with viewers.

Video Cassette Recorder: See VCR.

vignette: Visual special effect whereby viewers see images through a perceived keyhole, heart shape, diamond, etc. In low-budget form, vignettes are achieved by aiming camera through a cutout of a desired vignette.

vignetting: Undesirable darkening at the corners of a picture, as if viewer's peering through a telescope, due to improper matching of lens to camera—pickup's scope exceeds lens size.

VITC: (Vertical Interval Time Code) Synchronization signal recorded as an invisible component of the video signal, accessed for editing precision (See LTC).

VOD: (Video on Demand) Usually only heard in the context of delivering full-frame, full-motion video to a television; since most video on the internet is provided on-demand.

voiceover: (VO) Audio from an unseen narrator accompanying video, heard above background sound or music. Typically applied to edited visuals during post-production.

wav: A sound format for storing sound in files developed jointly by Microsoft and IBM. Support for WAV files was built into Windows 95 making it the de facto standard for sound on PCs.

WAV sound files end with a.wav extension.

waveform monitor: Specialized oscilloscope testing device providing a graphic display of a video signal's strength. Plus, like a sophisticated light meter, aids in precise setting of picture's maximum brightness level for optimum contrast.

Webcam: (Web camera) A small camera connected to a computer, usually through a USB port. Webcams usually produce small, progressive-scanned images.

whip pan: (swish pan) Extremely rapid camera movement from left to right or right to left, appearing as an image blur. Two such pans in the same direction, edited together—one moving from, the other moving to a stationary shot—can effectively convey the passage of time or a change of location.

white balance: Electronic adjustment of camcorder to retain truest colors of recorded image. Activated in camcorder prior to recording, proper setting established by aiming at white object.

wide-angle: Camcorder lens with short focal length and broad horizontal field of view. Opposite of telephoto, supports viewer perspective and tends to reinforce perception of depth.

wild sound: Nonsynchronous audio recorded independent of picture i.e., rain on roof, five o'clock whistle— often captured with separate audio recorder (see nonsynchronous sound).

windscreen: Sponge-like microphone shield, thwarts undesirable noise from wind and rapid mic movement.

wipe: Transition from one shot to another, where a moving line or pattern reveals the new shot. In its simplest form it simulates a window shade being drawn.

wireless mic: A microphone with a self-contained, built-in miniature FM transmitter that can send the audio signal several hundred feet, eliminating the need for mic cables.

workprint: Copy of a master videotape used for edit planning and rough cut without excessively wearing or otherwise jeopardizing safekeeping of original material. Also called "working master."

wow and flutter: Sound distortions consisting of a slow rise and fall of pitch, caused by speed variations in audio/video playback system.

XLR: (ground-left-right) Three-pin plug for three-conductor "balanced" audio cable, employed with high-quality microphones, mixers and other audio equipment.

Y: Symbol for luminance, or brightness, portion of a video signal; the complete color video signal consists of R,G,B and Y.

Y/C: Video signal type (also known as S-video) employed with Hi8 and S-VHS video formats and analog output -on digital camcorders. Transmits luminance (Y) and chrominance (C) portions separately via multiple wires, thereby avoiding picture quality degradation.

YUV: (y = luminance, u = B-Y or blue and v = R-Y or red) Video signal used to compose a component NTSC or PAL signal (see RGB).

zoom: Variance of focal length, bringing subject into and out of close-up range. Lens capability permits change from wide-angle to telephoto, or vice versa, in one continuous move. "Zoom in" and "zoom out" are common terms.

zoom ratio: Range of a lens' focal length, from most "zoomed in" field of view to most "zoomed out." Expressed as ratio: 6:1, for example, implies that the same lens from the same distance can make the same image appear six-times closer (see focal length, zoom)

Contributing Authors

Kyle Cassidy is a visual artist who writes extensively about technology.

Bill Davis writes, shoots, edits and does voiceover work for a variety of corporate and industrial clients.

Nathan Beaman is an Apple Certified Final Cut Pro 6, Level 2 Apple Certified XSAN for Pro Video and Apple Certified Motion Graphics Trainer.

Peter Biesterfeld is a video production college professor.

Tony Bruno produces independent films, is an occasional actor, and makes his living as a professional technical writer.

Andrew Burke works as an online media strategist and video producer.

Julia Camenisch is a freelance video producer and writer who successfully sells stock footage on several sites.

Earl Chessher is a veteran journalist and newspaper publisher with more than 30 years' experience. He is a career independent professional video services provider who has produced thousands of videos and written about creating and marketing videos for more than 20 years.

John Devcic is a freelance writer and videographer.

Edward B. Driscoll, Jr. is a freelance journalist covering home theatre and the media.

Doug Dixon covers digital media at Manifest-Tech.com.

Teresa Echazabal is a freelance video editor, writer, and producer.

Bill Fisher is a documentary video producer.

Michael Fitzer is an Emmy award-winning commercial and documentary writer/producer.

Charles Fulton is *Videomaker*'s Associate Editor.

Randy Hansen is an award-winning photographer and editor and is photo chief of a major market TV News station.

Mark Holder is a video producer and trainer.

John Joyner is a freelance editor, writer, and lecturer.

Mark Levy is an attorney specializing in intellectual property law. He has won many amateur moviemaking awards.

Laura Martone is a screenwriter, producer and co-founder of the LA Indie Film Group.

Mark Montgomery is a Web content specialist and produces instructional videos for a leading Web application developer.

Robert G. Nulph is an assistant professor of communication studies and an independent video/film producer/director.

Morgan Paar is an adjunct professor of film/video production and post-production at Bronx Community College in New York City and an independent cinematographer and editor specializing in international documentary production.

Brandon Pinard is an independent video producer.

Jennifer O'Rourke is *Videomaker*'s Managing Editor.

Jeanne Rawlings is an Emmy award winning sound recordist and documentary producer. Her clients have included the National Geographic Society, ABC and Discovery Channel.

Michael Reff is Director of Photography at Turner Broadcasting.

Hal Robertson is a digital media producer and technology consultant.

Tad Rose is a writer and independent producer.

Marshal M. Rosenthal is a technology/entertainment writer whose experience in the industry spans over 20 years.

Brian Schaller is an independent producer traveling around the world working on his documentary.

Stephen Smith is an award-winning producer and editor for Lone Peak Productions.

Dave Sniadak is an award-winning video producer. His clients include several Fortune 500 companies, professional sports franchises and small businesses.

Jim Stinson is the author of Video: Digital Communication and Production.

Randal K. West is the Vice President/Creative Director for a DRTV full service advertising agency.

James Williams is an independent filmmaker and video journalist.

Peter Zunitch is a post-production manager and editor working on every system from 16 mm film to Avid Symphony, utilizing many of today's advanced manipulation and compositing tools.

Index

A

A-roll footage 206, 239
AAC audio format 350
alpha channel 279, 281
alternative endings to films on
    DVD 383–4
American Civil Liberties Union
    (ACLU) 296–7
animatic storyboards 108
aperture settings 13, 147
archiving 18–19, 285
Attenborough, David 93
audio adjustment in
    post-production 266–9
audio cleaning tools 268
audio commentary on DVDs 383
audio interfaces 275
audio problems 124–5, 135,
    186–9, 266, 269
audio processors 268–9
audio recording equipment
    182–3, 188–9, 271, 275–7
audio recording levels 182–5,
    188
auditions 120–1
authoring
    of Blu-ray discs 369–75
    of DVDs 349–54, 359–68
autofocus 38
autoloader duplicators 380

B

B-roll footage 206, 239–40
back light 168

background noise 147, 186–7,
    206; *see also* noise, sources
    of
backup routines 17–19, 282–6,
    350
Baggs, Amanda 333
batteries 67–70, 138, 181
    rechargeable 70
    smart 59
behind-the-scenes features on
    DVD 385–6
Benjamin Button 221
Berkeley, Busby 27
Big Mini-DV Festival 314
Billy Jack 309
The Blair Witch Project
    341
blockbusters 220–1
blocking of action 217–18,
    226
blogs and blogging 333–4
Blu-ray discs 360
    authoring of 369–75
    burning of 373, 375
booms 140, 161, 275
bounced light 174, 178
Brando, Marlon 385
BRATS 310–12
Braveheart 29
Breaking Ten 273
Brightcove 335–6
Brown, Ryan 326
budgeting 112, 117, 130,
    203–4, 211–13

bugs
    in the corner of the screen
        280–1
    in software 366
burning of discs 349–51, 354–5,
    373–7
Burns, Ken 92
Buzz
    in audio signals 188
    from promotion of a video 341

C

cable tv channels 209, 287–90
cameras
    cases for 6
    choice of 10–11, 307
    maintenance and cleaning of
        3–6
    positional moves 159–63
    preparation for shooting 139
    program mode and *manual
        control* 147
Cameron, James 8
Canon EOS 5D Mark II camera 31
casting 120–2, 130
Castle, William 312
CDs (compact discs) 16, 18
    burning of 349–50
cease and desist letters 344
celebrities, privacy rights of 346
characters in film 78–81
charge-coupled devices (CCDs)
    7–10
Choi, Hahn 10–11

cinema vérité 203, 322
citizen journalism 293–6
clapboards 253–5, 272, 275–6
cleaning cloths 5
cleaning solutions 4–5
clipping of digital audio 183
clothing patterns 198
cloud storage 18
CNN (Cable News Network) 294
color choice for costuming
    197–8
color correction 22, 258–61
Comic Sans typeface 263
Commercial Advertisement
    Loudness Migration (CALM)
    Act 185
communication 115–18
compact discs *see* CDs
complimentary metal-oxide
    semiconductors (CMOS)
    7–11
compositing 278–81
compression of video 323–7, 369
    open-source software for 327
computers recommended for
    video editing 71–4
concept proposals 116–17
configuration of computers 72–3
contacts for individual shoots
    140–1
continuity 224
contrast ranges 177–8
convergence in 3D 229–31
copy protection on DVDs 360
copyright 343–6
costs of filmmaking 111–14; *see
    also* budgeting; hard costs
Craigslist website 222
cranes 27–8, 161
CreateSpace 306, 336
creativity 91–4, 133
Creator software 360
credits 241
cropping 281
cutaways 136, 207
cutting in action 224–6

D
Dali, Salvador 150
Dasein: the Art of Being 33
de-interlacing 265
deleted scenes from films on
    DVD 383
delivery dates 307
demonstrations, on-screen 94
depth of field (DoF) 14, 38–9,
    221
design elements 116
Di Caprio, Leonardo 247
diffusion of sunlight 180–1
digital asset management (DAM)
    15

digital audio workstations
    (DAWs) 268
Digital Juice 252
digital versatile discs *see* DVDs
director's cuts 383
Dirty Jobs 45–6
Discovery Channel 209, 258
distributors 303, 339
diversity receivers 51–2
divine proportion 150, 152
documentaries 92–4, 201–13,
    305
    distribution of 337–42
    funding of and budgeting for
        110–14
    subject matter of 213
Dod Mantle, Anthony 221
Dolby Digital audio 350, 360
dollies 26–7, 29, 43, 161
dress
    for interviewees 192
    for *pitching* 86
    for *talent* 197–8
dual system sound 275
DVD Architect software 361–2
DVD Flick software 362
DVD-lab software 361
DVD Maker software 366–8
DVD Movie Factory software
    361
DVDit software 361–2
DVDs (digital versatile discs) 16,
    18, 258, 276, 319–20, 351–5
    authoring of 351–4, 359–68
    burning of 349–51, 354–5
    duplication of 305, 376–81
    extra features added to 382–6
DVDStyler software 368
dynamics processors 267

E
Easter eggs 386
Edison, Thomas 13
edit suites for audio 183–4
editing 59–60, 134–6, 148, 350
    computers recommended for
        71–4
    in-camera 148
    on-site 16–17
    organization of 232–6
    planning of 135–6
    shortcuts in 253–7
    of titles and graphics 262–5
editors 137
educational television and video
    211, 288
Elements software 238
Elliot, Sean D. 295, 297
The Empire Strikes Back 270
Encore software 362, 369–70,
    373
expert presenters 93–4

extended versions of films on
    DVD 383
extension cables 140

F
Facebook 303, 333
Federal Communications
    Commission (FCC) 296
Fibonacci sequence 150–1
file-based recording 16
file types, support for 363
fill light 167–70, 179–80
film, drawbacks of 220
Film Commission 208
film festivals 114, 208, 305,
    313–18, 337–9
filters 4, 21–2, 221
Final Cut software 238, 326, 362
Fiscal Sponsor Directory 113
flash players 331
flashlights 58
Flickr 333
"floating head" syndrome 178–9
floating stabilizer devices 161
fluorescent lighting 124, 148,
    199, 216
flying camera supports 156–7
focal length 162
focus 147; *see also* rack focus
Foundation Center 113, 212
four-walling 308–12, 341
frame rates 13
framing of shots 150–2
freeware for authoring of DVDs
    364–8
French flags 22
fuel cells 69–70
fuel gauges for batteries 59
funding of filmmaking 112–14,
    130, 204, 211–12
fur windscreens 187

G
gain control 9, 13–14, 147–8,
    181, 186
Galanis, Toli 195
Gaussian blur 265
gels 173, 181
GenArts 251–2
generic material common to
    several edits 233–4
Gilson, Murphy 316–17
gliding camera stabilizers 28–9
Goring, Trevor 109
government television channels
    288
grants for film and video making
    113
graphics 264
graphics accelerators 73–4
green screen environment
    215–18

The Guardian 194–5
Gumbel, Bryant 195

H

hand-held shooting techniques
    161–2
hard costs of filmmaking 213
hard drives 18, 74, 284–5
hard light 168, 170
hashtags 321
headphones 140, 187
Heffner, Richard 195
Herzog, Werner 107
Hester, Grinner 303
high-key lighting 168–71
high-pass filters 267–8
Hildebrandt, Paul 34
Hitchcock, Alfred 27, 106–7,
    109
Hofmeister, Kent 28
hot zone on a DVD 352
hum in audio signals 188

I

iDVD software 366
image sensors 7–10
image stabilization 157–8
images, online sources of 85
iMovie software 148, 238, 324
"in" points used in editing
    255–6
Independent Television Service
    (ITVS) 208
index cards 83–5, 109, 202–3
interlaced video 372–3; *see also*
    de-interlacing
interocular distance 229, 231
interviews 92–3, 190–5, 206,
    295
    best and worst examples of
        194–5
    planning of and preparation
        for 191
Iowa 208

J

Jarvis, Chase 33–4
JAWS 27
jibs 27–9, 43–4

K

key light 165–6, 167–71, 173,
    178
keyboard shortcuts 255, 257
keyframes 250, 272–3
Kickstarter website 107
Kjergaard, Kevin 293–8
Knoll Light Factory 251–2
Kristofferson, Kris 310
Kunaki.com 306
Kurosawa, Akira 106

L

labeling routines 32–3, 350,
    380–1
Lamb, Brian 195
lantern-style lights 58
Laughlin, Tom 309
layers, use of 280–1
lectures, on-screen 94
Led Zeppelin 183
legal issues 343–8
lens accessories 20–3
lens adapters 221
lens caps 4
lens cleaners 4
lenses, interchangeable 36–9
Leonardo da Vinci 150
Levey, Ryan Bruce 312
light kits, care of 181
lighting conditions 124, 148,
    165–77
lighting equipment
    cine-type 222
    for green screen environment
        216–17
    portable 54–8; *see also* three-
        point lighting
limiters for digital audio signals
    183
lithium ion (Li-ion) batteries 69
LiveJournal platform 334
locations 88–9, 102, 123, 126–7,
    130, 140, 177, 230
Long, J. Michael 303, 306
The Lord of the Rings 385
Lost 262, 264
loudness standards 184–5
low-key lighting 168, 171
low-pass filters 267
lower thirds 279–80
luminance levels 259–60

M

macro lenses 21, 38
makeup 198–200
marketing
    of an idea or concept 306
    of a video 301–7, 338–9
"marrying" of special effects 252
master copies 17
matte-box system 22
Mecca, Bill 303, 306
Media Encoder software 326,
    373
media management 17, 33, 285
Melies, George 279
memory and memory cards 19,
    73
menu customization on DVDs
    360
Michael Wiese Books 111
microphones 45–9
    balanced or *unbalanced* 47–8

bidirectional 47
boundary-type 47–8
built in to cameras 147,
    187–8, 271
cardioid 46, 48
directional or *non-directional*
    46–7
lavaliere-type 48
shotgun-type 46–8, 188
signal levels from 188–9
testing of 139
wireless 50–3
Midwest Independent Film
    Festival 314
Miller, Patti 202
mixers 139
moiré effect 197–8
monitors 59–63
    camera-mounted 62–3
    field type 62
    LCD type 59–60
    NTSC type 61, 258
    production type 61–3
monopods 44, 156
Moore, Michael 203, 205
Movie Maker software 148, 238,
    324–5
MP3 discs 349–50
music, *copyright-protected* or
    royalty-free 345
Musil, Donna 310–12
MySpace 333

N

Nero Multimedia Suite 360–1
Nerve.com 195
neutral density (ND) filters 22,
    174
Newton, Sir Isaac 259
niche markets for video 302
nickel cadmium (NiCd) batteries
    68
nickel metal hydride (NiMH)
    batteries 68, 79
night scenes 181
noise, sources of 124–5, 147,
    186–7
noise reduction 267–8

O

Old Spice 322
online video platforms 335–6
open-source software 327,
    366–7
organization of files and footage
    232–6, 238, 283
O'Rourke, Jennifer 295–6
"out" points used in editing
    255–6
outdoor videography 176–81
outlines of projects 117, 129,
    203–4, 211

P

pacing of video 240, 245–8
panning 160, 248
Papyrus typeface 263
parallel cuts 225
Partially True Tales of High Adventure! 316–17
ParticleIllusion 252
pay rates for video work 307
pedestal positions 161
permission to shoot 126
persistence of vision 13
pickup shots 135
Pirates of the Caribbean 385–6
pitching 86, 211
pixel counts 9
planning
　of the edit 135–6
　enemies of 132–3
　of the shoot 128–32; *see also* pre-production
Plant, Robert 183
PluralEyes software 35
podcasts 333
polarizing filters 22
post-it-notes 83, 85
post-production 132–6, 266–9
posture for shooting 155
Power Producer software 360–1
power supplies 124, 189
pre-production 82–6, 101, 128–9, 132, 204
pre-visualization
　software for 103
　in 3D 108, 230
Premiere software 325–6, 362, 369–70, 373
preparatory work 127, 145–7
presentation methods and styles 91–4
press kits 319
The Price 108
privacy, right of 346–7
production managers 136–7
production meetings 117
progressive scan nonitors 372
promotional activities 332–6
Psycho 106
public access tv channels 208, 287–91, 340

Q

QuickTime player 325

R

raccoon eye light 178
rack focus 162
Ran 106
Red Giant 251–2
Red Vic theater 341
redundant array of independent disks (RAID) 35, 285–6

reenactments 206–7
reflectors 56–7, 164–6, 178–81
　indoor use of 166
release forms 126–8, 213, 346–8
remote-controlled camcorders 22
replication of discs 381
reshooting 135
resource requirements 116
Richards, Keith 386
Riggs, Rita 106–7
Rodriguez, Robert 280
rolling shutters 10
Romeo-Theater.com 340–1
Rowe, Mike 45
RSS (really simple syndication) feeds 340–1

S

Salmon, Christopher 108
Sapphire software 250–2
Saving Private Ryan 29
scary movies 81
scene cards 108
scheduling 87–90, 104, 116, 118, 130
　software for 130
Scorsese, Martin 120
scouting 126–7, 130, 177–8, 181, 230
scream appeal 81
screen direction 223–7
　175-degree rule 223–6
screen resolution 60
screenplays 96, 129
screenwriting software 99
script supervisors 137
scripts 78, 94–9, 117–18, 129–30, 133, 136
　benefits from use of 97–8
　formality of 96
SD cards 18–19
search engines 334, 339
selectable frequencies 51–2
serif and *sans serif* typefaces 264–5
shaky shots 24
shot lists 101, 103–4, 129, 135, 146–7, 253–5
ShotPut Pro 283–4
shutter angle 221
shutter speed 12–14, 147
Silverlight software 331
simultaneous rolling 286
Slumdog Millionaire 221
Snyder, Zack 278
social networks 333; *see also* Facebook
soft light 168–71, 178
Softpedia certification 365, 367
solid-state storage 18, 74
Sonic Scenarist software 360

Sound Advice 50
sound effects 270–3
　libraries of 271
Spartan Epic, 295 278
speakers for audio editing 184
special effects 129–30, 249–52, 280
　lenses for 22
Spielberg, Steven 27
split-screen effects 280
sponsorship 204
spyware 365
Squeeze 8 software 326–7
squelch controls 52
stabilization tools and techniques 24–30, 154–8, 222
Star Wars 106, 221, 280, 386
status displays 52
Steadicam 28–9, 157, 161, 222
storyboard artists 101, 109
storyboarding software 101, 108–9
storyboards 88, 94, 101–9, 129, 146, 203, 230
　examples of 105–9
　types of 107–8
streaming video 209, 328–31
sunlight 148, 165–6, 177–80
Superman Returns 385
surround sound 277
sweet spots 151–2, 320
switchers 64–6
synchronization of sound 35, 274–7
syndication 340–1

T

T-bars 66
talent to appear on-screen 89–90, 116, 119–22, 147, 181
　dress for 197–8
　evaluation of 121
　recruitment of 119–22
　sources of 120
tape-based production 139
　advantages and disadvantages of 16
tape compression 183
tapeless production 15–17, 19, 255
Tascam DR-05 audio recorder 277
tax ememption 113
tele-extenders 21
telephoto lenses 37–8, 146
television *see* cable tv channels; public access tv channels; user-generated content
television advertisements 321–2
Tequila, Tila 333
thirds, rule of 151–2

3D, shooting in 228–31
three-point lighting 167–71, 178, 181
Thunderbolt interface 74
tilting the camera 160–1
time, manipulation of 240
time management 193
timecode 254–5
timelines 272, 276–7
timing
  of shoots 125–6
  of video footage 88
Titanic 247
titles, editing of 262–4
transcoding programs 329–30, 363
treatments 78, 83–6
A Trip to the Moon 279
tripods 25–6, 139, 156, 162
  buying guide 40–9
trombone shots 43
Tulsa Overground festival 314
tweets 320–1
Twitter 303, 320–1
two-column script format 96, 129
typeface, choice of 263–4

U
ultra-violet (uv) filters 22
United States Supreme Court 290
uploading to the web 320–1, 334
user-generated content 293–4

V
vectorscopes 259, 260
Vertigo 27
vertigo shots 43
vidcasting 210
video
  differences from film 219–20
  made to look like film 221–2
video forums 306
video portals 333; *see also* YouTube
video servers 18
Vimeo.com website 241
VodPod website 333
voice-overs 92
volume envelopes 267–8

W
Walker, Amy 333
wardrobe 196–8
Warshawski, Morrie 113
WAV files 276
waveform monitors 259
weather conditions 133
web designers 334–5
web video 319–22
  compression software for 323–7
  promotion of 332–6
websites
  for distribution of videos 304
  for particular videos 339
  for streaming video 209

of video producers 333–5
white-balance correction 261
wide-angle lenses 20–1, 36–7, 146, 231
wind noise 187
window lighting 173–4
Winslet, Kate 247
wipes 280
Wiseman, Frederick 92
Withoutabox.com 316, 338
The Wizard of Oz 77–80
workflow 31–5
  definition of 32
working copies 17–18
workspace layout 236
workstation systems 71–2
WorldFest Houston Film Festival 314
Wright, Mary 199
Wurtz, Timothy 310–12

Y
Yaskin, Keith 293, 295, 298
YouTube 241, 284, 303, 319–22, 329, 333, 366

Z
Zahedi, Caveh 309–10
Zoom H2 audio recorder 277
zoom lenses 38–9, 146–7, 155, 162, 231
zoom-through adapters 20